HITTING THE HEAD

Goff Books
Published by Goff Books. An Imprint of ORO Editions
Gordon Goff: Publisher

www.goffbooks.com
info@goffbooks.com

Author: Andre Howard
Book design by Olivia Grey Smith
Collages by @coverartssucks
Managing Editor: Jake Anderson

10 9 8 7 6 5 4 3 2 1 First Edition

ISBN: 978-1-961856-79-0

Prepress and Print work by ORO Editions Inc.
Printed in China

Goff Books makes a continuous effort to minimize the
overall carbon footprint of its publications. As part of this
goal, Goff Books, in association with Global ReLeaf,
arranges to plant trees to replace those used in the
manufacturing of the paper produced for its books. Global
ReLeaf is an international campaign run by American
Forests, one of the world's oldest nonprofit conservation
organizations. Global ReLeaf is American Forests'
education and action program that helps individuals,
organizations, agencies, and corporations improve the local
and global environment by planting and caring for trees.

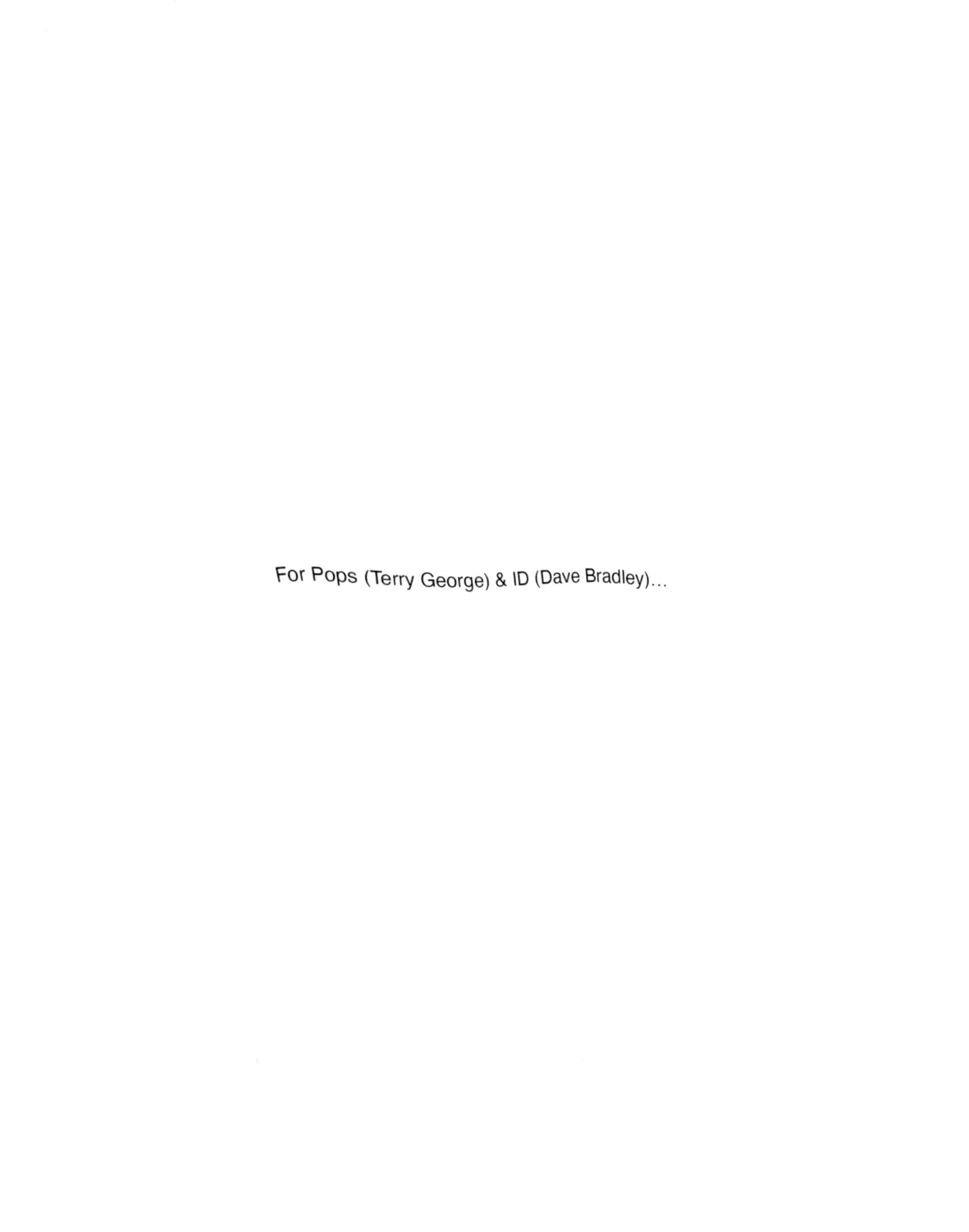

For Pops (Terry George) & ID (Dave Bradley)…

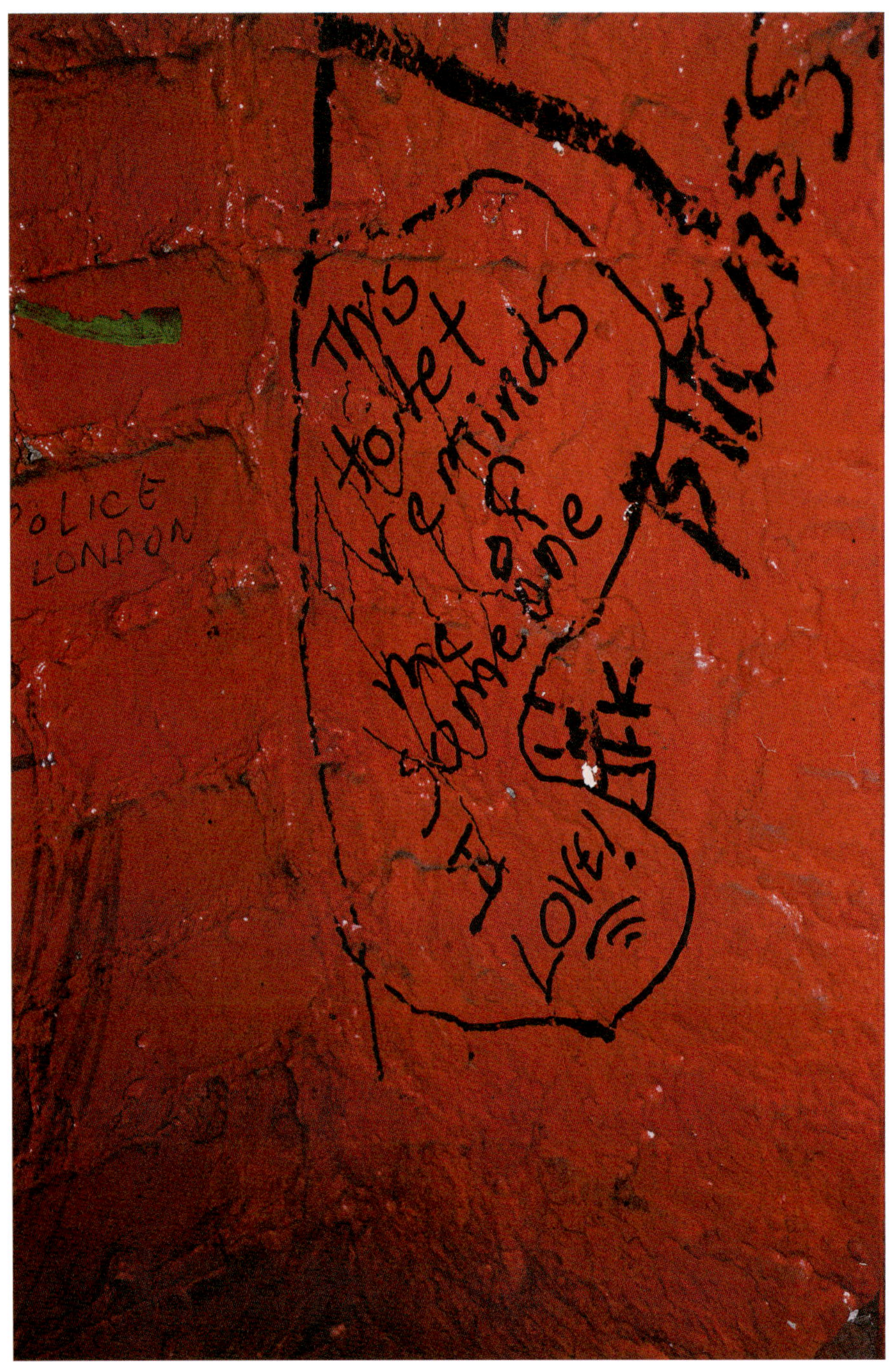
THIS
TOILET
REMINDS
ME OF
SOMEONE
I
LOVE!
POLICE
LONDON

Love Letter To NYC

Over the course of two years, I hit up over 100 dive bars
across all five boroughs—partly to shine a light on
mom-and-pop spots… but also, let's be real, to drink
and have a good time! LOL. The *Hitting The Head* project
came out of a genuine fascination with NYC's dive bar
culture, counterculture, and finding beauty and art in
the everyday and overlooked.

The original idea was to showcase dive bars across all
five boroughs, but it quickly morphed into something
more personal. These spots became the focus because
they're the ones I kept coming back to — places where
I made memories with friends and colleagues, caught
some amazing performances, and, of course,
got absolutely shitfaced!

Putting this book together took me down memory lane.
A lot of these spots don't exist anymore, and I've lost a
few loved ones along the way too. I just hope you enjoy
flipping through it as much as I enjoyed bringing it to life.

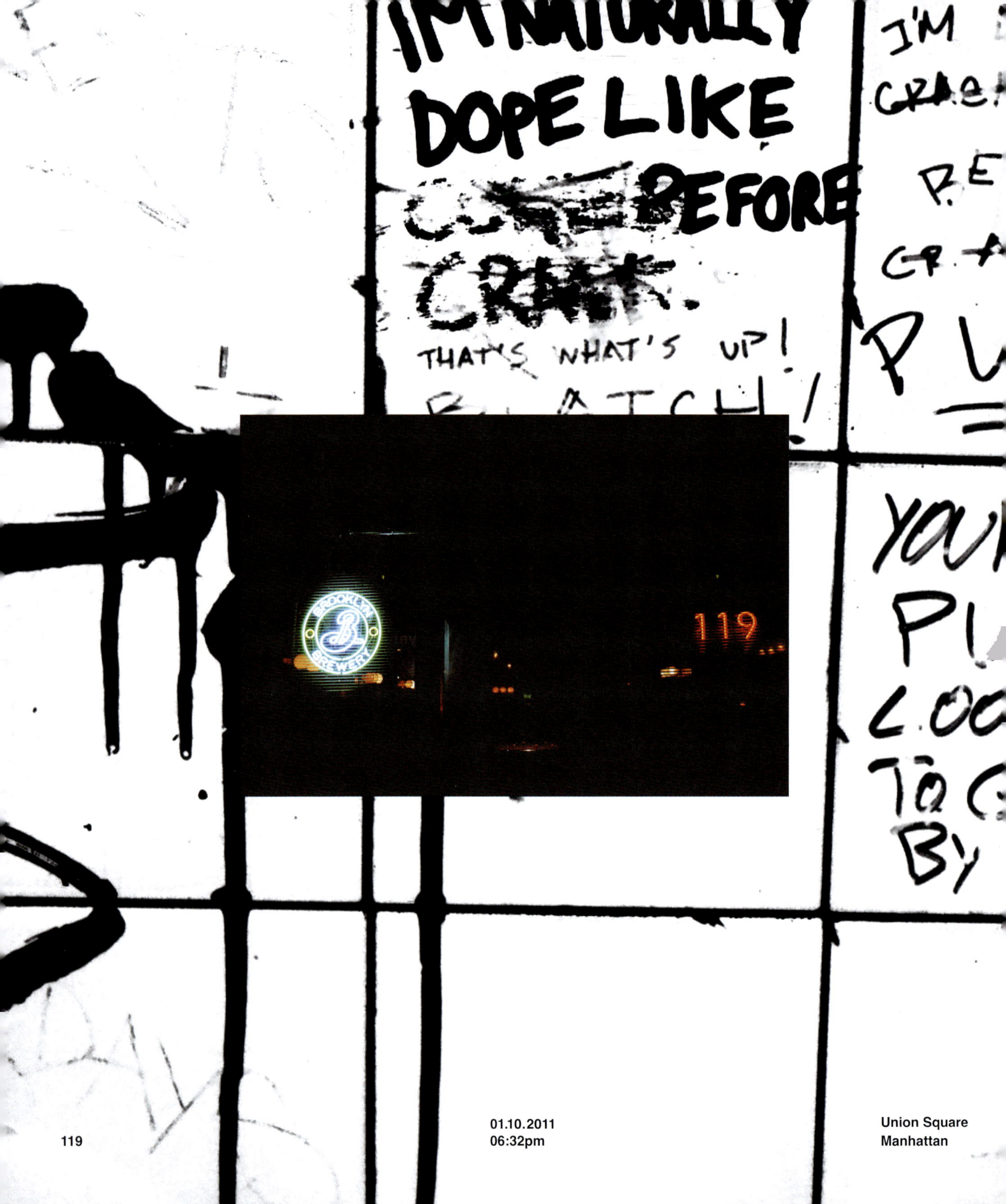

01.10.2011
06:32pm

Union Square
Manhattan

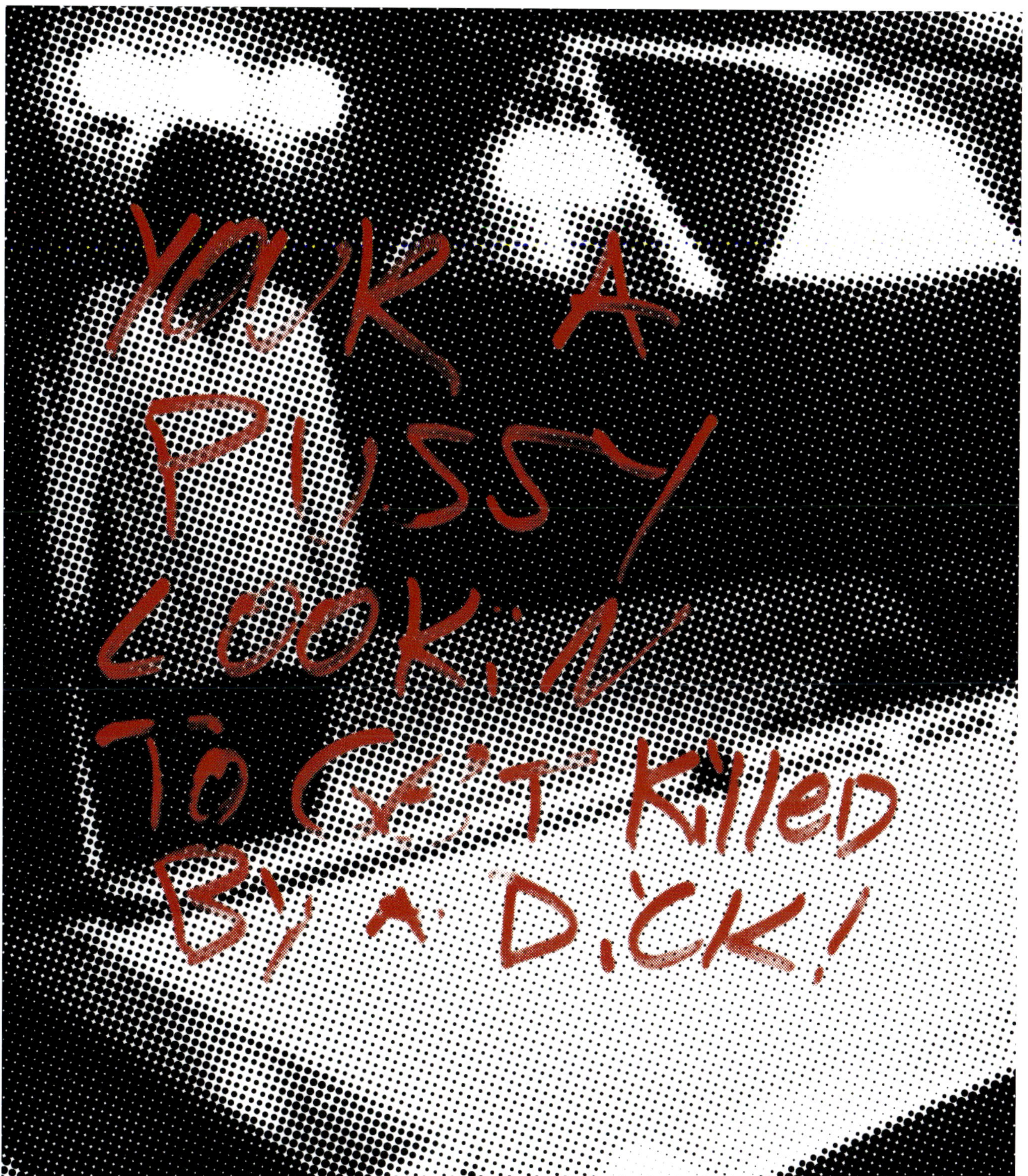
YOU'K A
PUSSY/
LOOKIN/
TO GET KILLED
BY A DICK!

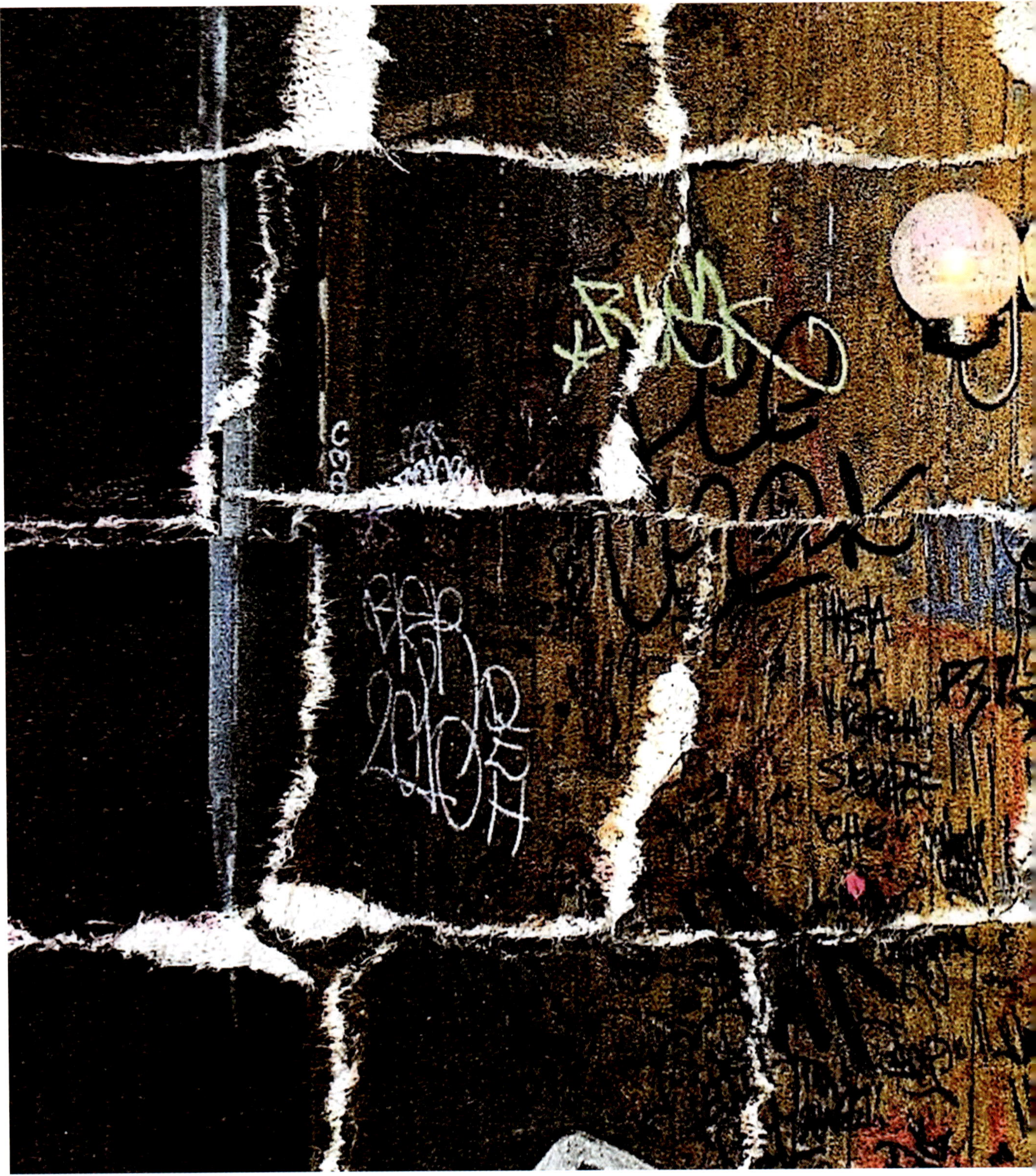

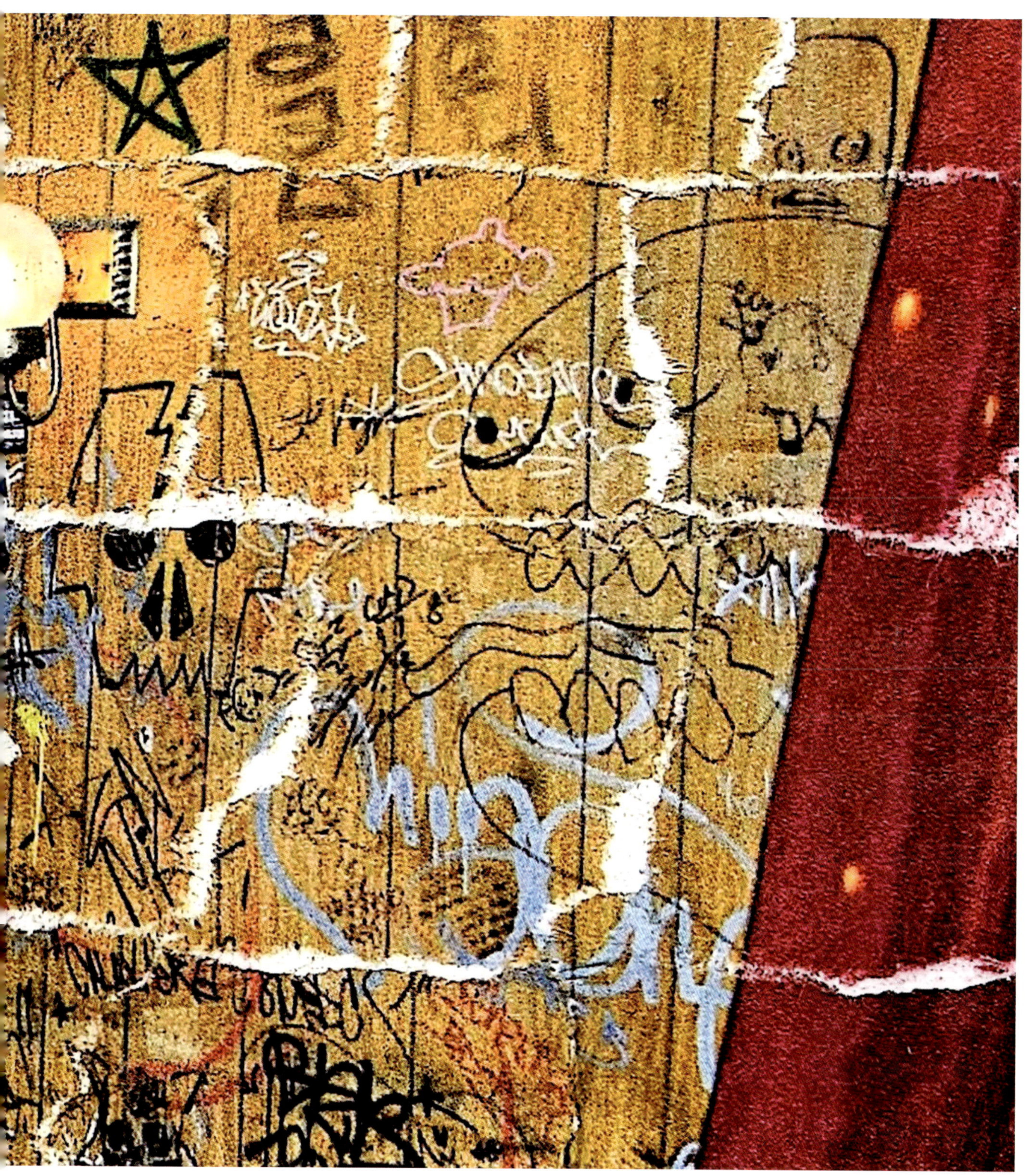

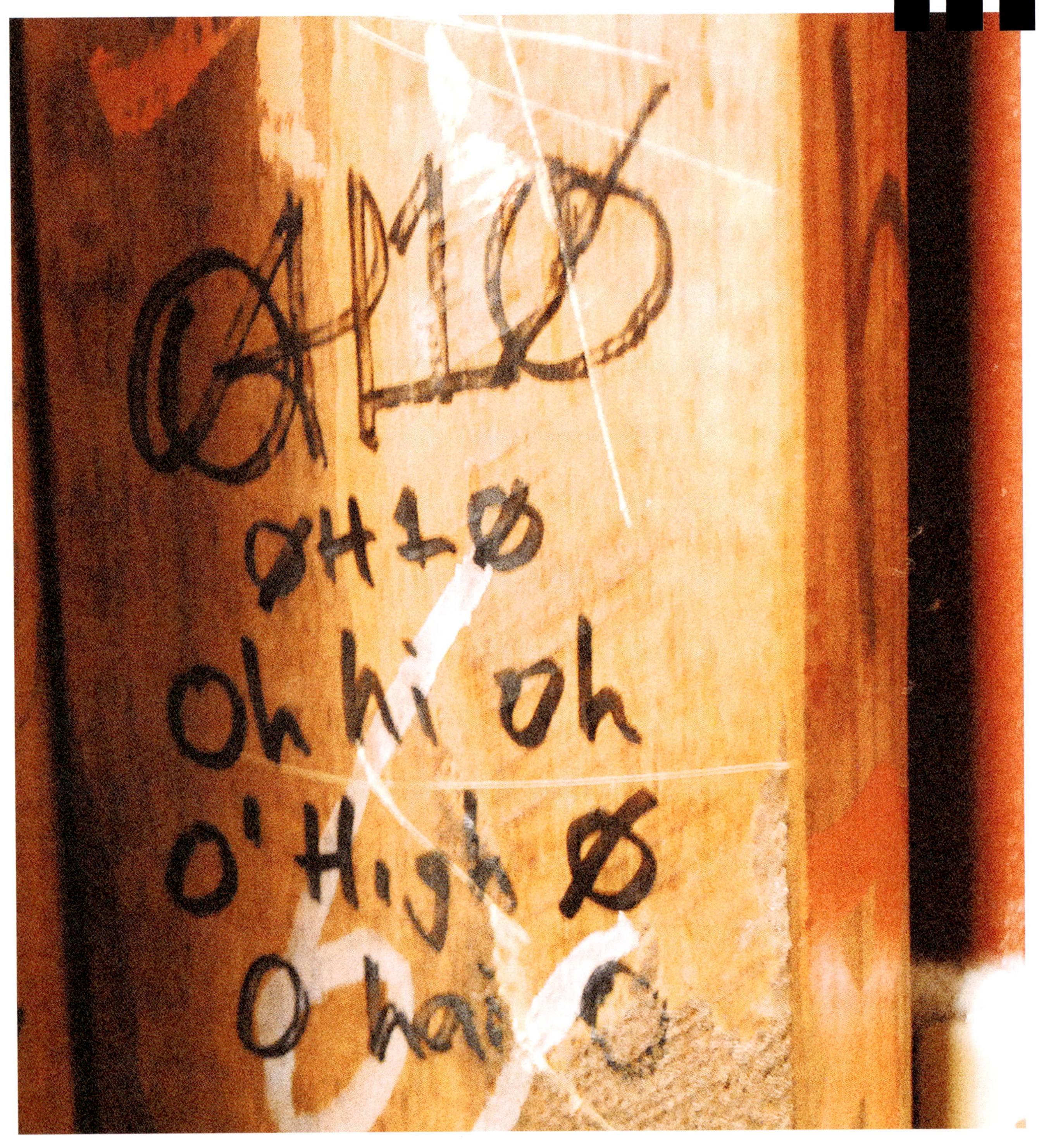

Alligator
Bar

06.01.2011
01:42pm

Williamsburg
Brooklyn

the Ext

fine Shit

you Love

nigga Boston

I SEE YOU SHITTING...DAMN YOU LOOK GOOD... I WISH I COULD TAKE A SHIT TOO BUT I DON'T HAVE AN ANUS.

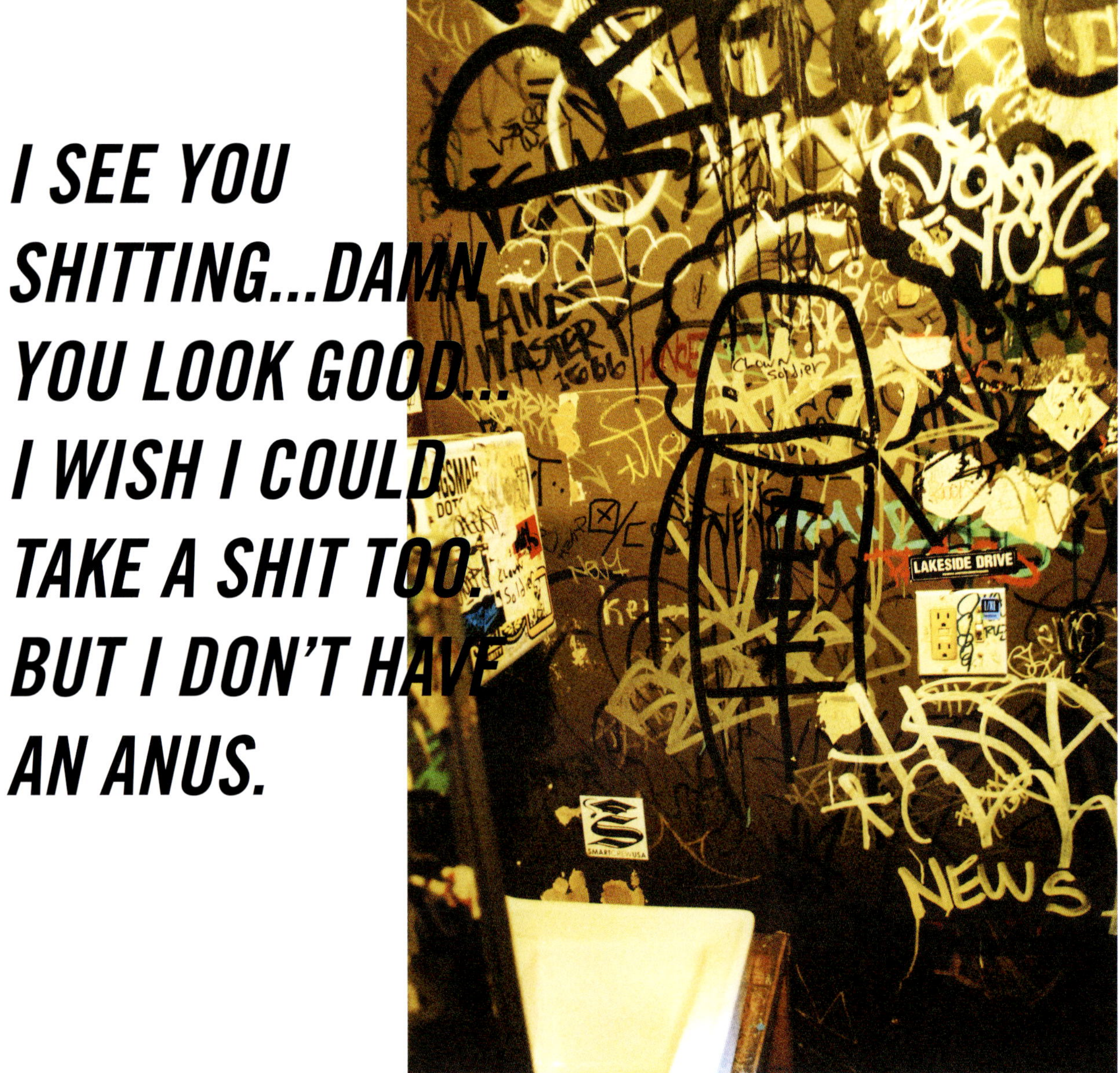

12.04.2010
02:30pm

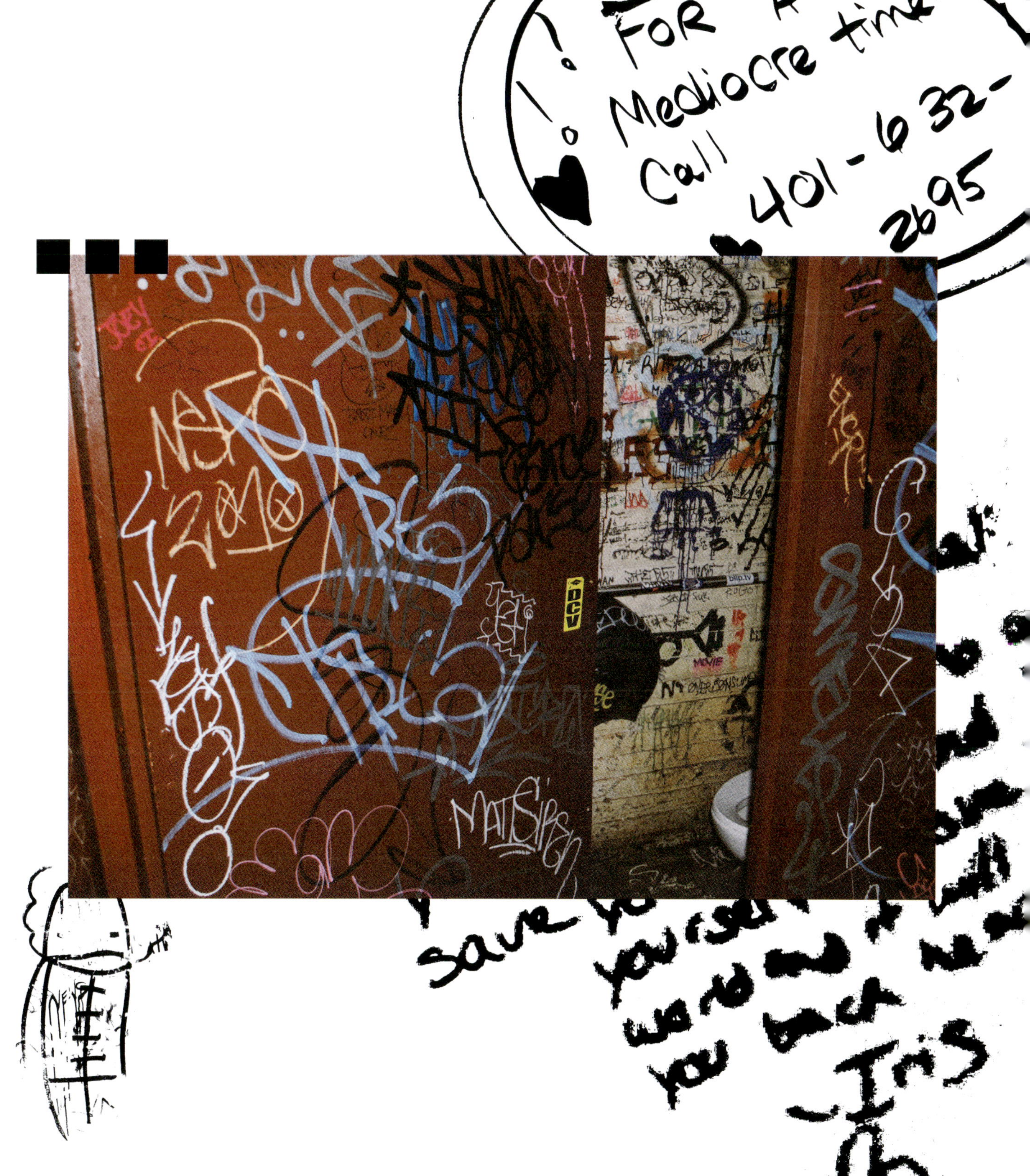
FOR A
Mediocre time
Call
401 - 6 32 -
2695
save yo
you'sa
wa no
you
Iris

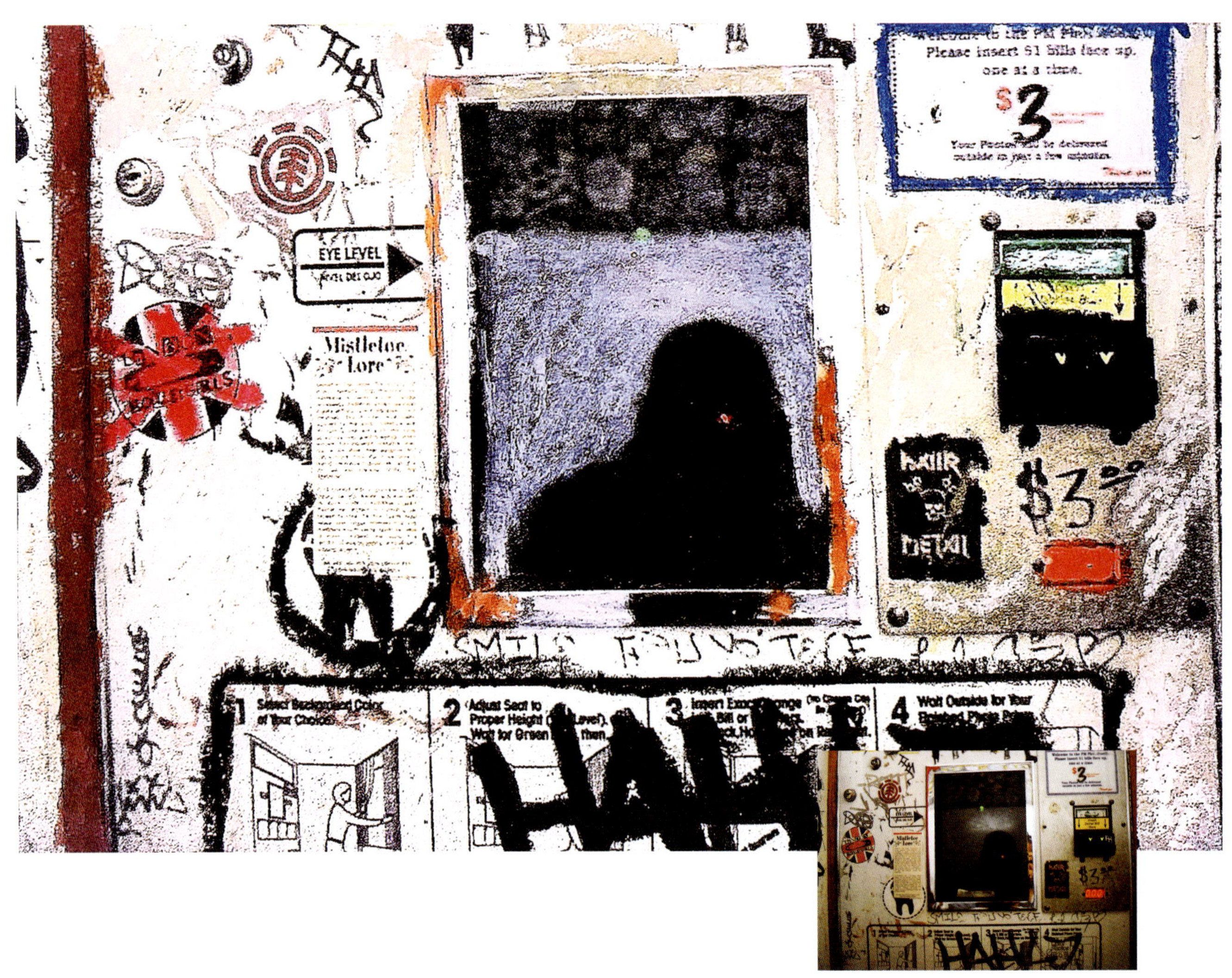

EYE LEVEL
NIVEL DEL OJO
Mistletoe Lore
$3
$3

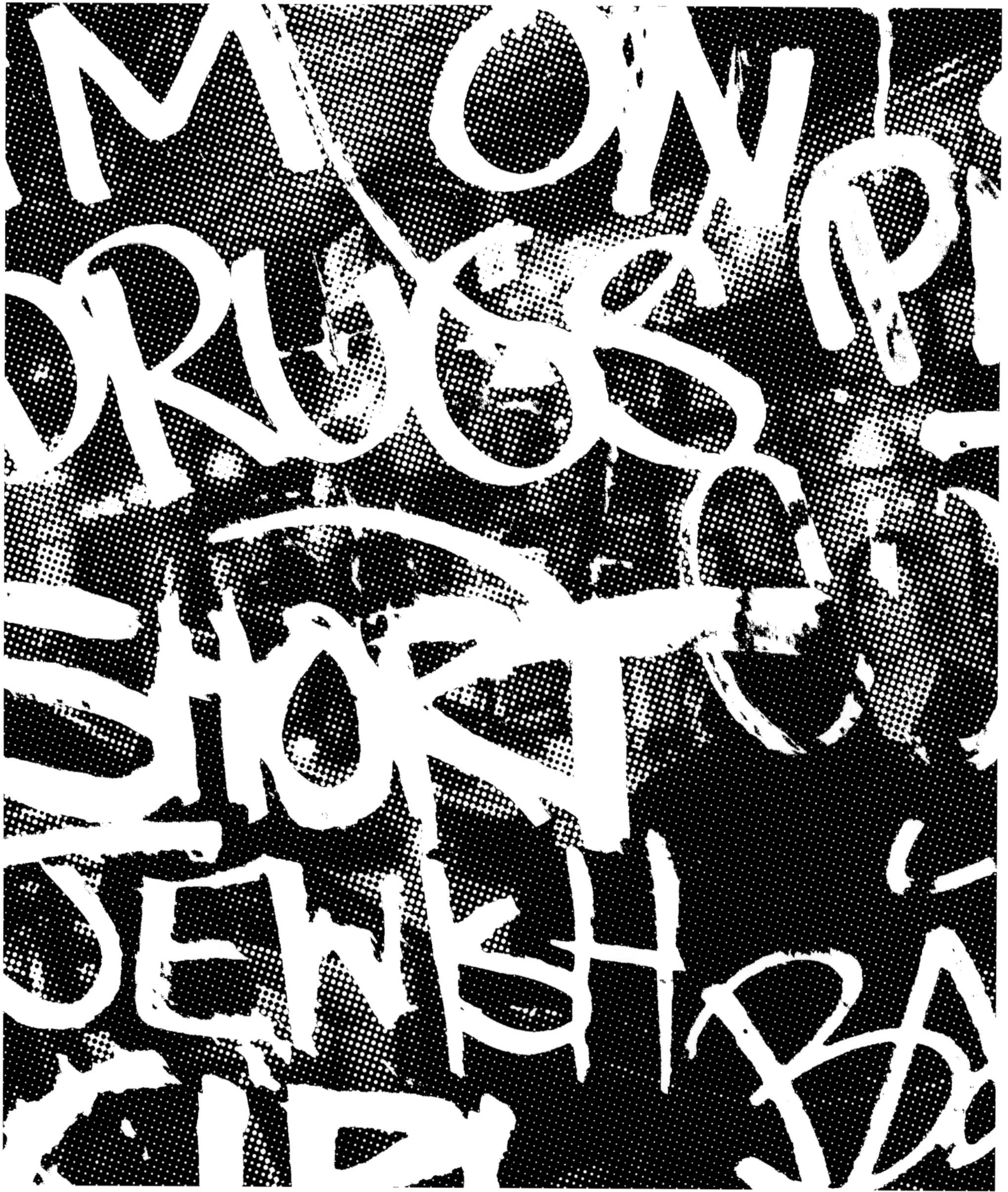

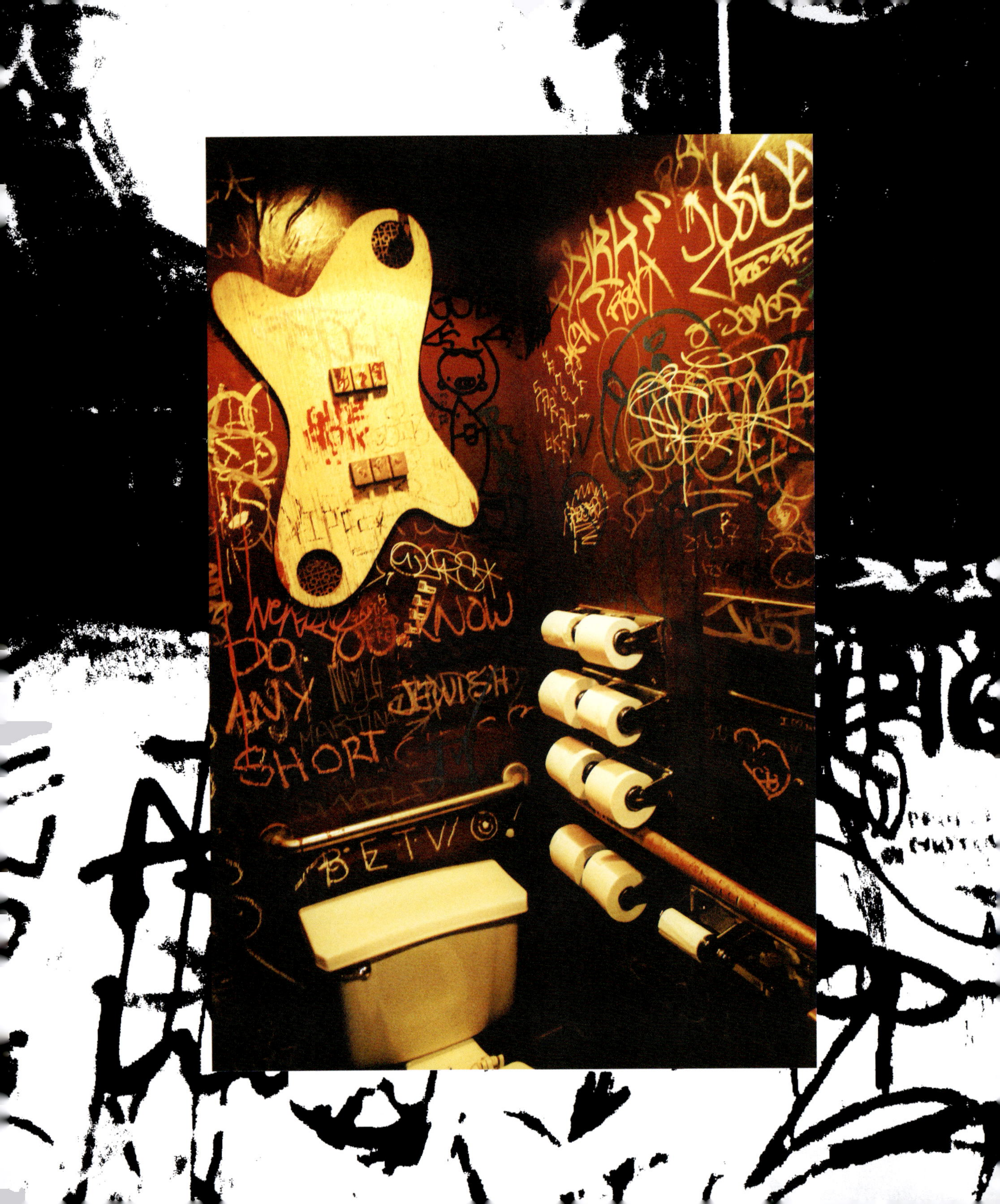

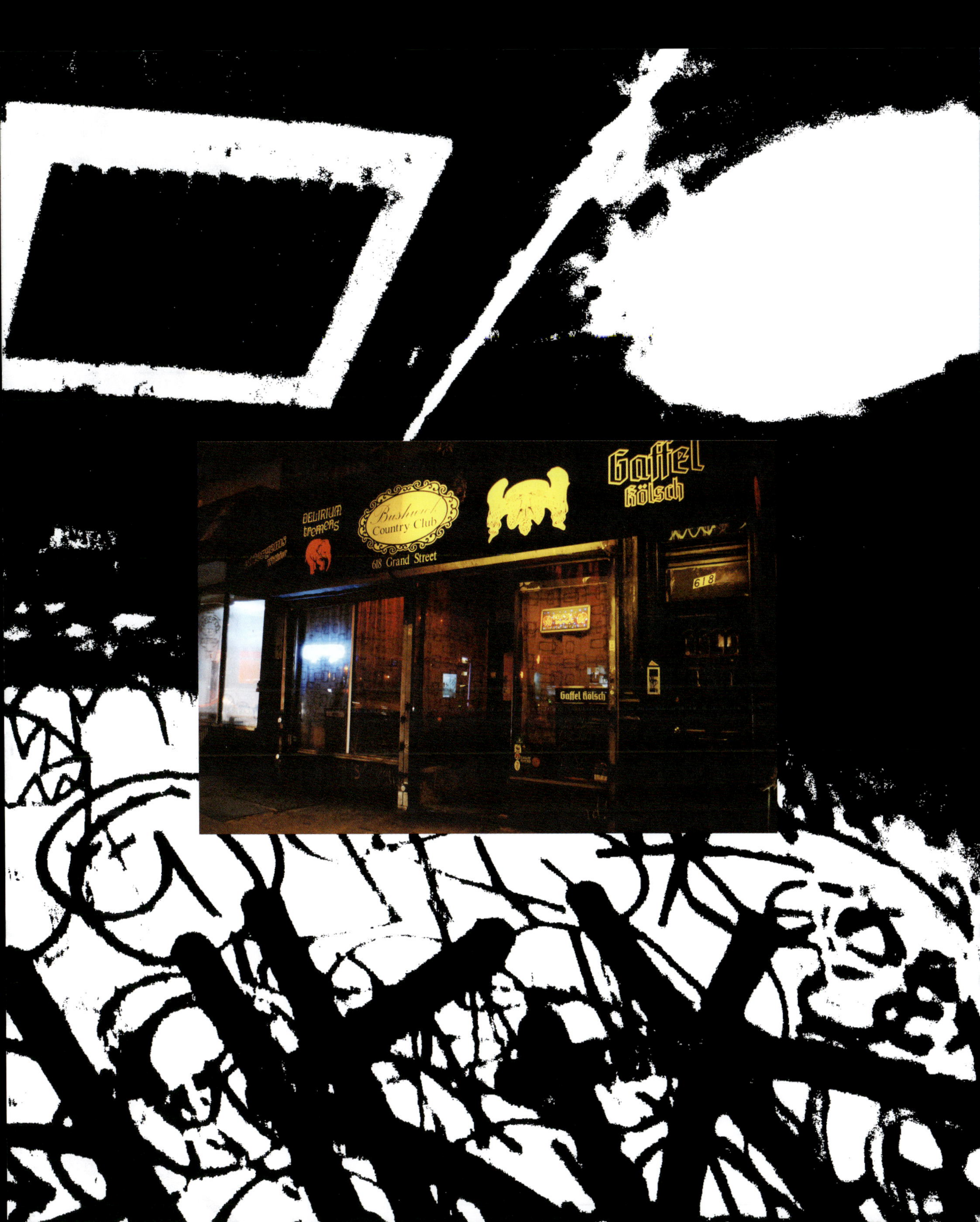

DELIRIUM tremens
Bushwick Country Club
618 Grand Street
Gaffel Kölsch
618
Gaffel Kölsch

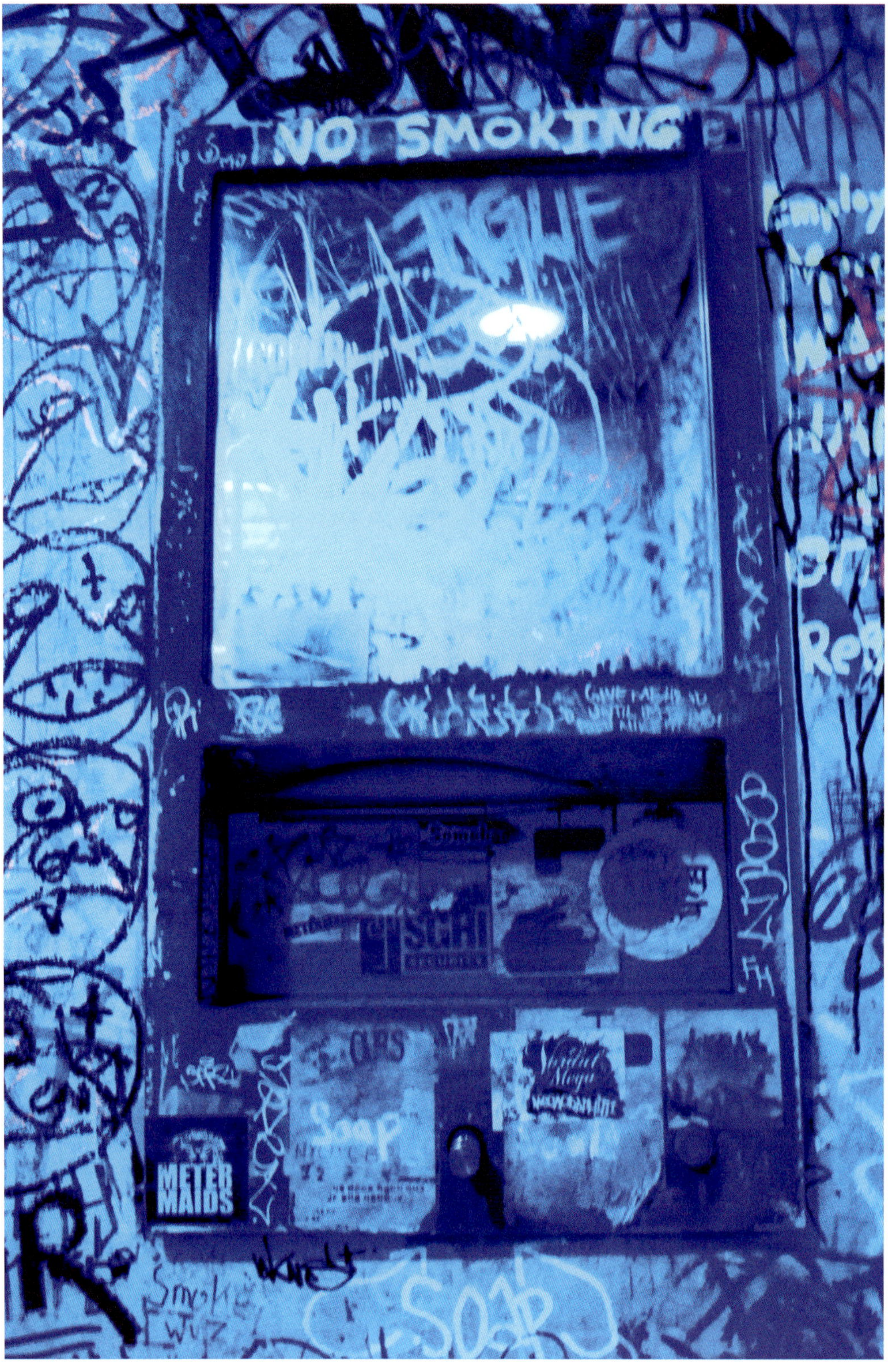
NO SMOKING
METER MAIDS
Soap

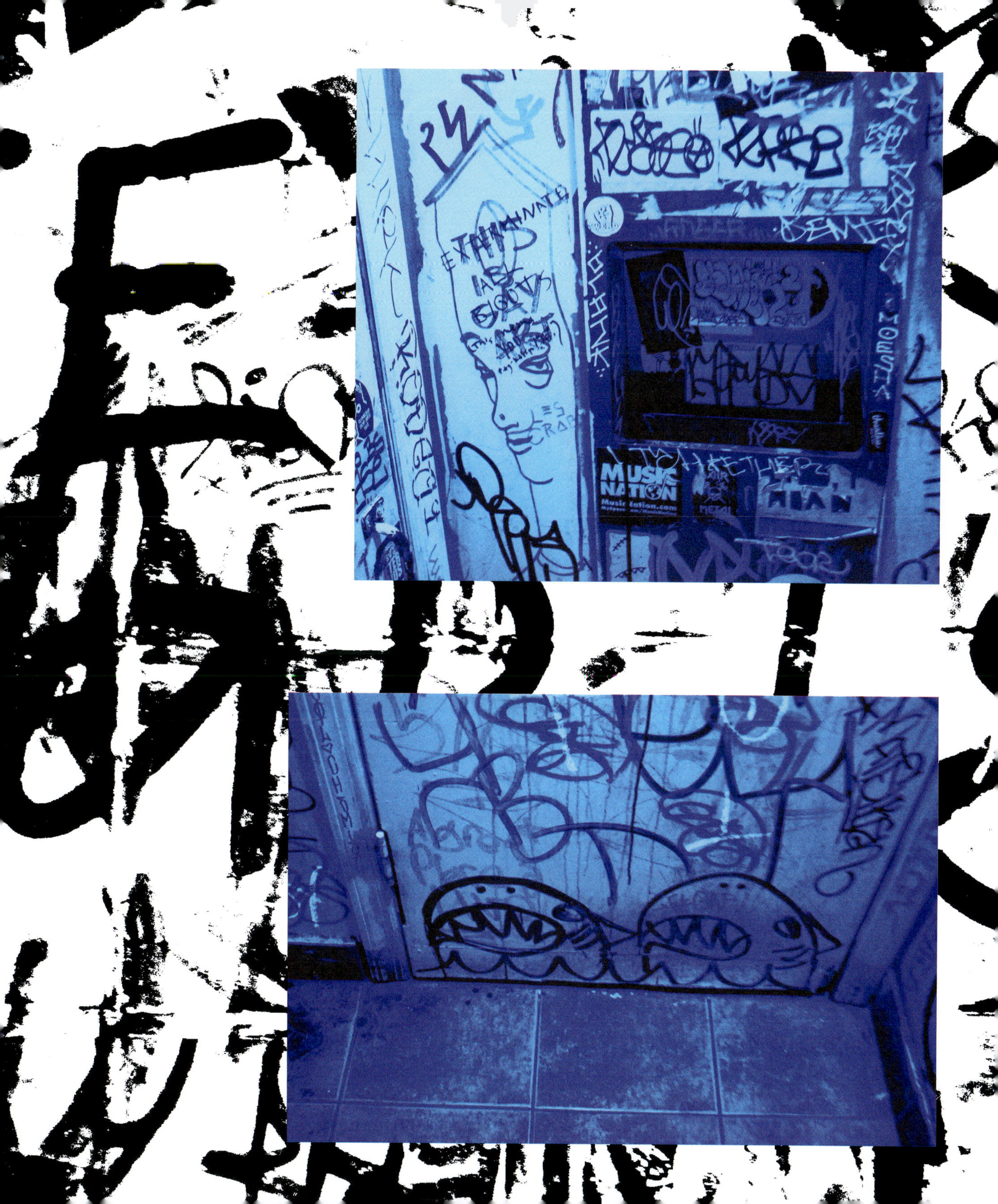

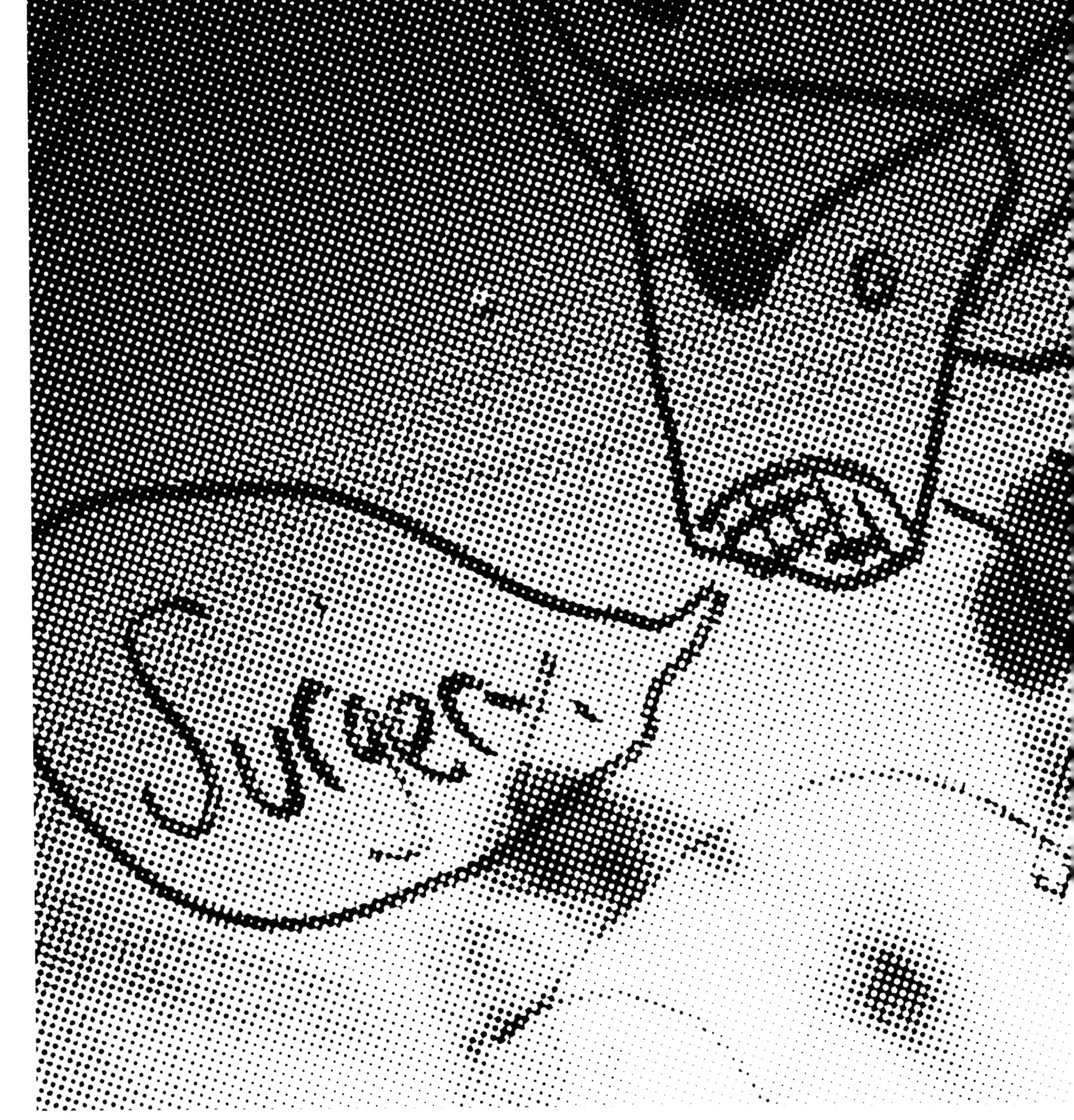

Sweet

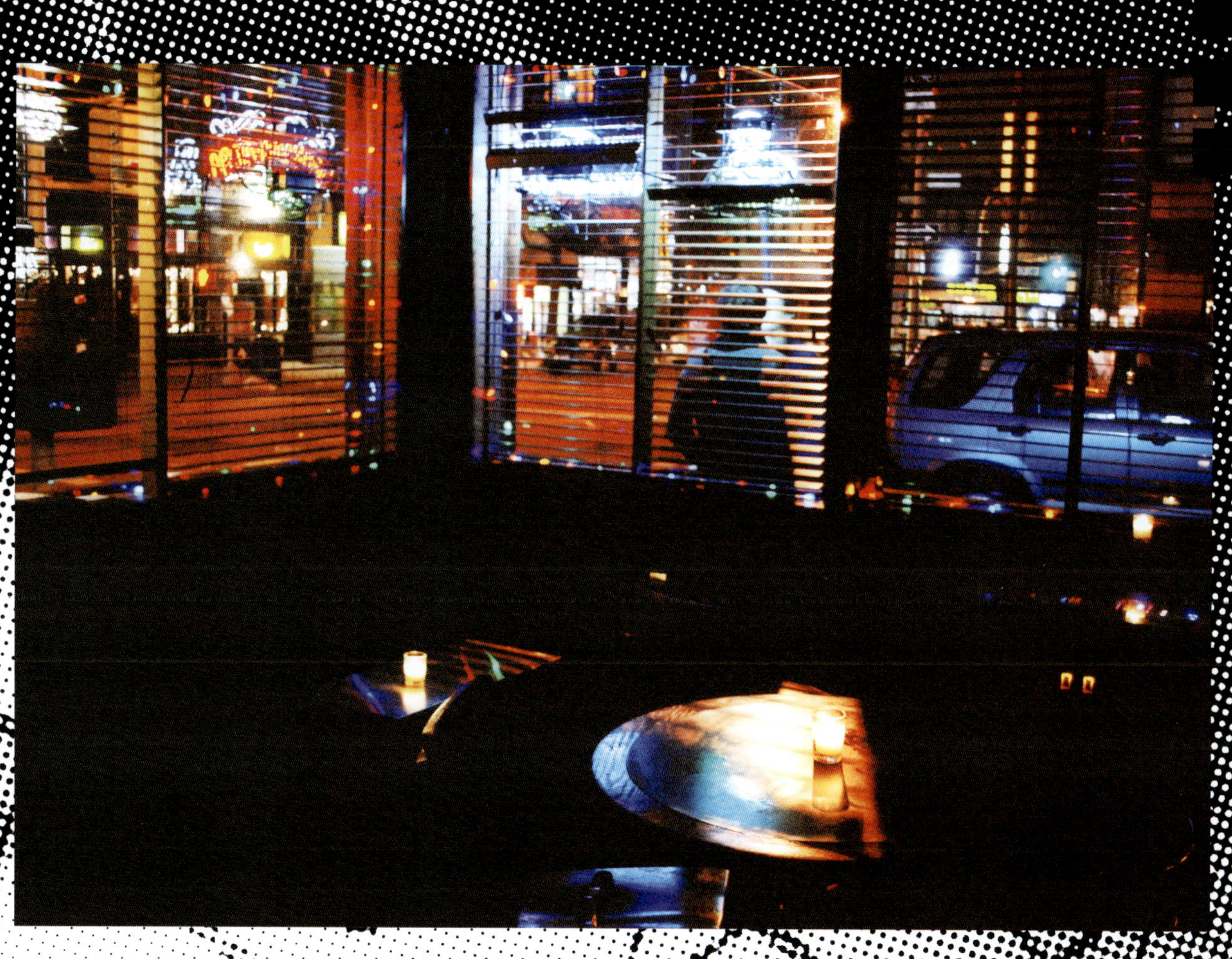

" YOU'RE NOT
DRUNK IF YOU
CAN LIE ON THE
FLOOR WITHOUT
HOLDING ON"

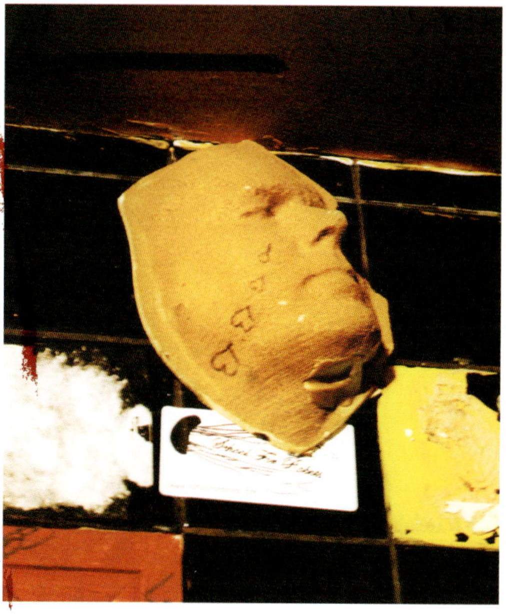

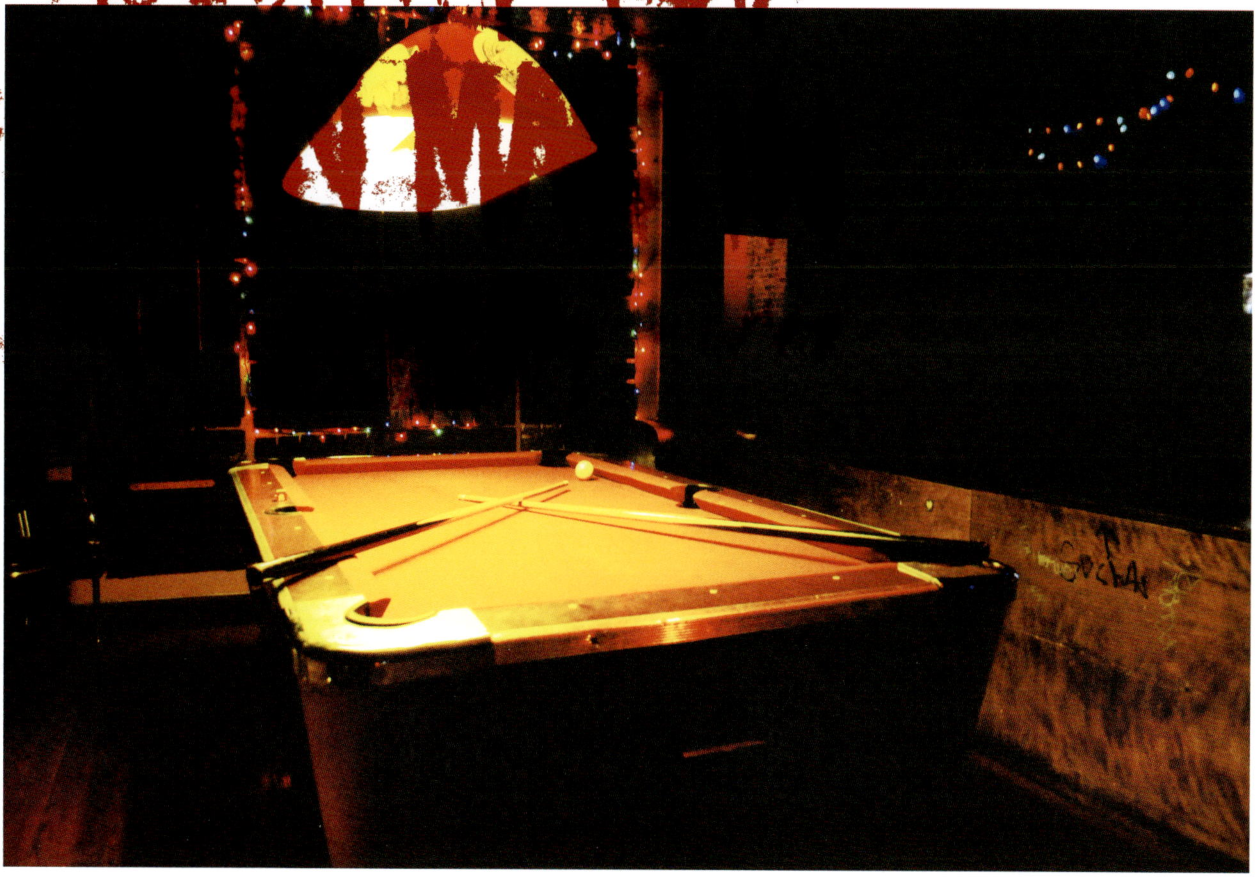

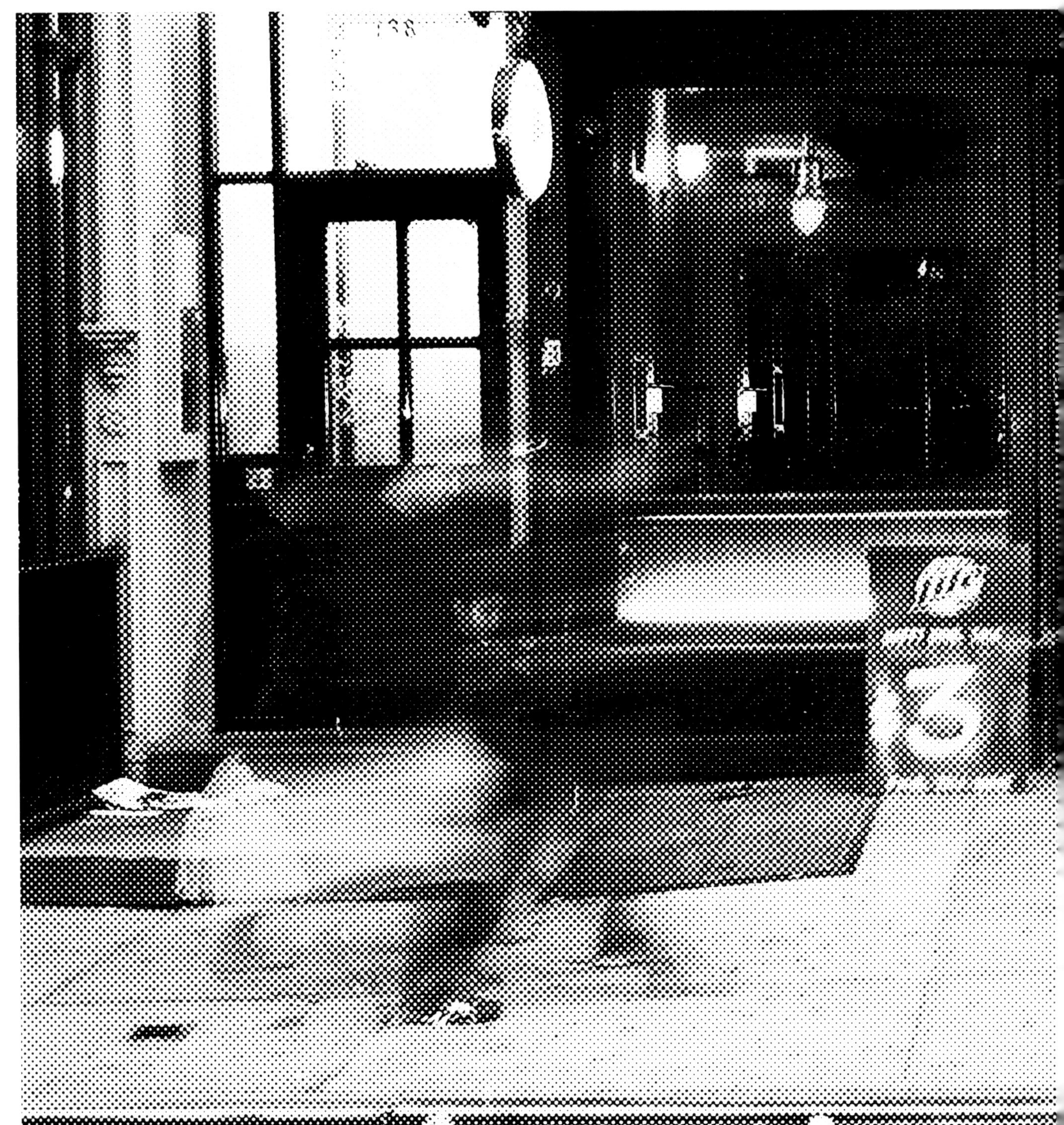

Local 138

11.13.2010
04:50pm

Lower East Side
Manhattan

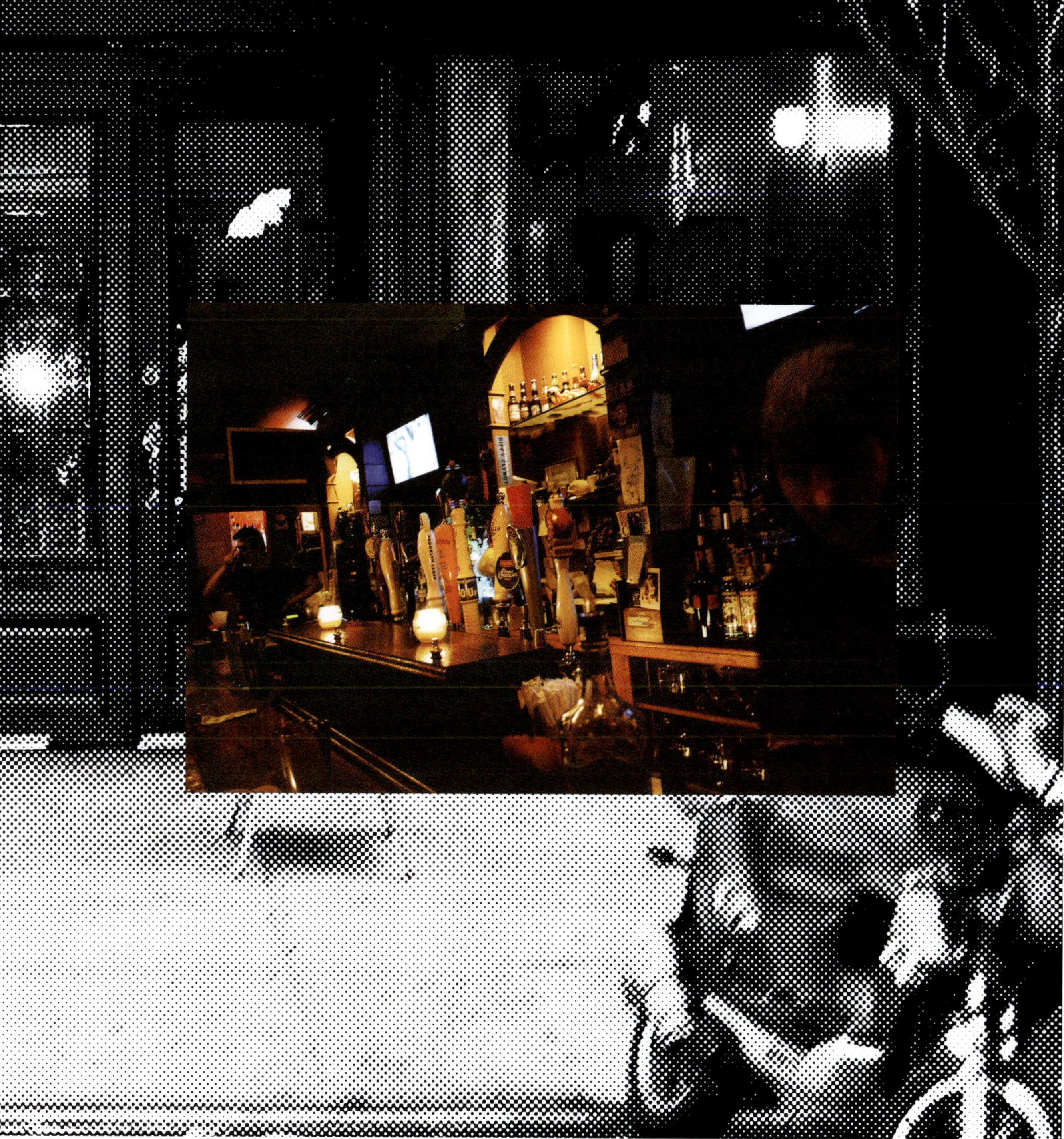

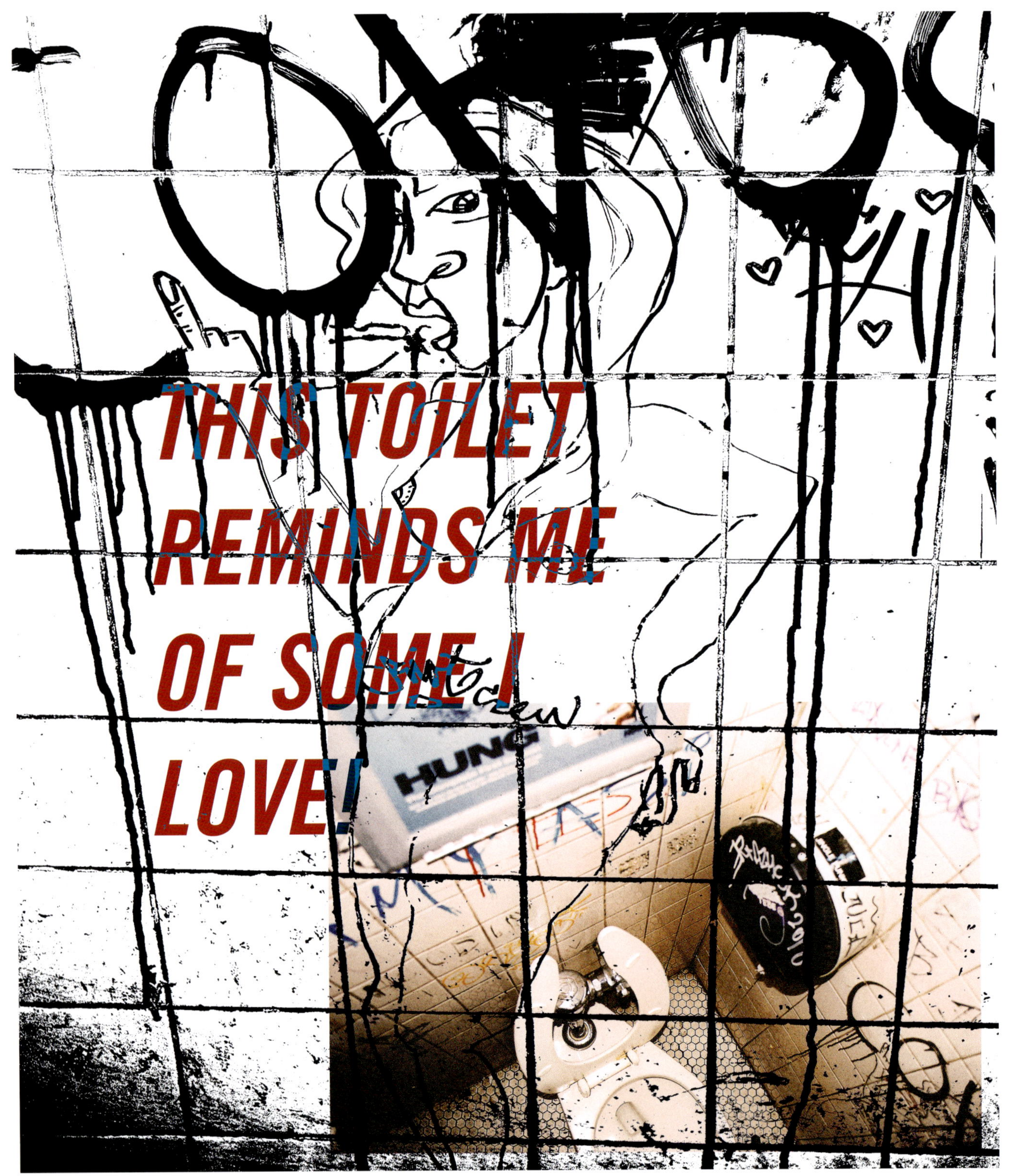

THIS TOILET
REMINDS ME
OF SOME I
LOVE!
HUNG

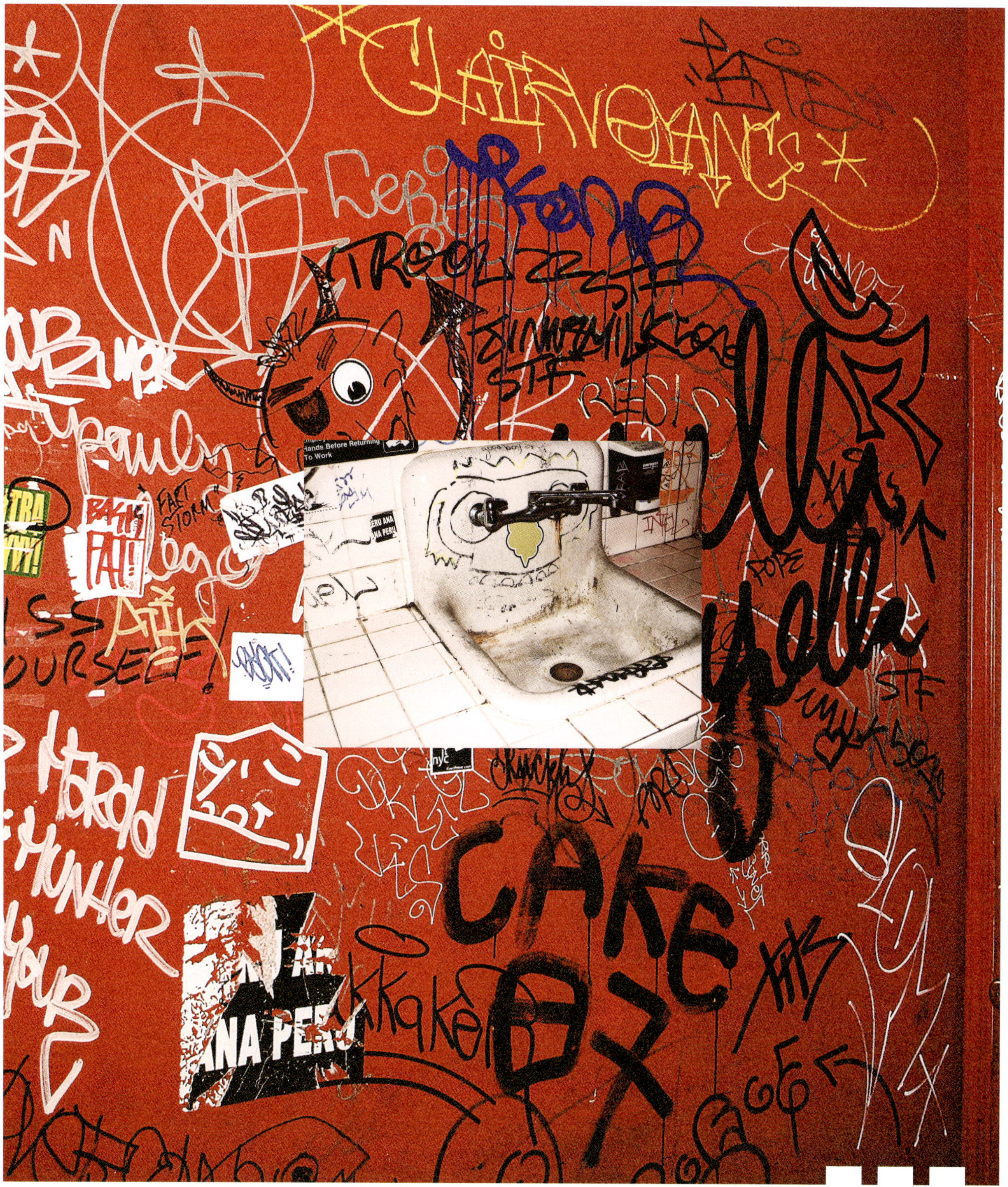

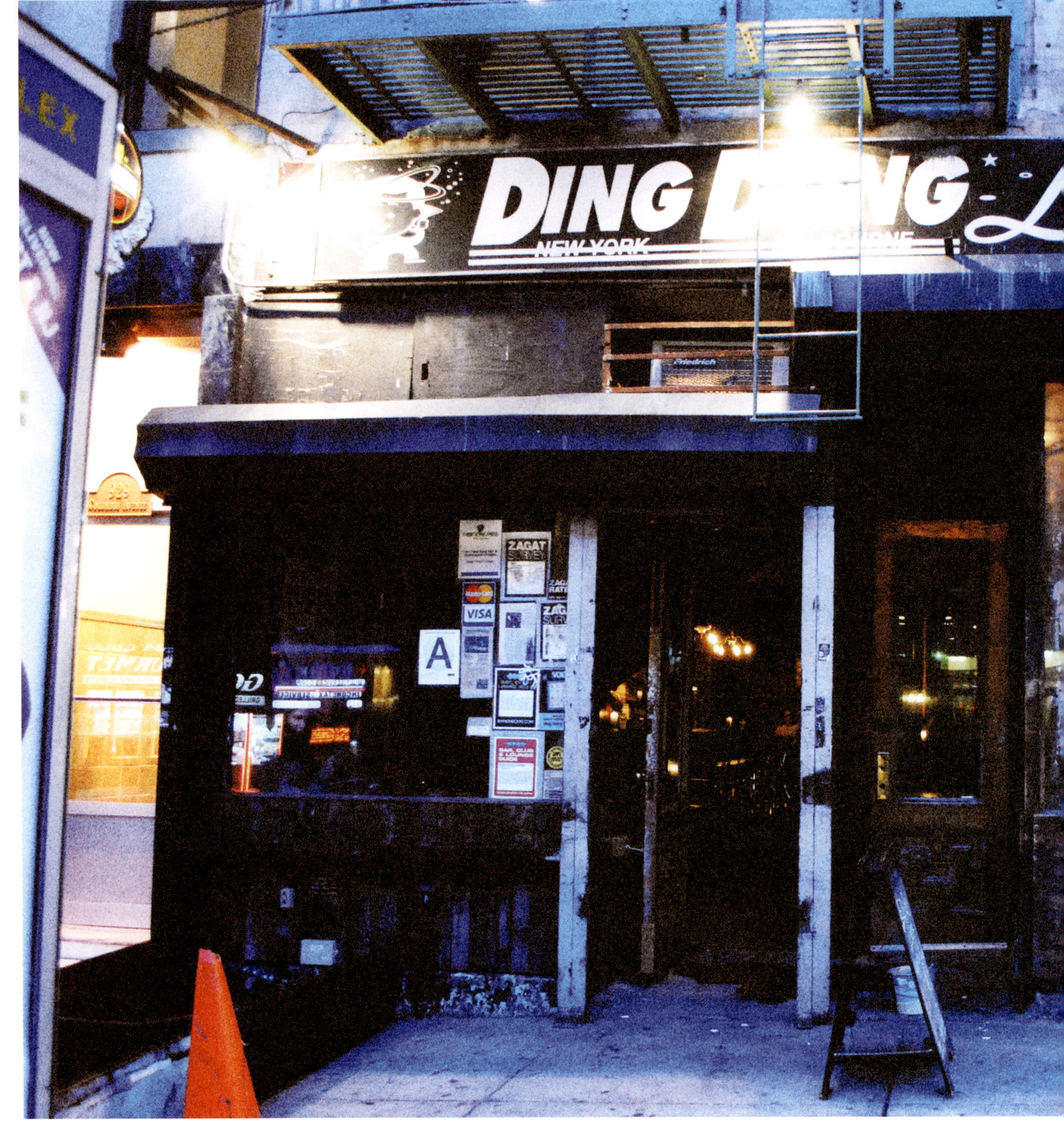

Ding Dong Lounge

04.11.2011
07:44pm

Upper West Side
Manhattan

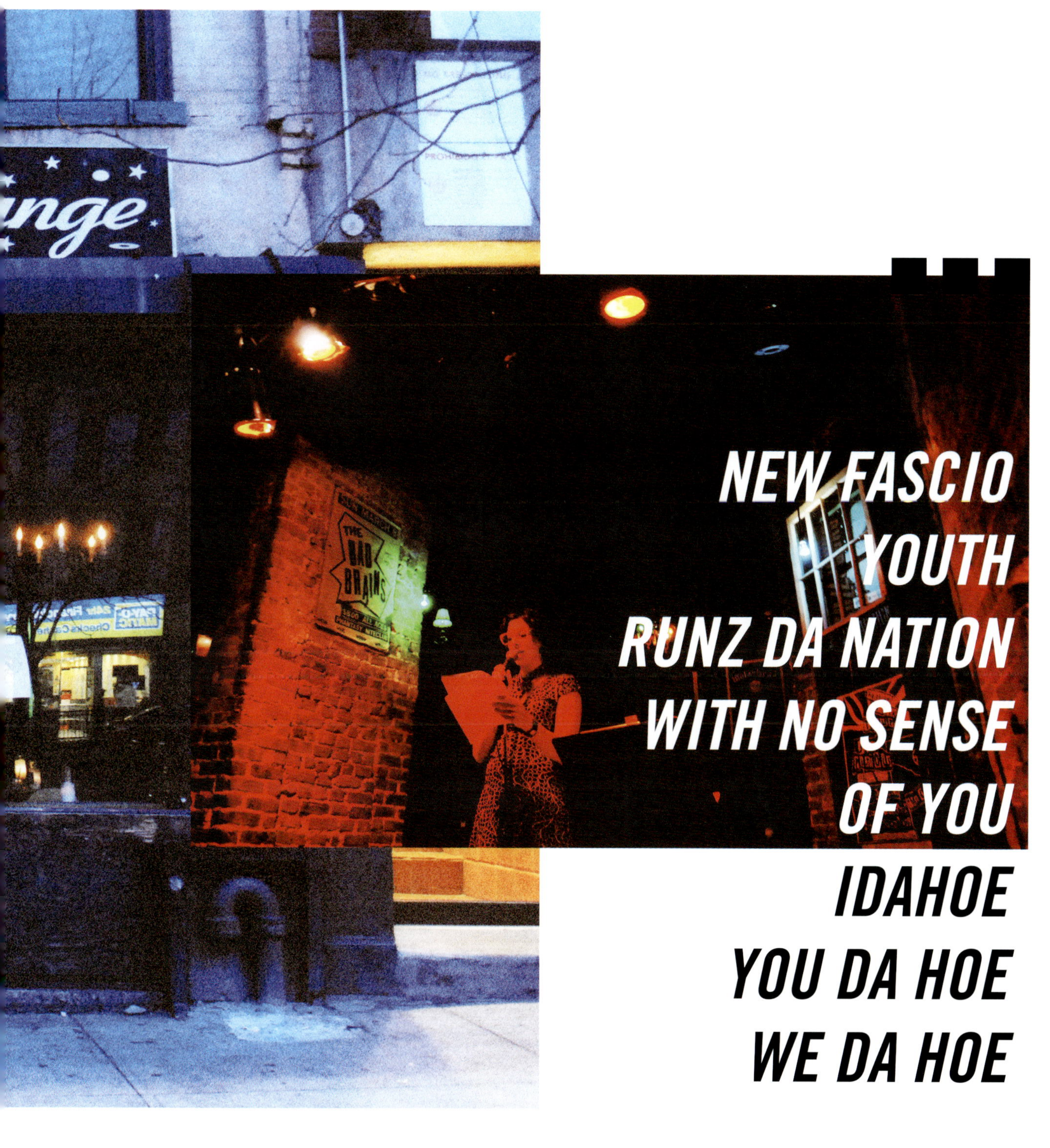
NEW FASCIO
YOUTH
RUNZ DA NATION
WITH NO SENSE
OF YOU
IDAHOE
YOU DA HOE
WE DA HOE

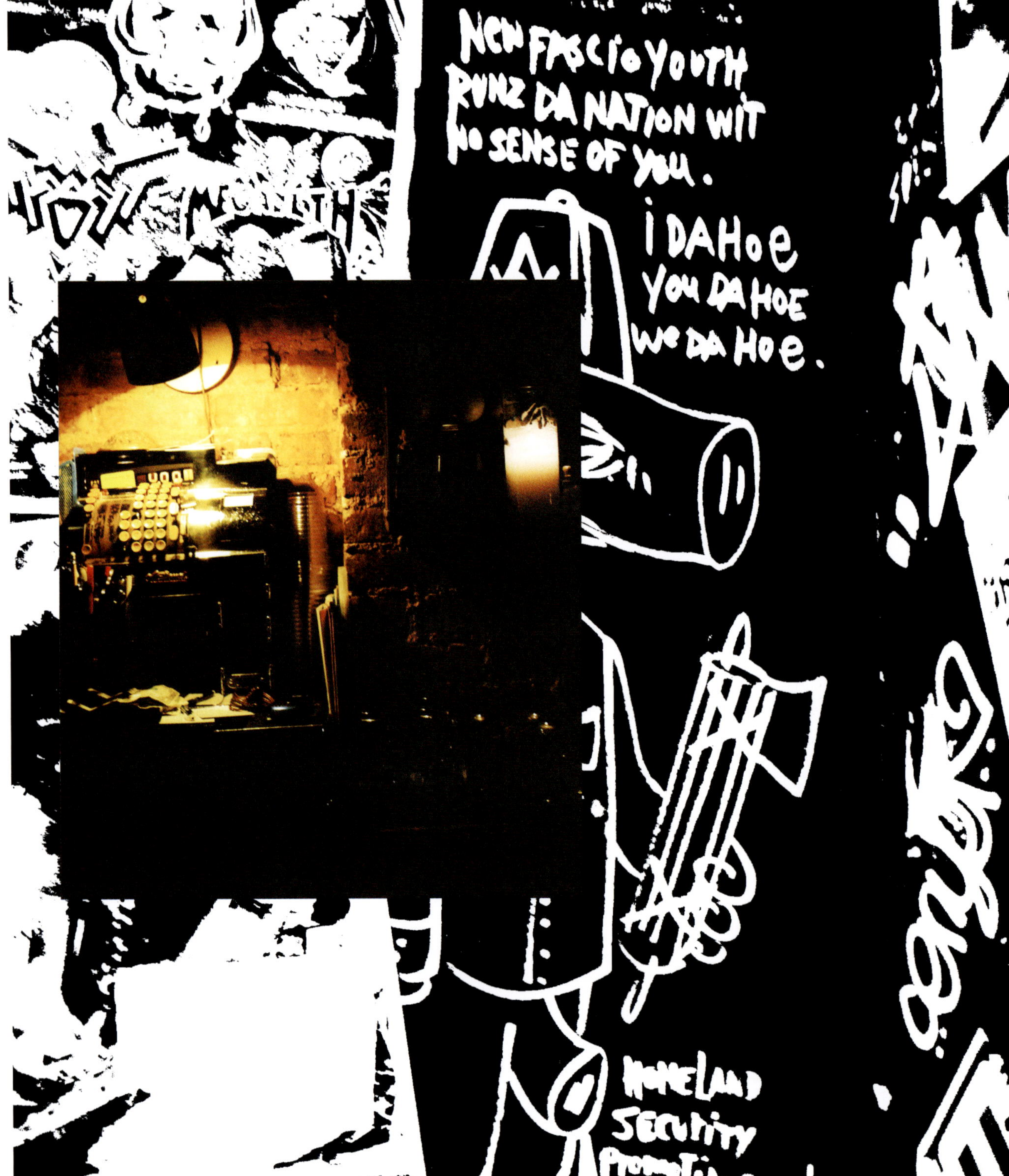

NEW FASCIO YOUTH
RVNZ DA NATION WIT
NO SENSE OF YOU.

i DAHoe
You DA Hoe
WE DA HoE.

HOMELAND
SECURITY

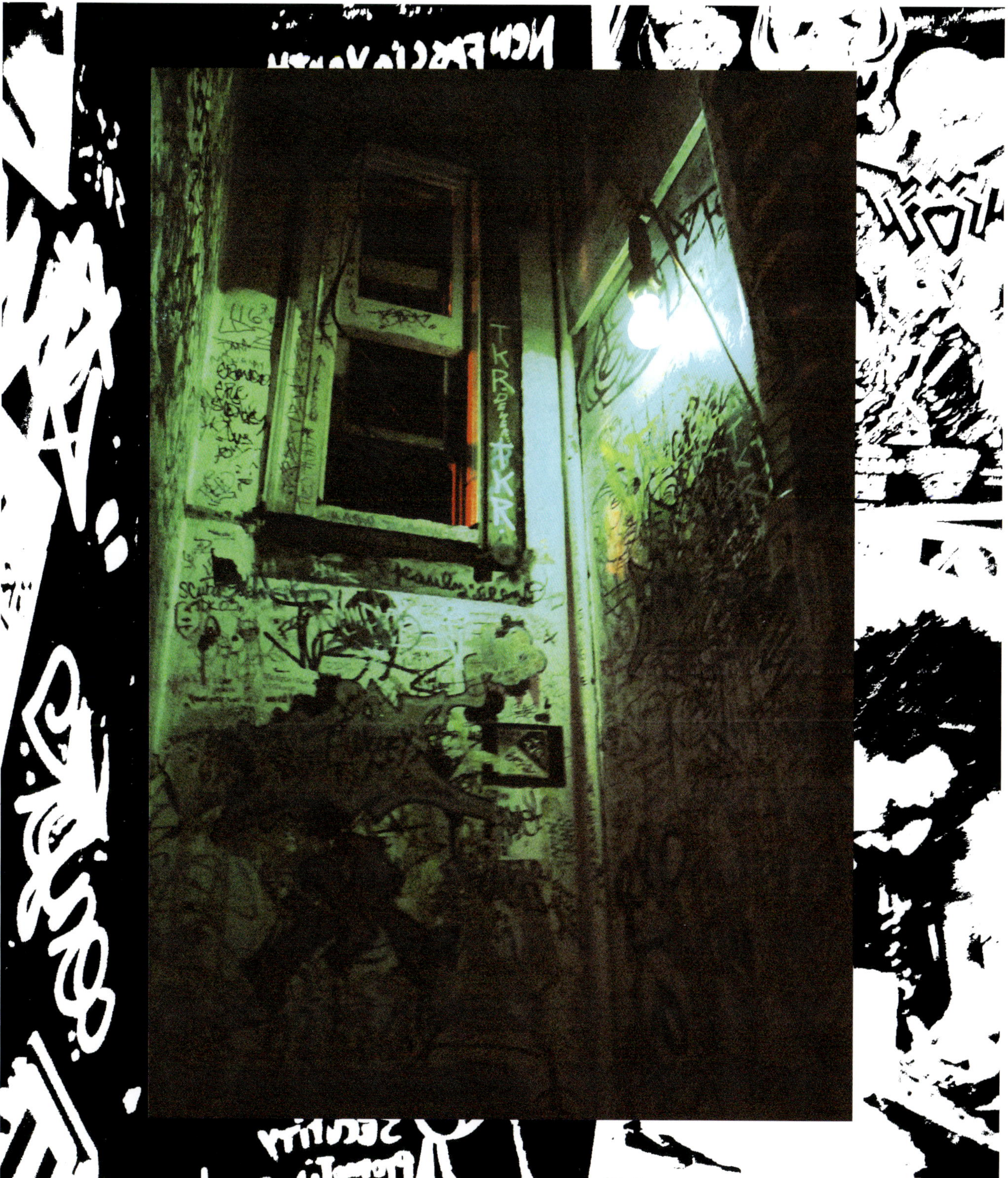

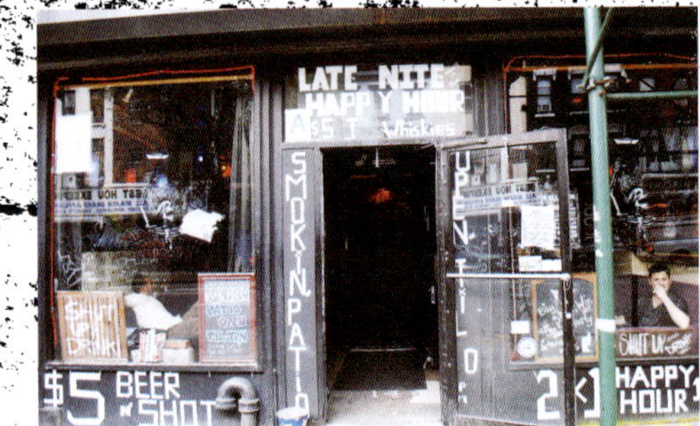

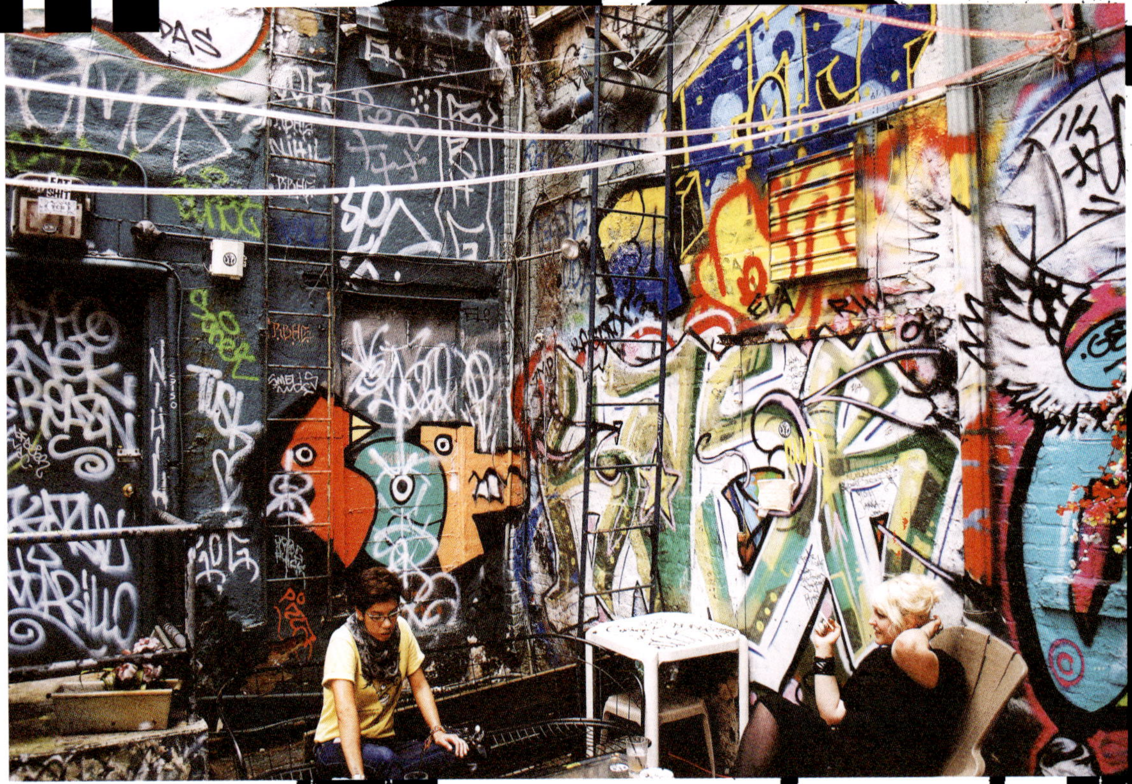

Double Down Saloon

04.11.2011
02:04pm

Lower East Side
Manhattan

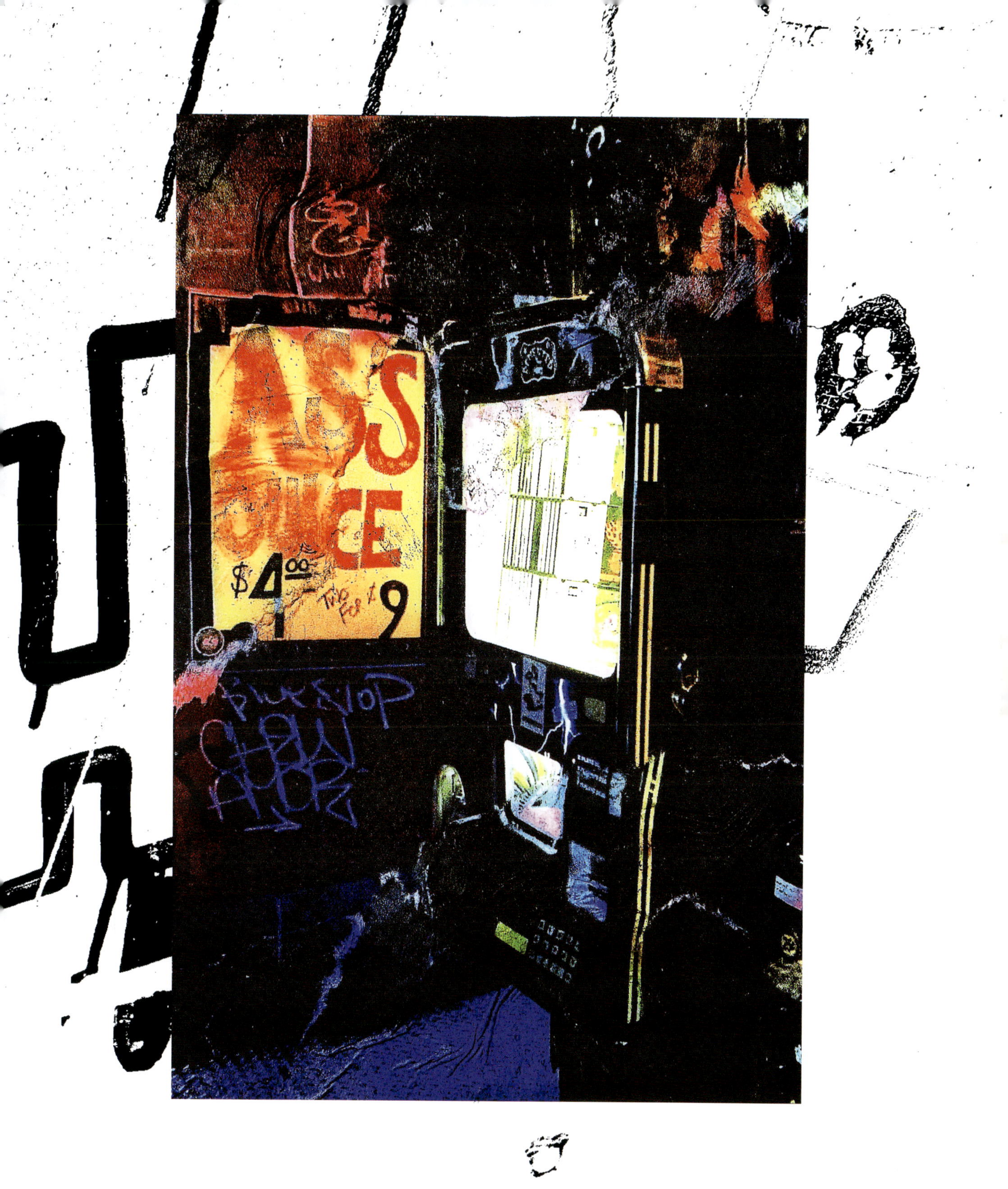

JUICE
$4.00
TWO FOR 9

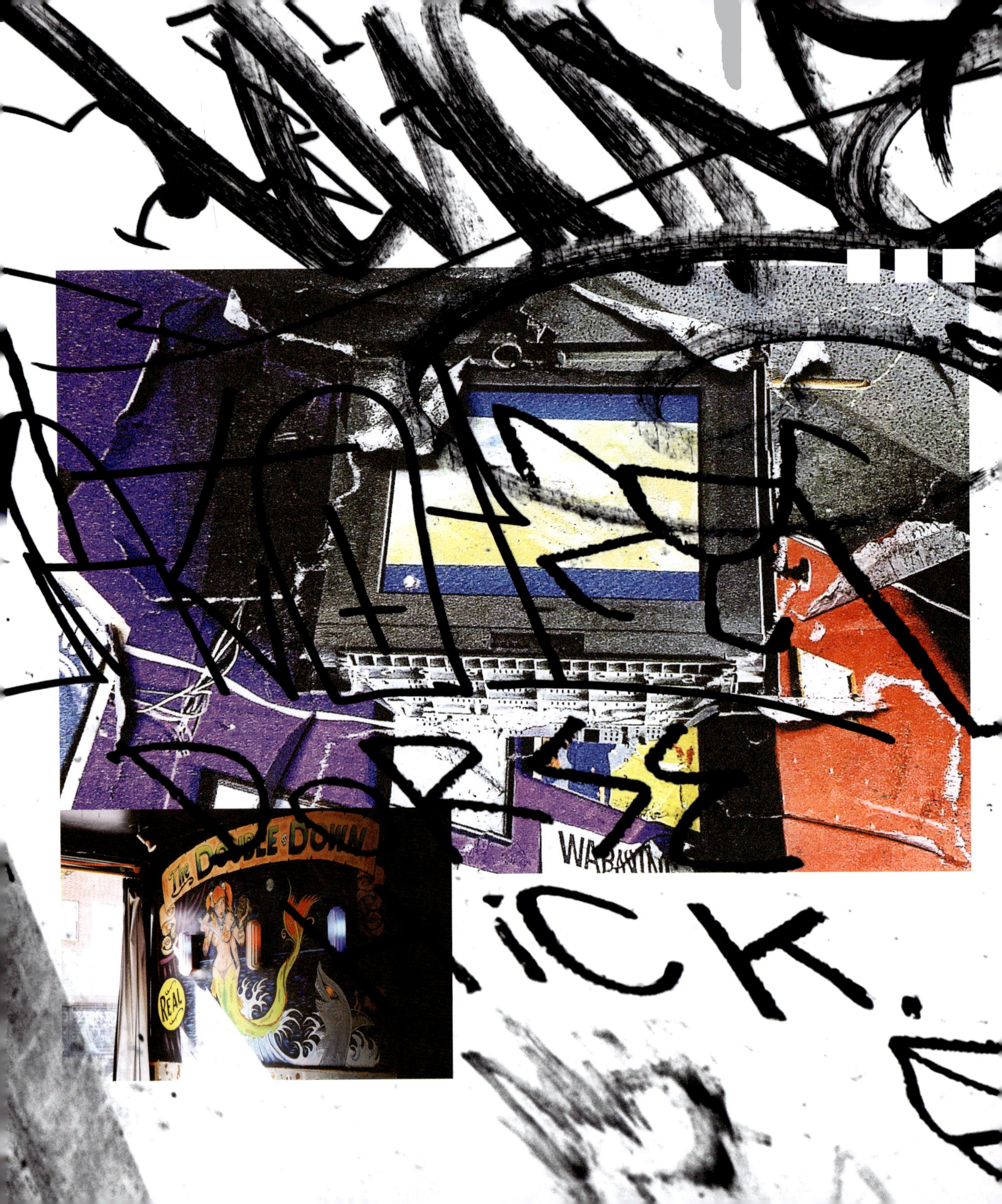

The DOUBLE DOWN
REAL

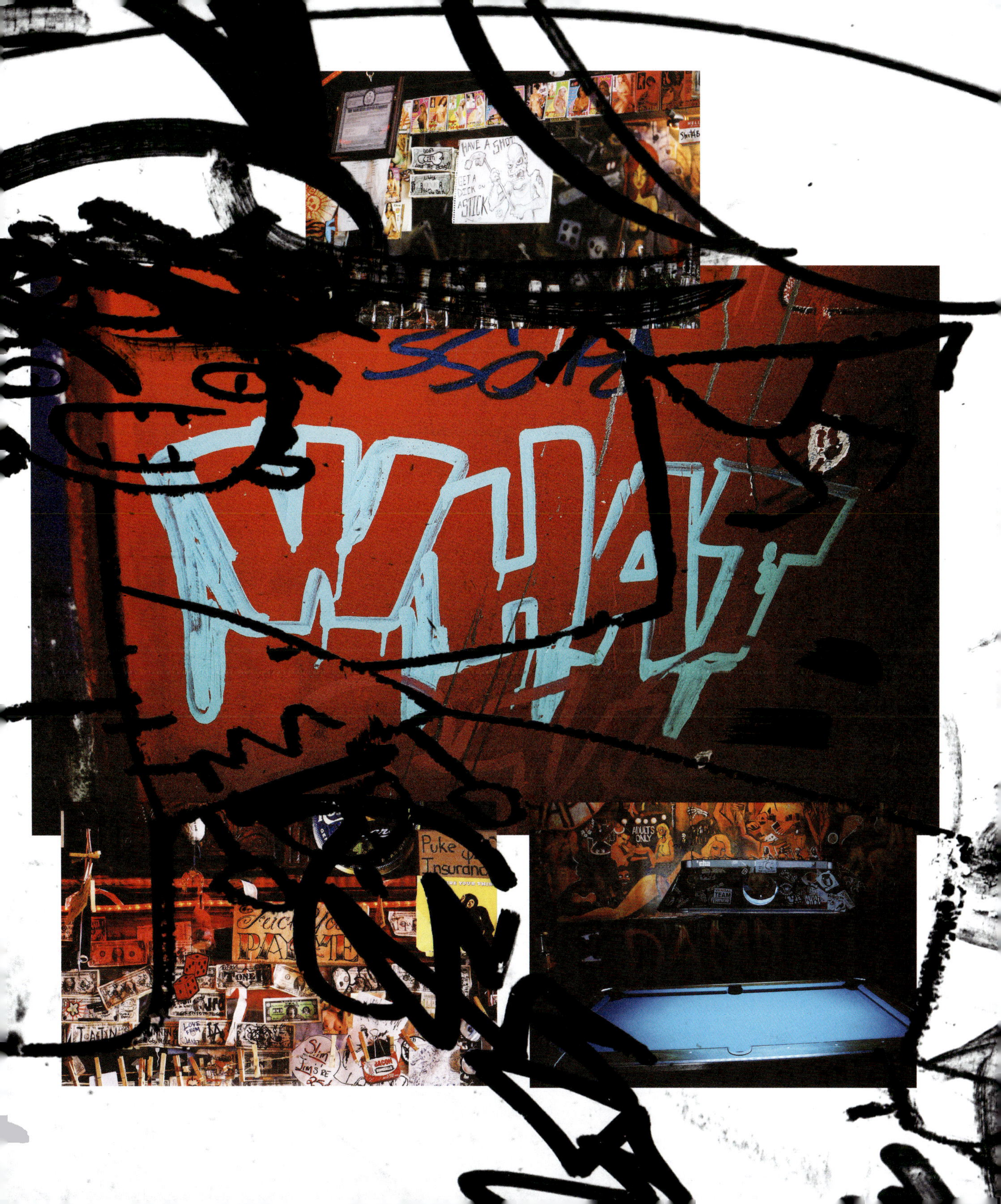

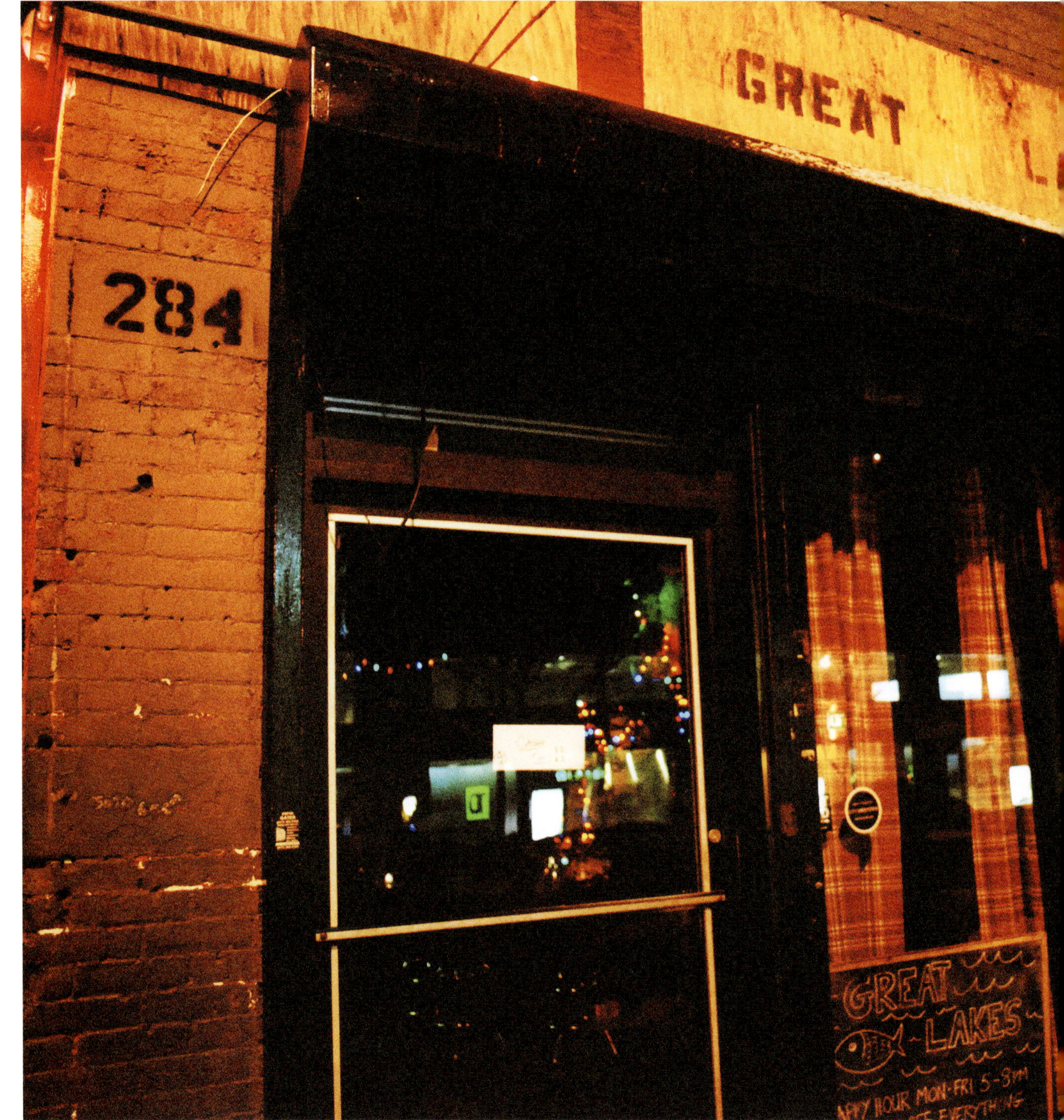

Great Lakes

01.29.2011
07:23pm

Park Slope
Brooklyn

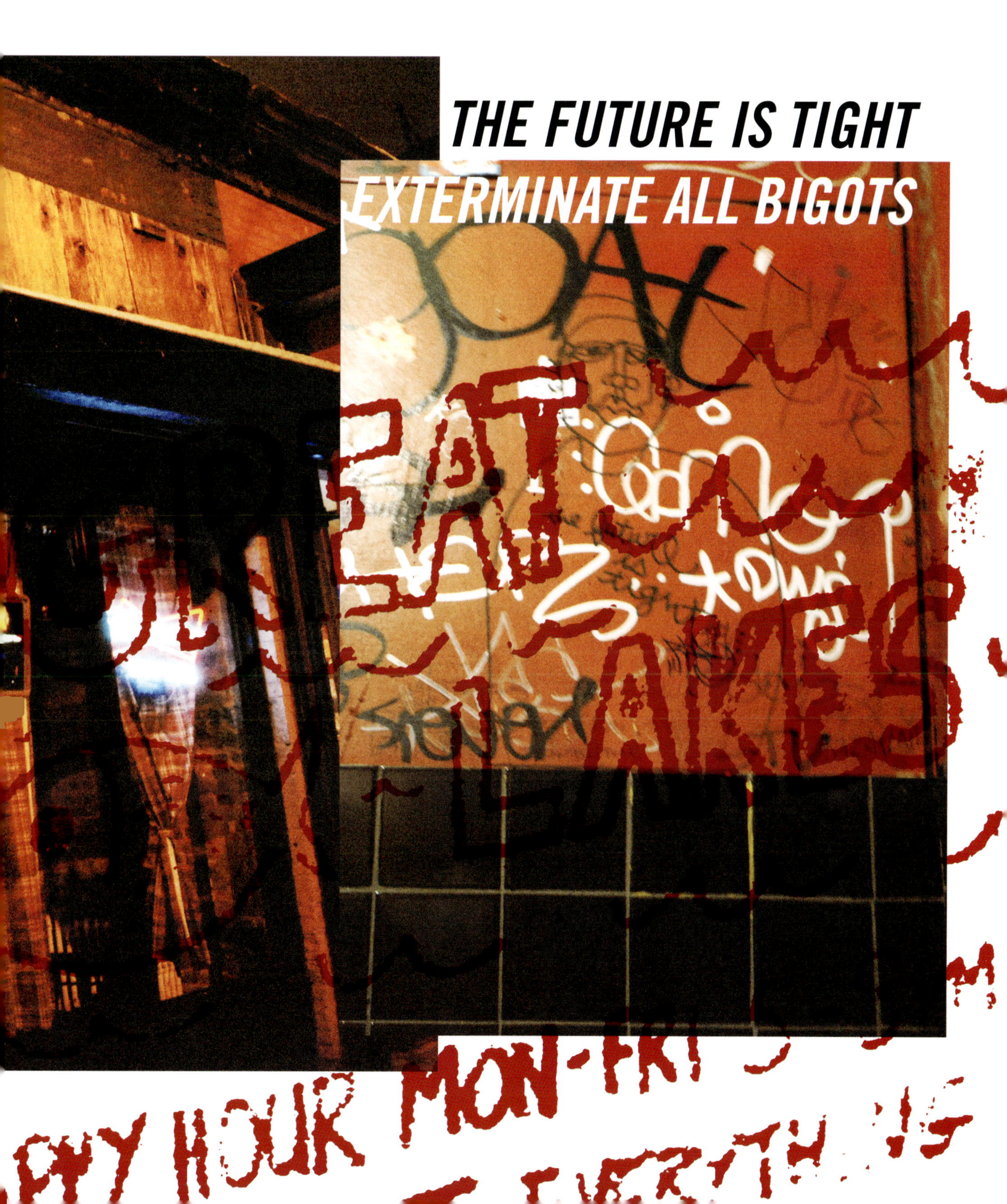

THE FUTURE IS TIGHT
EXTERMINATE ALL BIGOTS
HOUR MON-FRI

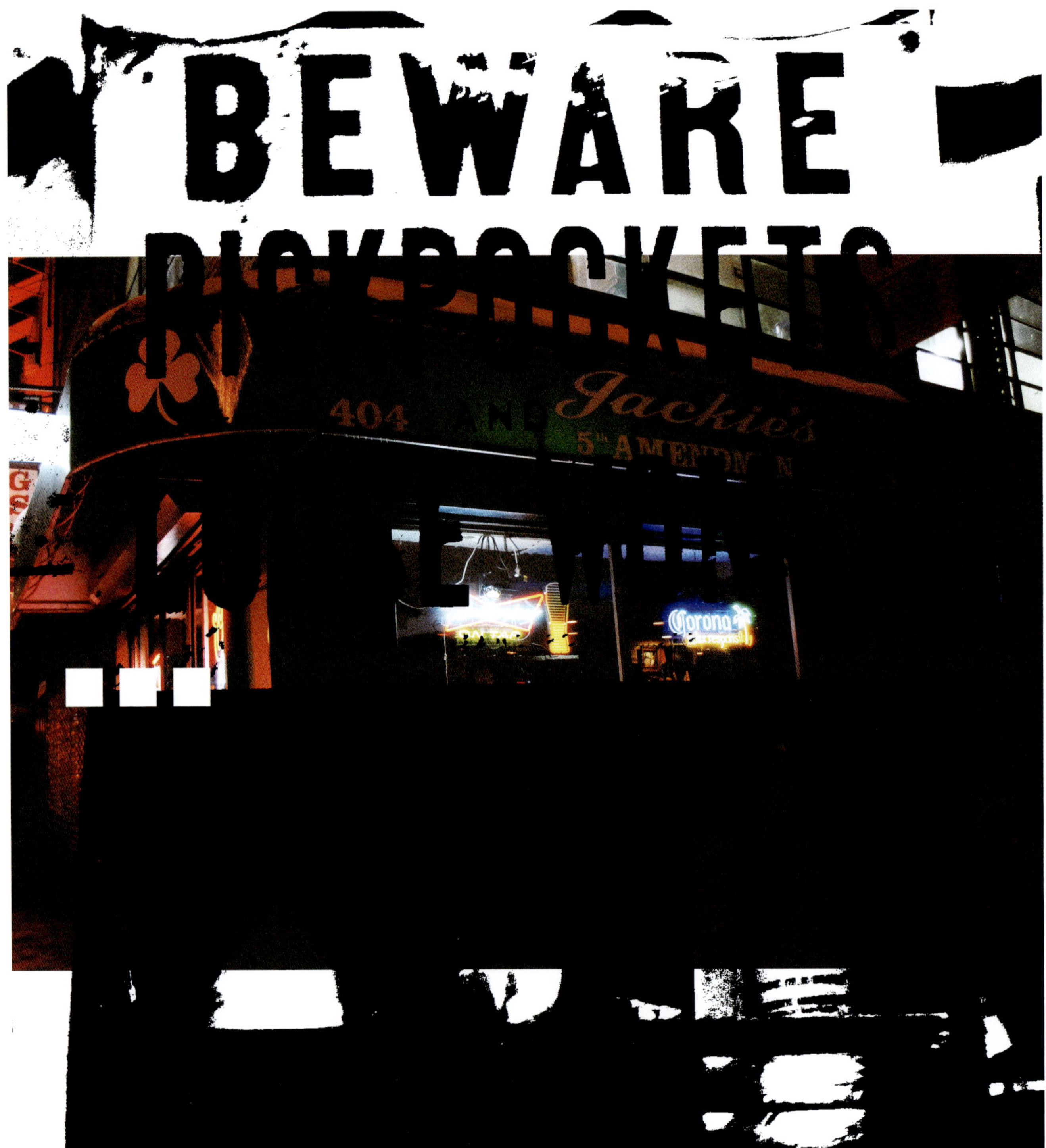

01.29.2011
07:23pm

Jackie's 5th Amendment

Park Slope
Brooklyn

Community

Dive bars have always been a staple of communion
& culture...customers come & go.

Time changes everything.... weight, wardrobe, decor and
definitely price...which in turn affect patronage. Depending
on how long an establishment has been open, there's a
generation of folks who can attest to a time before when
the beer was cheaper, the shots were stronger and the
music was better.

Drink specials & shots, jukeboxes playing Van Halen,
The Strokes, Wu-Tang Clan or Sinatra, quarters lined up
on the pool table...frat boys, mixed in with Lower East
side residents. This scene is replicated from The Village,
Upper East Side to Bushwick to Astoria.

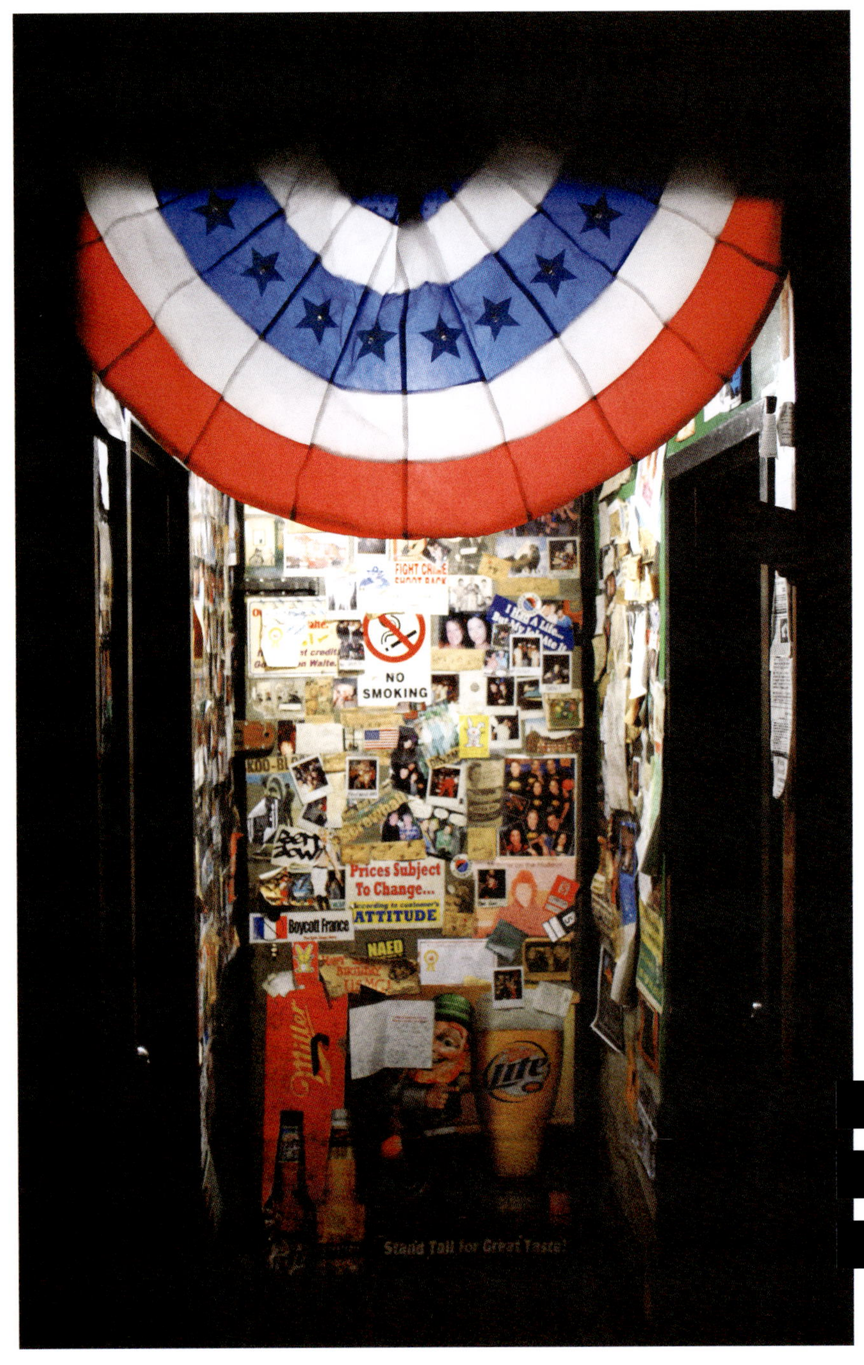

NO SMOKING
Prices Subject To Change...
according to customer's ATTITUDE
Boycott France
Miller
lite
Stand Tall for Great Taste!

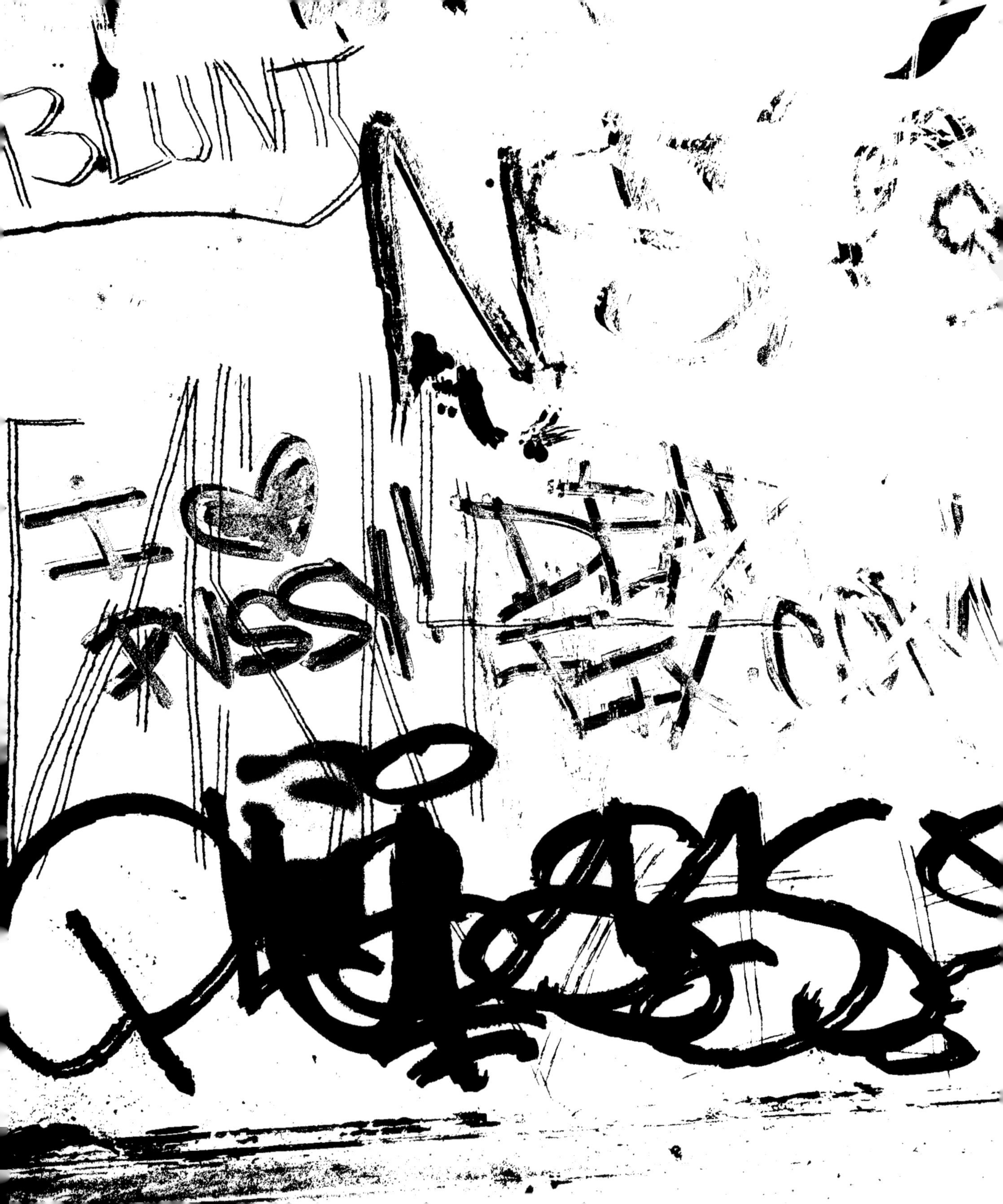
BLUNT

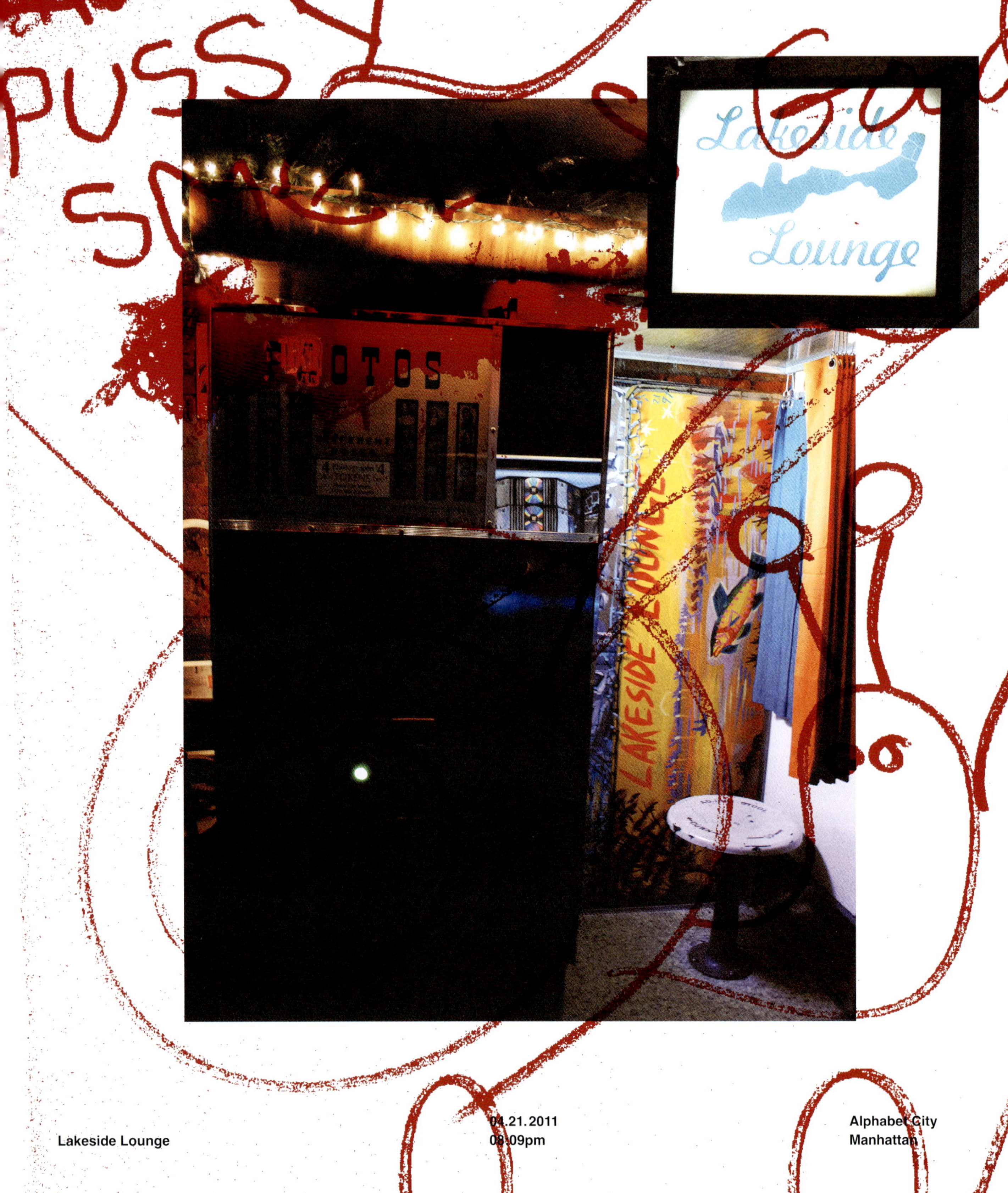

04.21.2011
08:09pm

Alphabet City
Manhattan

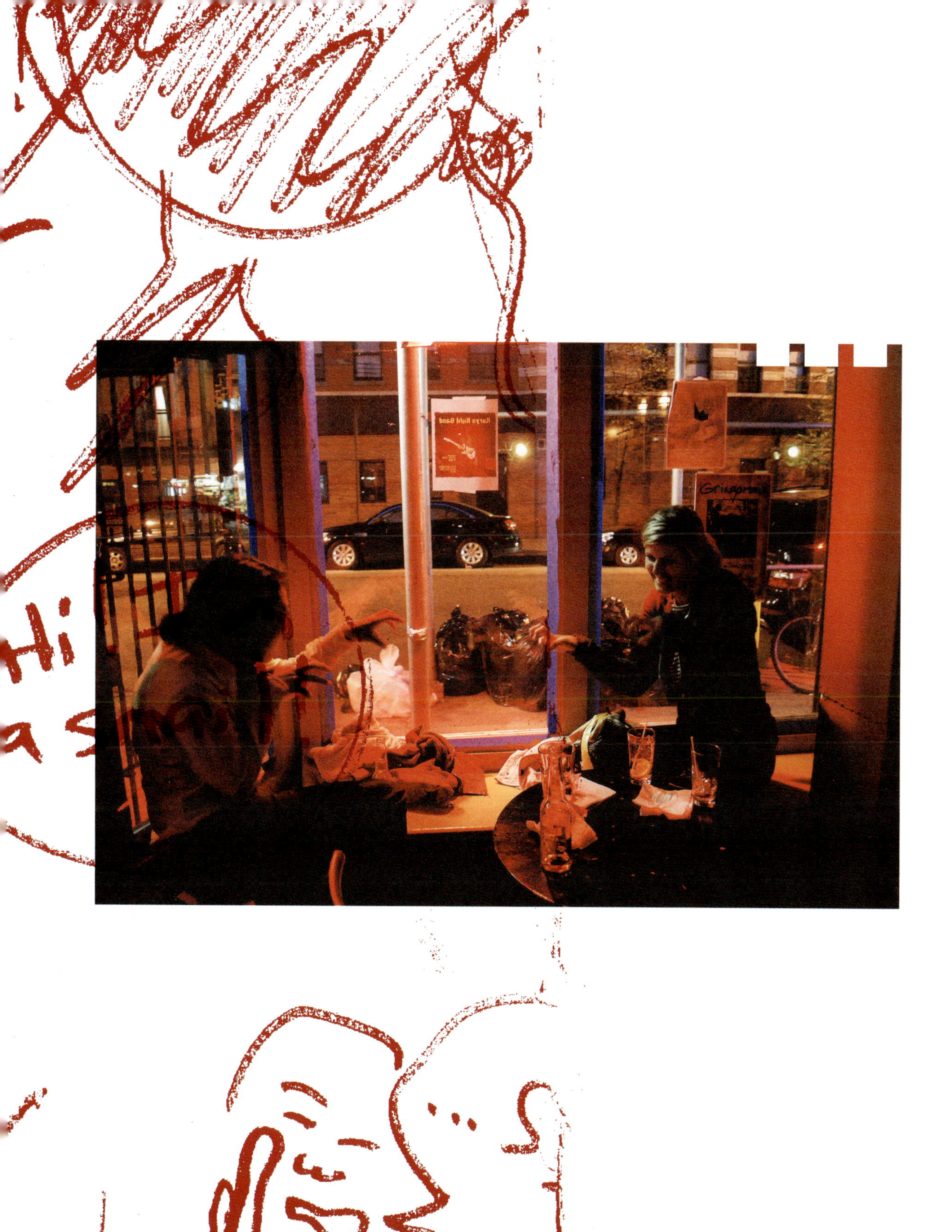
Harya Night Band
Gringronu

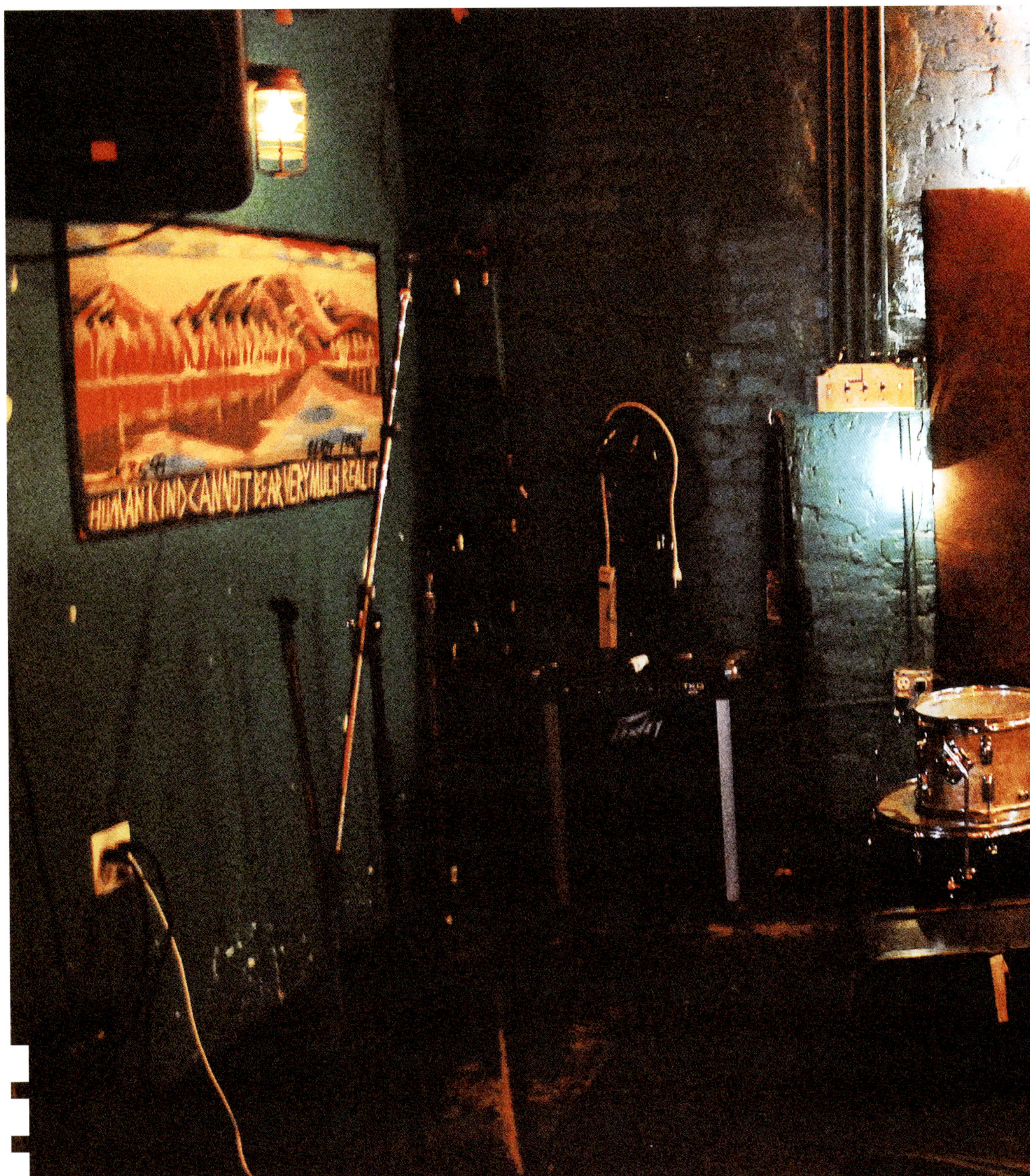
HUMAN KIND CANNOT BEAR VERY MUCH REALITY

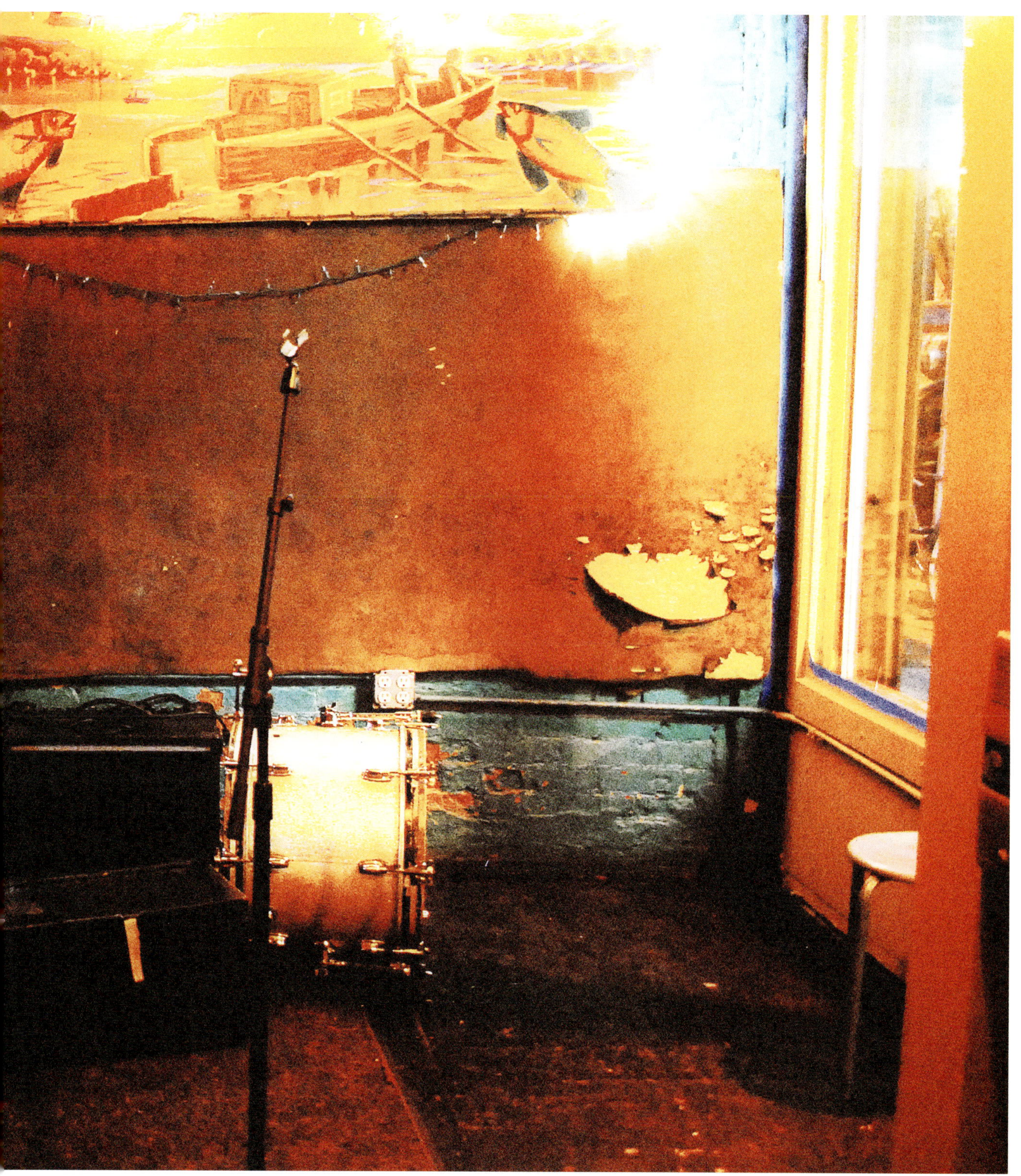

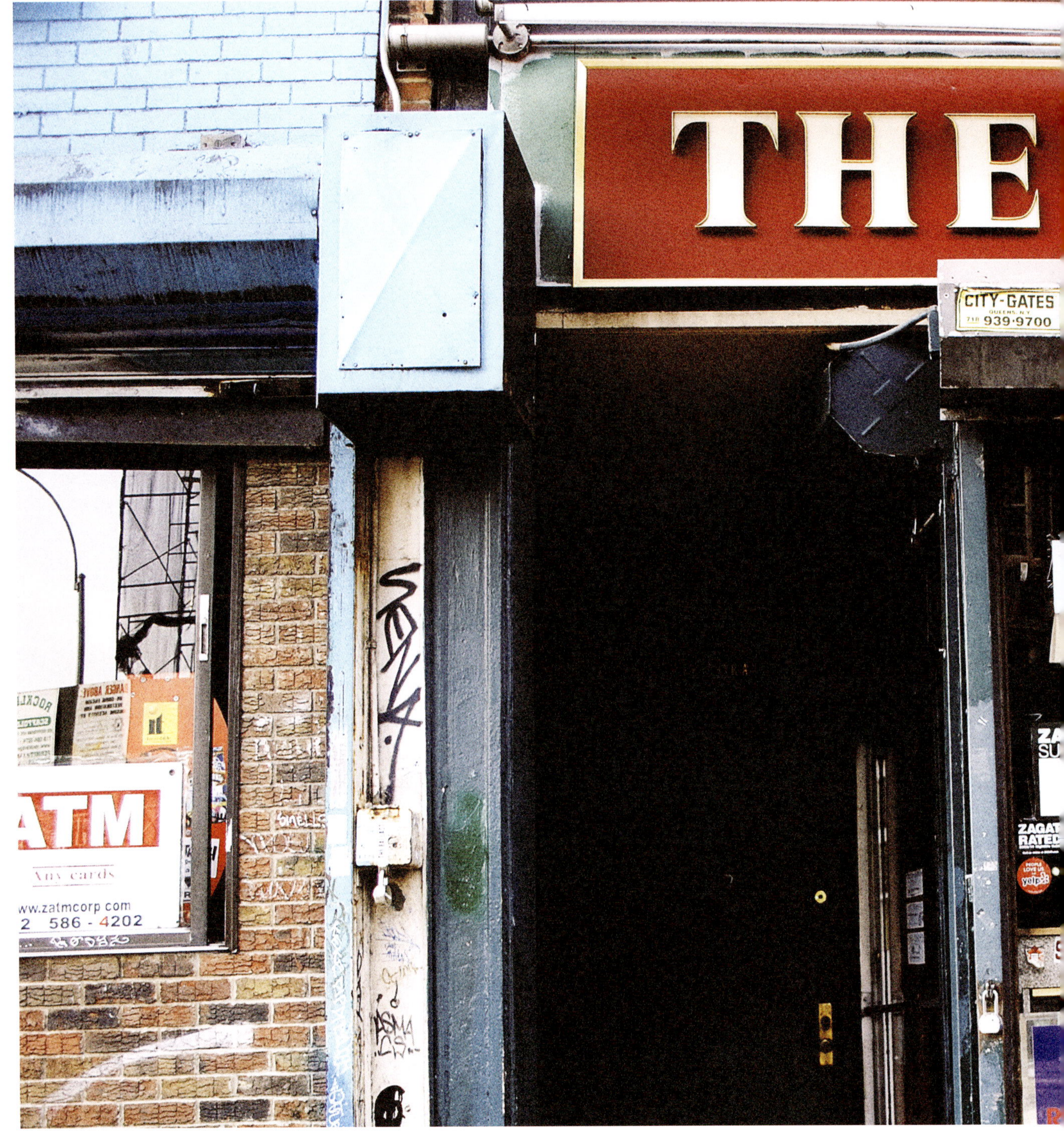

The Library

07.28.2011
07:33pm

Lower East Side
Manhattan

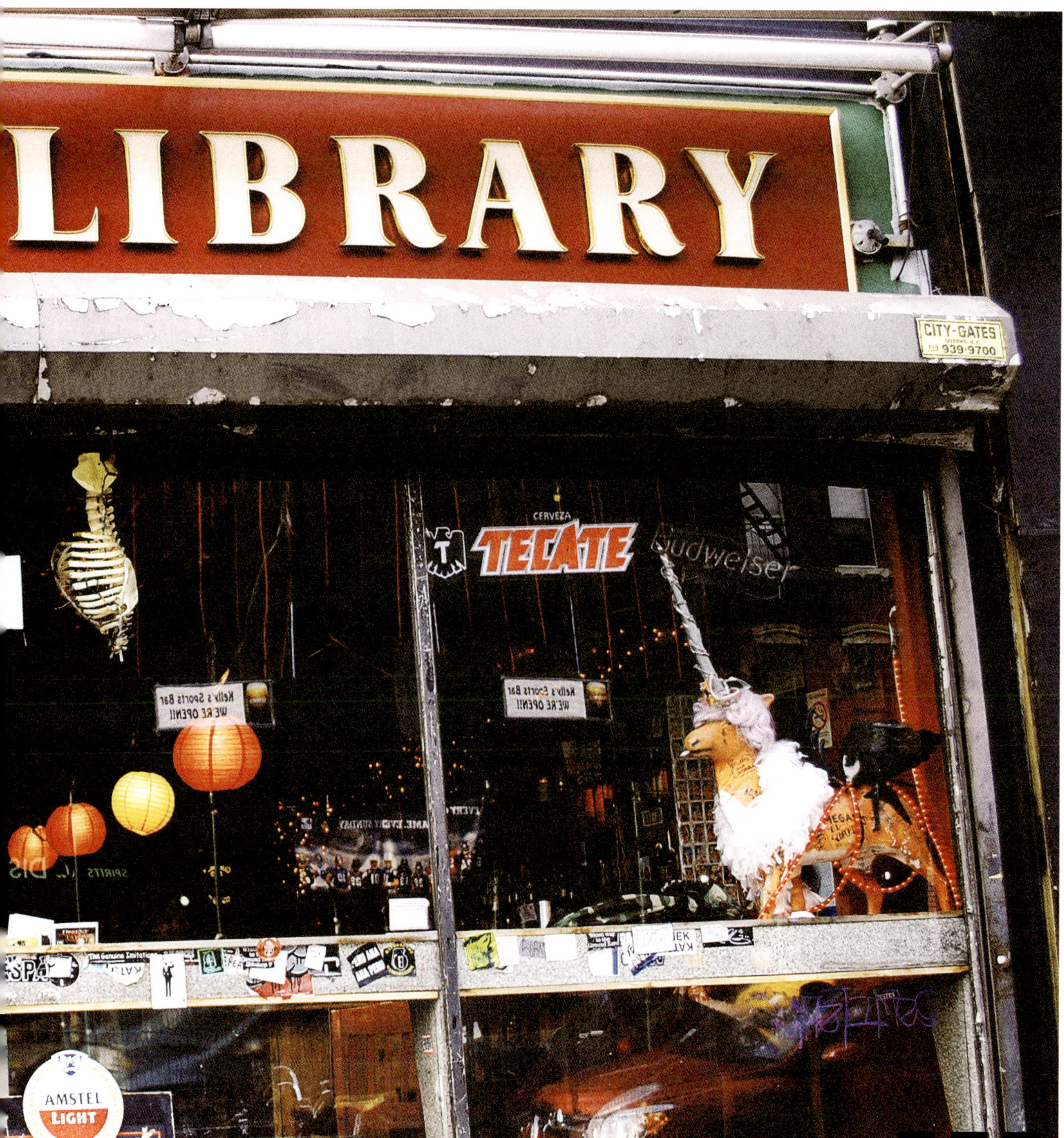

LIBRARY
CITY-GATES
QUEENS, N.Y.
718 939-9700
CERVEZA
TECATE
Budweiser
Kelly's Sports Bar
WE'RE OPEN!!
Kelly's Sports Bar
WE'RE OPEN!!
AMSTEL
LIGHT

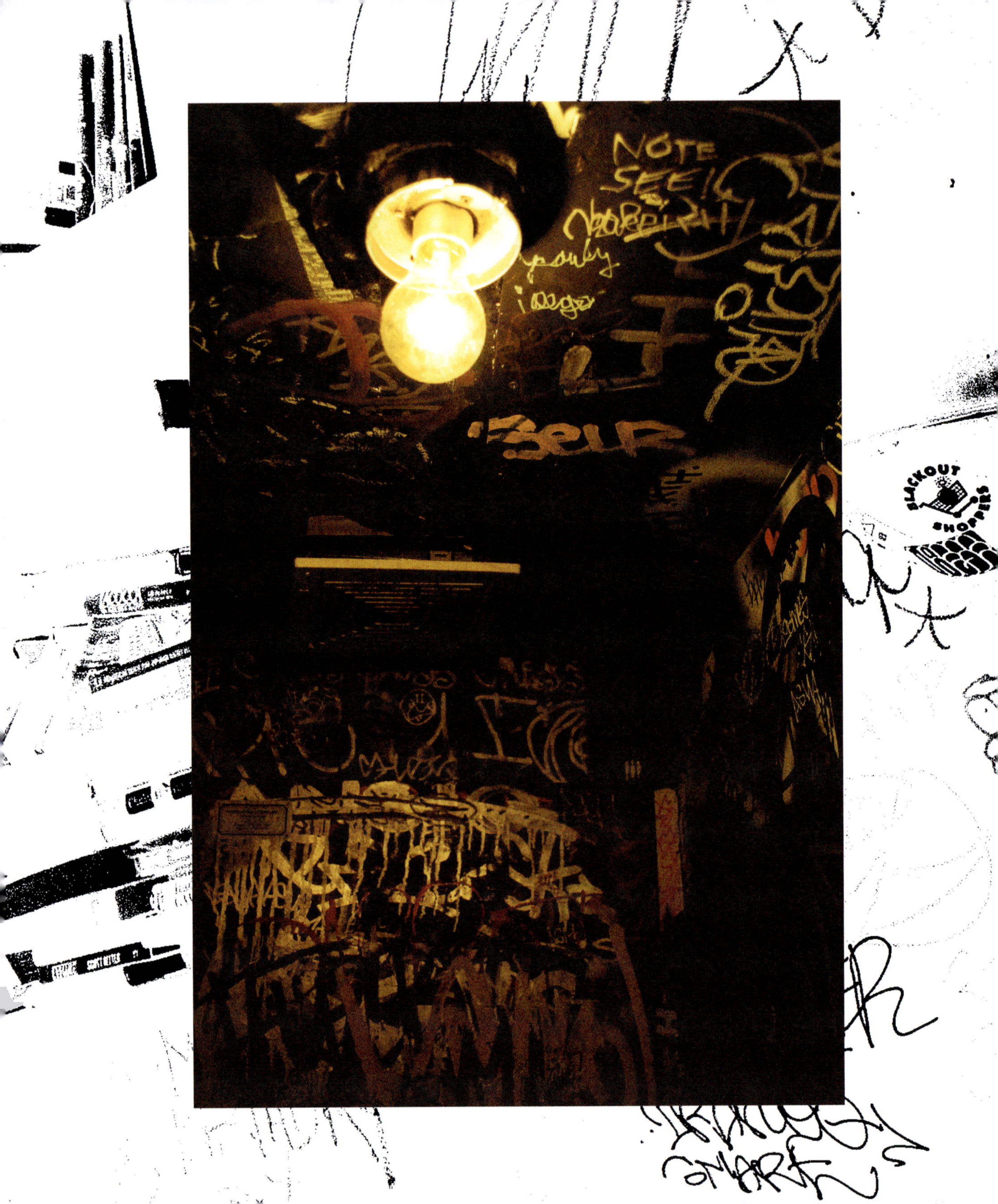

NOTE
SEE!
i oega
BELR
BLACKOUT SHOPPERS

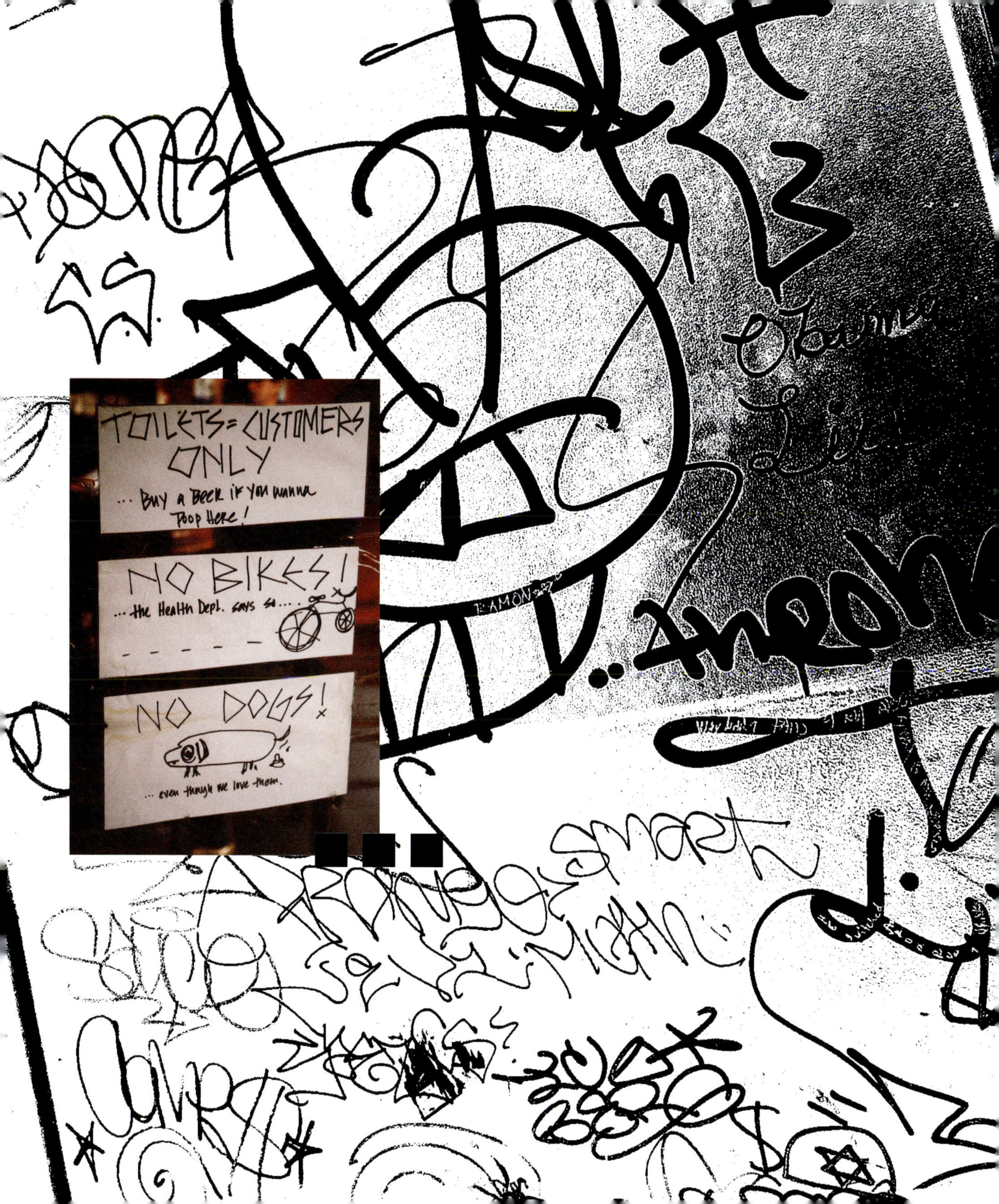

TOILETS = CUSTOMERS ONLY
... Buy a Beer if you wanna poop here!
NO BIKES!
... the Health Dept. says so ...
NO DOGS!
... even though we love them.

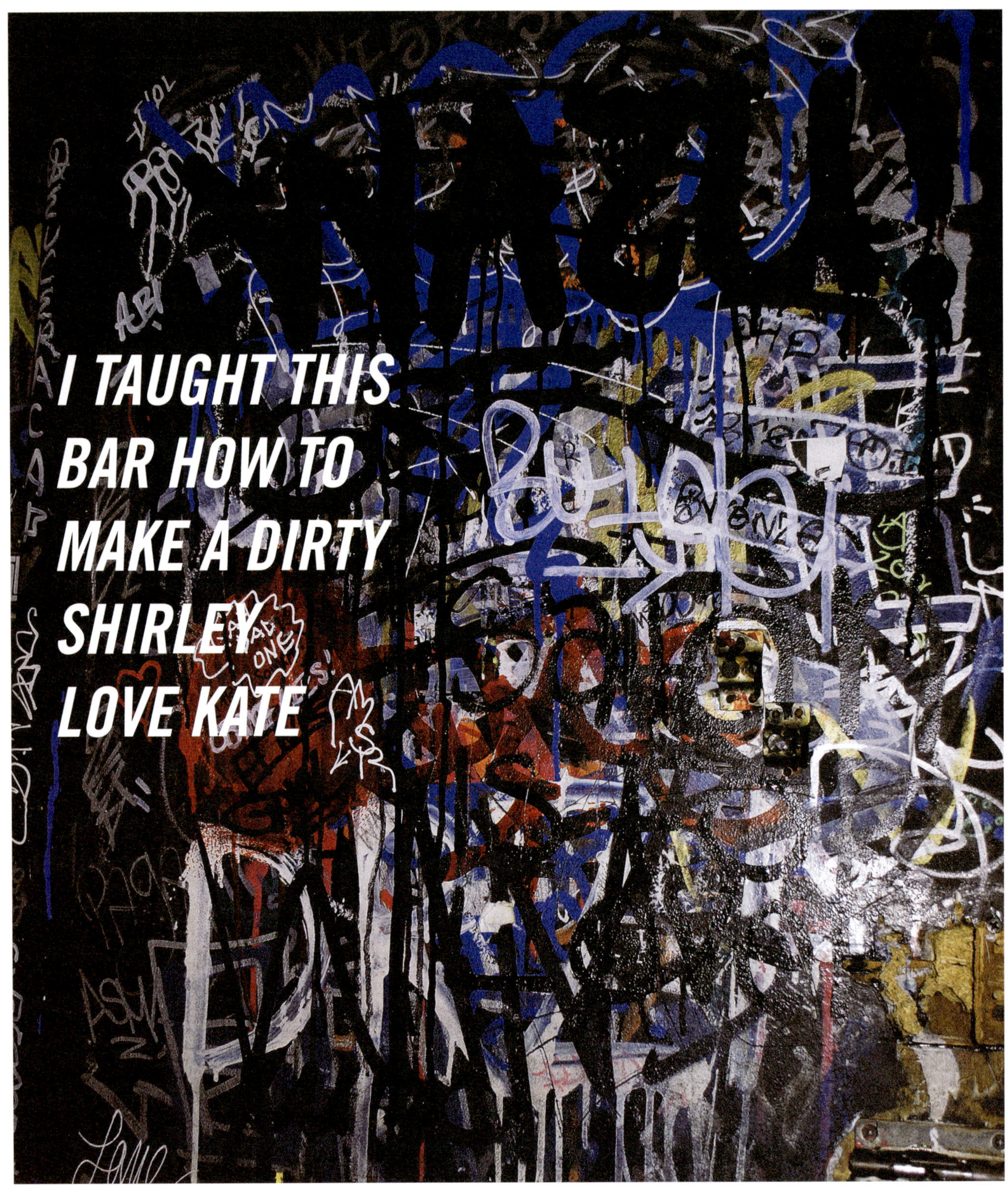
I TAUGHT THIS
BAR HOW TO
MAKE A DIRTY
SHIRLEY
LOVE KATE

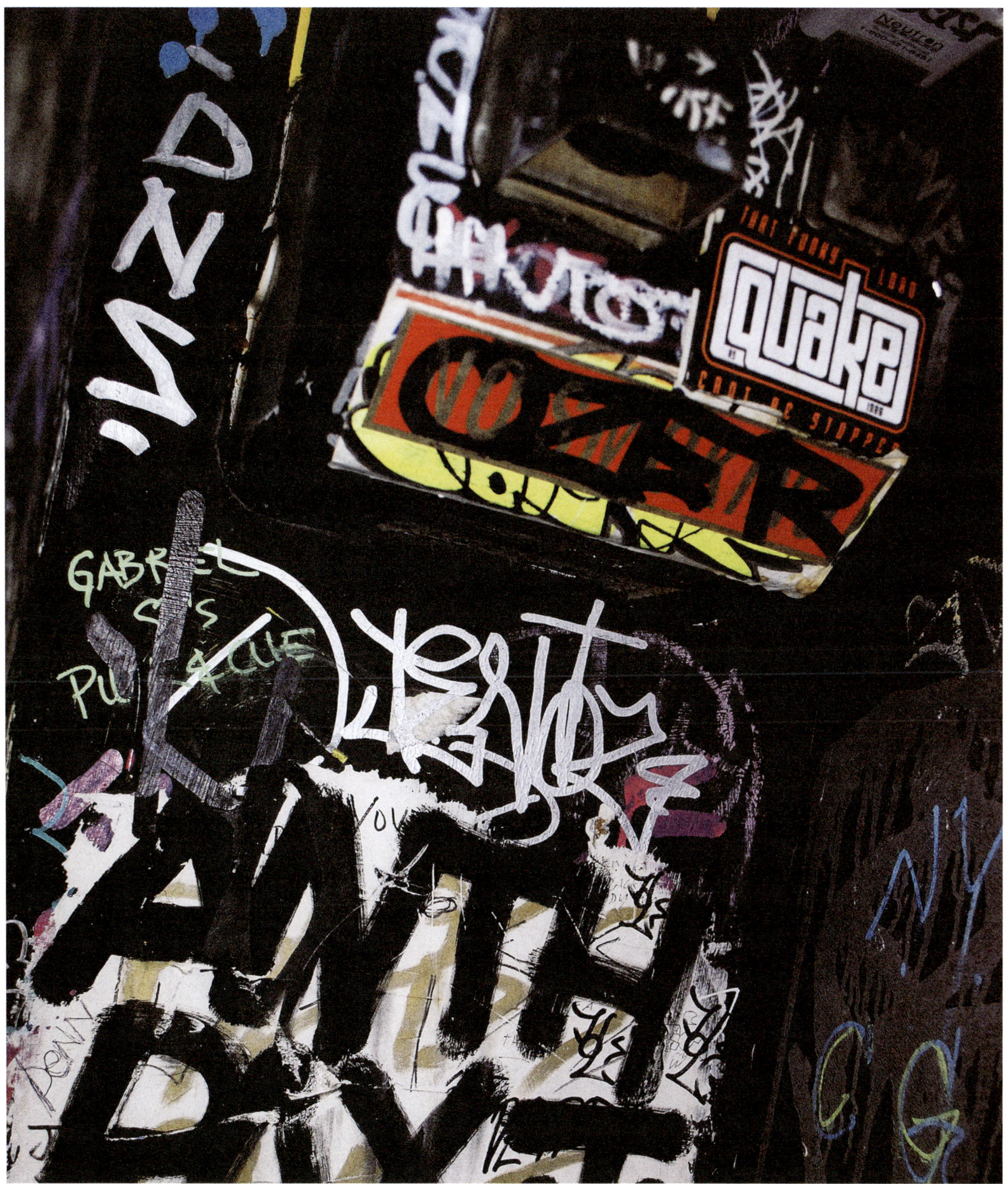

QUAKE
NY
GABRIEL

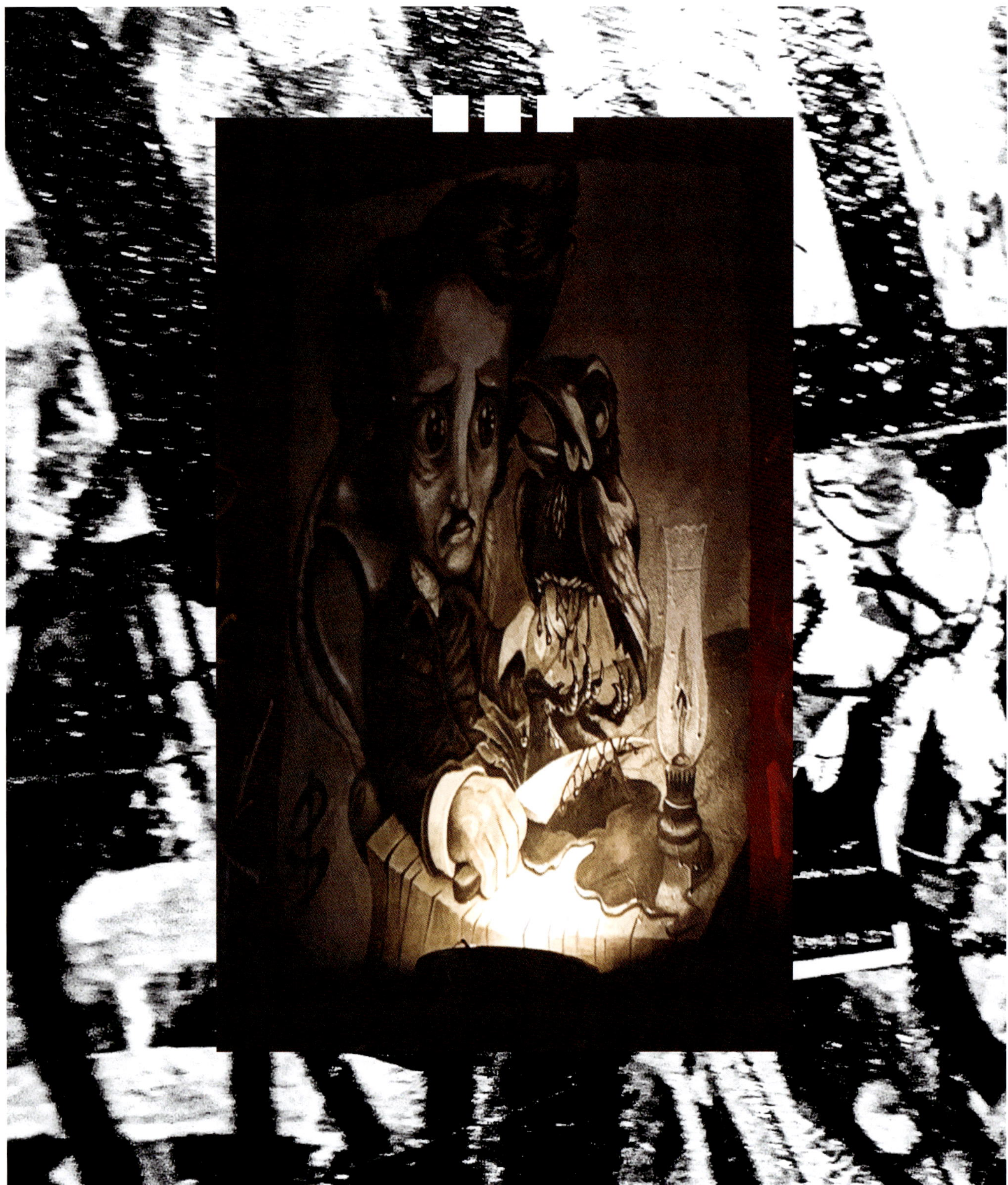

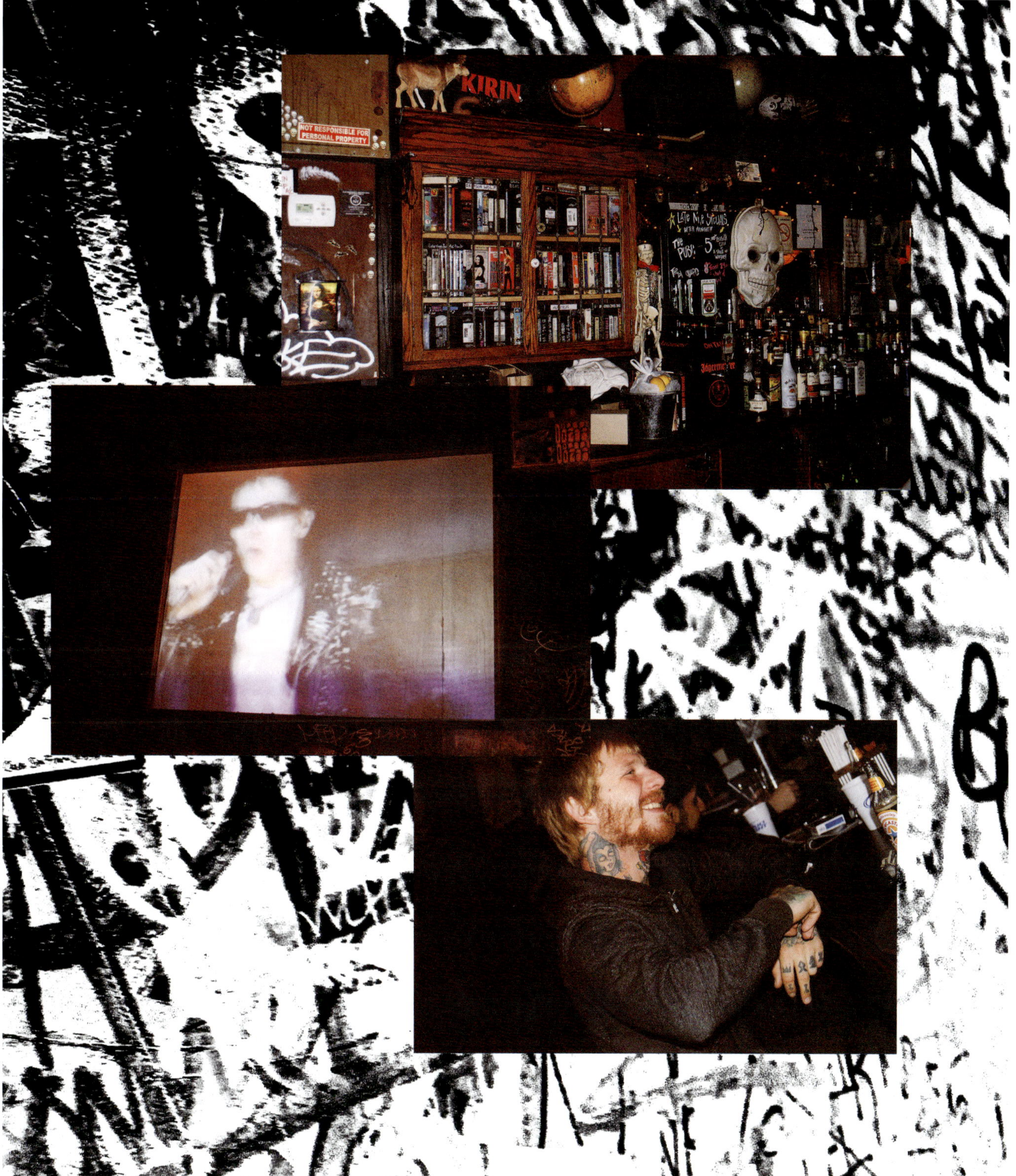

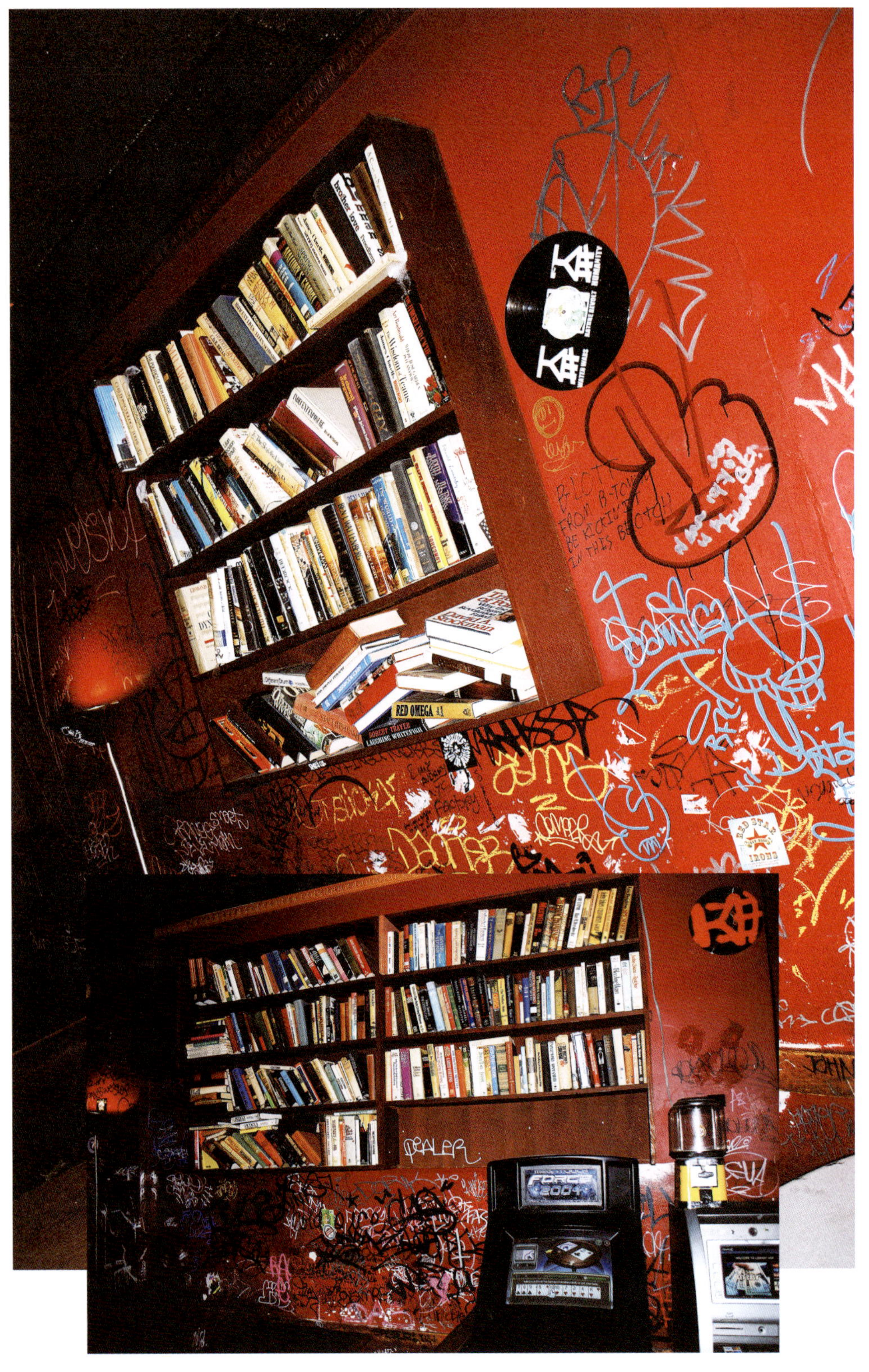

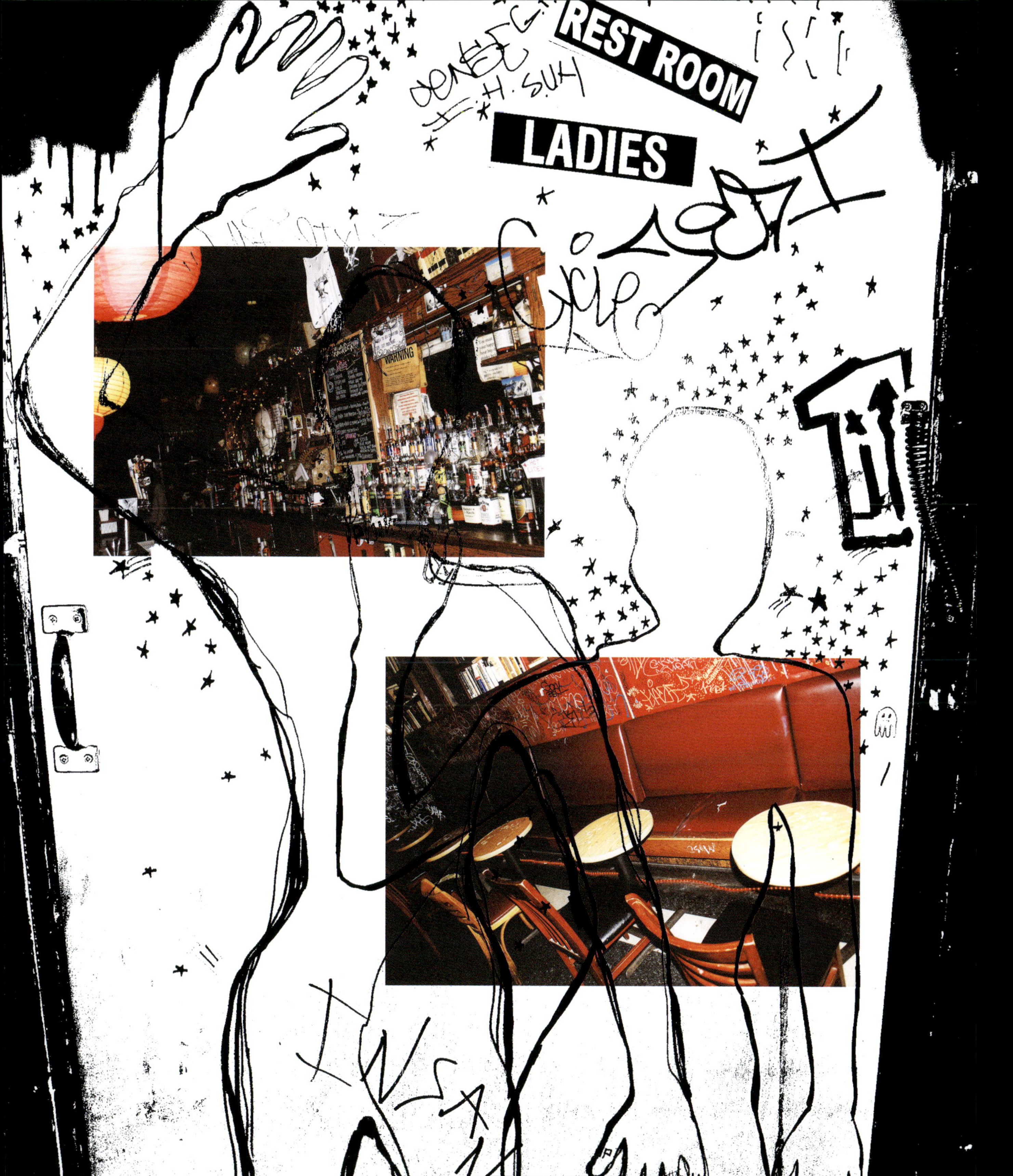
REST ROOM
LADIES
WARNING

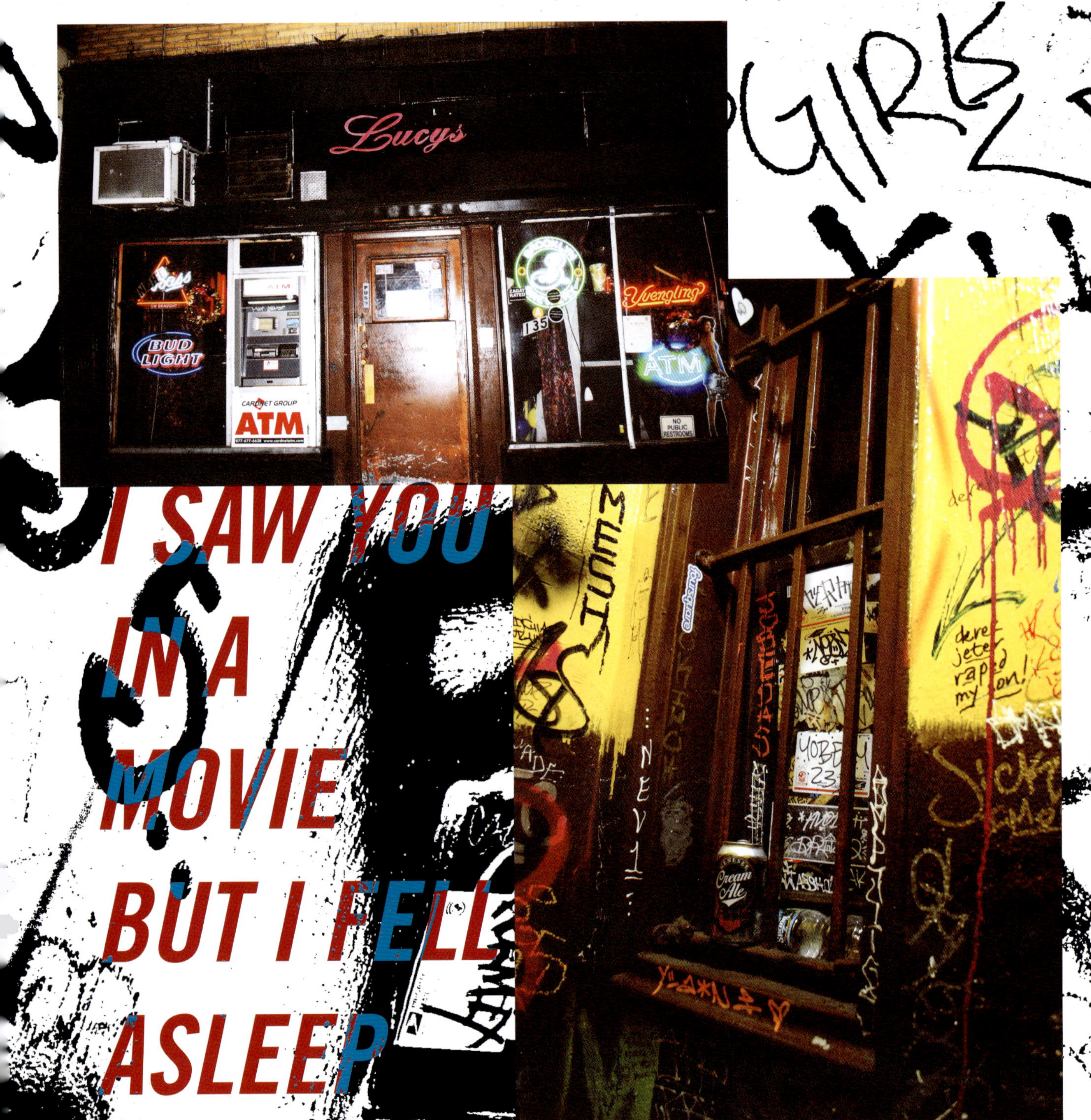

01.08.2011
06:43pm

Lucy's

East Village
Manhattan

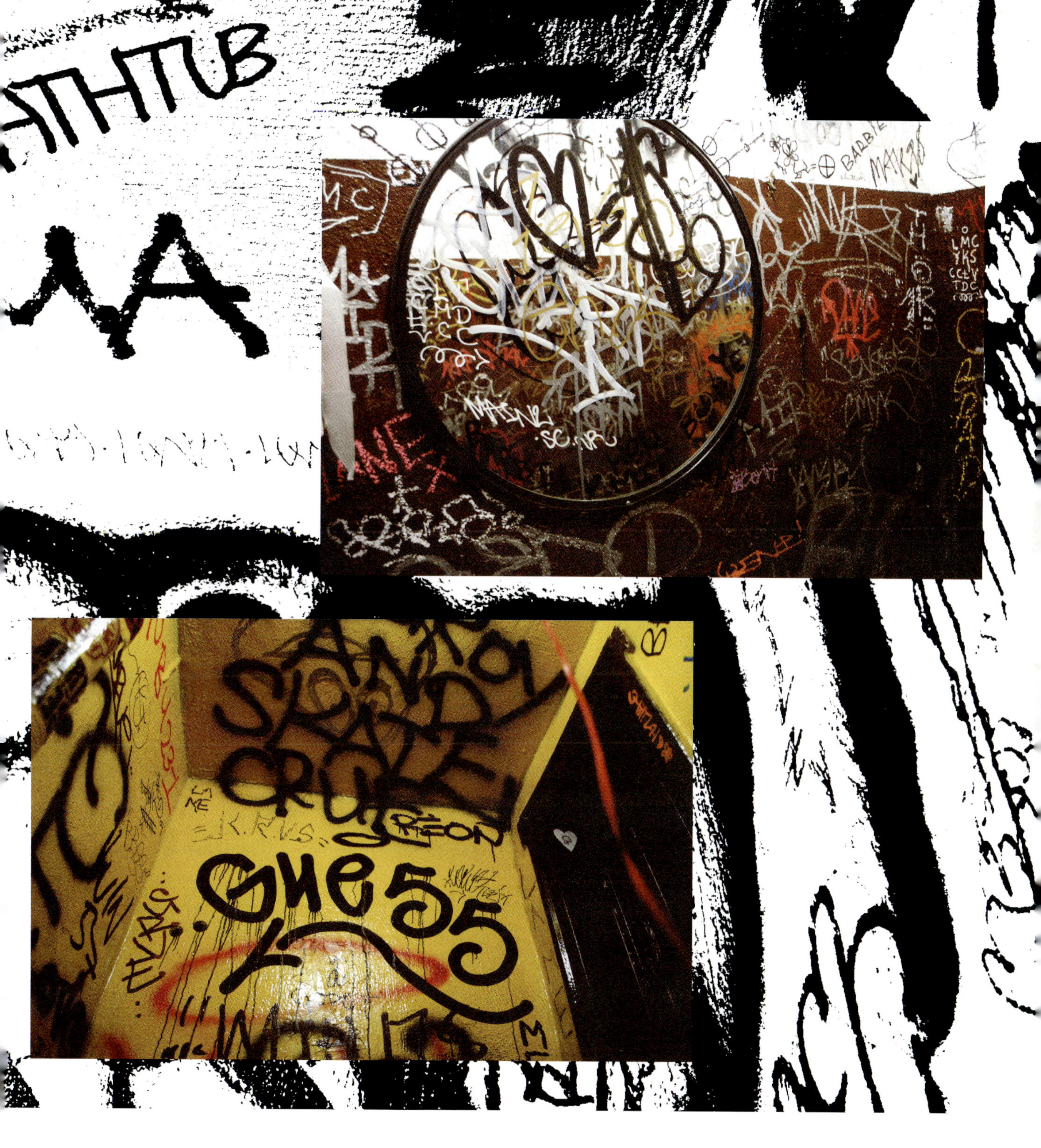

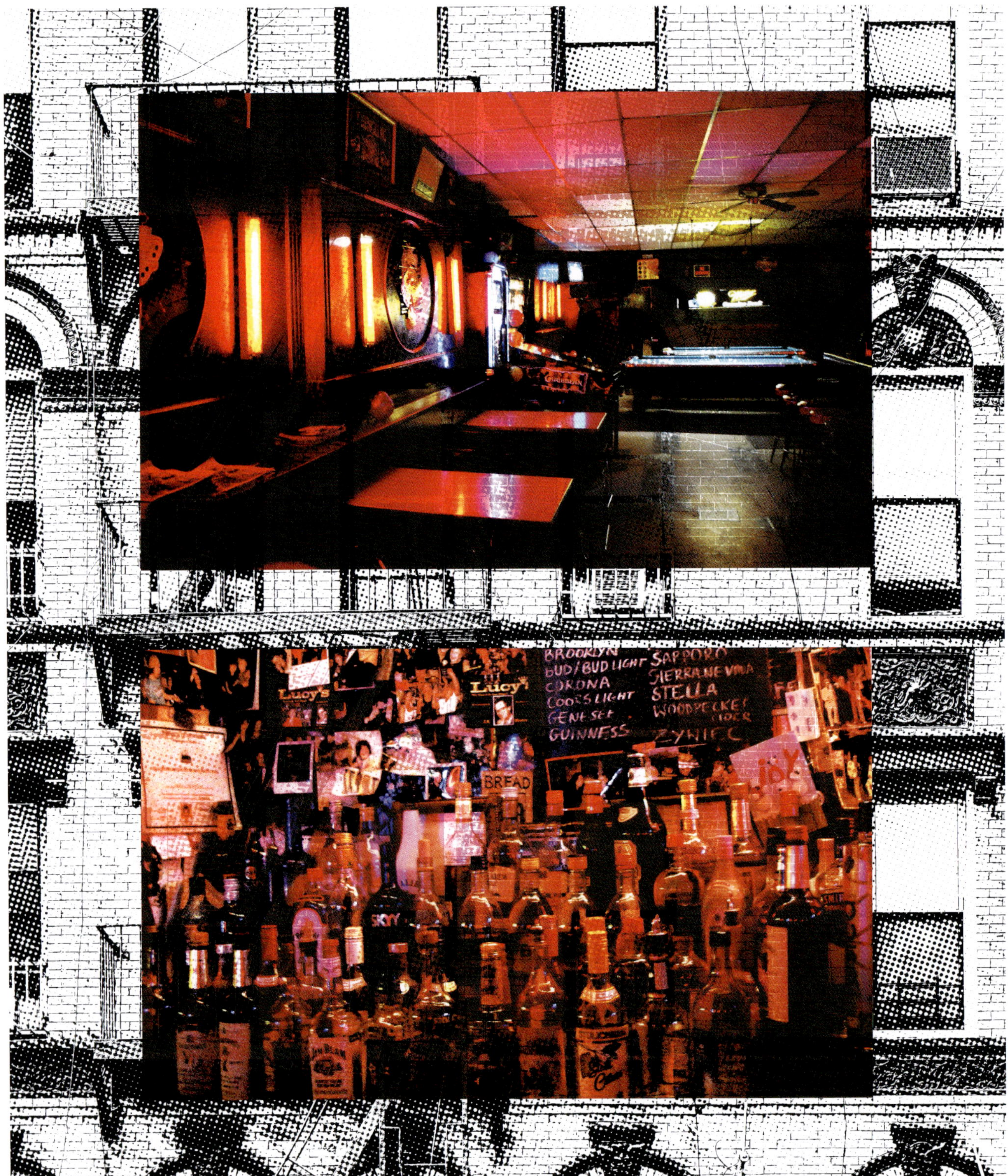
BROOKLYN
BUD / BUD LIGHT
CORONA
COORS LIGHT
GENESEE
GUINNESS
SAPPORO
SIERRA NEVADA
STELLA
WOODPECKER CIDER
ZYWIEC
BREAD
Lucy's

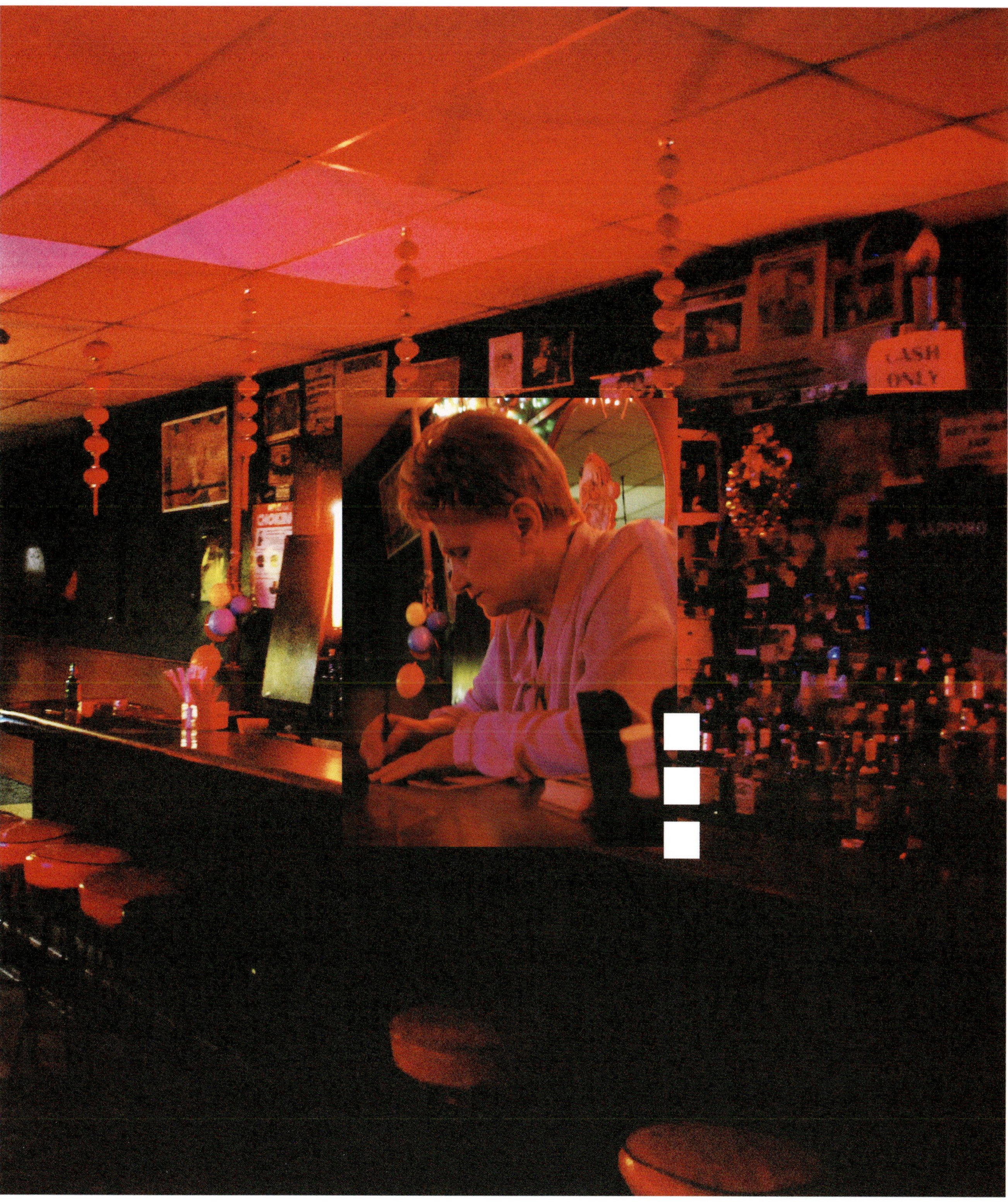

MESH
WILLIAM
CORDOVA
IS A
SLUT
2000
NOV
NAGEL

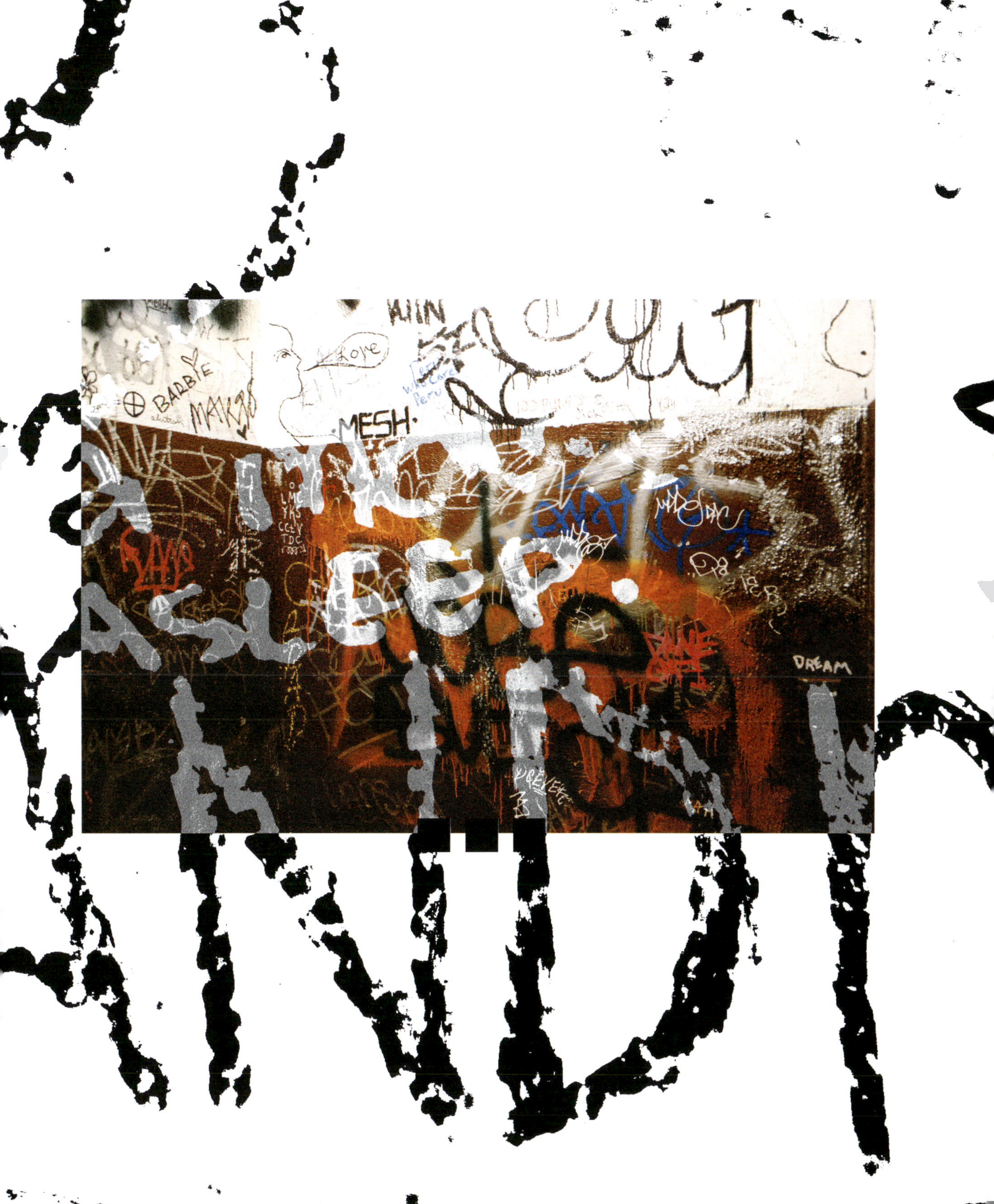
MESH.
BARBIE
MAK
DREAM
ASLEEP

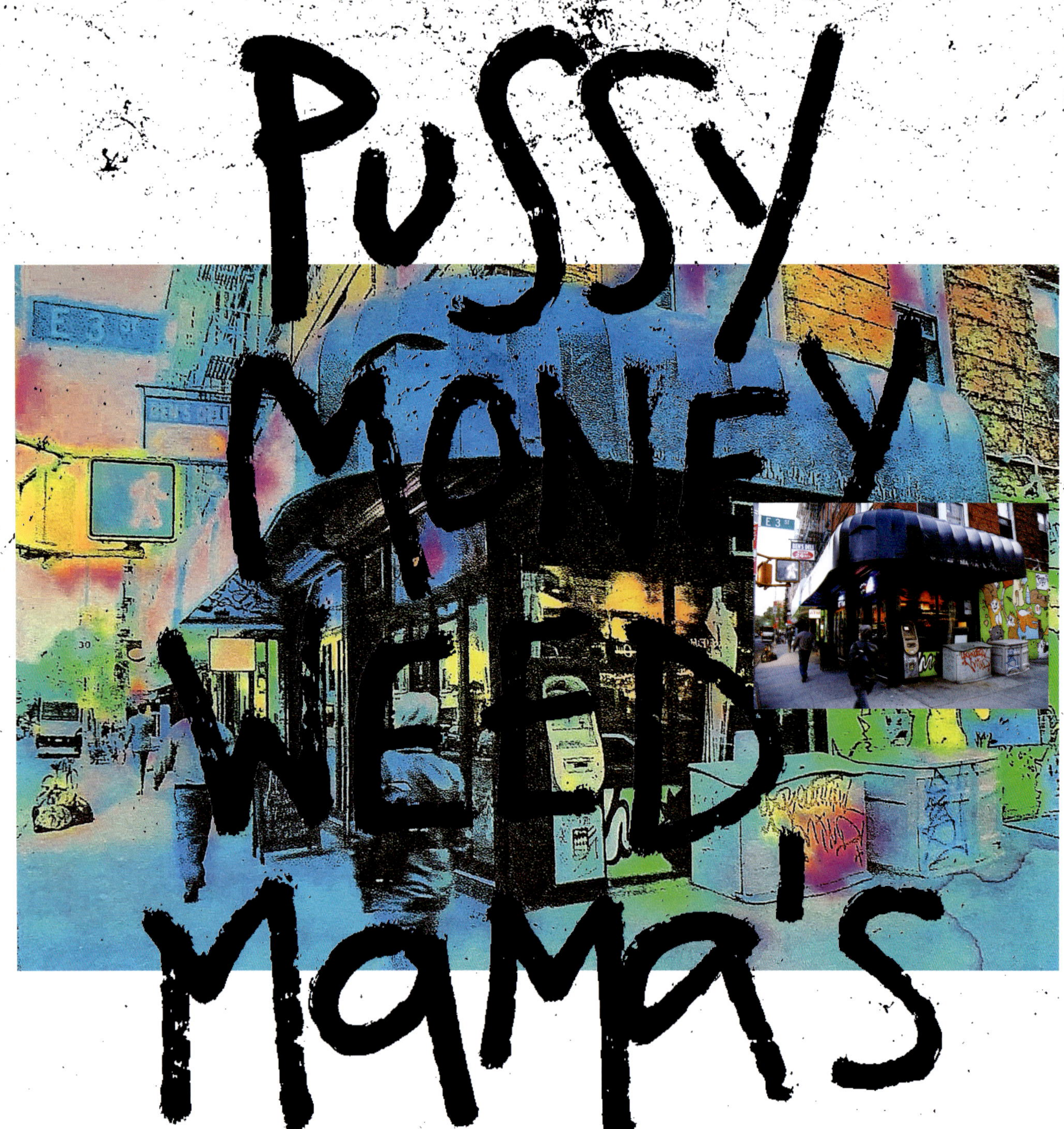

Mama's

04.21.2011
07:47pm

Alphabet City
Manhattan

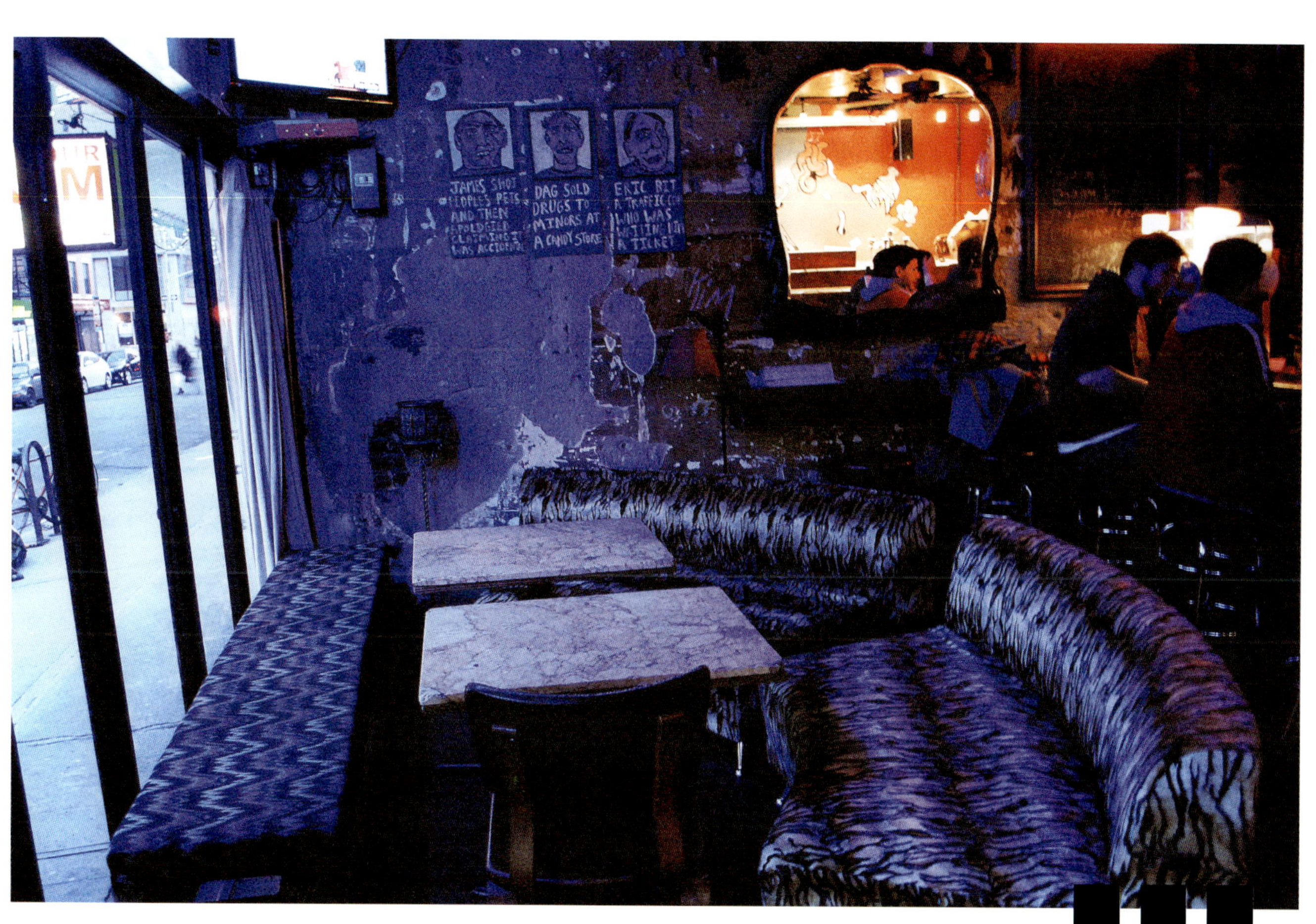
JAMES SHOT
PEOPLE'S PETS
AND THEN
APOLOGIZED
CLAIMING IT
WAS ACCIDENTAL
DAG SOLD
DRUGS TO
MINORS AT
A CANDY STORE
ERIC BIT
A TRAFFIC COP
WHO WAS
WRITING HIM
A TICKET

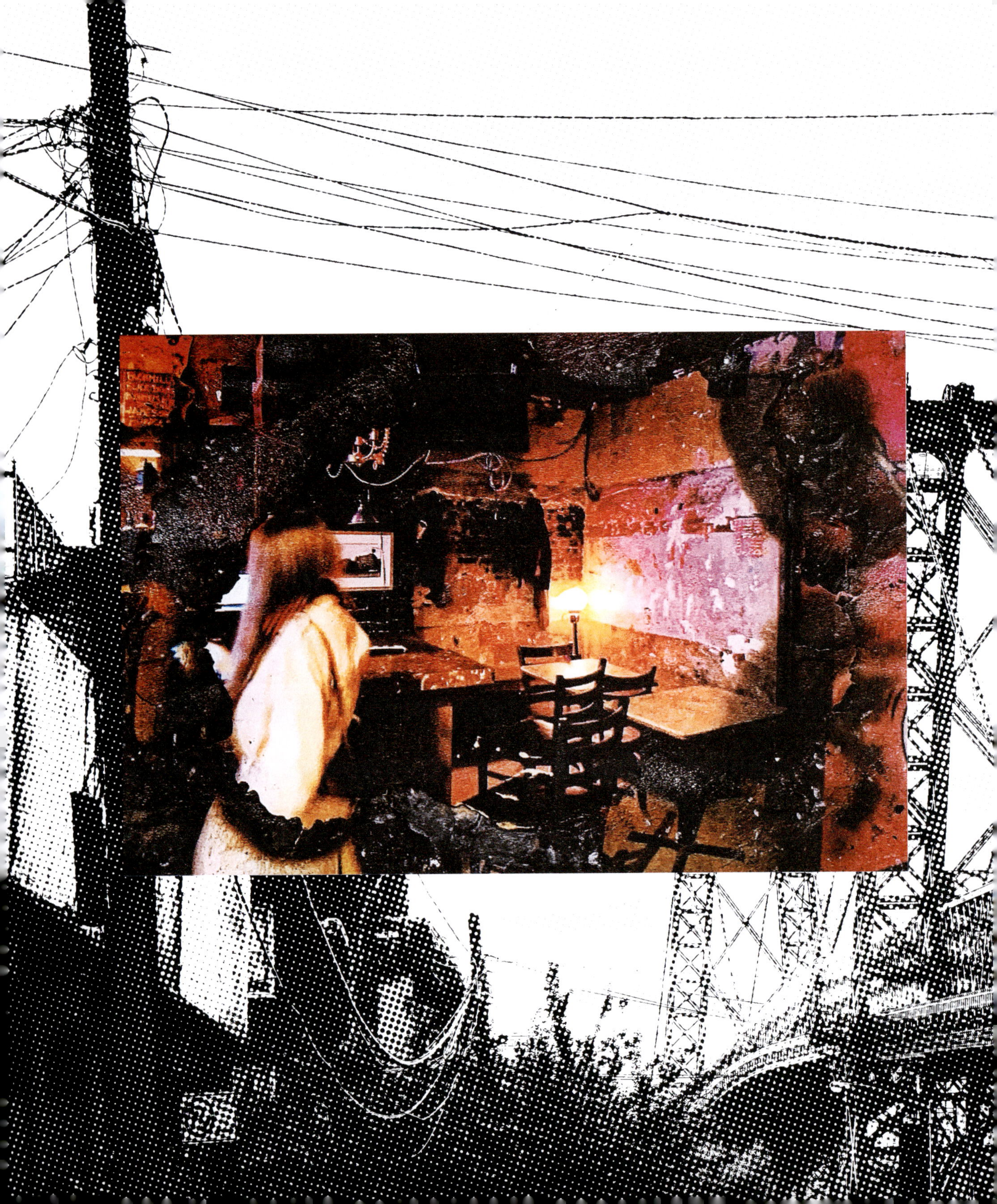

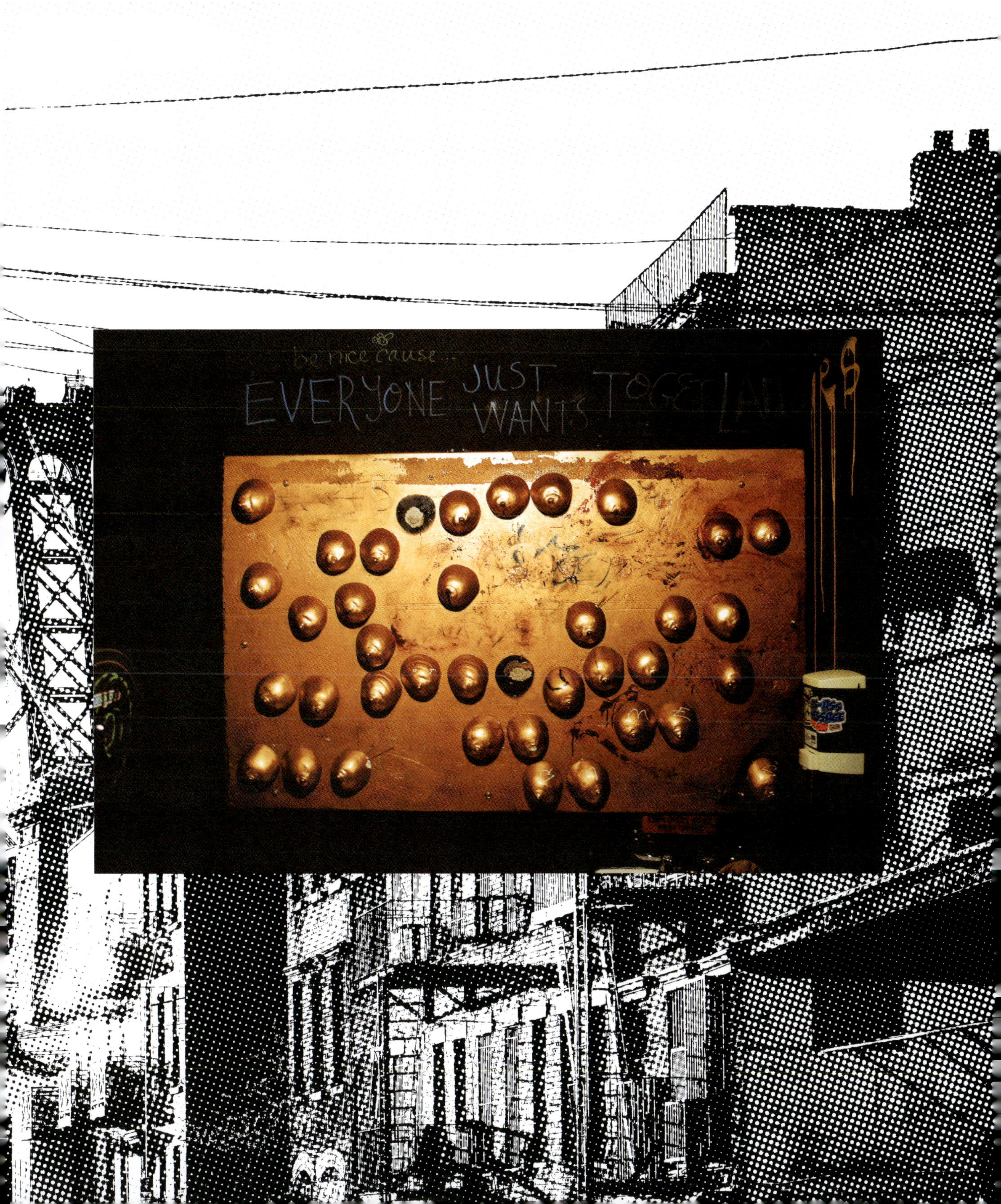

be nice cause...
EVERYONE JUST WANTS TOGETHER

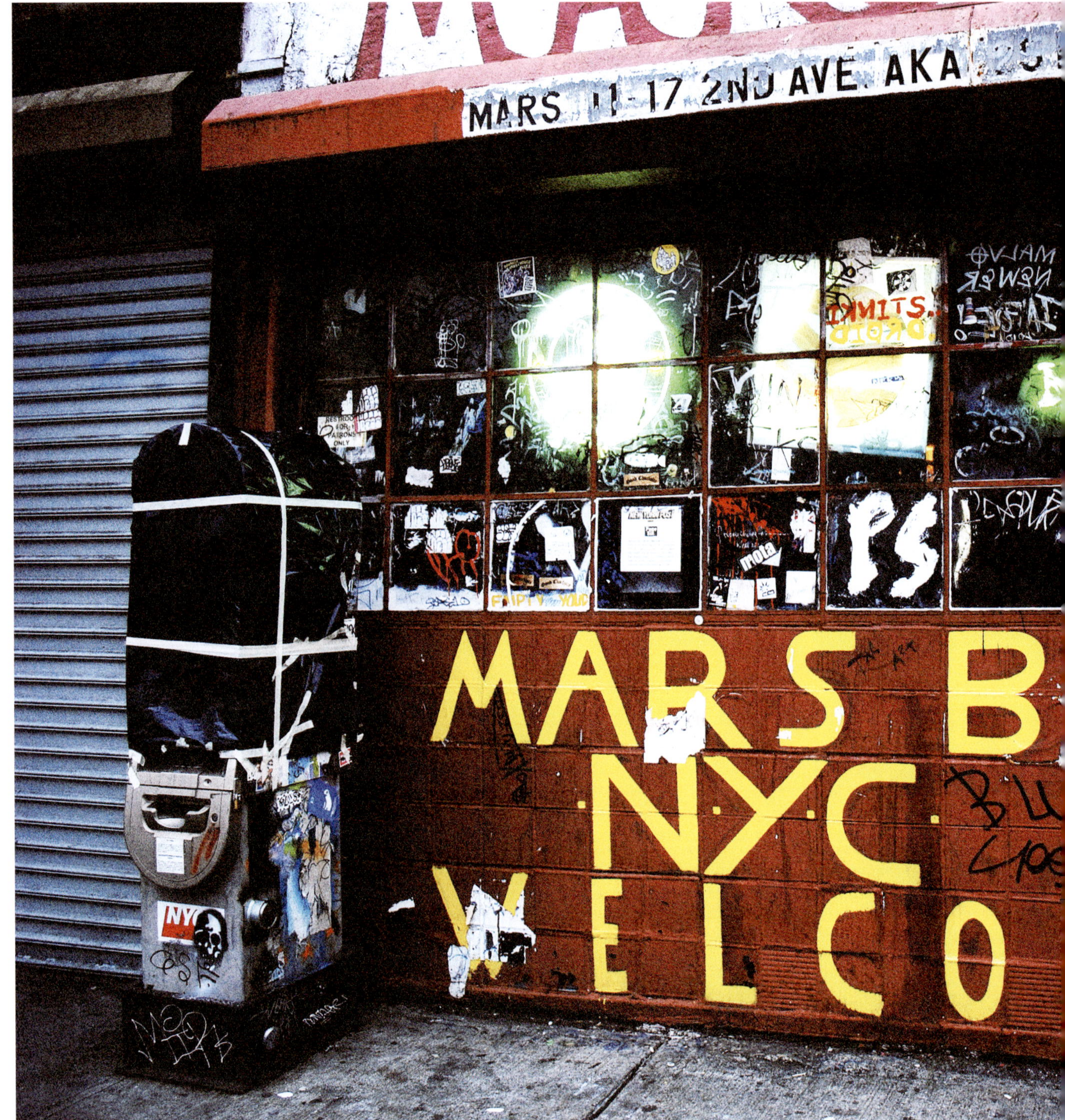

01.08.2011
03:15pm

Mars Bar

East Village
Manhattan

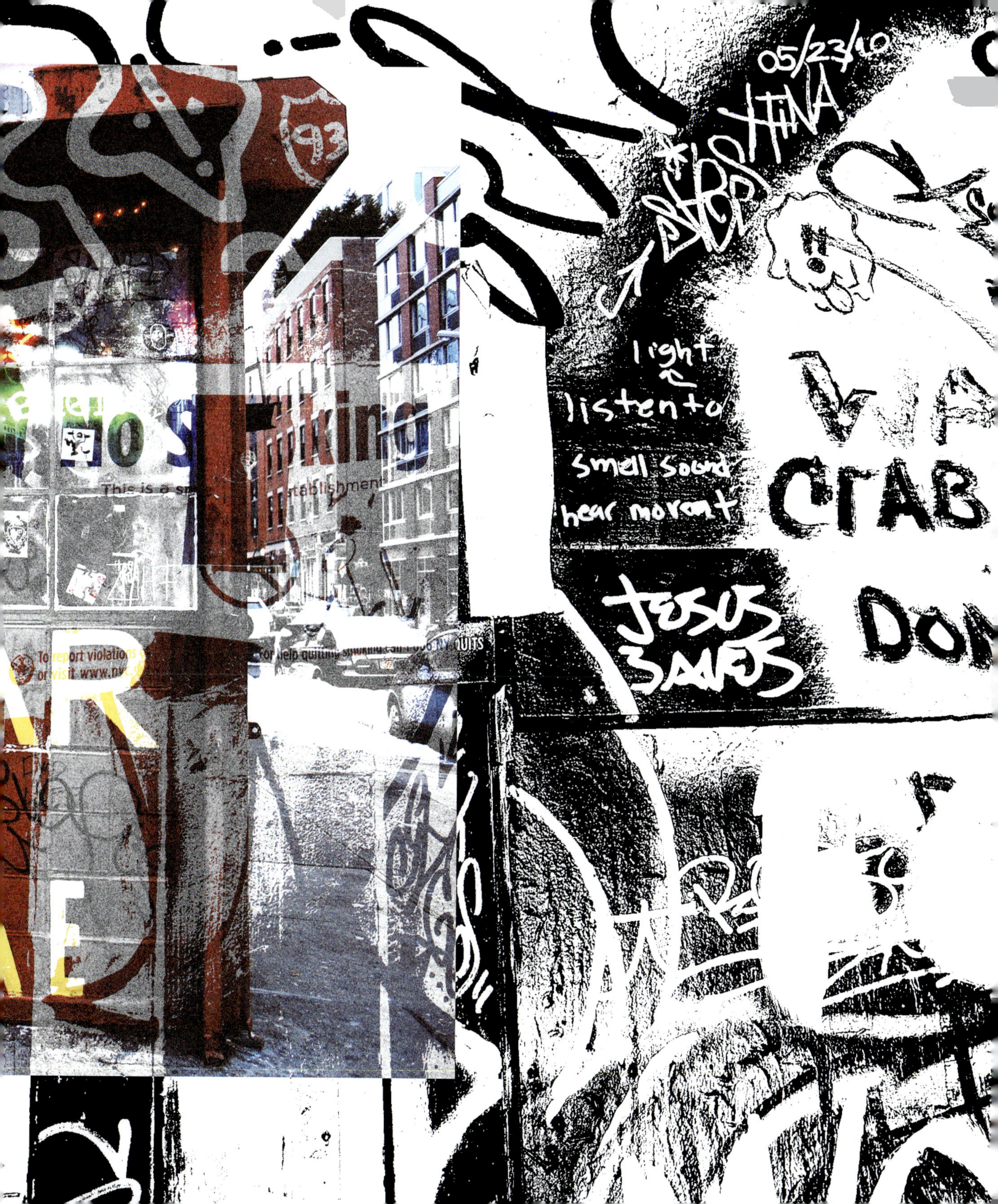
93
NO SMOKING
This is a smoke free establishment
To report violations or visit www.nyc
For help quitting smoking call 1-866-NY-QUITS
05/23/10
XTINA
light
listen to
smell sound
hear movment
JESUS SAVES
VA
CrAB
DON

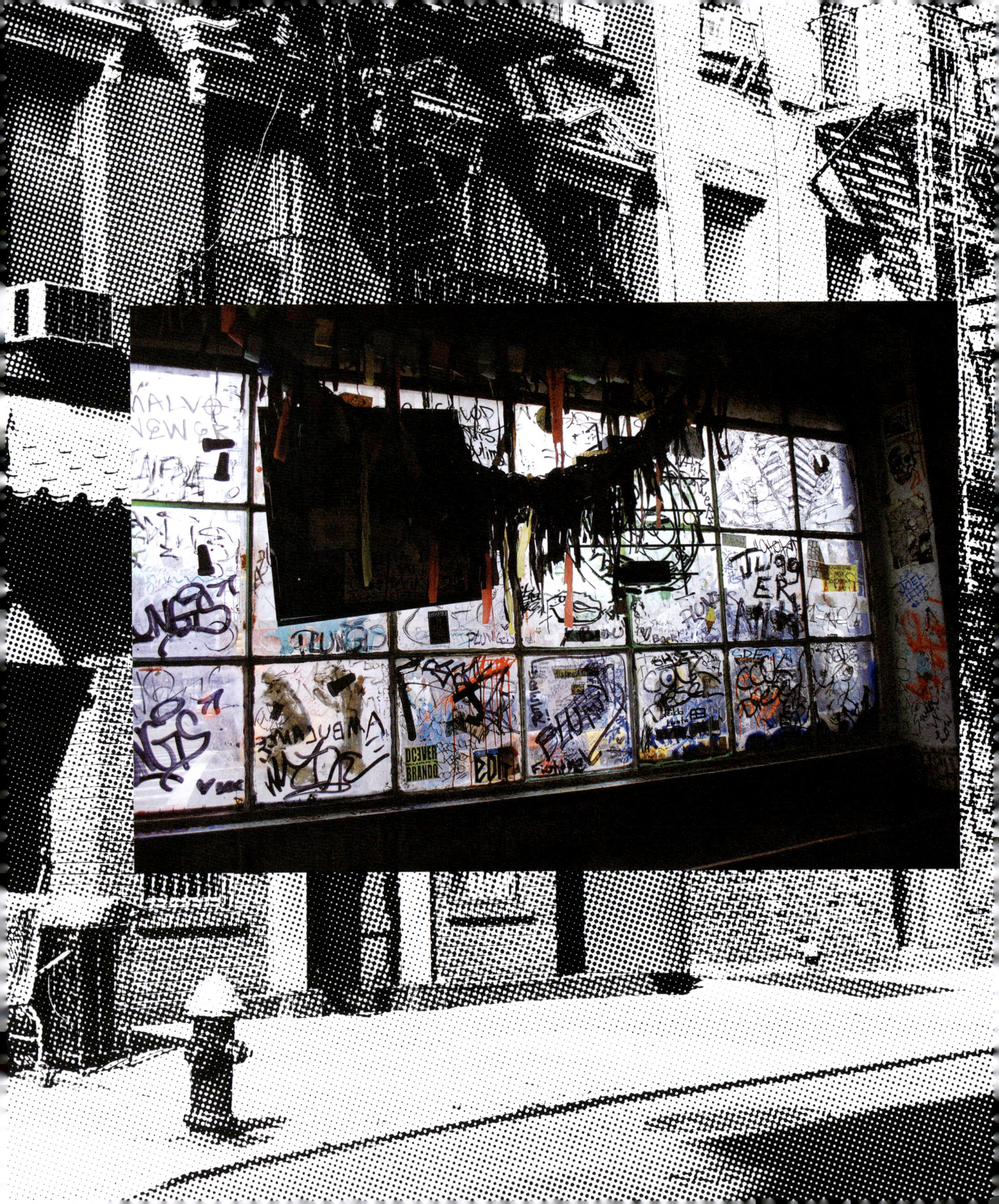

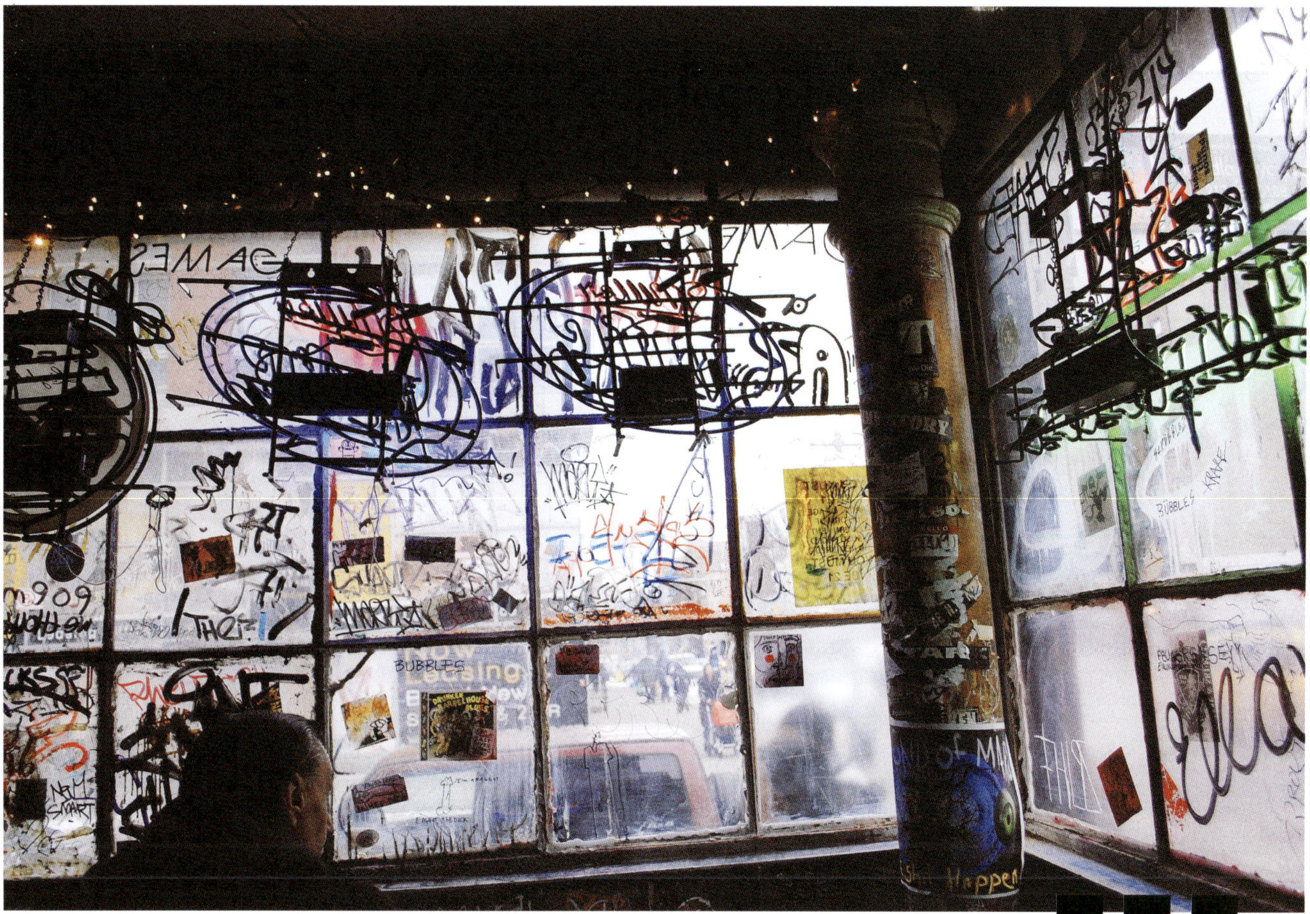

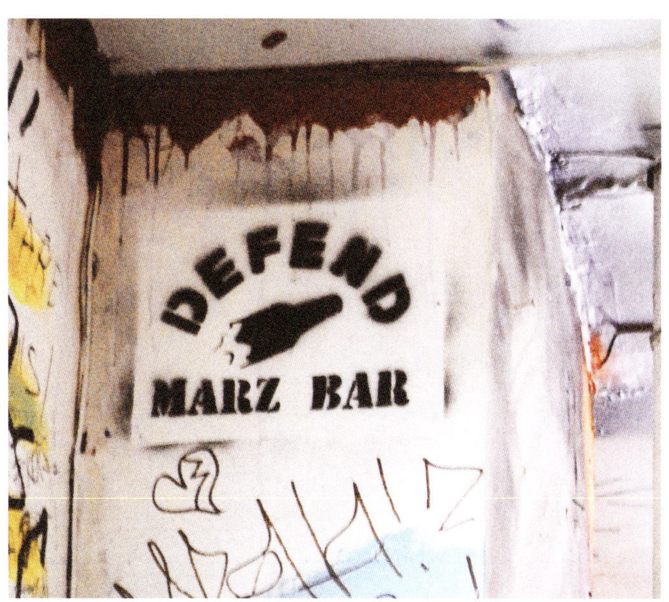
DEFEND
MARZ BAR

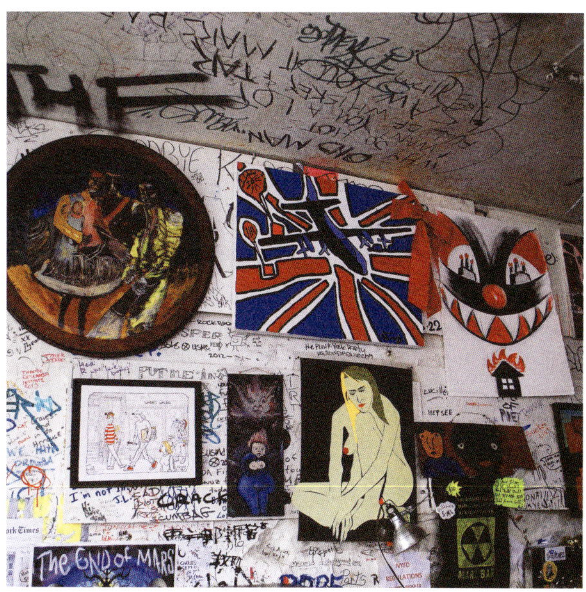
THF
THE END OF MARS

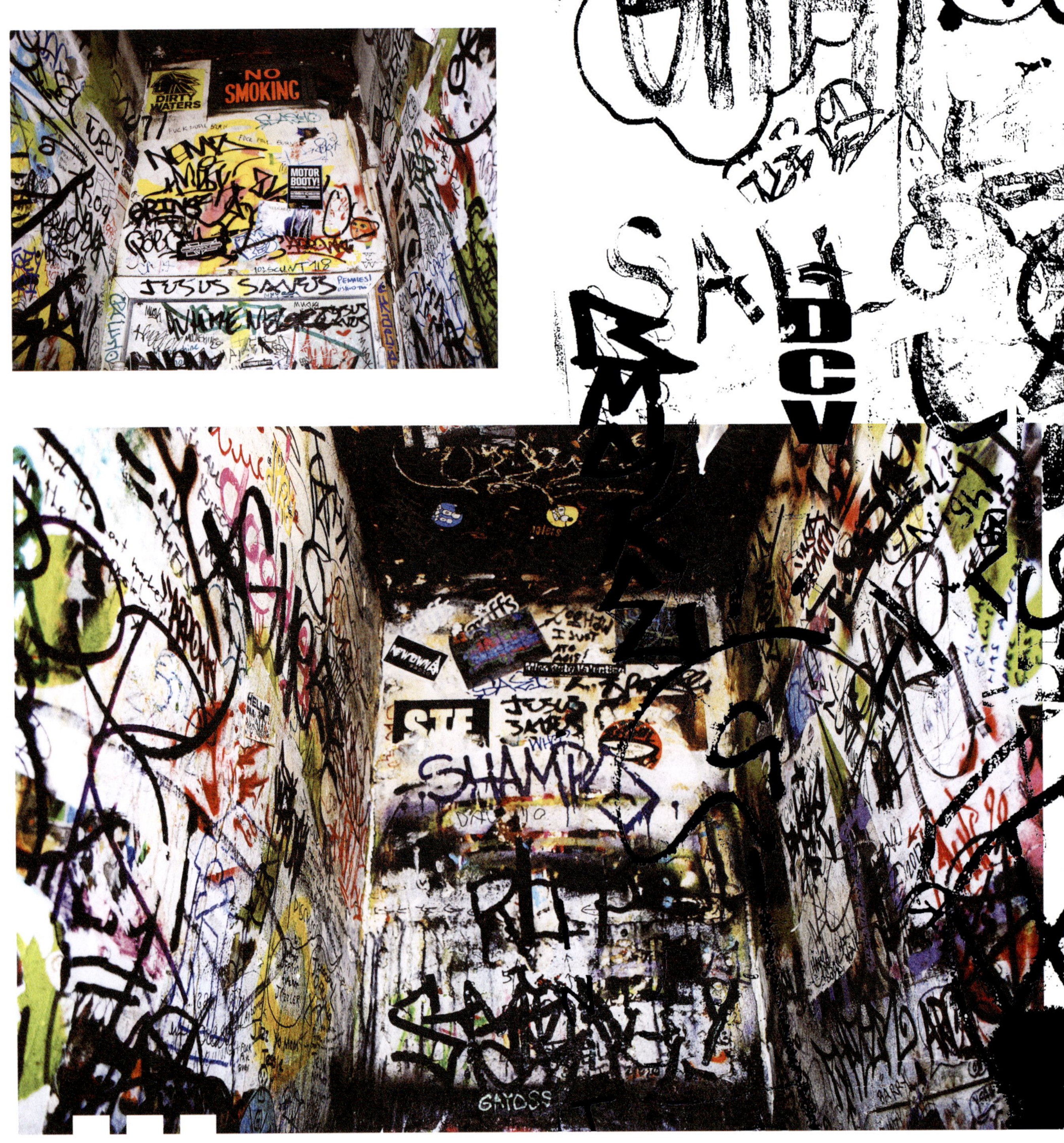

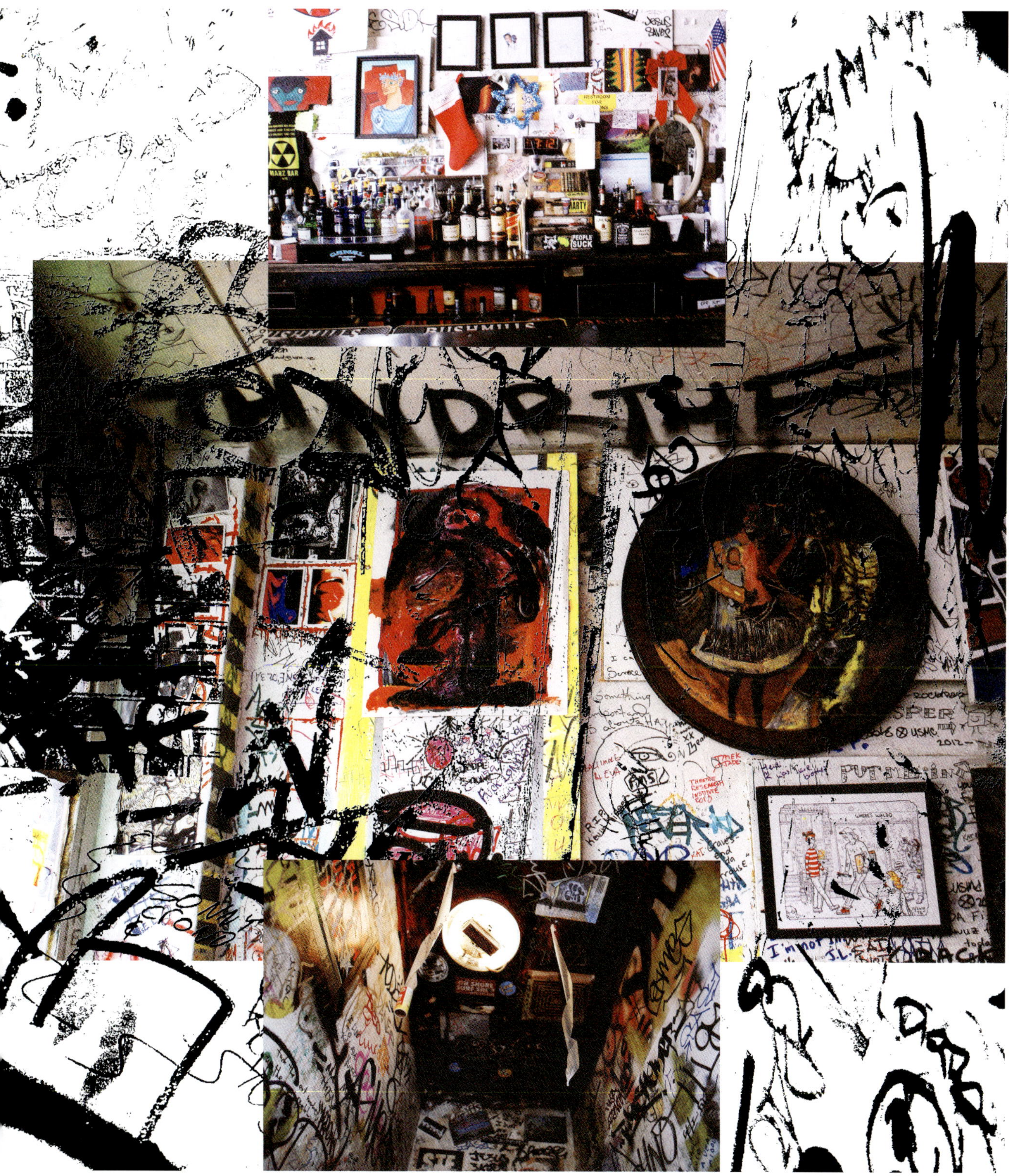

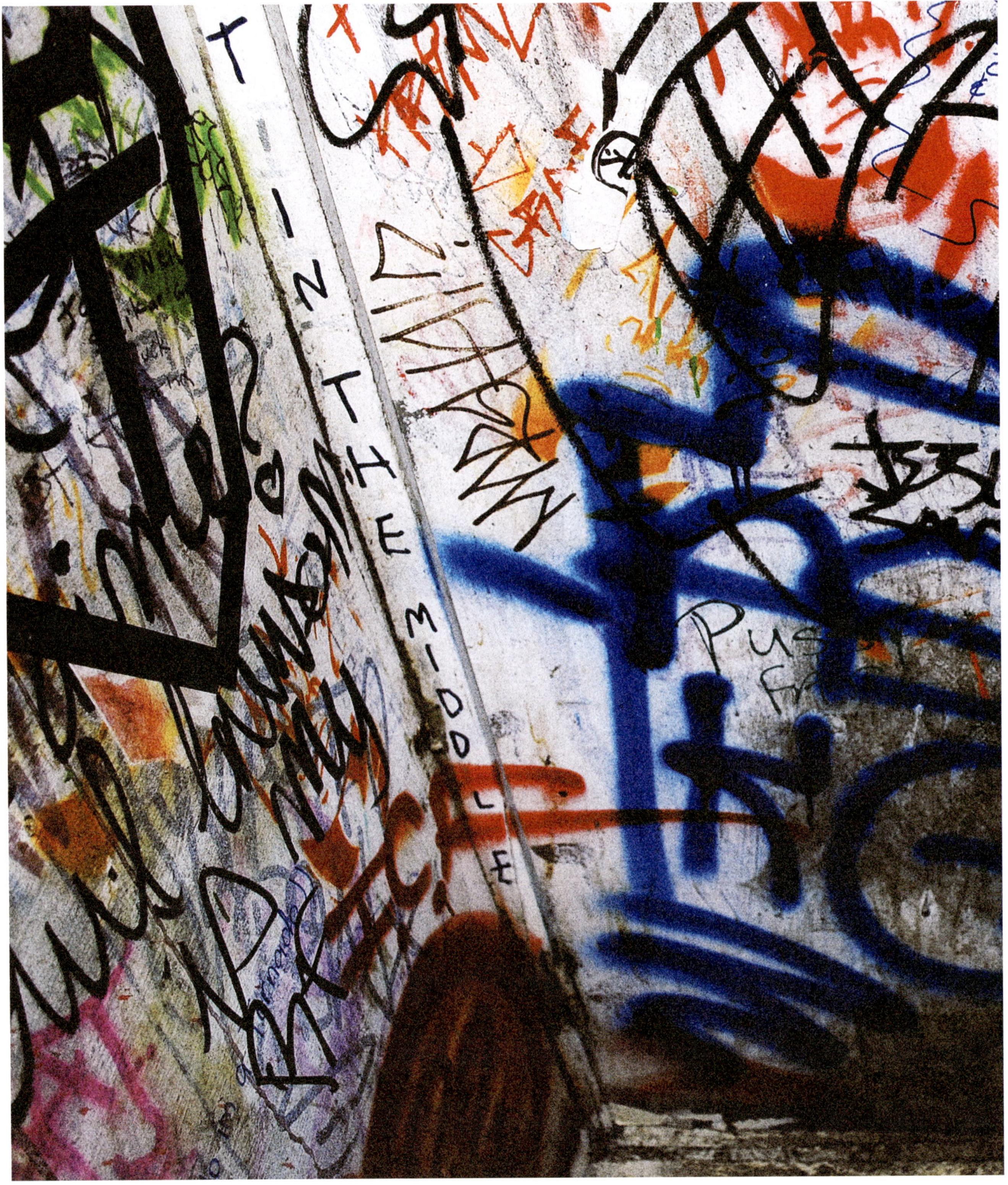
IN THE MIDDLE

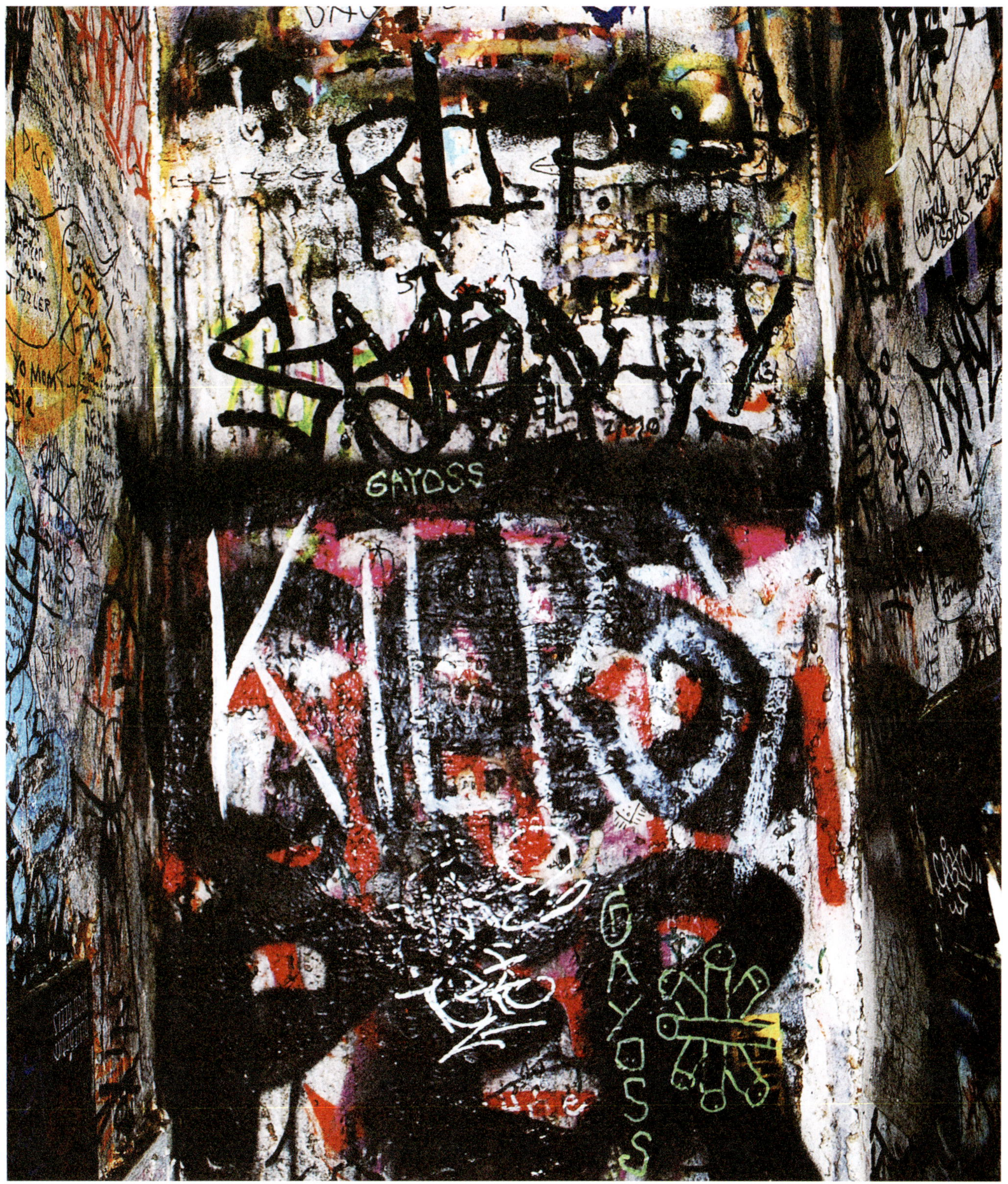

IMAGINAL

"And Yaweh said unto Avram, "I own you, bitch!"
— The Talmud

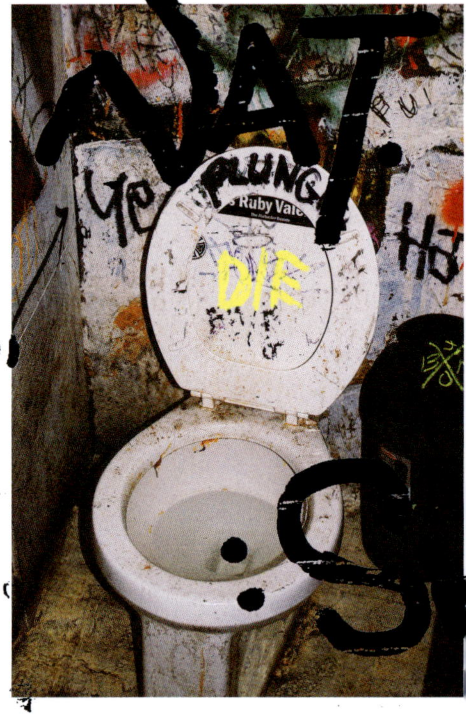

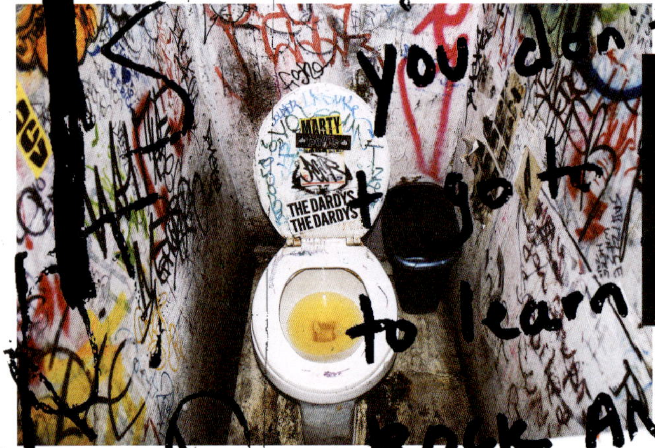

you don't have to go to 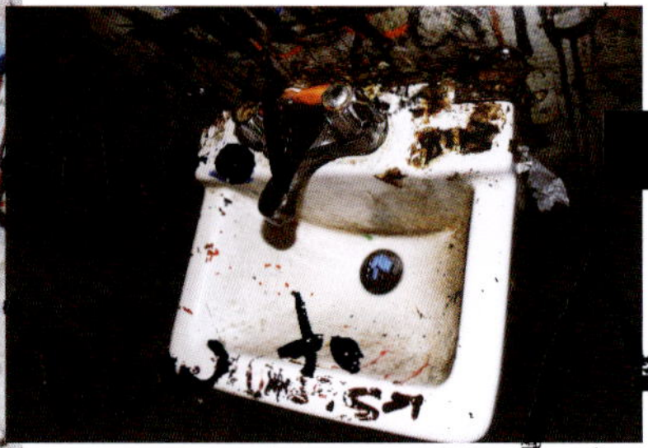 to learn
ROCK AND ROLL!!

— CALIFORNIA . .
SOUL —

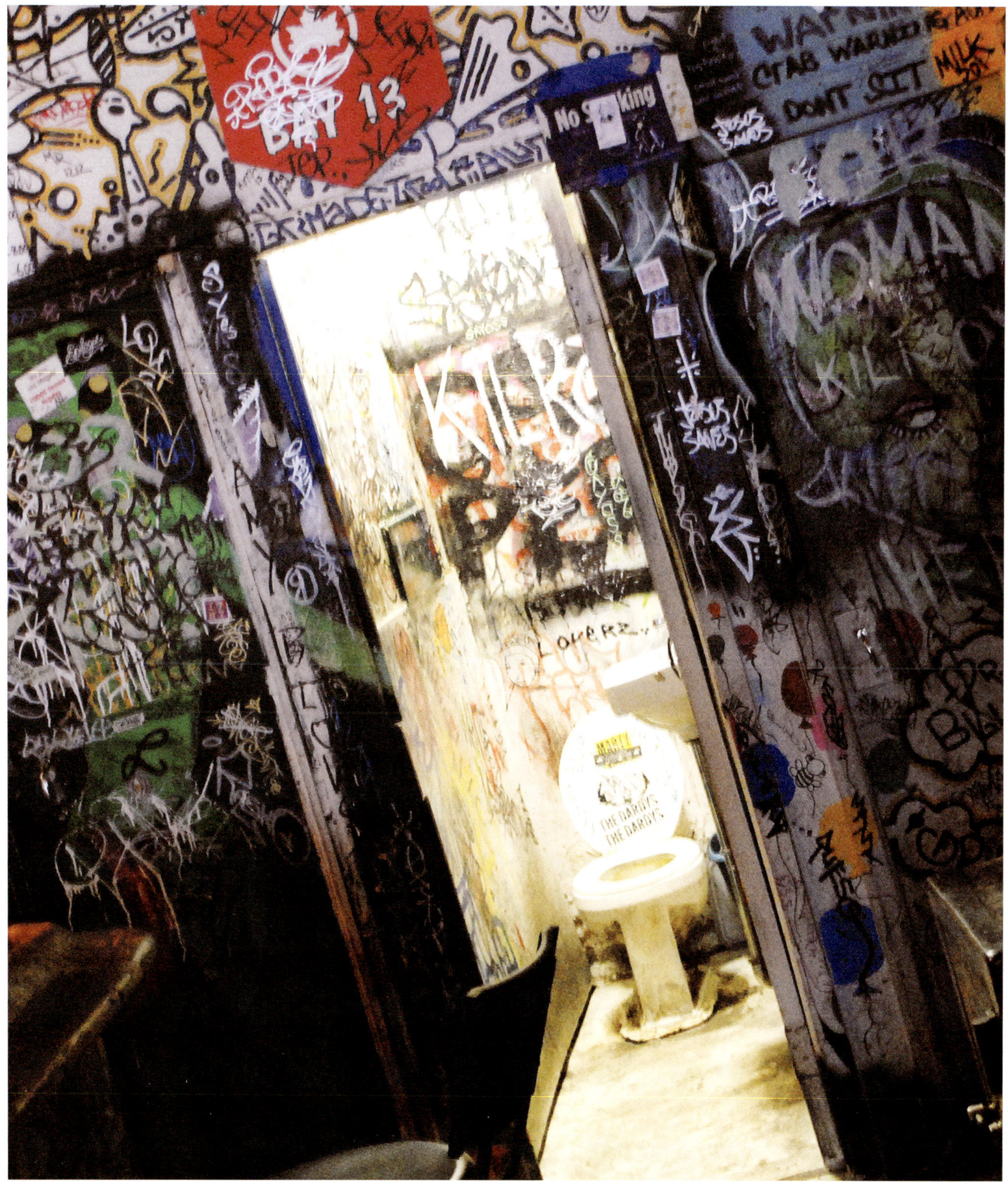

BAY 13
No Smoking
WARNING
CTAB WARNING
DON'T SHIT
MILK
JESUS SAVES
WOMAN
KILLER
KILLER
LOVERZ
THE DARDYS
THE DARDYS

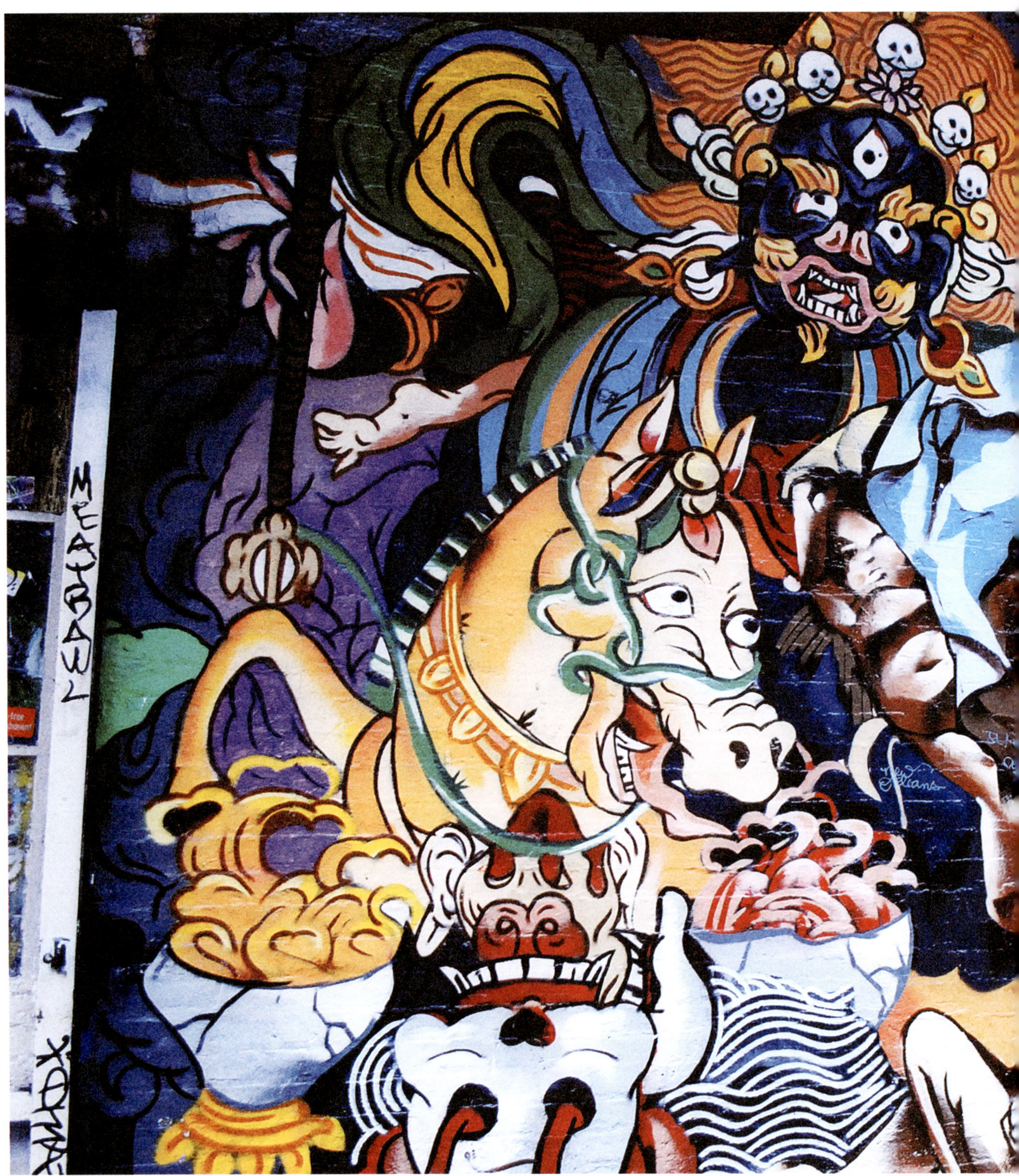

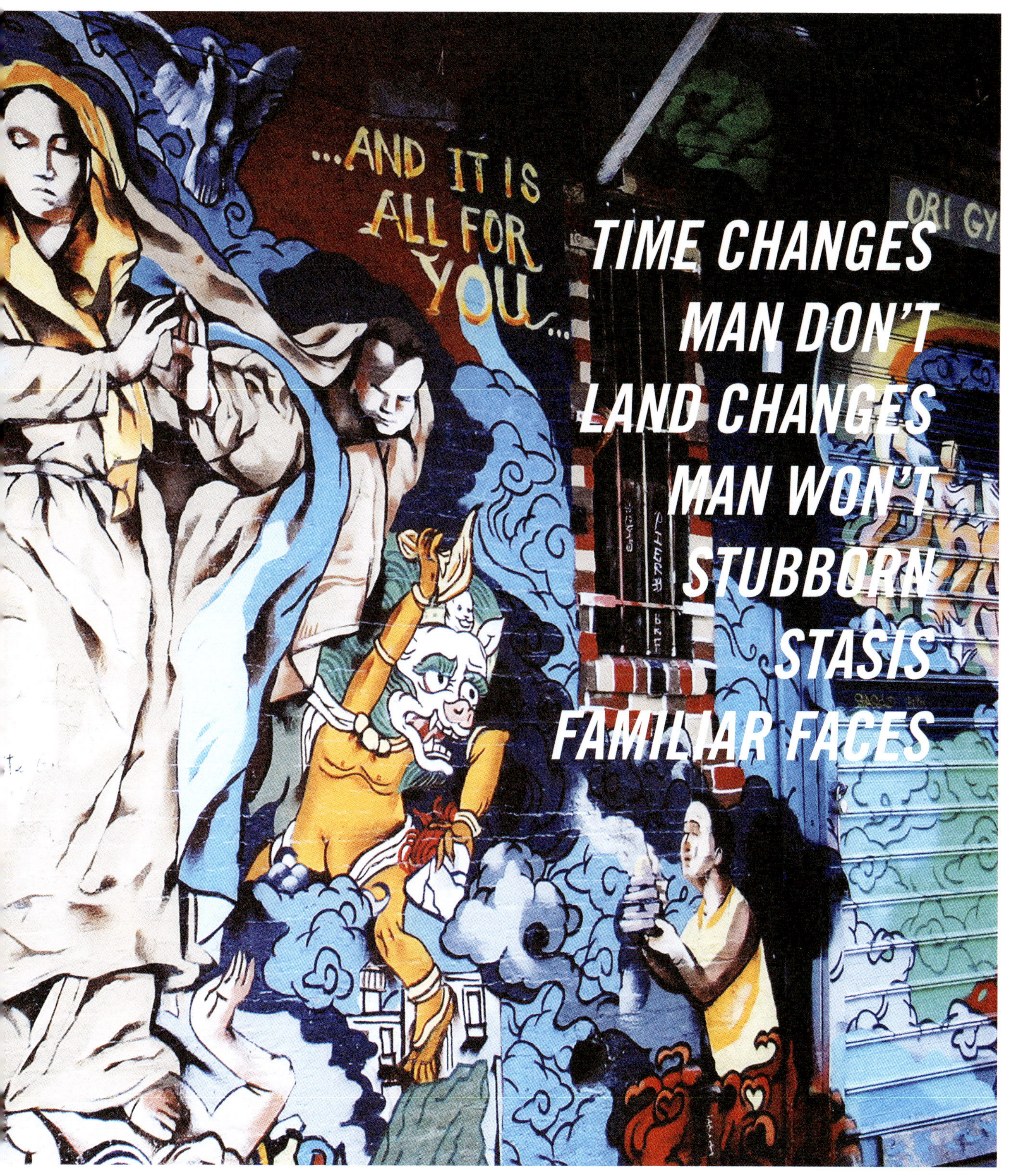

...AND IT IS ALL FOR YOU...
ORI GY
TIME CHANGES
MAN DON'T
LAND CHANGES
MAN WON'T
STUBBORN
STASIS
FAMILIAR FACES

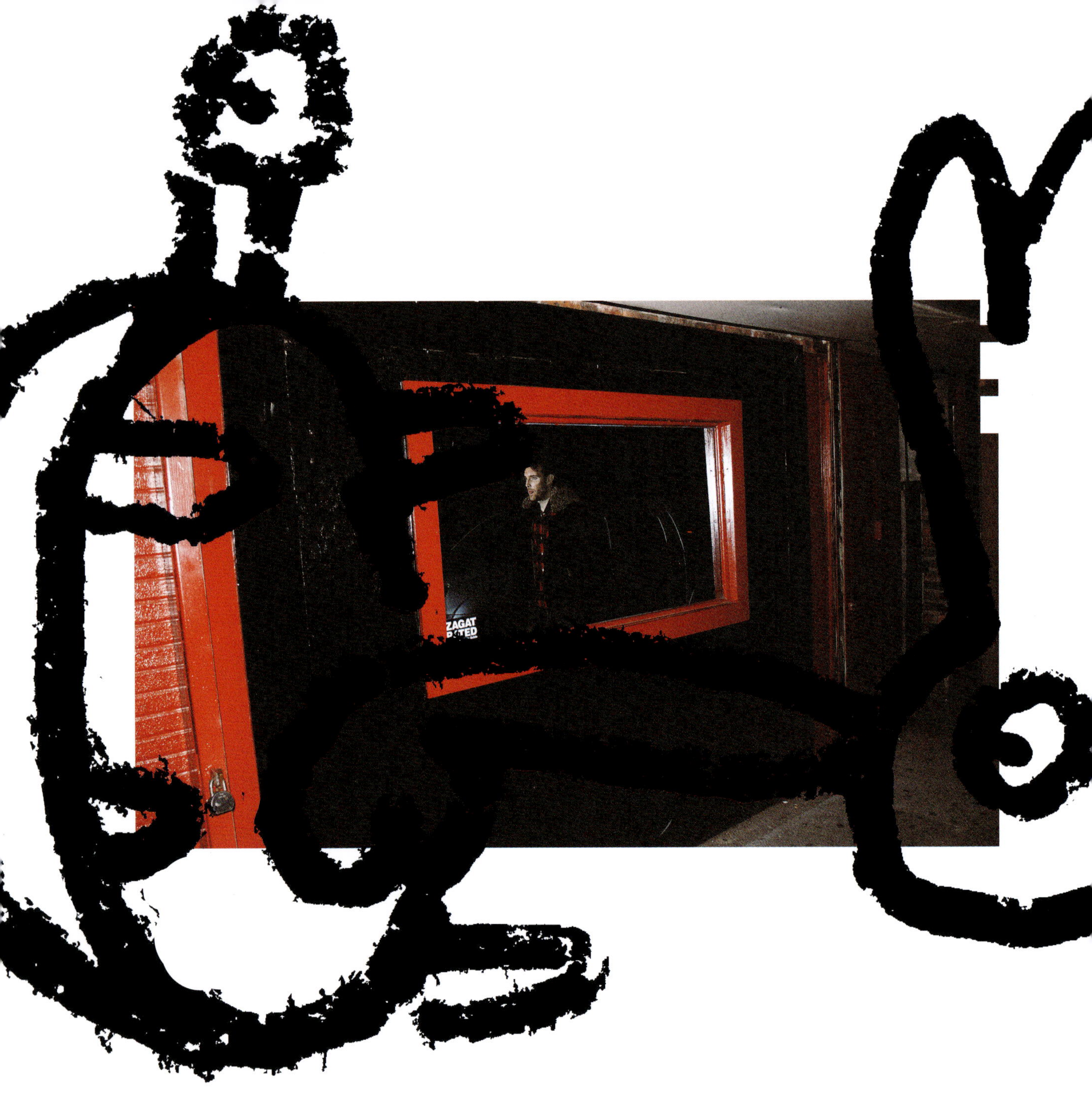
ZAGAT
RATED

Metropolitan

12.04.2010
04:50pm

Williamsburg
Brooklyn

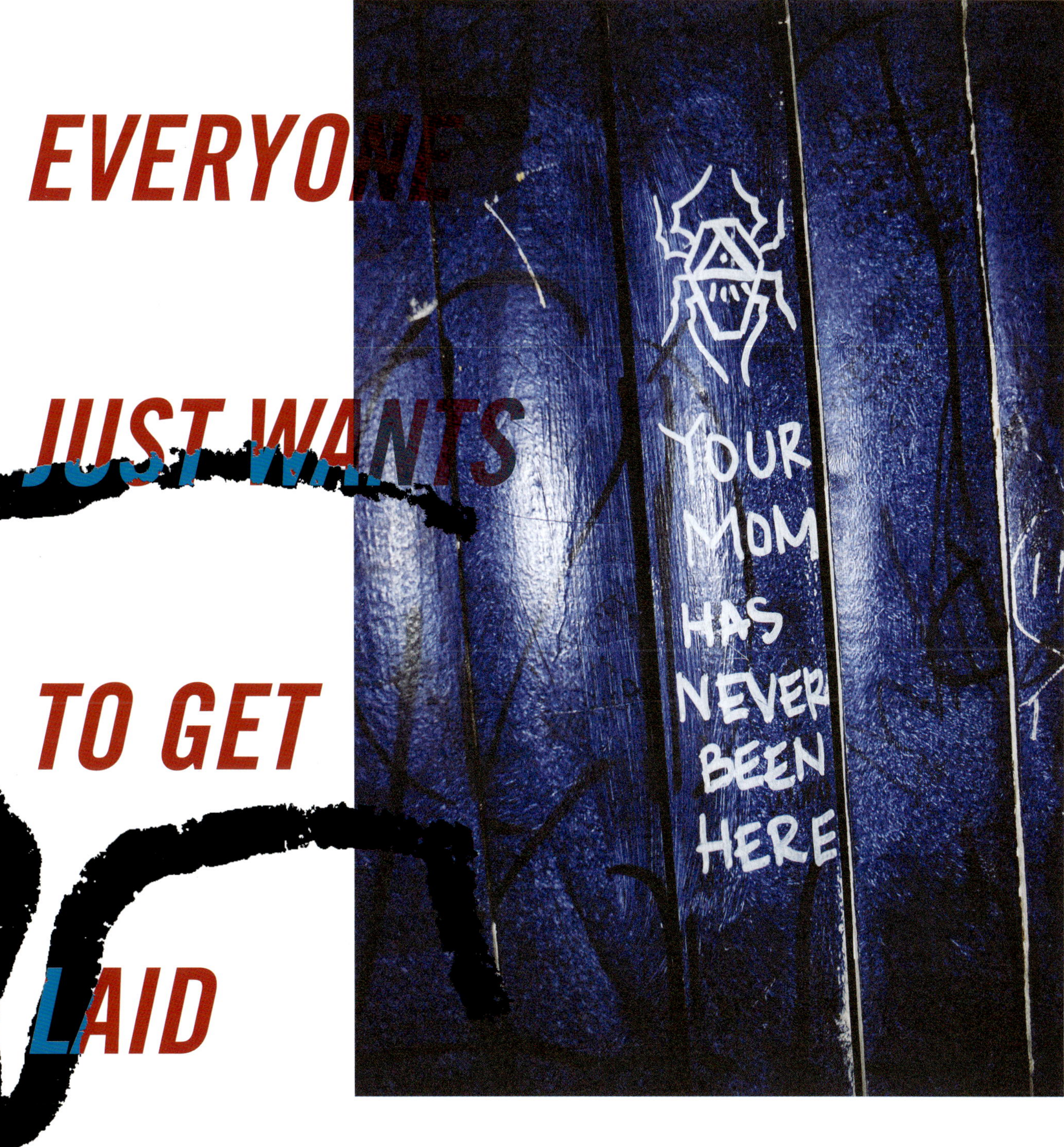

EVERYONE

JUST WANTS

TO GET

LAID

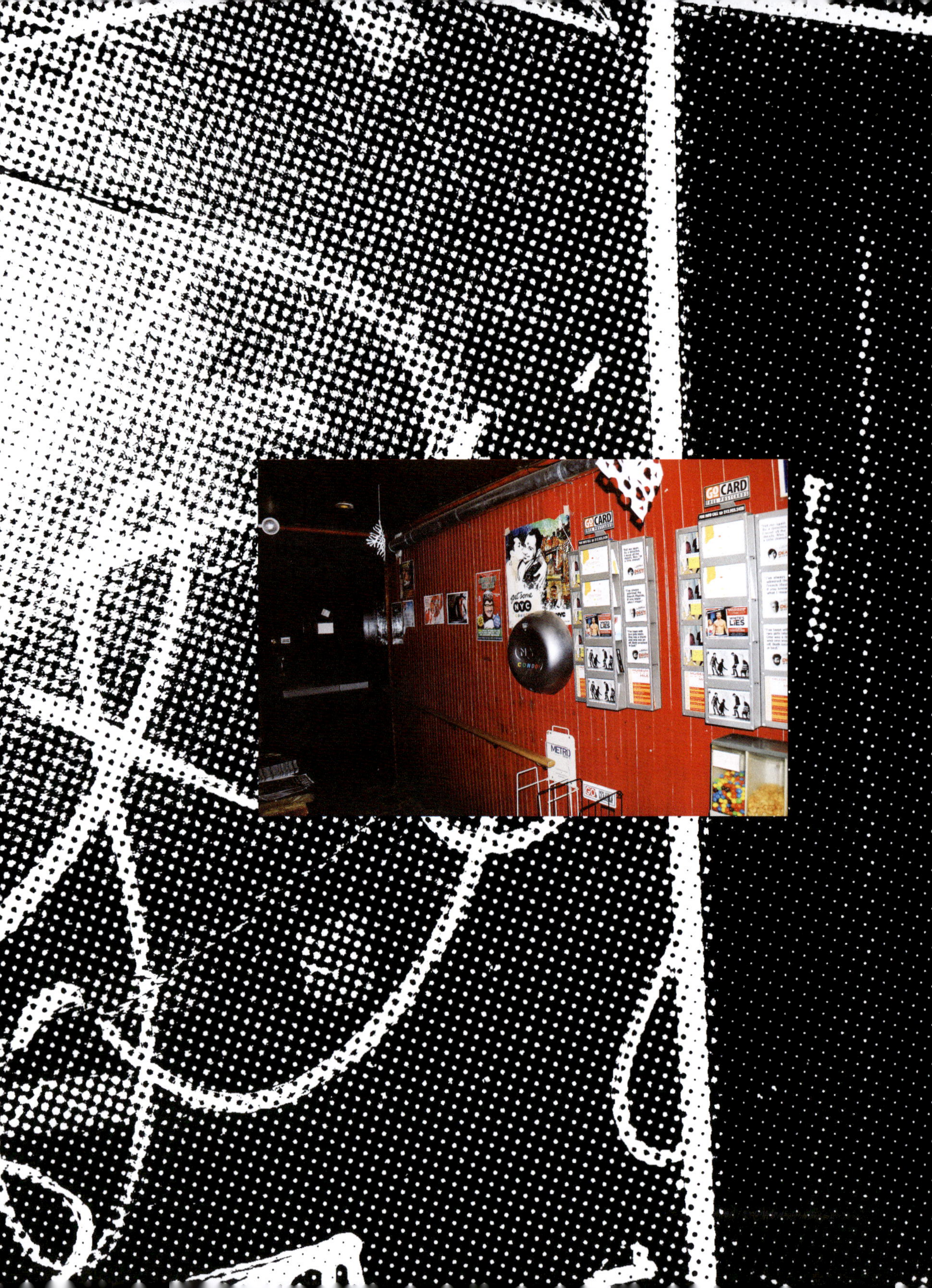
GO CARD
GO CARD
METRO
PRINTED LIES

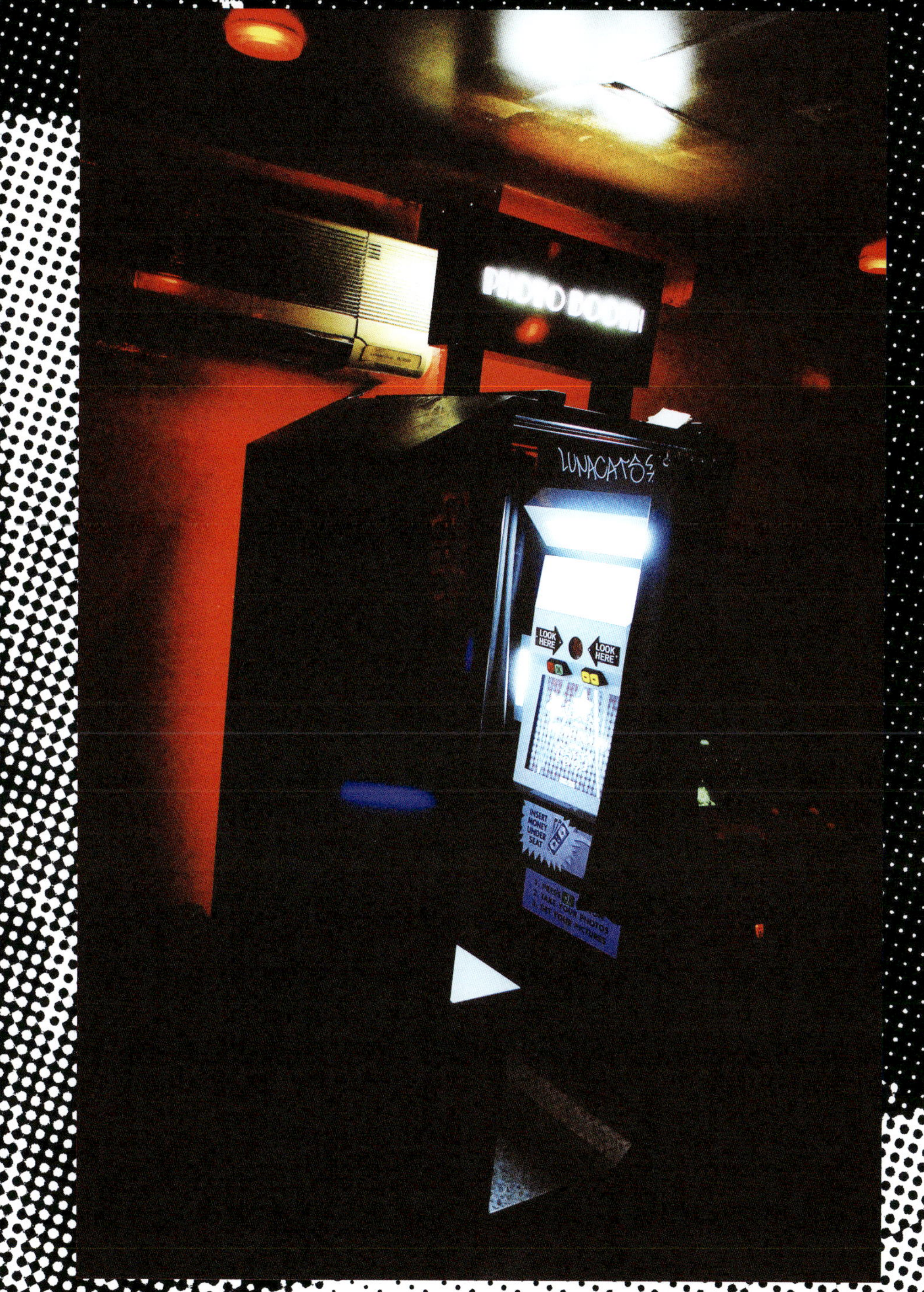

PHOTO BOOTH
LOOK HERE
LOOK HERE
INSERT MONEY UNDER SEAT

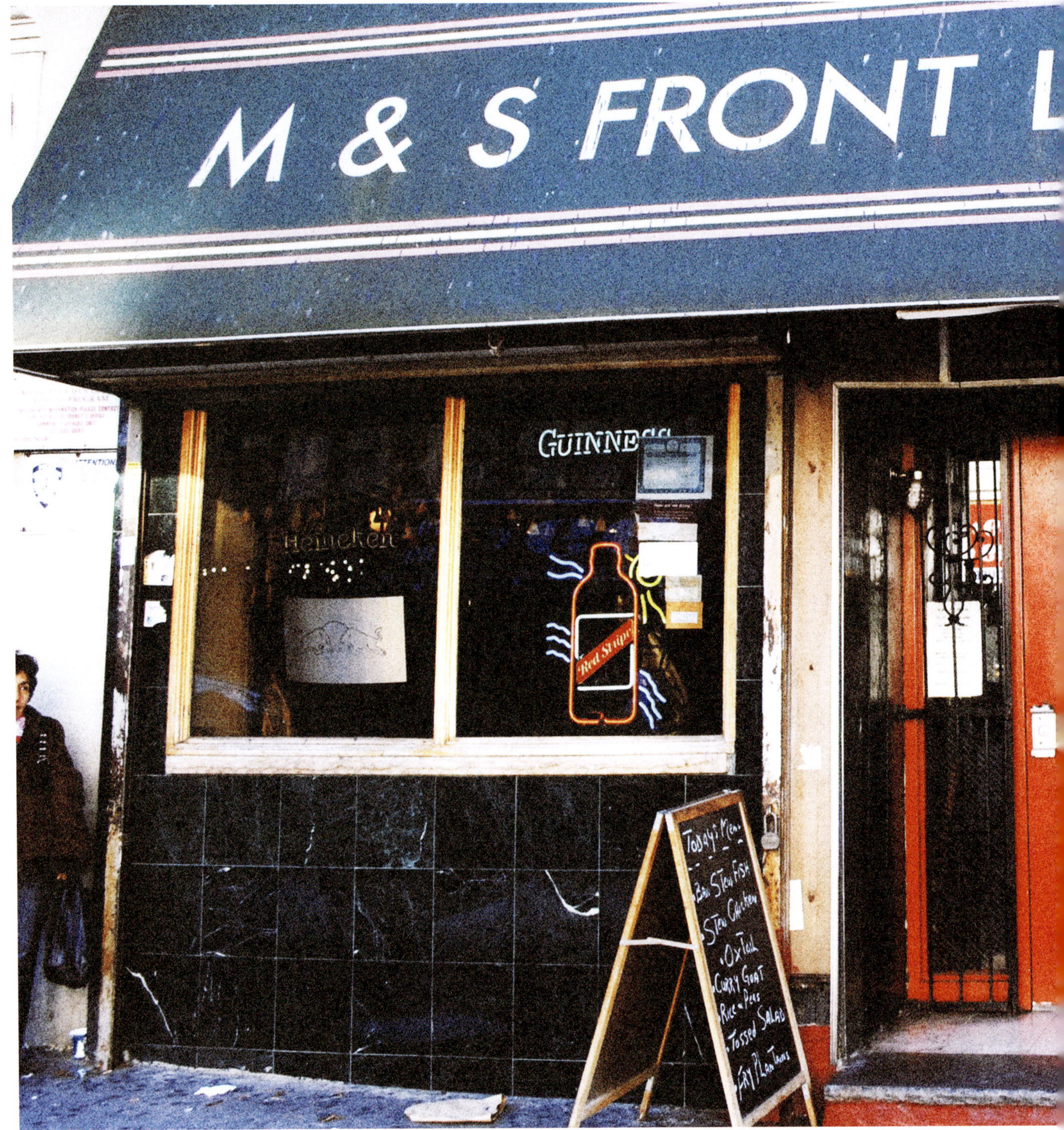

M&S Front Line Company

11.06.2010
04:26pm

Harlem
Manhattan

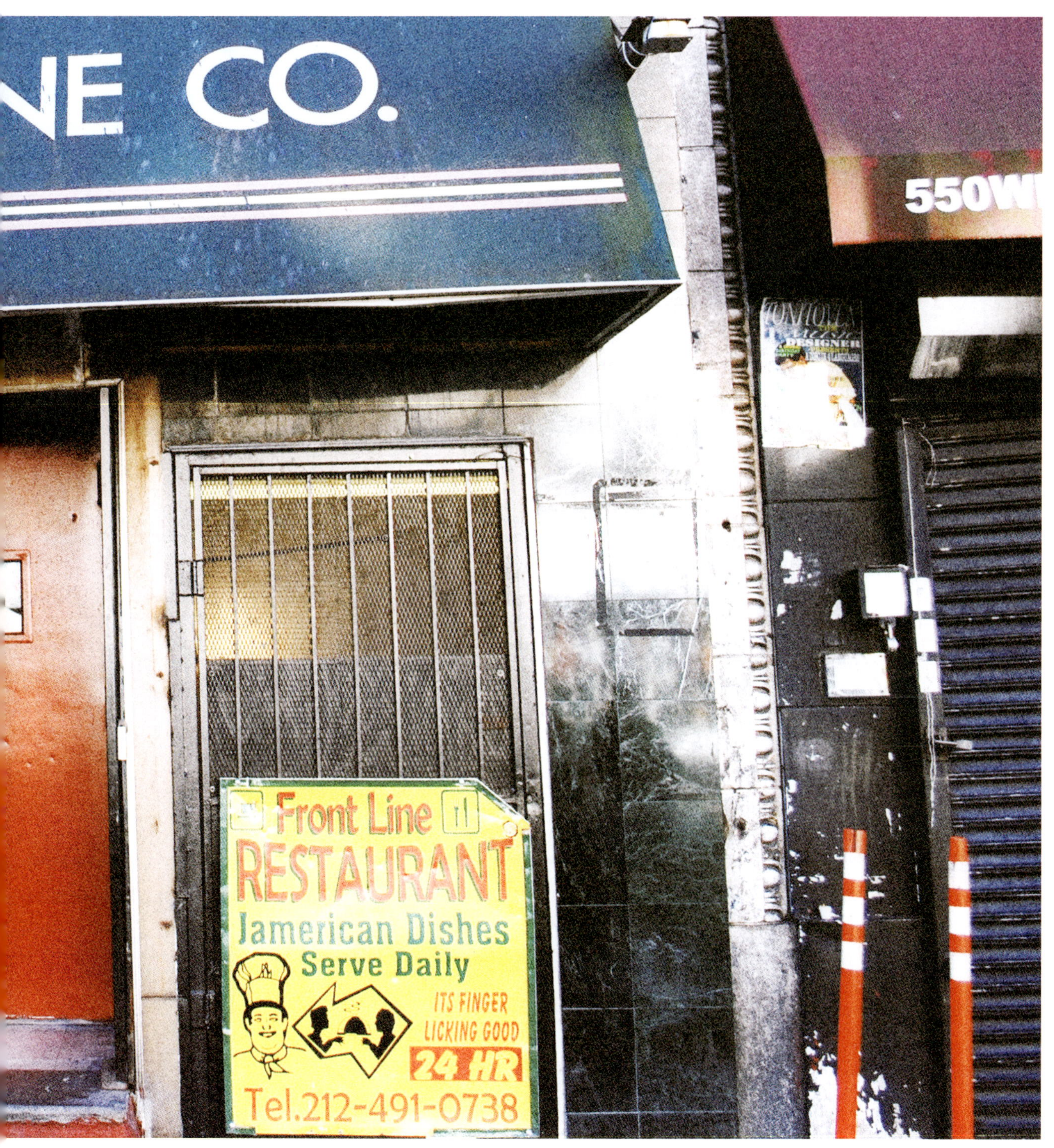
NE CO.
550W
Front Line
RESTAURANT
Jamerican Dishes
Serve Daily
ITS FINGER
LICKING GOOD
24 HR
Tel.212-491-0738

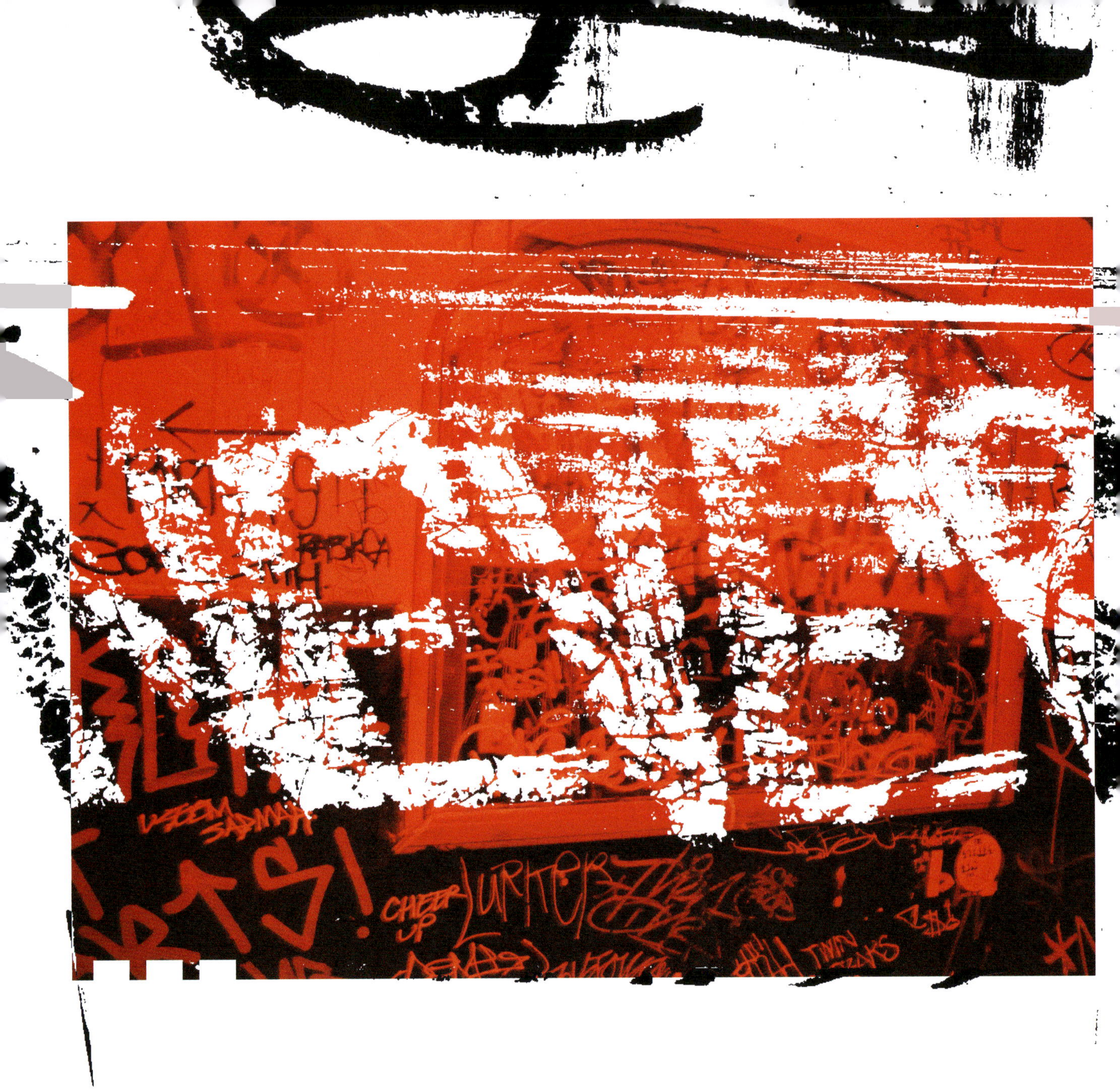

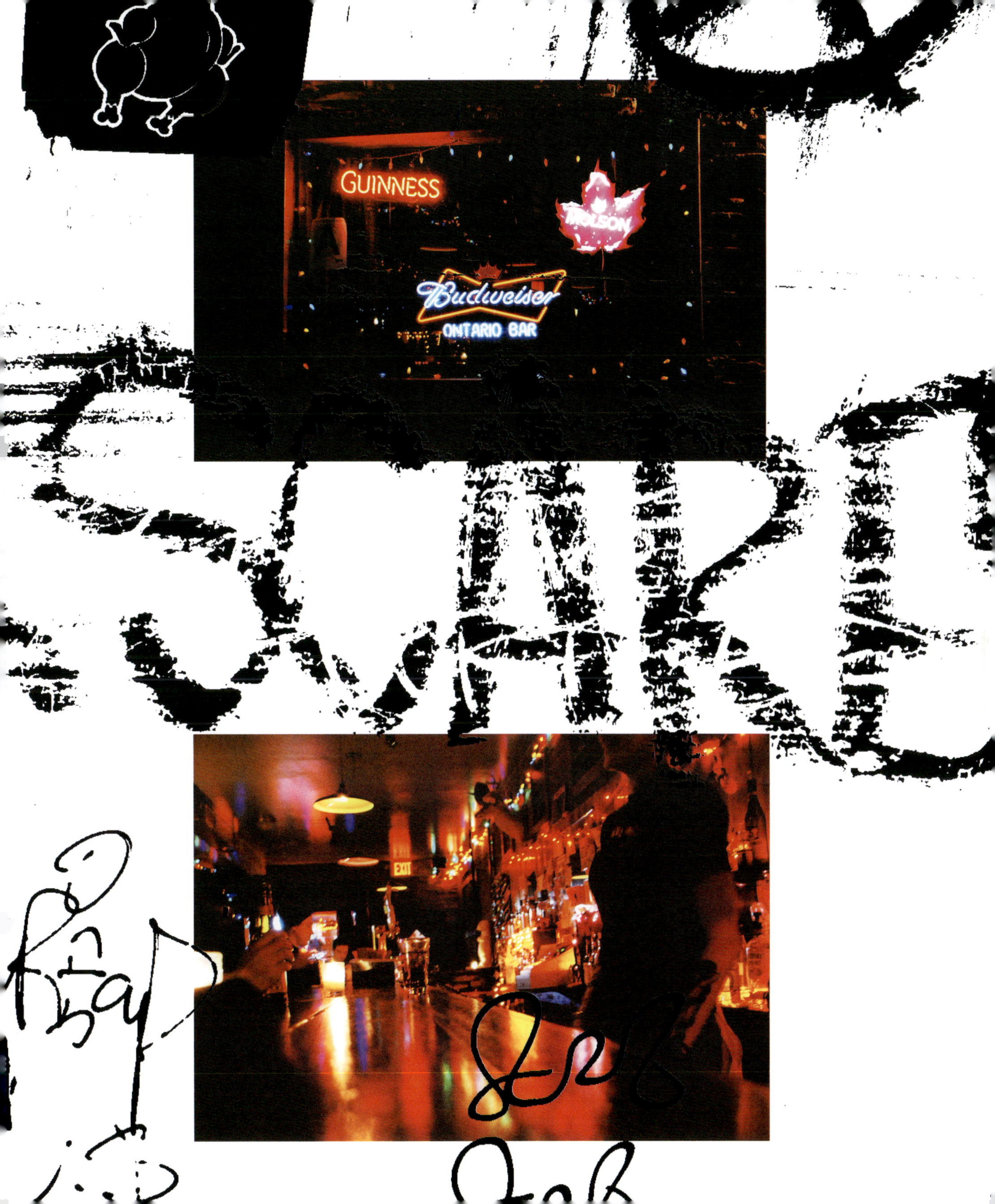

GUINNESS
MOLSON
Budweiser
ONTARIO BAR

EXIT

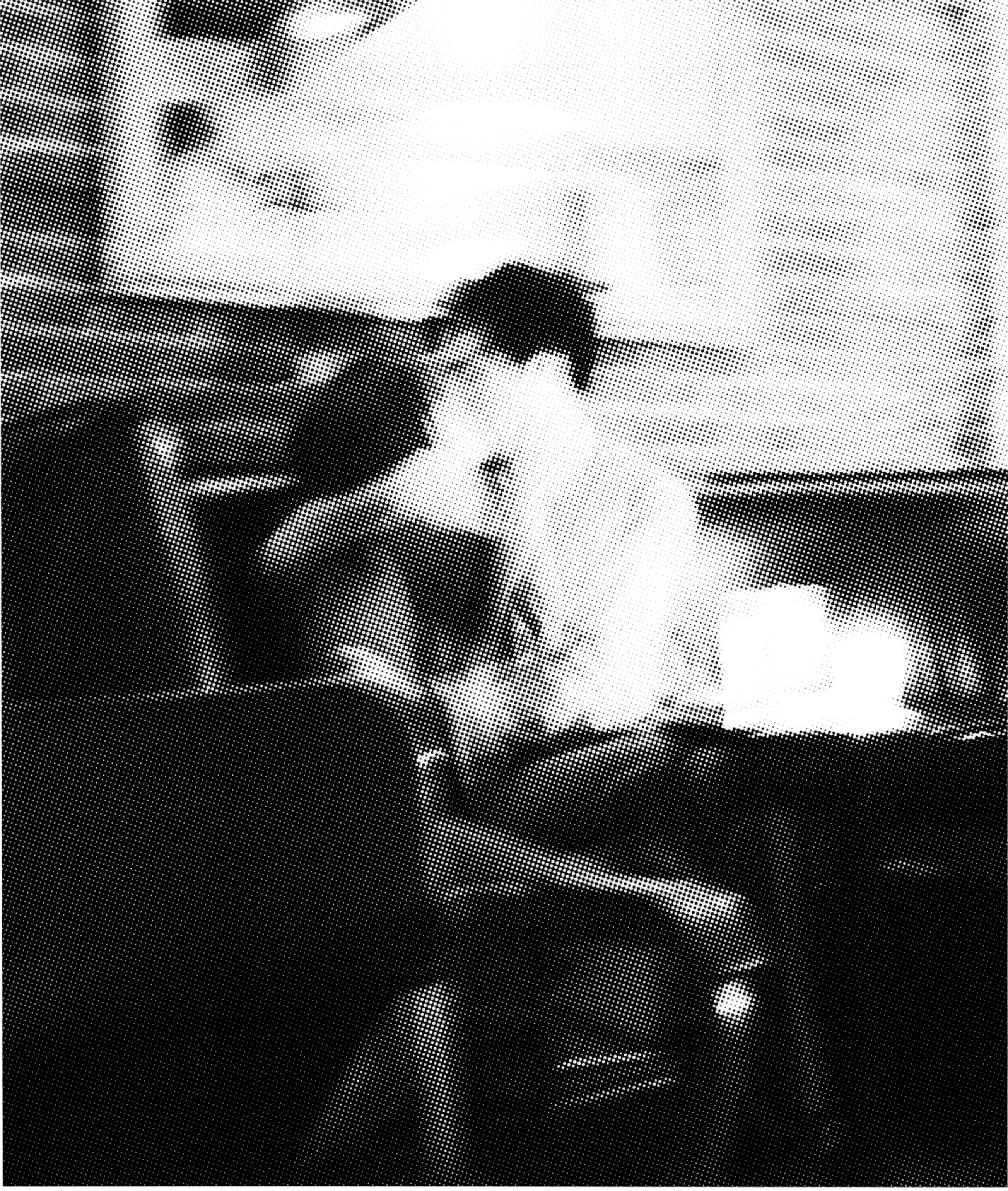

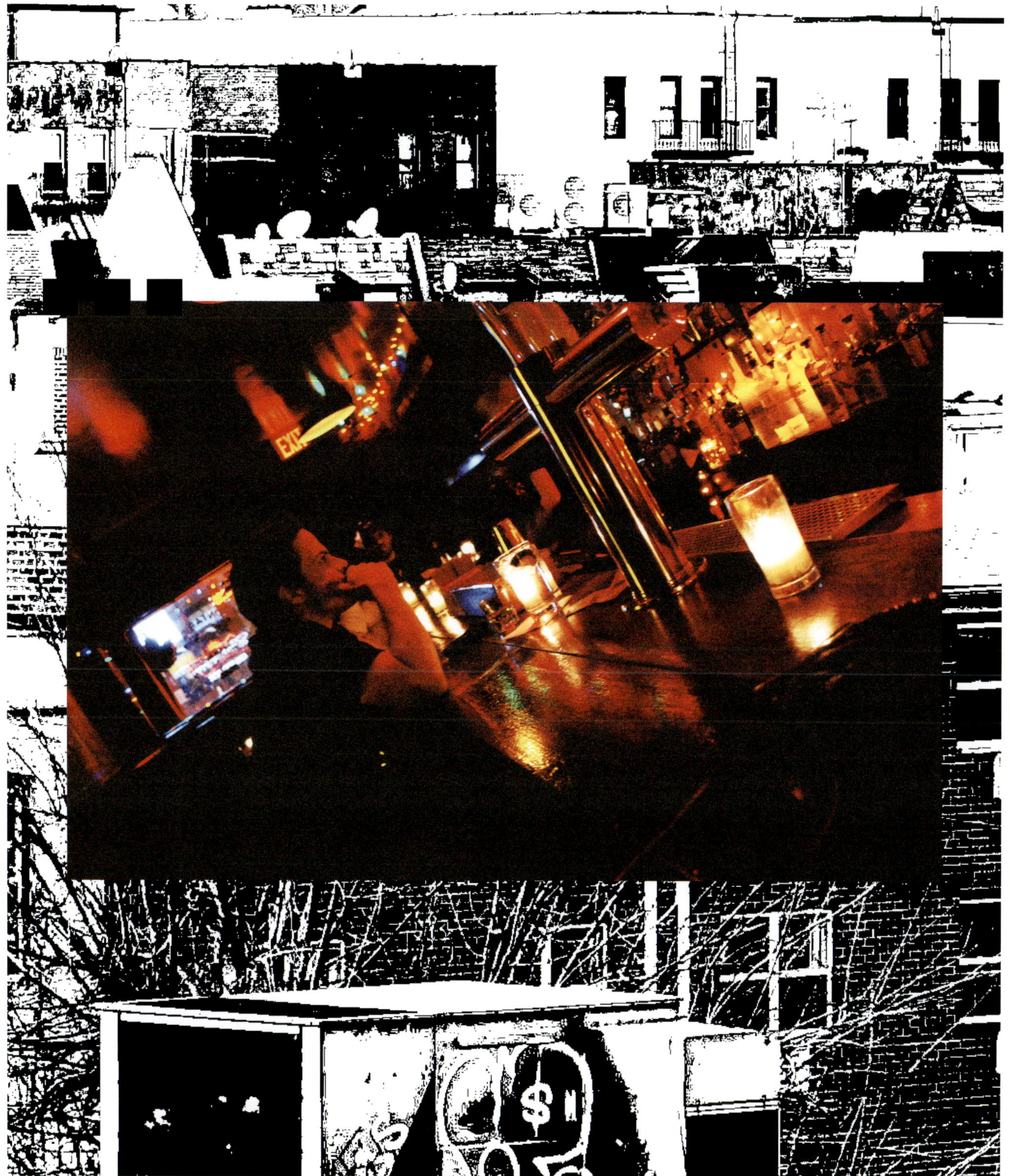

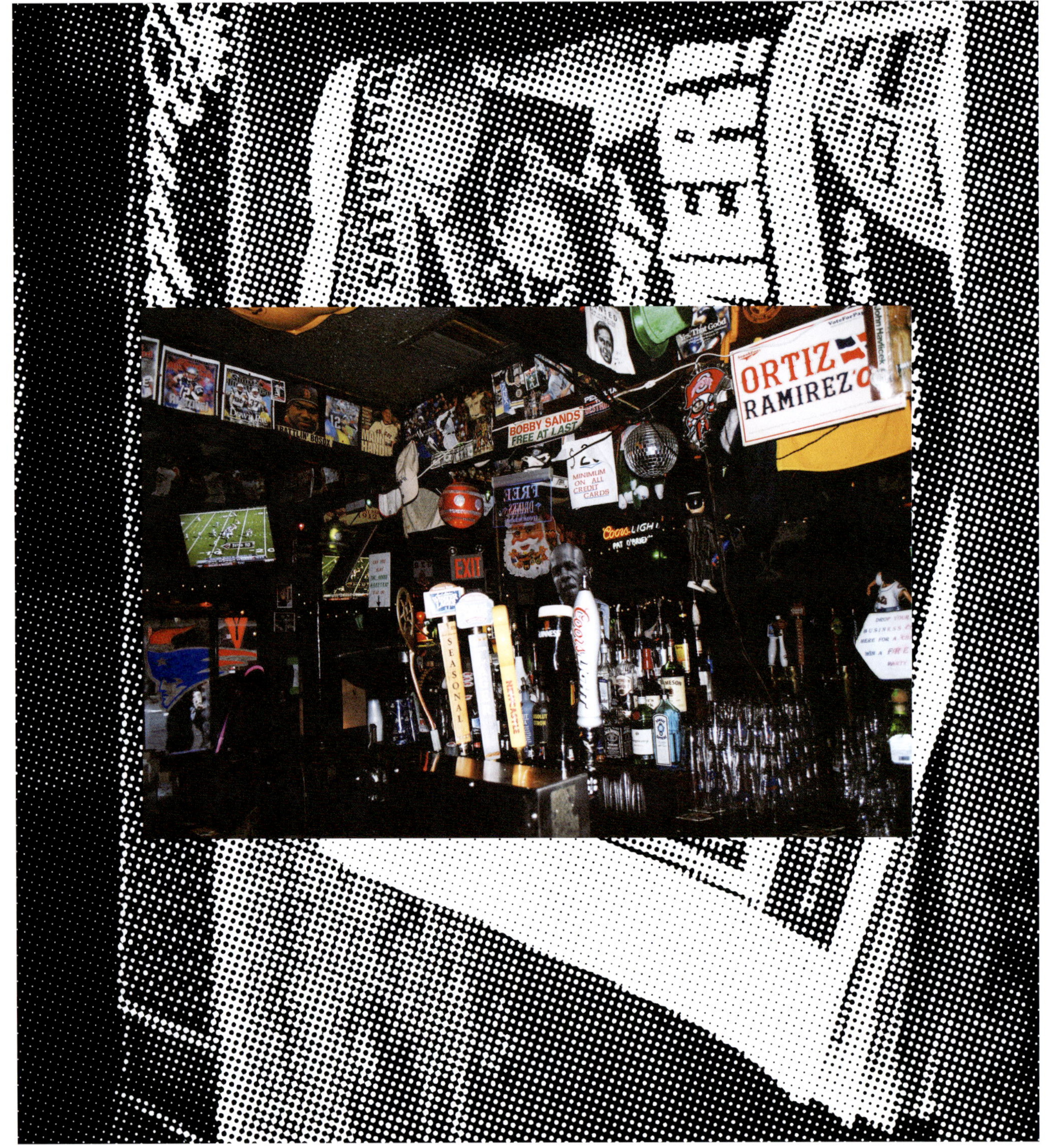

Pat O'Briens

12.18.2010
03:52pm

Upper East Side
Manhattan

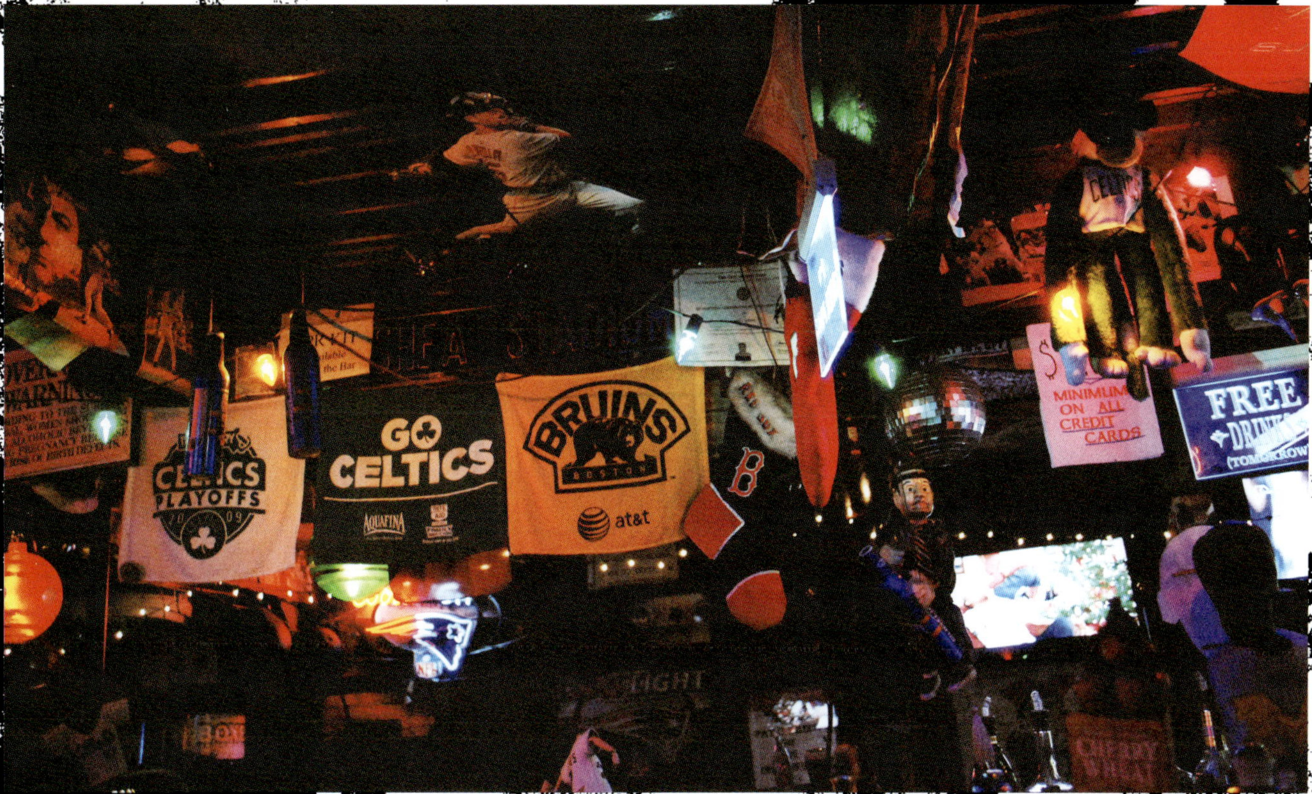

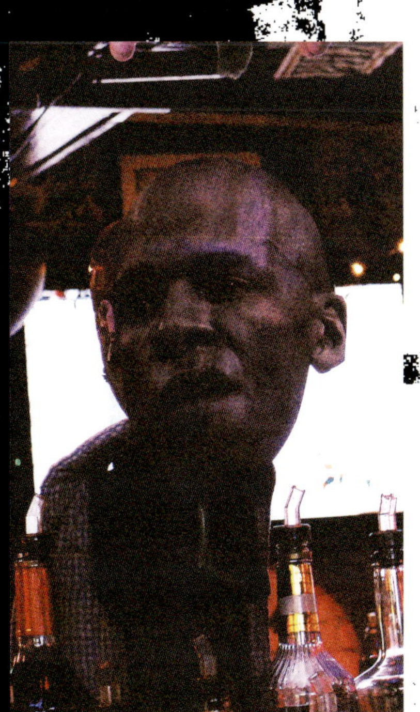
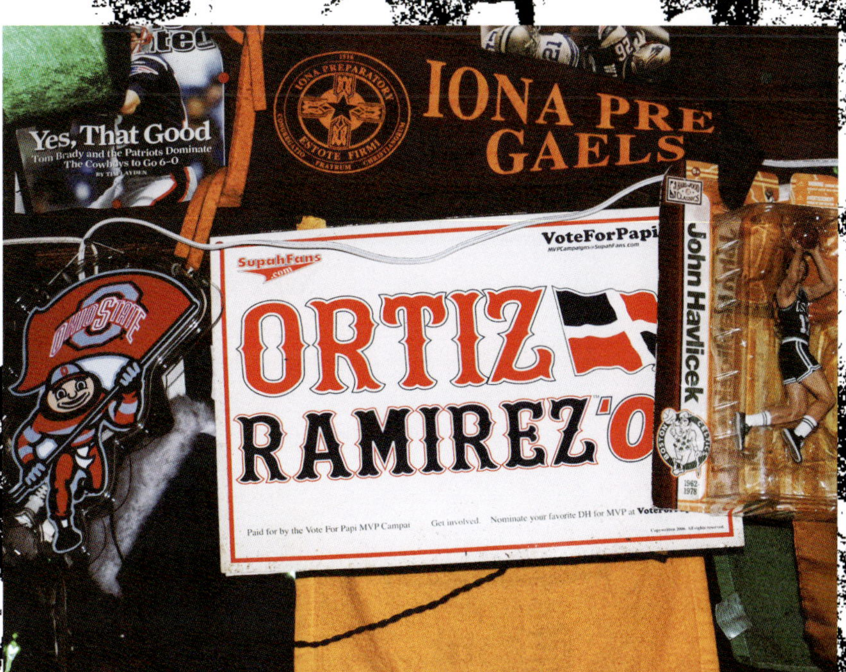
Yes, That Good
Tom Brady and the Patriots Dominate
The Cowboys to Go 6-0
IONA PREP
GAELS
OHIO STATE
SupahFans.com
VoteForPapi
ORTIZ
RAMIREZ'O
John Havlicek

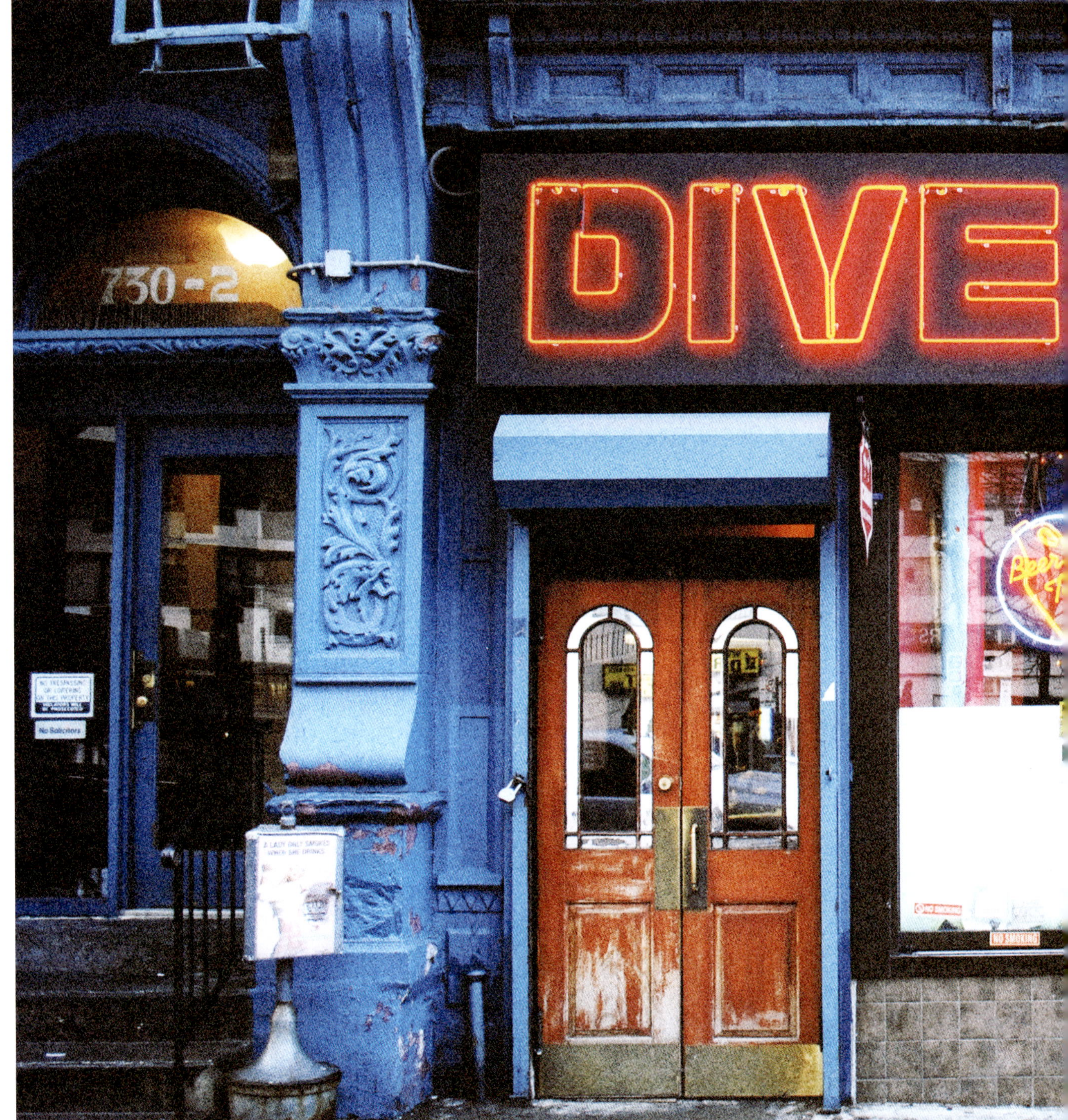

Dive Bar

12.30.2010
04:13pm

Upper West Side
Manhattan

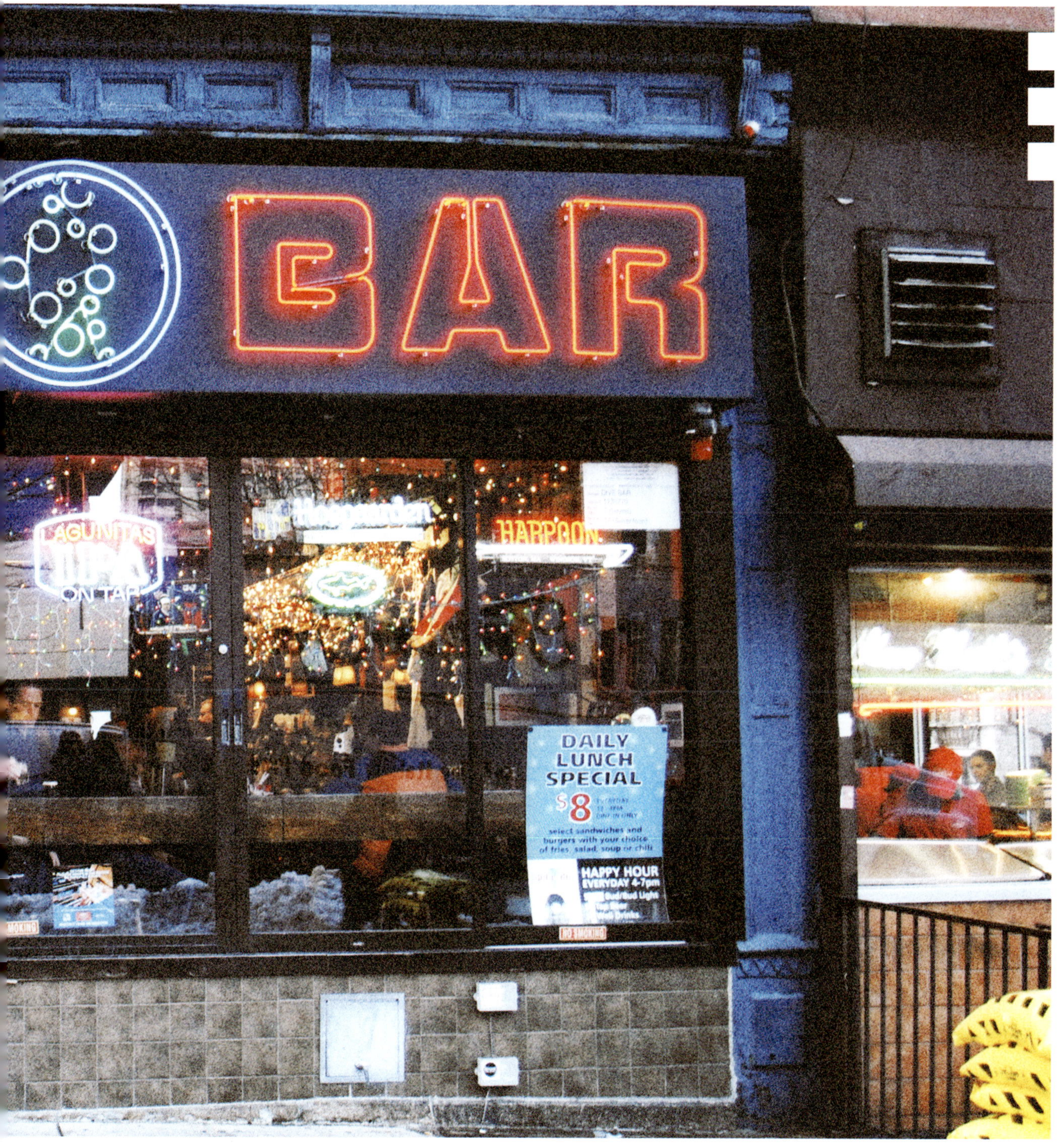

BAR
LAGUNITAS
IPA
ON TAP
HARPOON
DAILY
LUNCH
SPECIAL
$8
select sandwiches and
burgers with your choice
of fries, salad, soup or chili
HAPPY HOUR
EVERYDAY 4-7pm
NO SMOKING

08.29.2011
03:39pm

Pregame

"Meet me at…" was basically a catchphrase. I spent a lot of nights posted up at one of these spots—sometimes way earlier than planned. Whether it was 2-for-1 happy hours, after-work hangs, or full-on after-hours, we all collected those random little trinkets they handed out for buybacks—checkers, chess pieces, wooden nickels, old subway tokens, you name it. St. Jerome's had a $2 Bud/Bud Light deal from 2pm till midnight, a DJ spinning in the front window, and a projector that sometimes played porn at night, depending on the bartender's mood. There was even a tiny 3x3 box with a dance pole across from the bar—Lady Gaga (back then just Stefani Germanotta) used to dance there on weekends. Her boyfriend at the time, Lüc Carl, tended bar—looked like Nikki Sixx and rocked leather pants year-round, dead of summer included. After that, we'd maybe hit 151, Johnson's, or Local 138. And that was just the warm-up. The night usually wrapped at a show—maybe Black Rebel Motorcycle Club at Warsaw, James Blake at Terminal 5, or Bad Brains at Irving. It was a time… and the memories still hit.

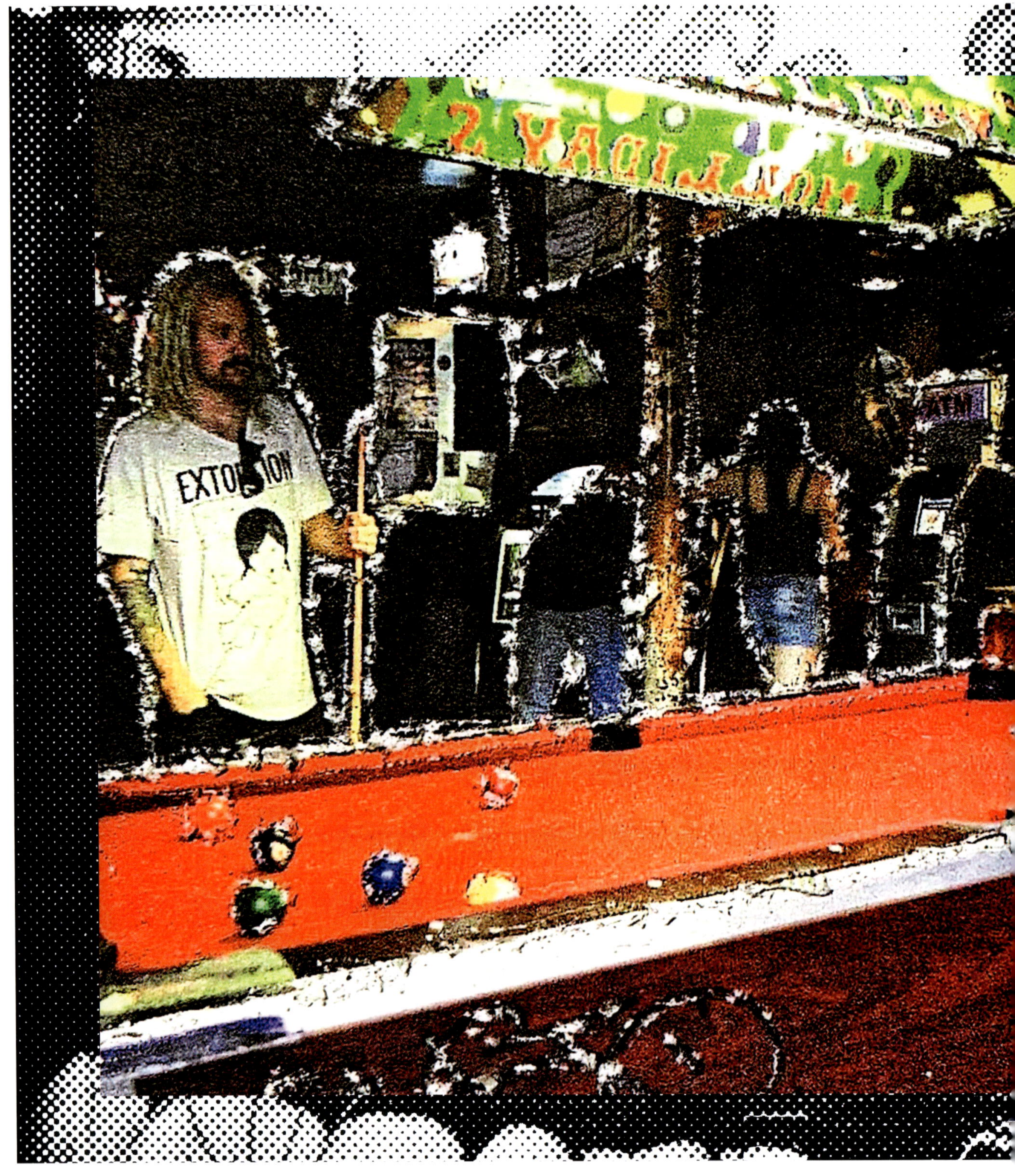
HOLIDAYS
EXTORTION

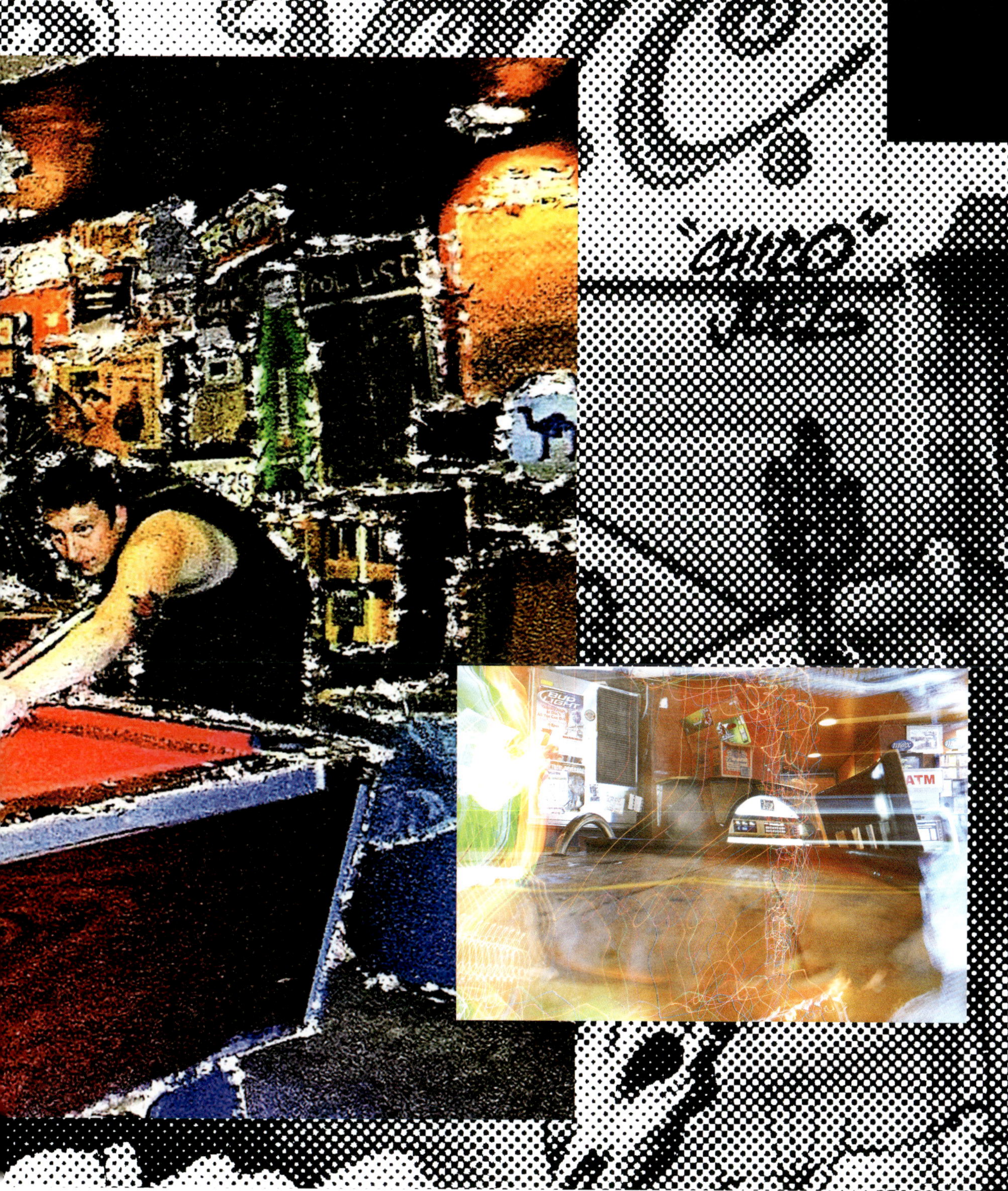
"CHICO"

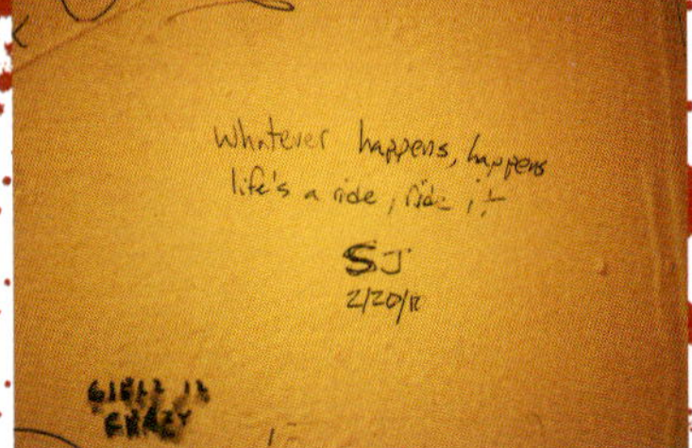
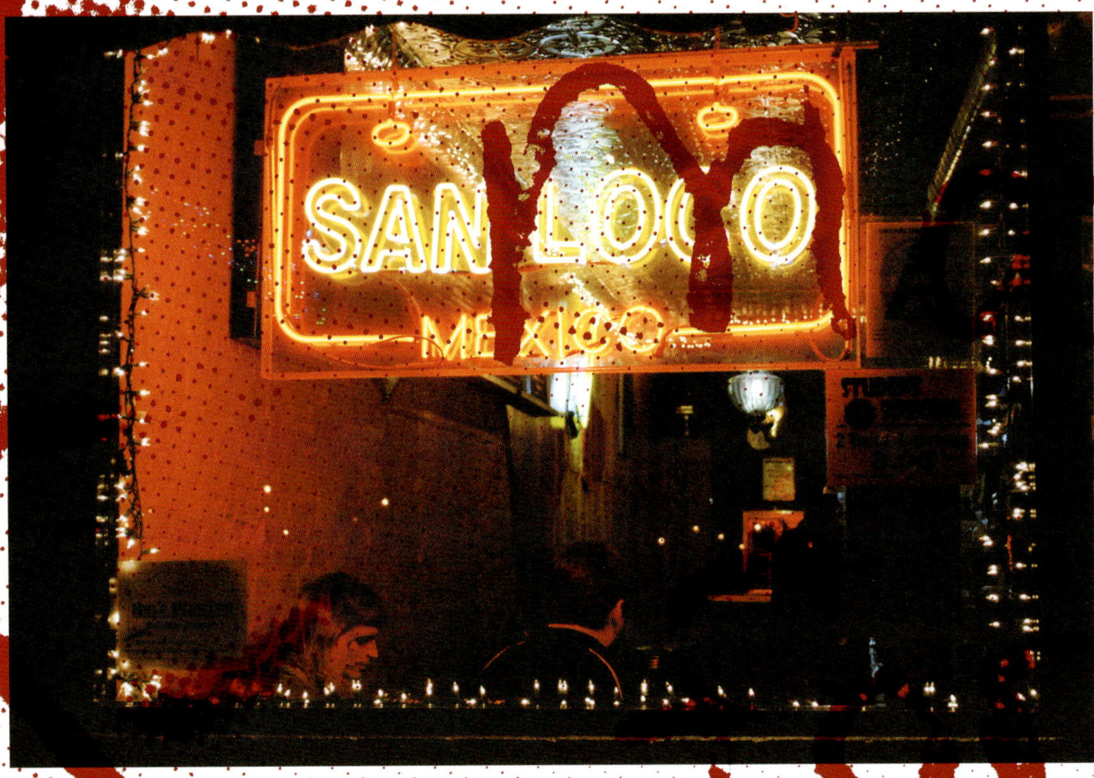

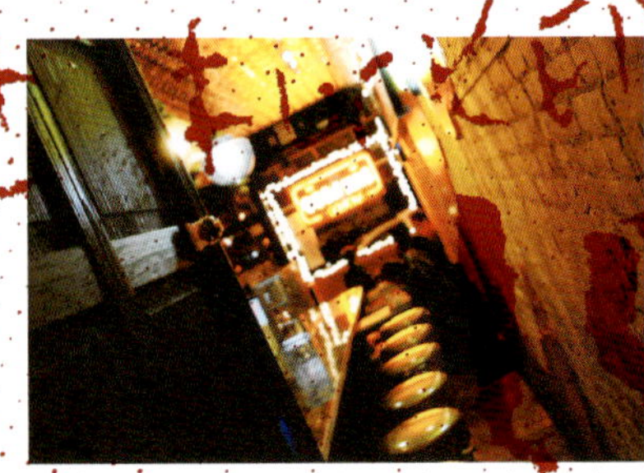

San Loco

01.08.2011
06:35pm

East Village
Manhattan

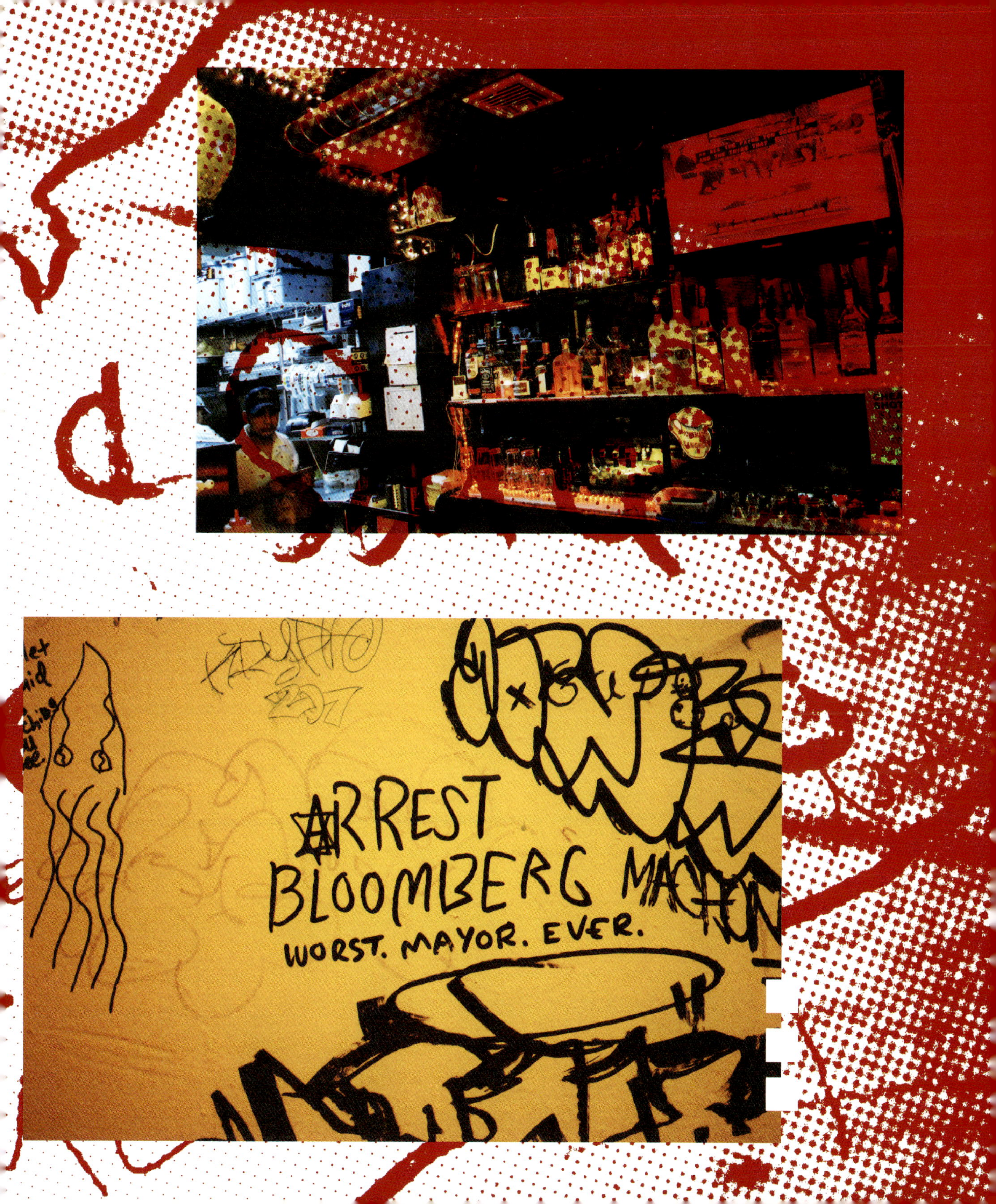

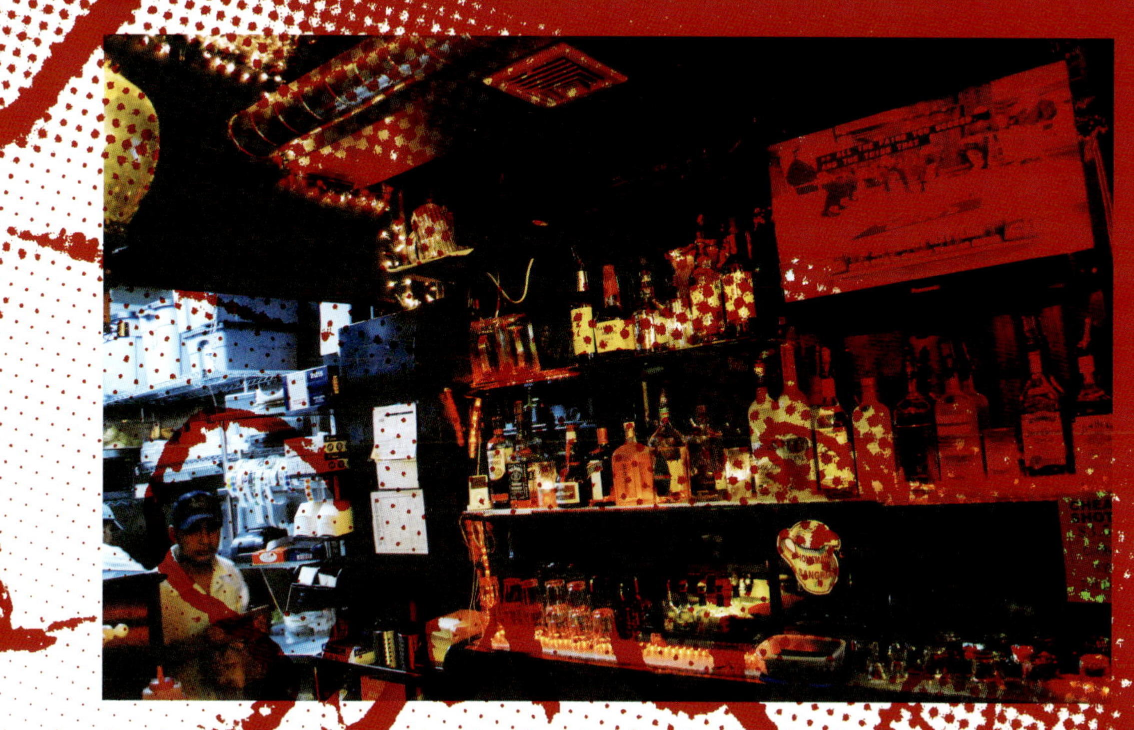
ARREST
BLOOMBERG MACHON
WORST. MAYOR. EVER.

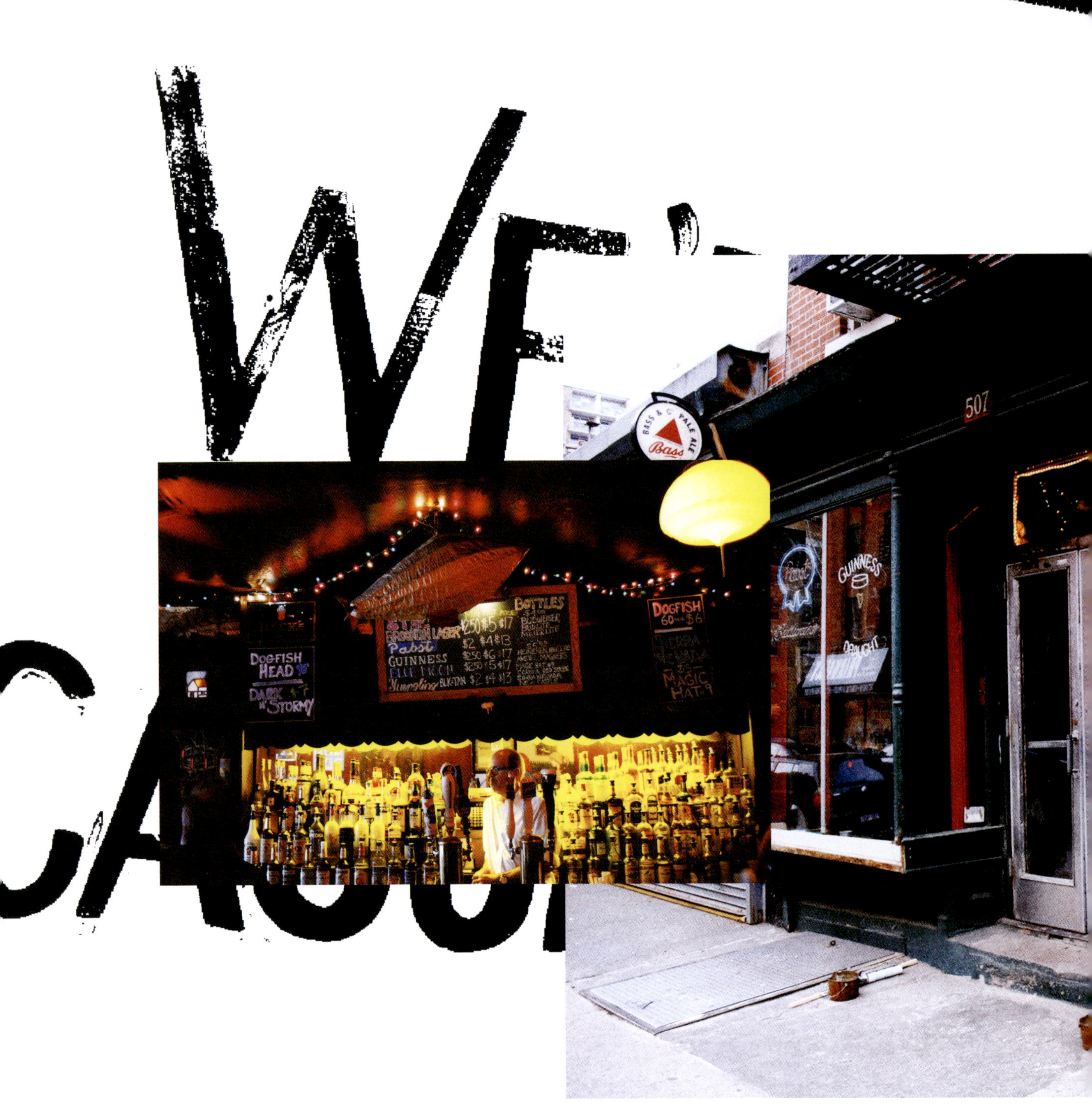
507
BASS & Co PALE ALE
Bass
Pabst
GUINNESS
DOGFISH
HEAD
DARK N STORMY
BOTTLES
BROOKLYN LAGER
Pabst
GUINNESS
BLUE MOON
Yuengling BLK-TAN
DOGFISH
60
SIERRA
NEVADA
MAGIC
HAT

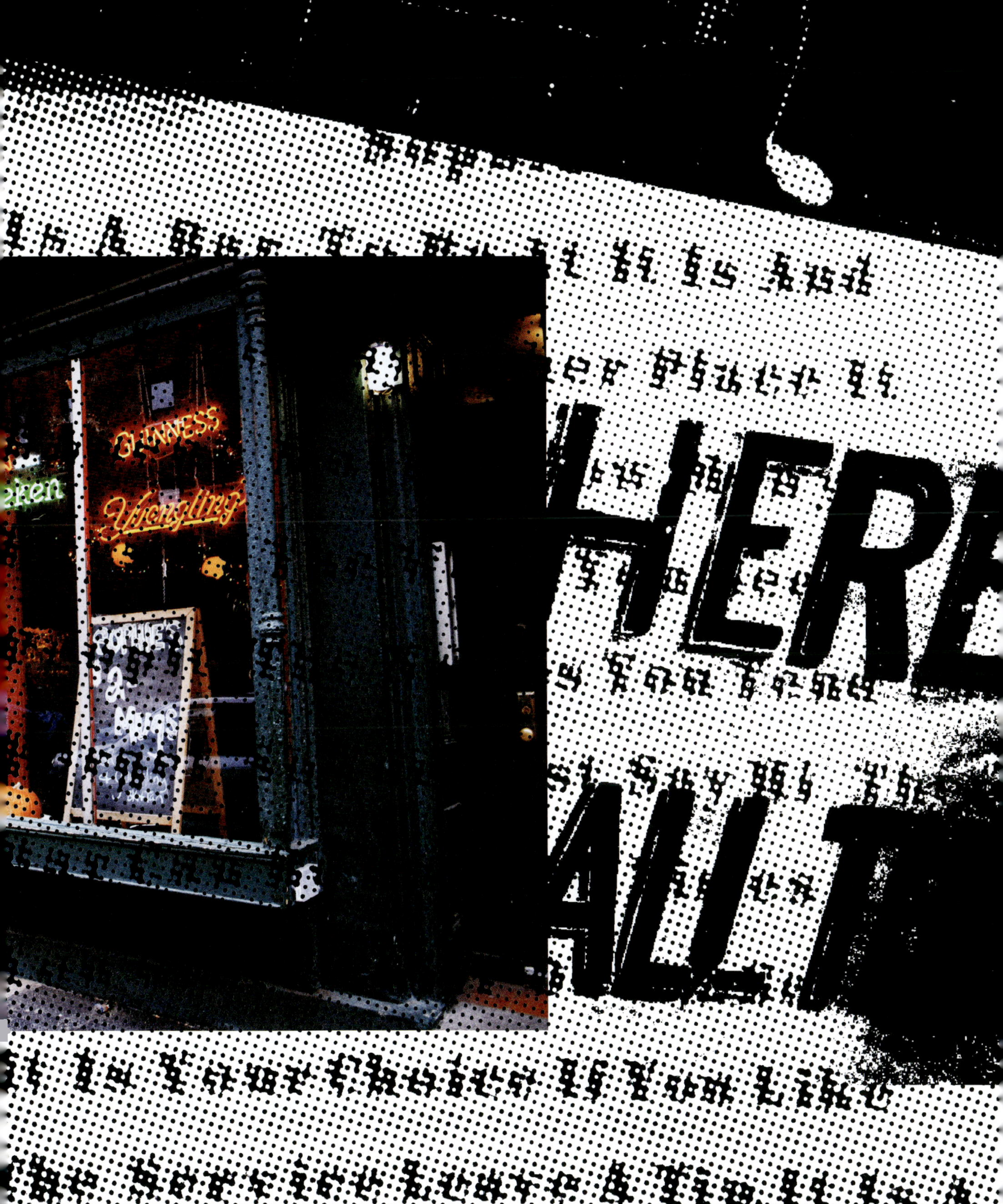
GUINNESS
Yuengling
eken
HERE
ALL
It Is Your Choice If You Like
The Service Leave A Tip It Is A

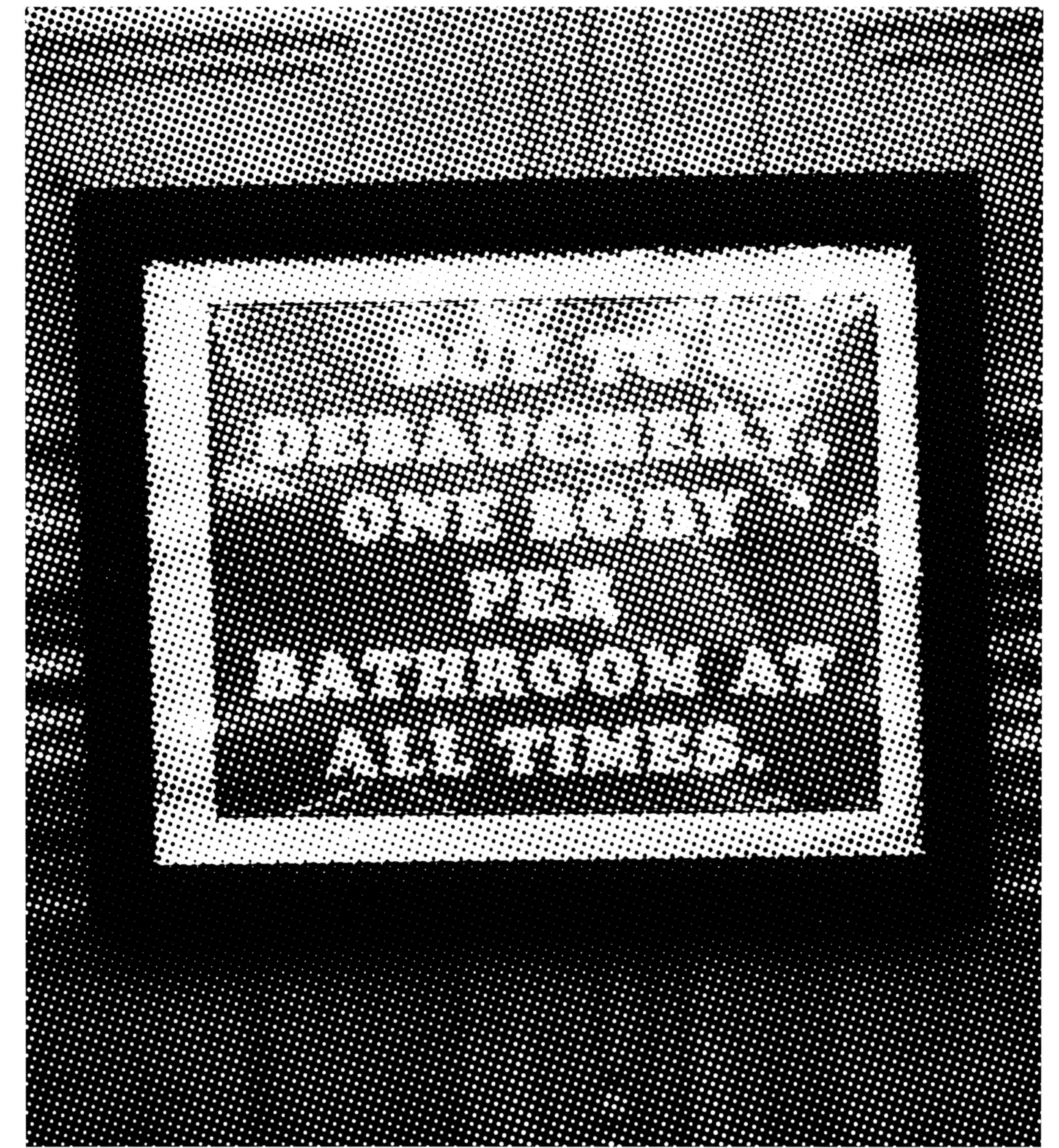
ONE FOOT
IN
BATHROOM AT
ALL TIMES.

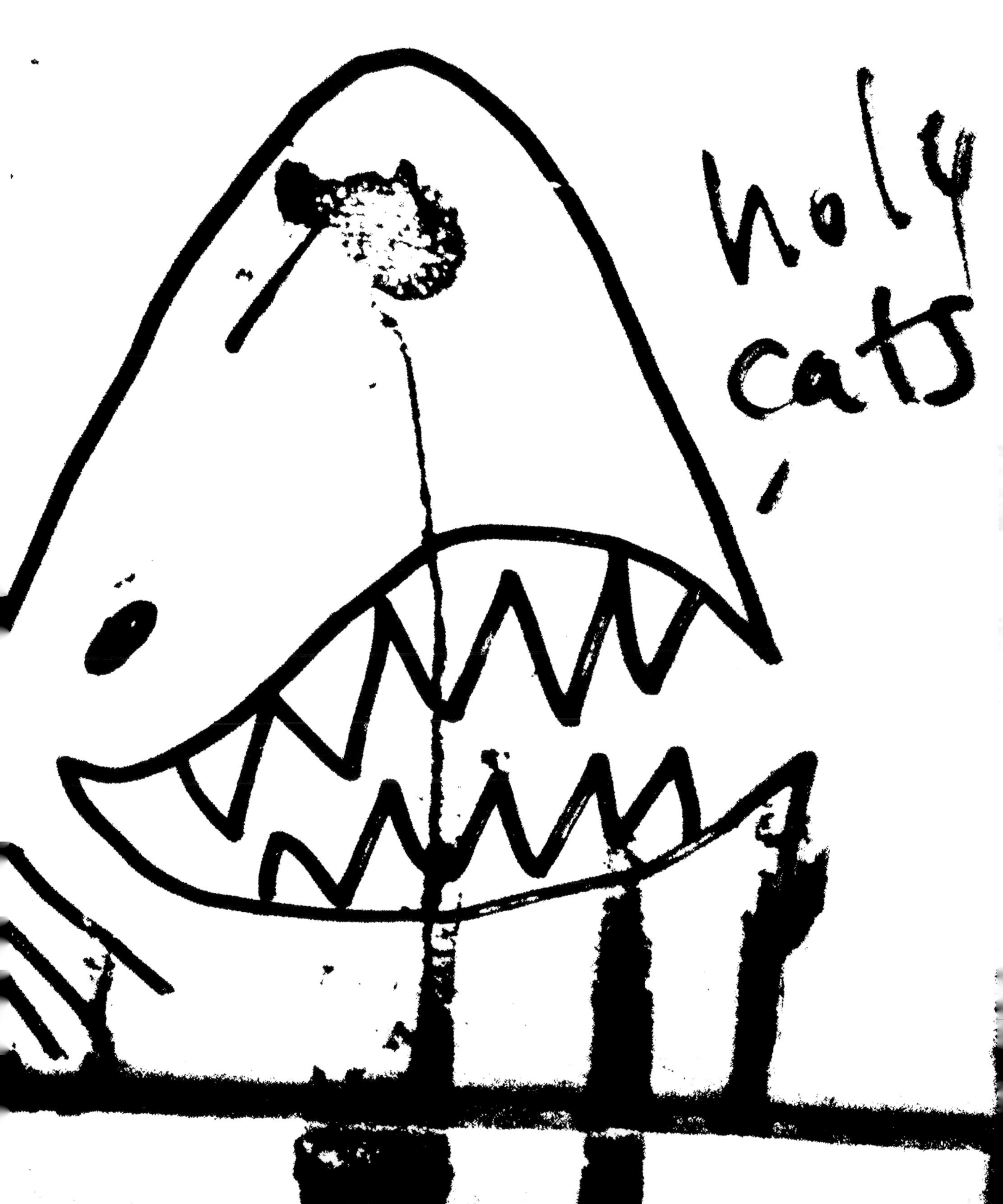

holy
cats

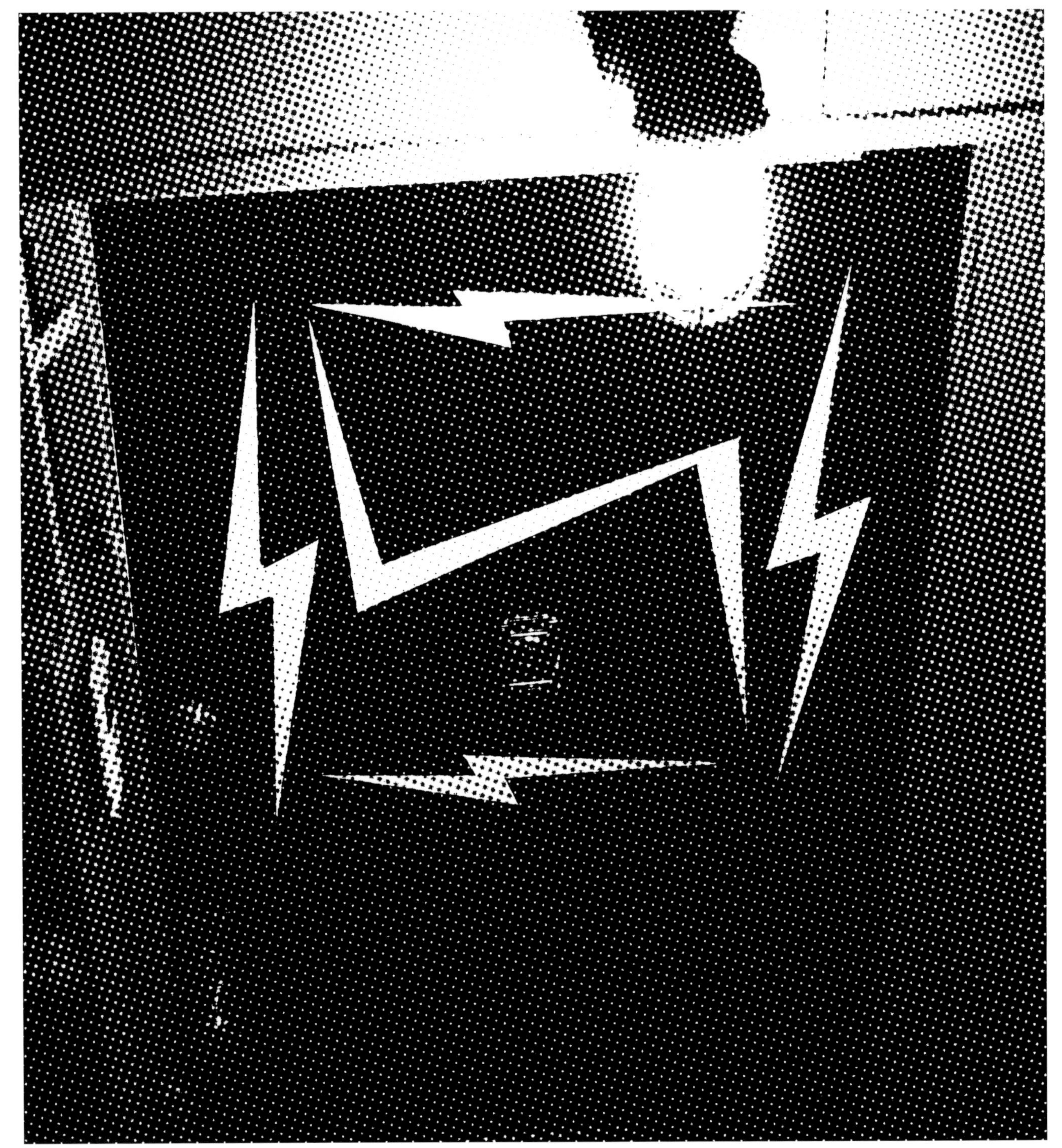

01.30.2010
08:17pm

Lower East Side
Manhattan

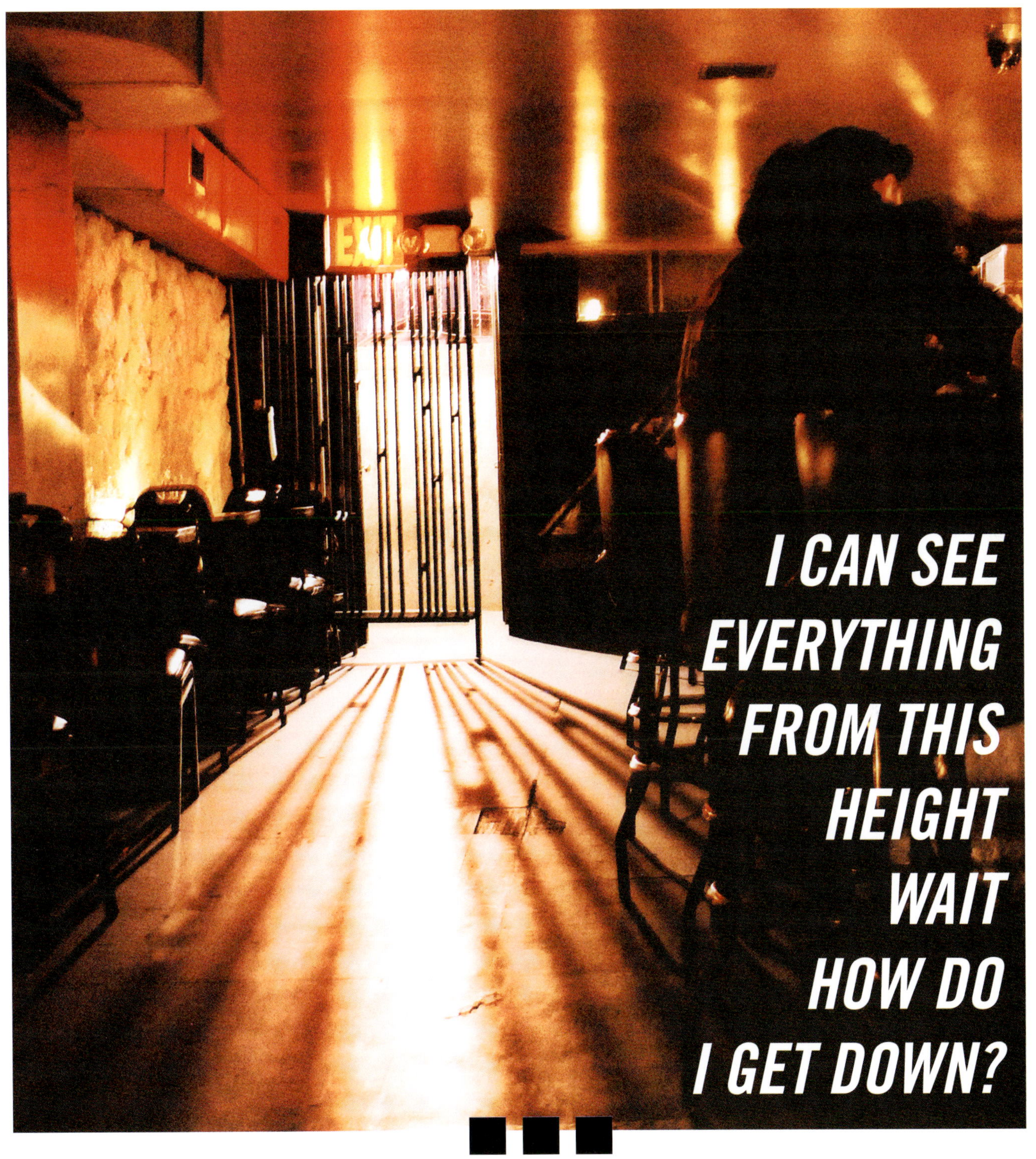

EXIT
I CAN SEE EVERYTHING FROM THIS HEIGHT WAIT HOW DO I GET DOWN?

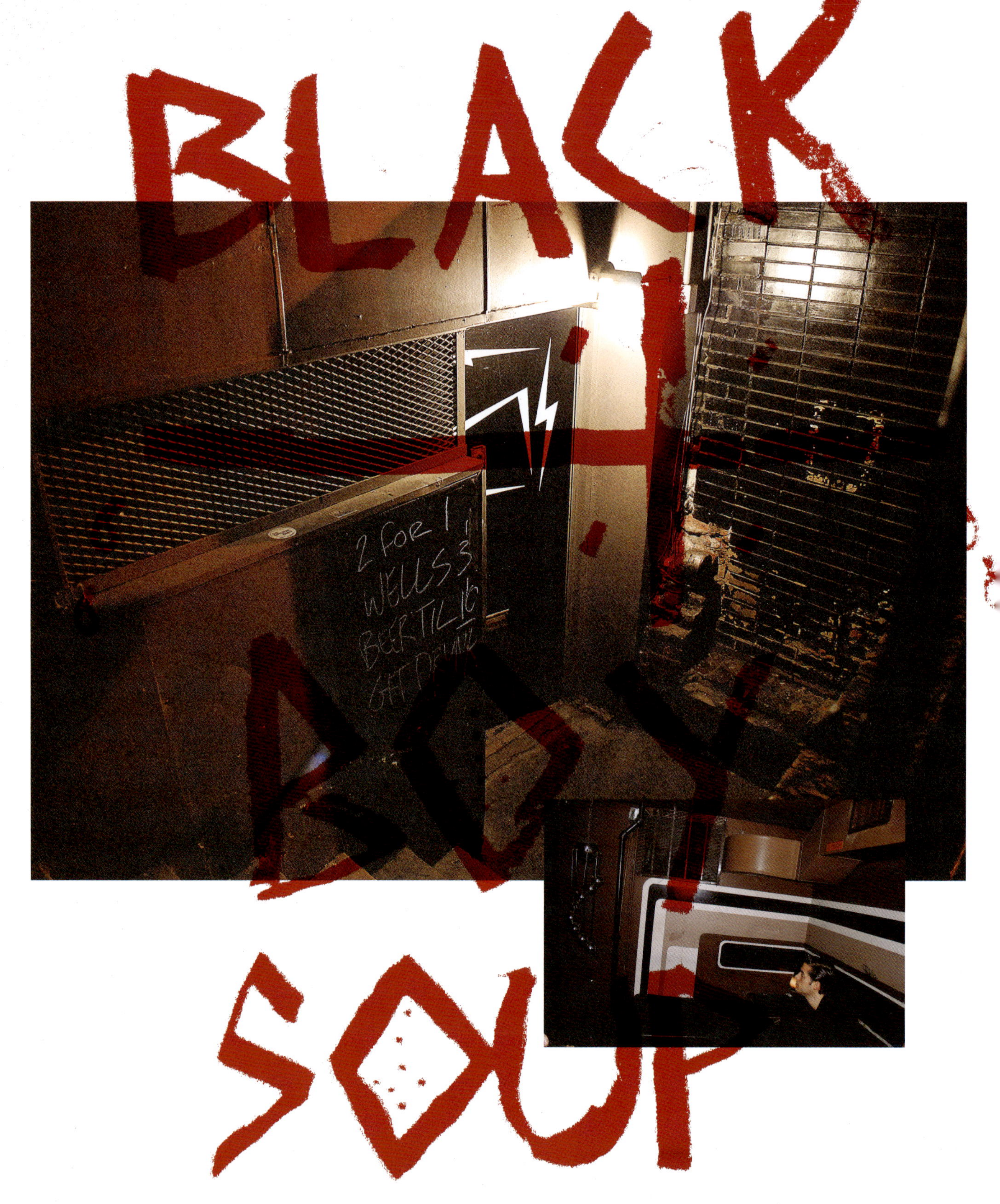

BLACK
SOUP
2 for 1
WELLS 3
BEER TIL 16
GET DRUNK

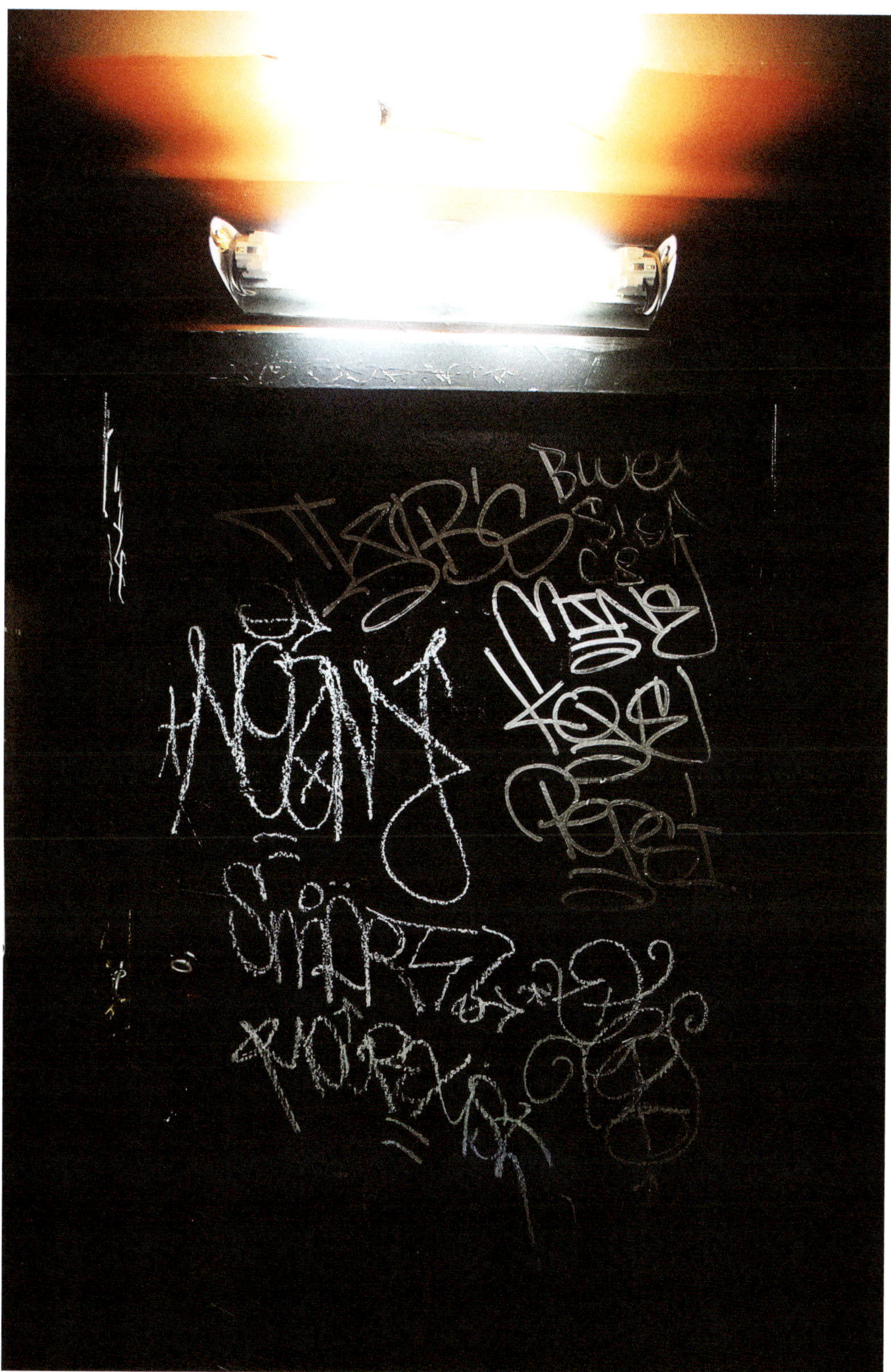

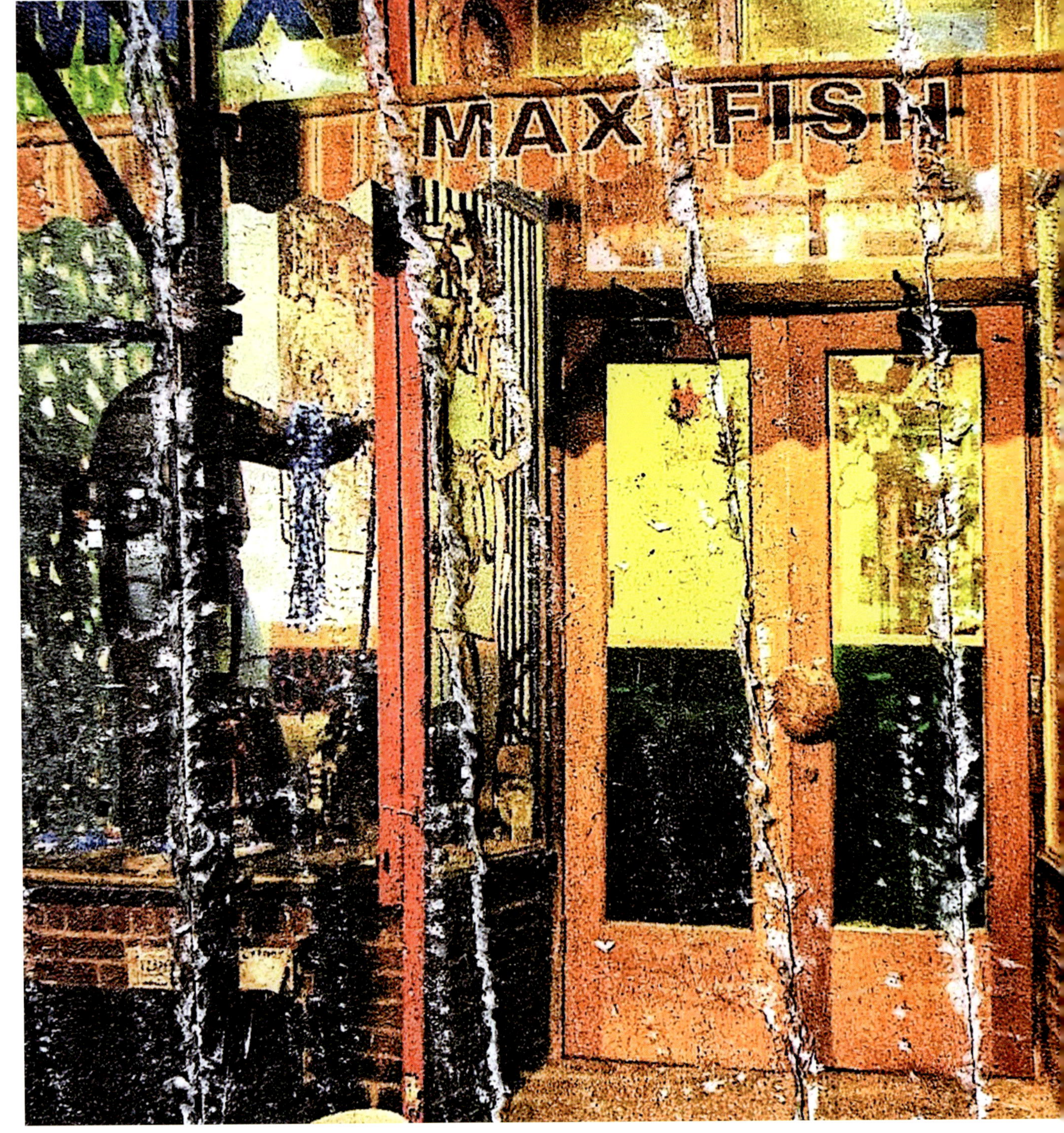

Max Fish

01.03.2011
07:23pm

Lower East Side
Manhattan

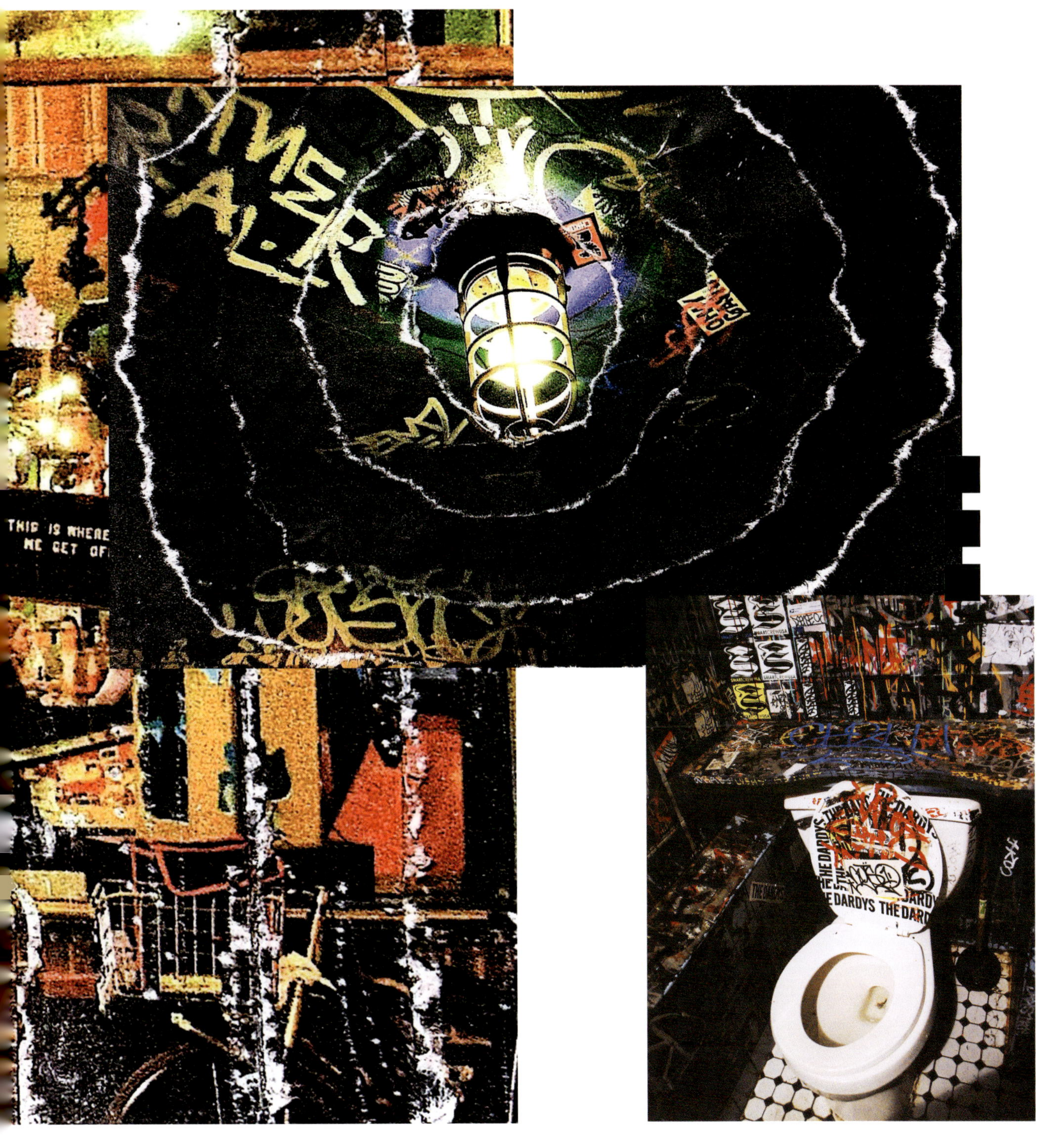
THIS IS WHERE
WE GET OF
THE DARDYS
THE DARDYS THE DARD

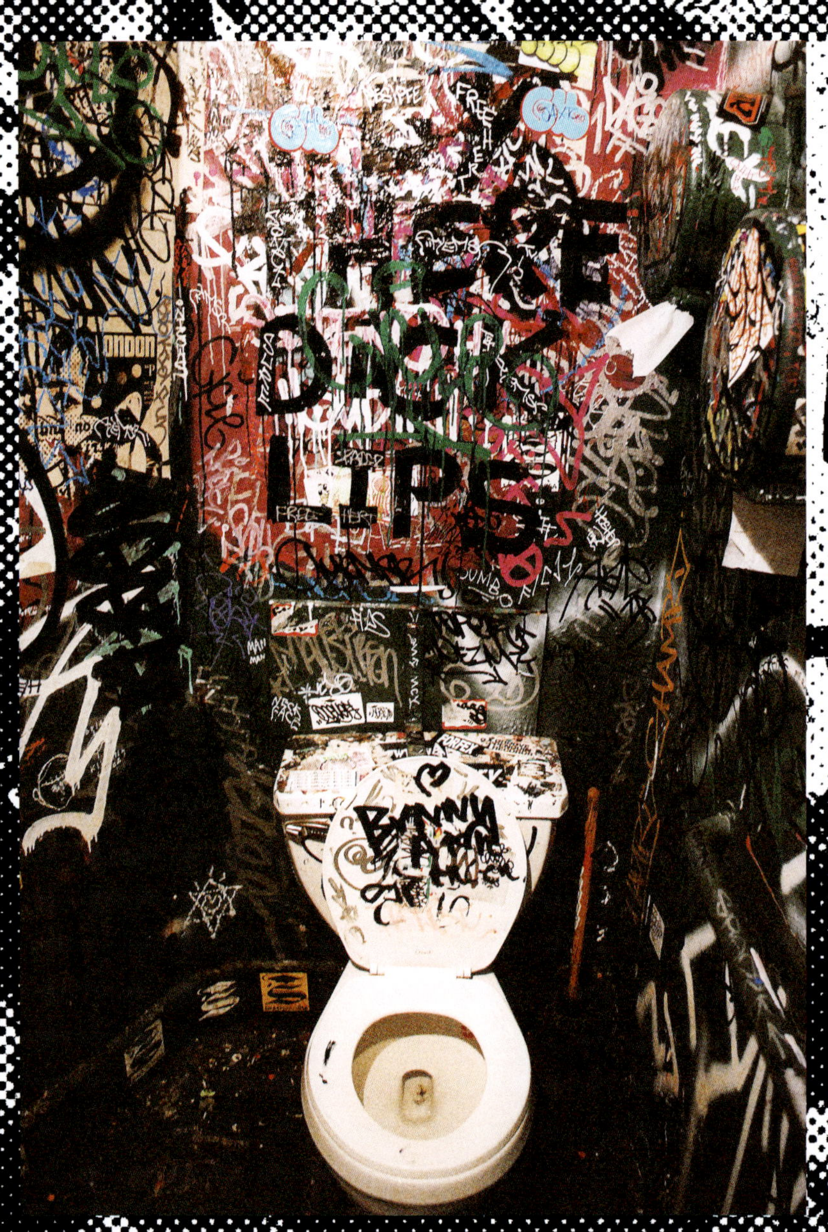

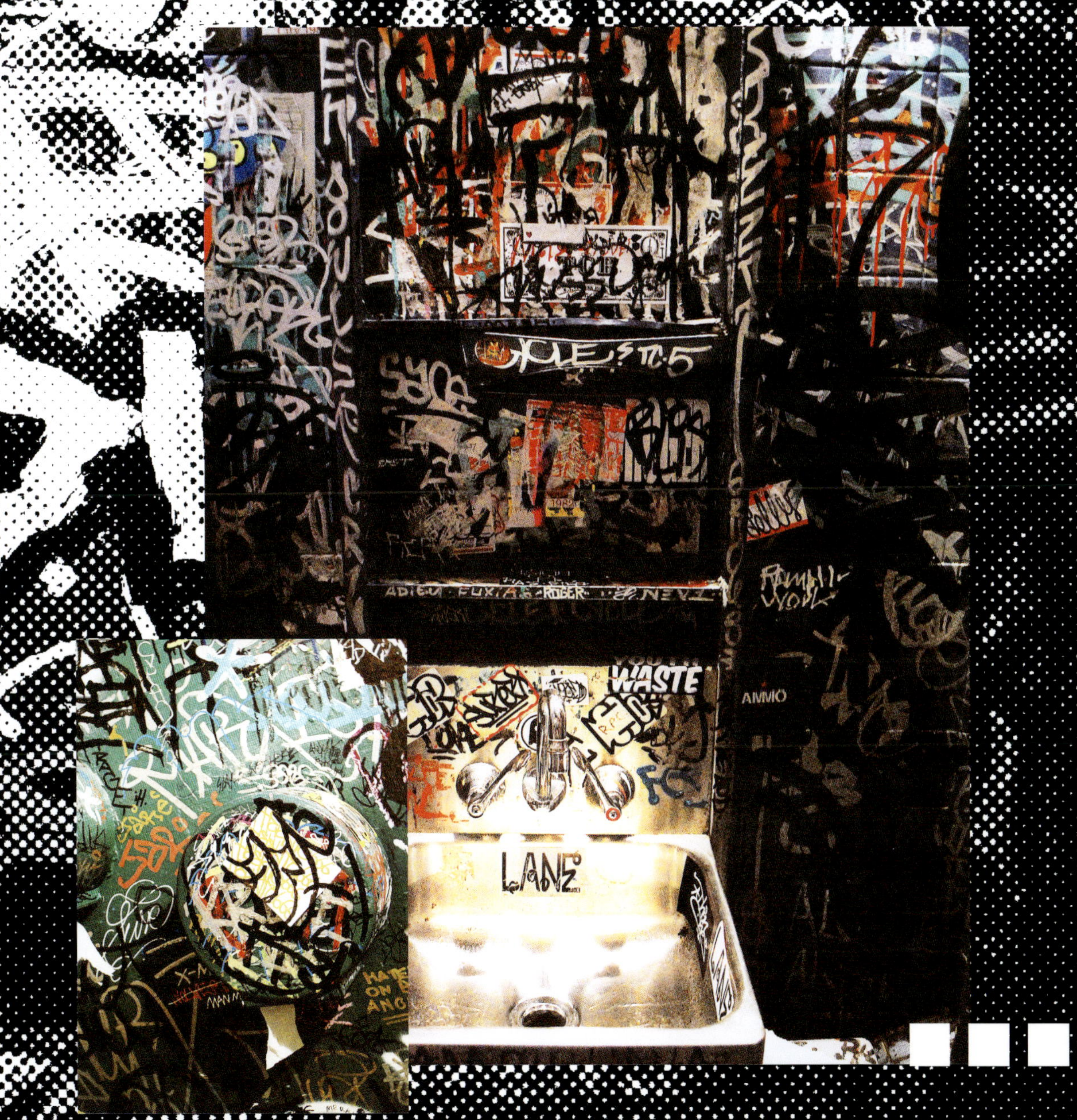

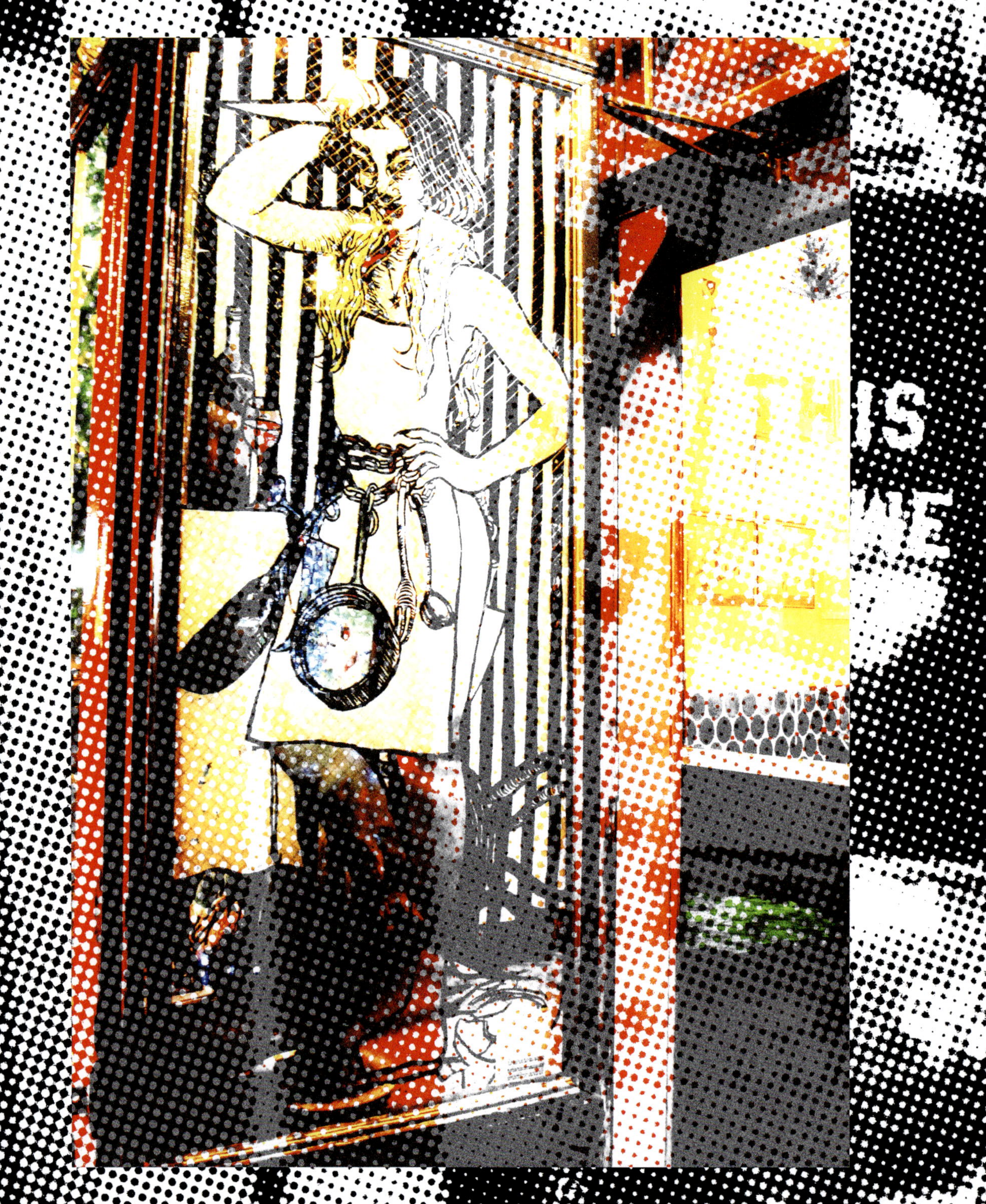
THIS
IS
NE

WHERE
ET

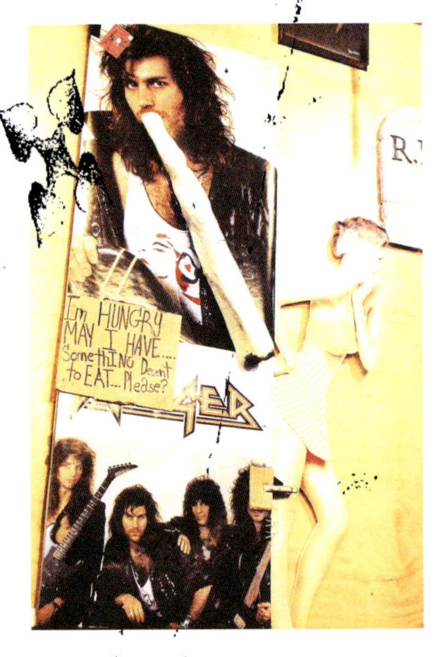

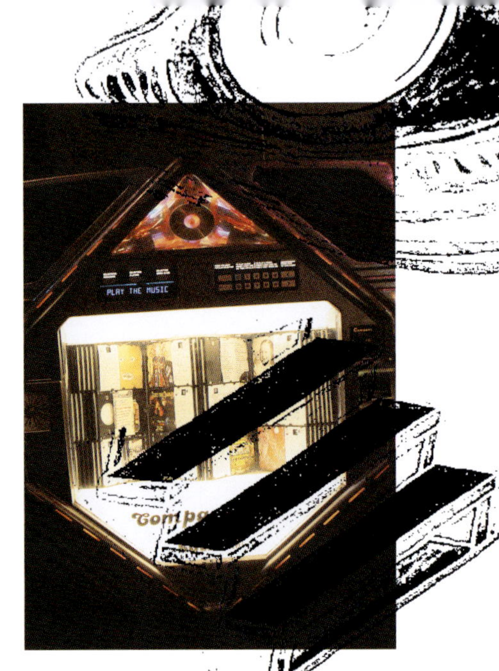

IT'S
GOING
TO BE
OK
TRUST ME

Or wa

Or wa

way 2

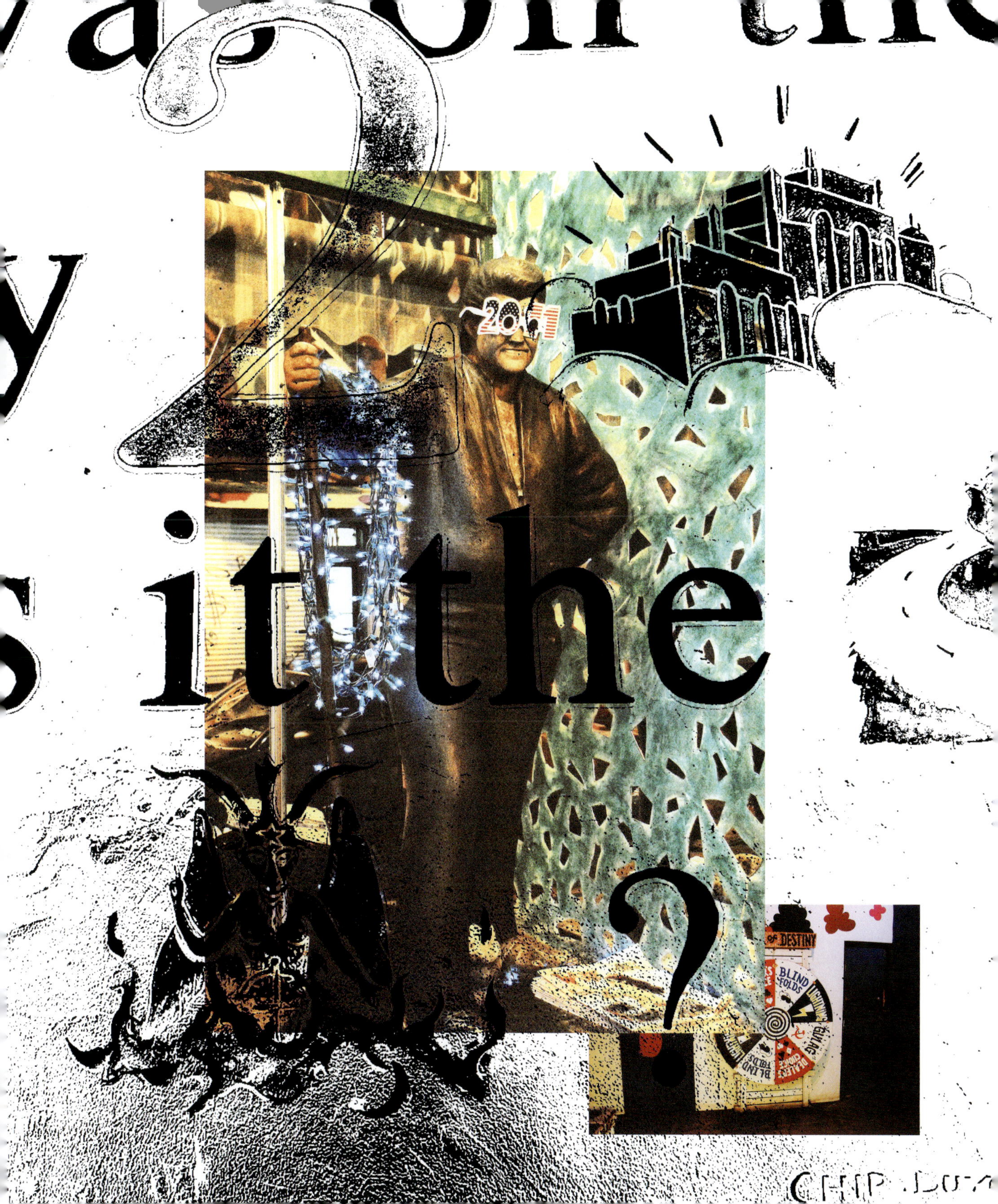
y as on the
y
s it the
it the
?
2001
OF DESTINY
BLIND
FOLDS
CHIP.DU

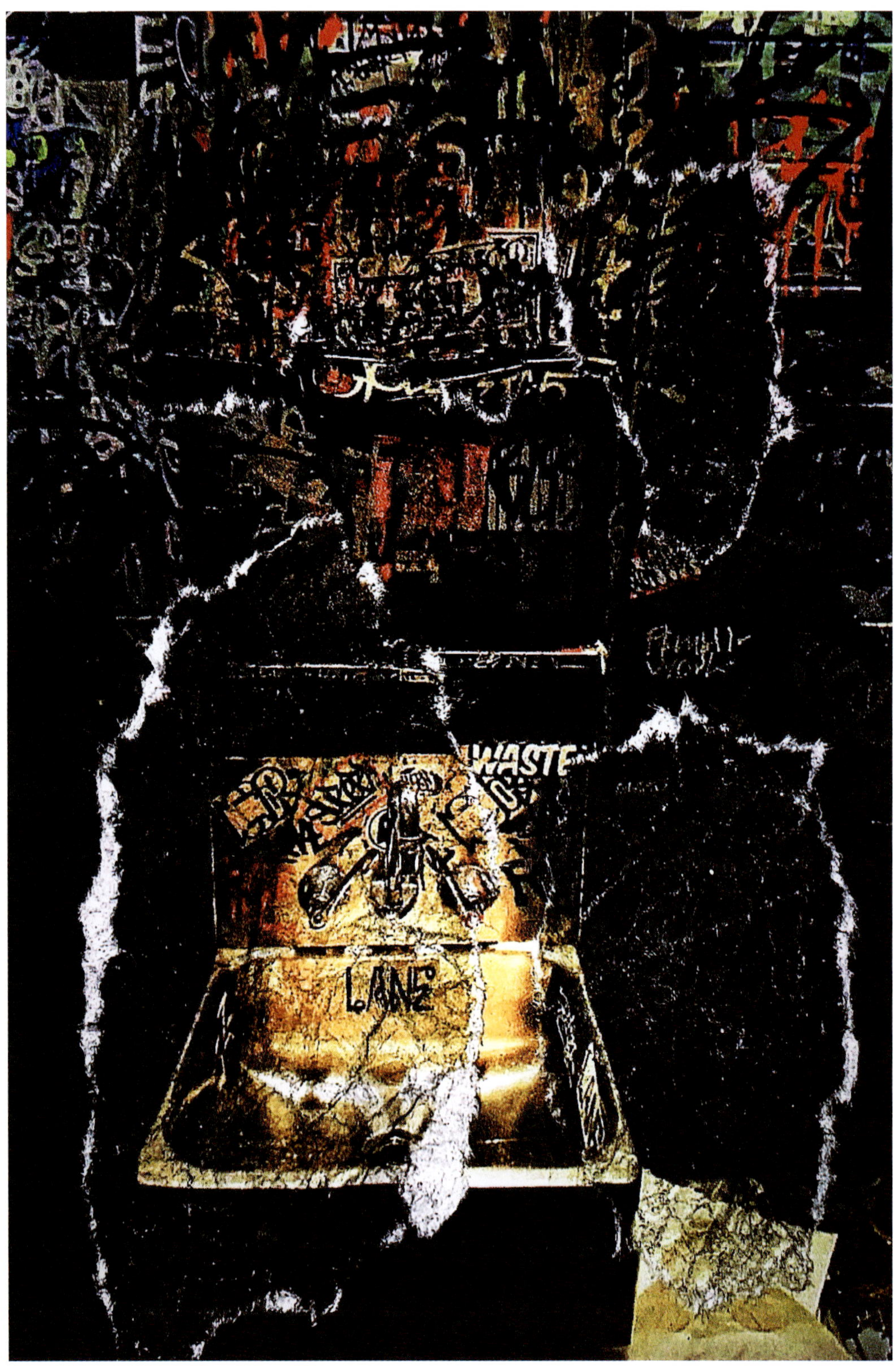

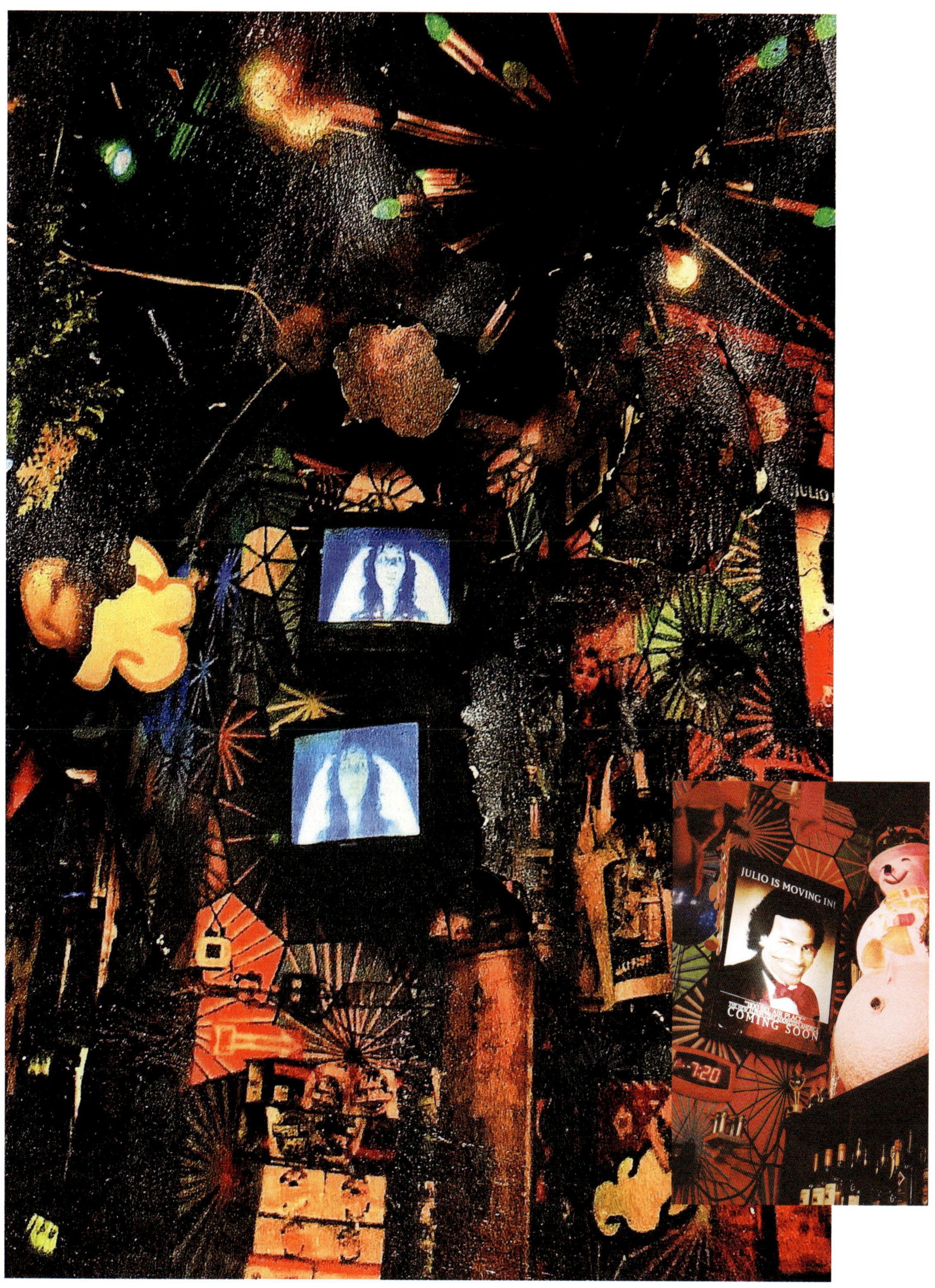

JULIO IS MOVING IN!
COMING SOON
7:20

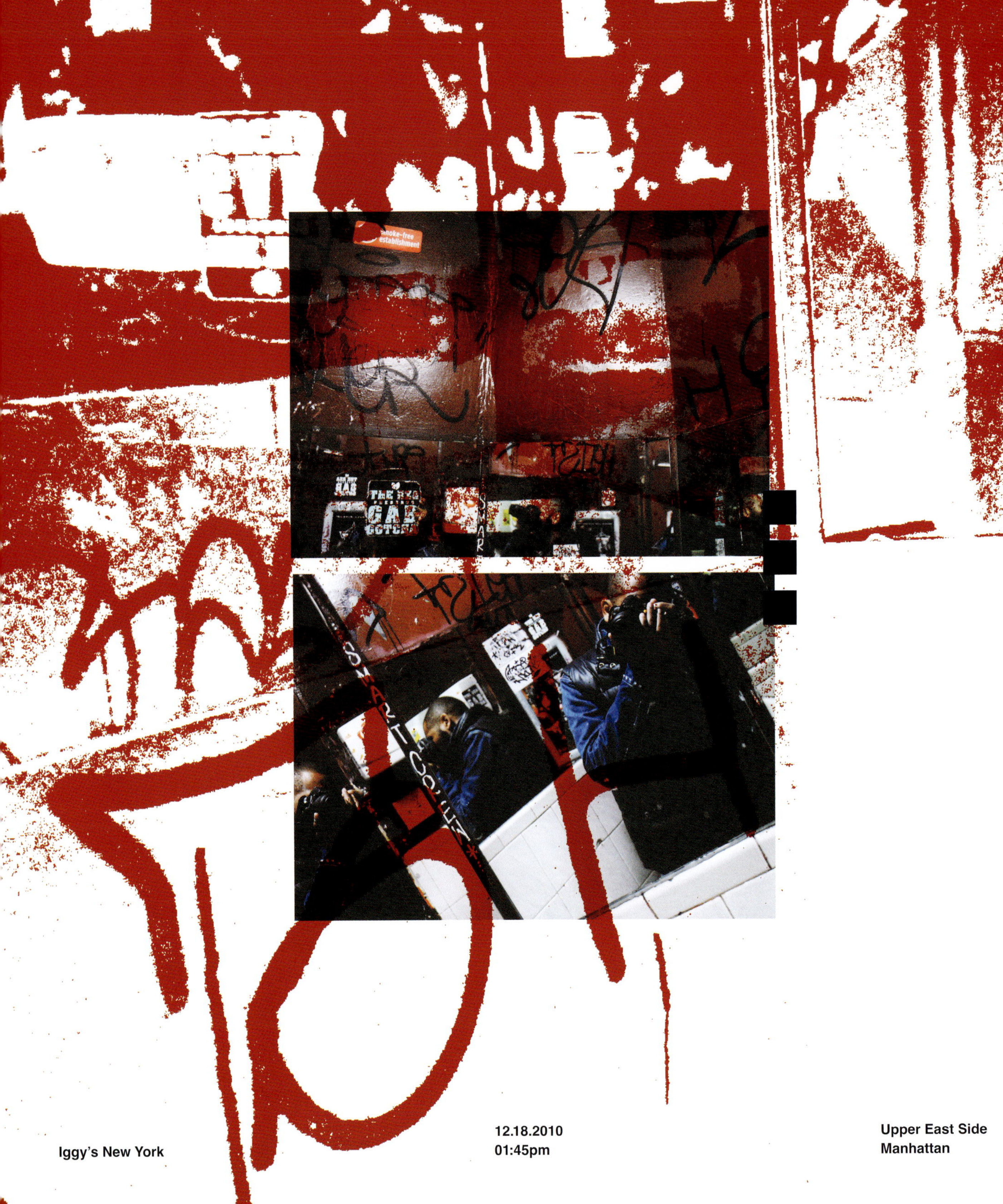

12.18.2010
01:45pm

Upper East Side
Manhattan

Iggy's New York

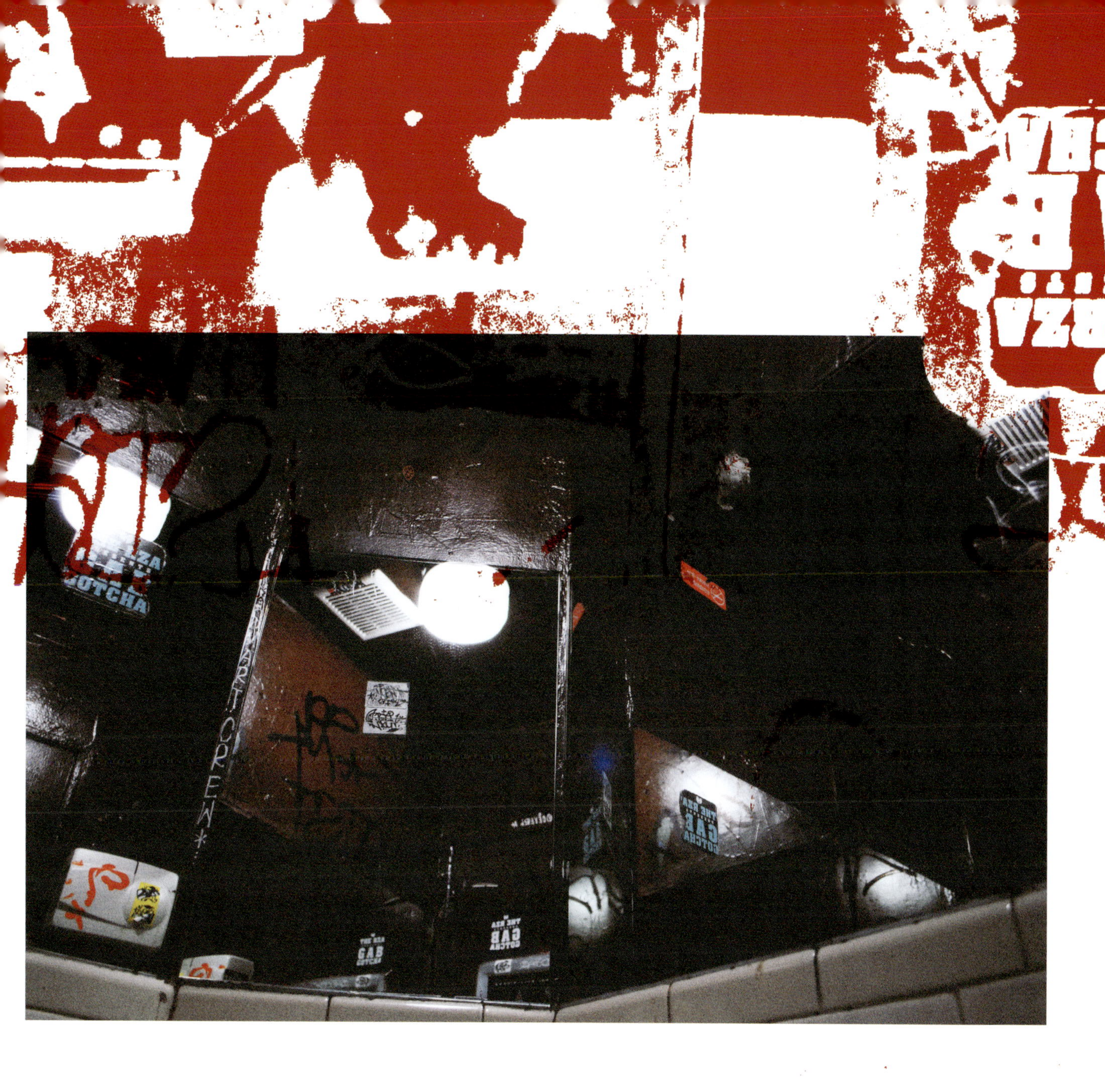

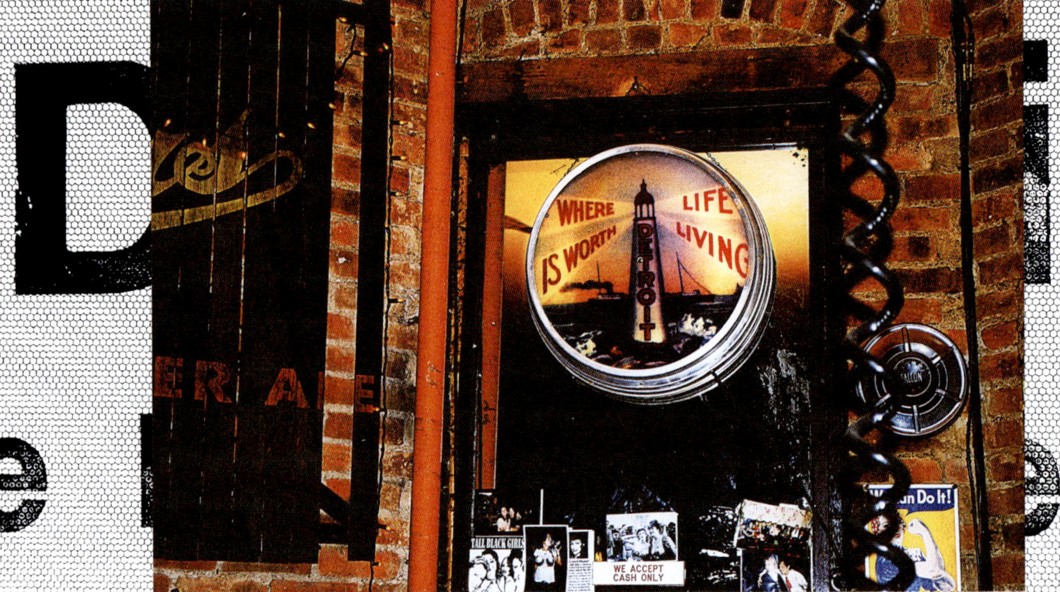

11.13.2010
07:50pm

Motor City

Lower East Side
Manhattan

Urbanization

Urbanization is a weird term to use for NYC. It's a
complete, concrete, urban playground. However,
gentrification altered the city in a weird way, some
would say for the better, most would say for the worst.
The 70s saw a bombed out, almost abandoned NY...the
times shaped resilient people and built the framework
for Hip-Hop & punk rock. The 80s saw the opulence of
capitalism, Wall Street and designer drugs, coming into
the 1990s the AIDS & crack epidemics wreaked havoc on
the city. Then came Guilani and his Gestapo- like tactics
that "cleaned" up NYC. Bloomberg "Disney-fied" the city
and ushered in gentrification. With gentrification parts of
NY "vanishing", rents spiked, transplants arrived...but
the spirit remained...besides you'll always need a place
to find cheap beer and well liquor.

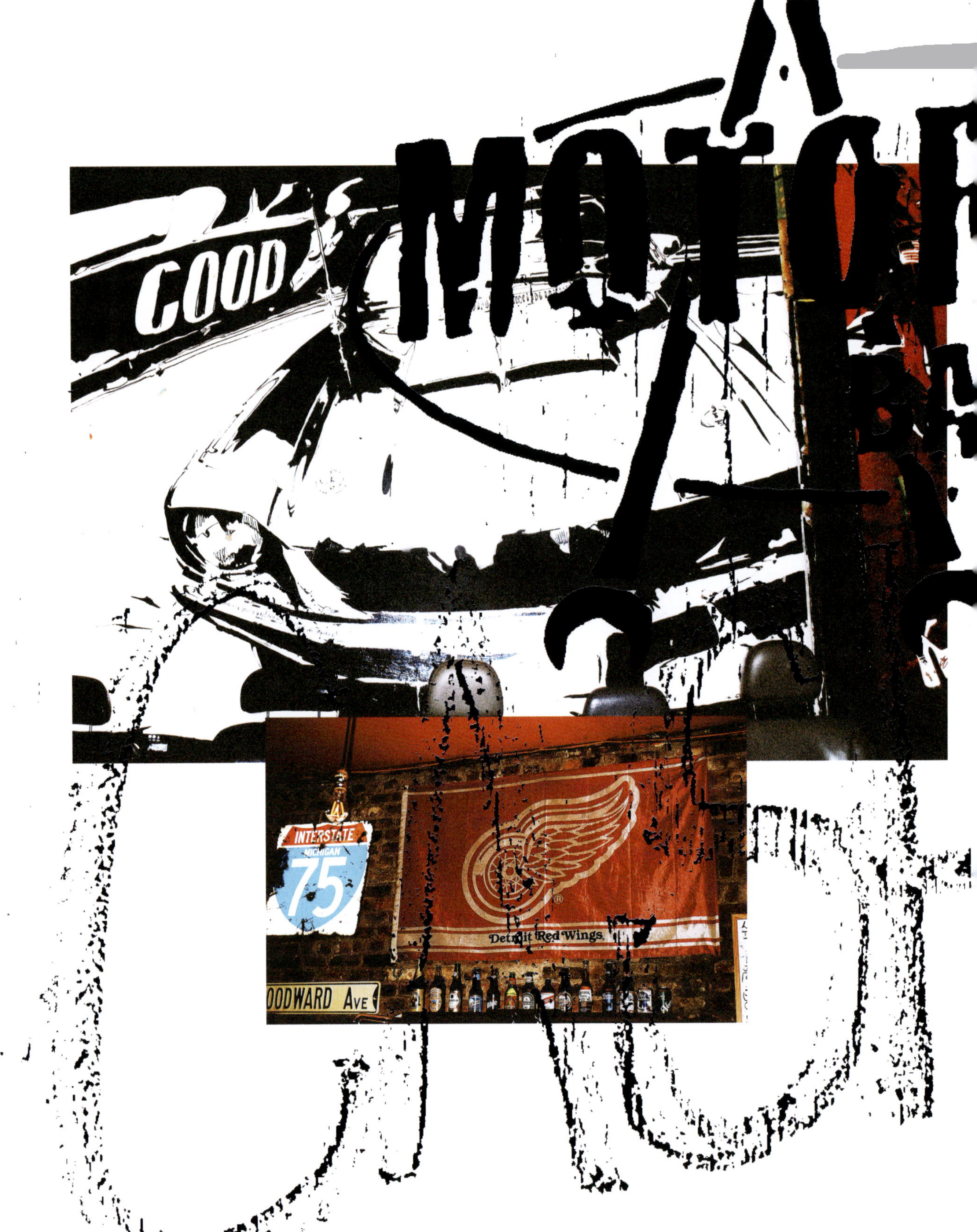
GOOD
MOTOR
INTERSTATE
MICHIGAN
75
Detroit Red Wings
OODWARD AVE

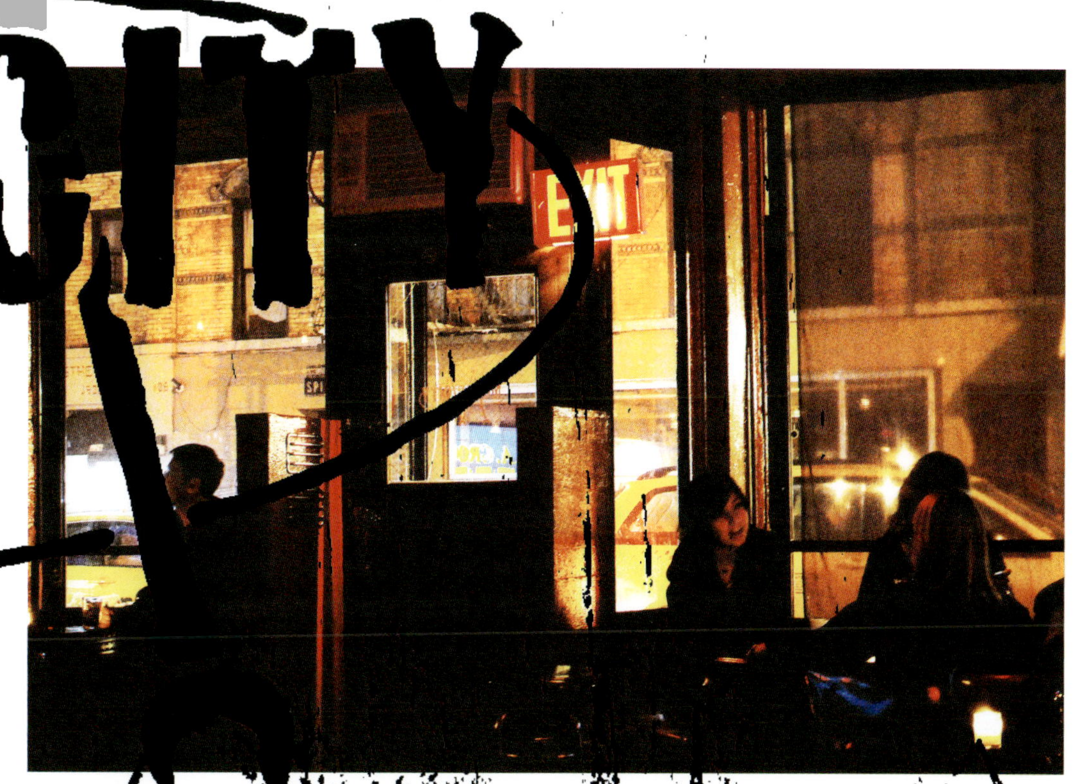

EXIT

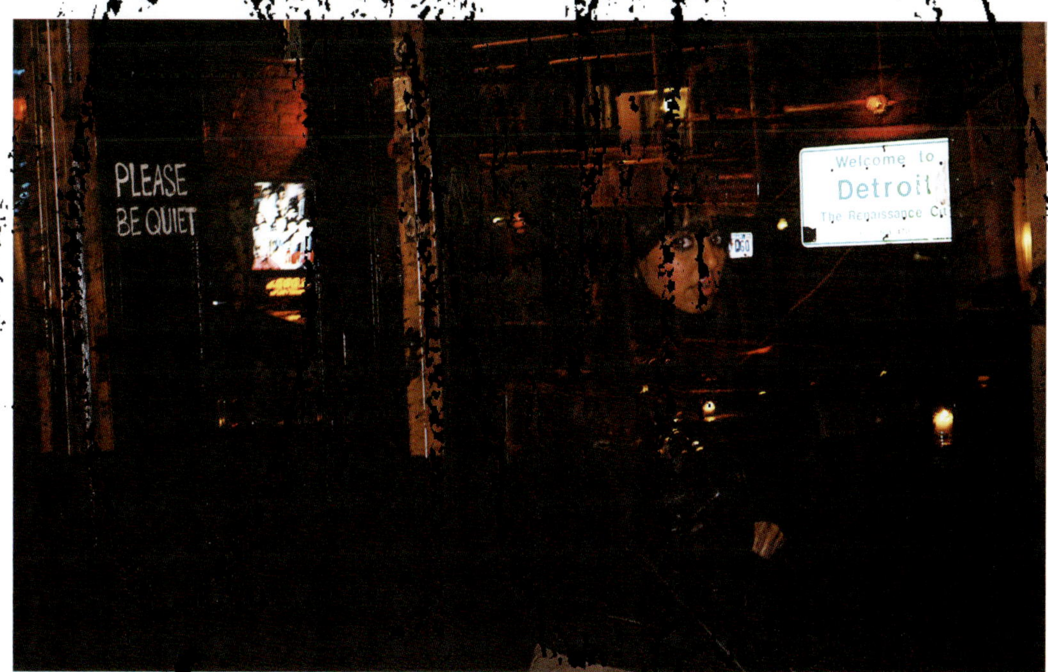

PLEASE
BE QUIET
Welcome to
Detroit
The Renaissance City

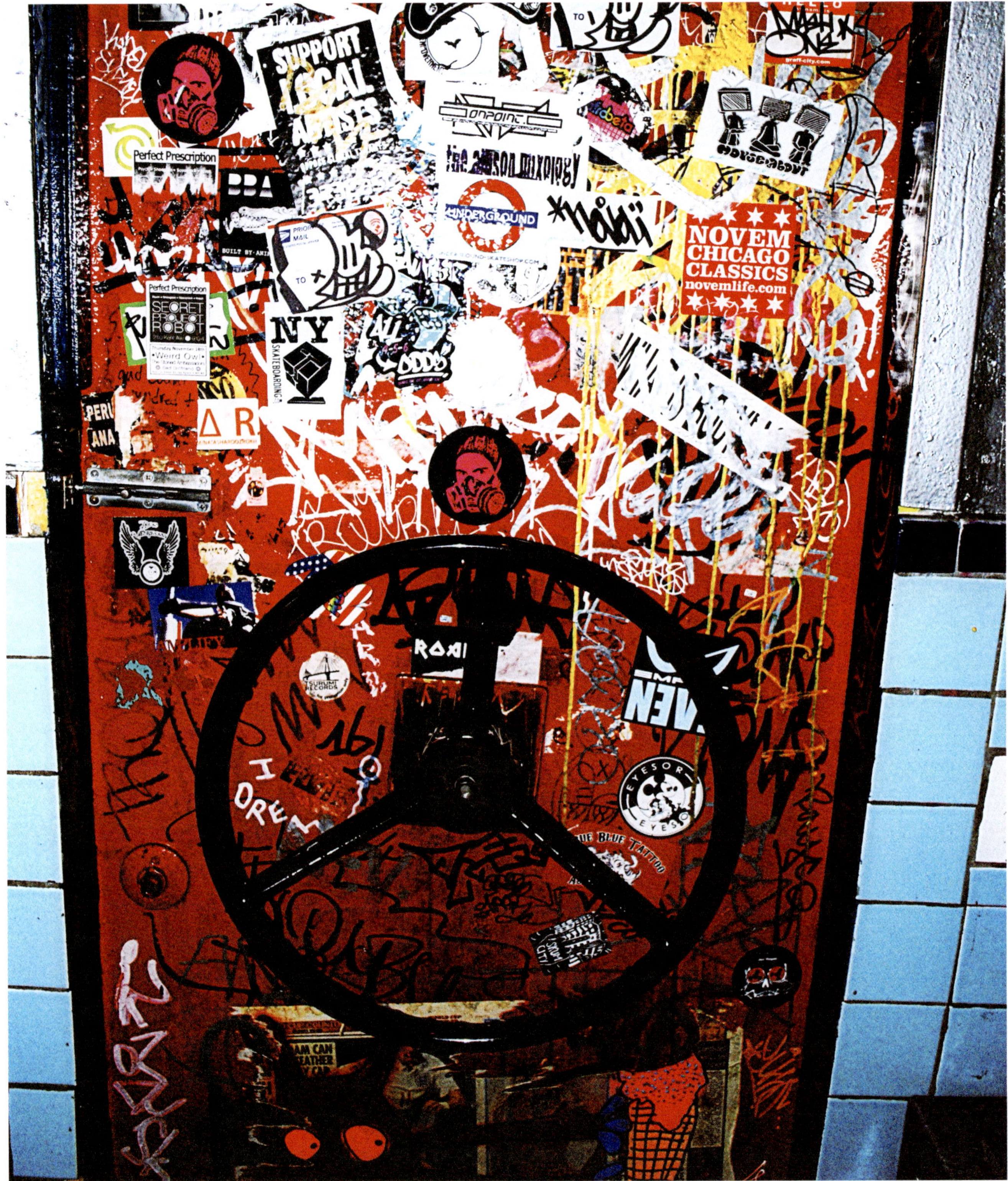
SUPPORT LOCAL ARTISTS
Perfect Prescription
ONPOINT
the Anderson mixology
UNDERGROUND
NOVEM CHICAGO CLASSICS
novemlife.com
SECRET PROJECT ROBOT
NY SKATEBOARDING
Δ R
PERU ANA
I OPEN
ROAI
EYESORE EYESORE
BLUE BLUE TATTOO

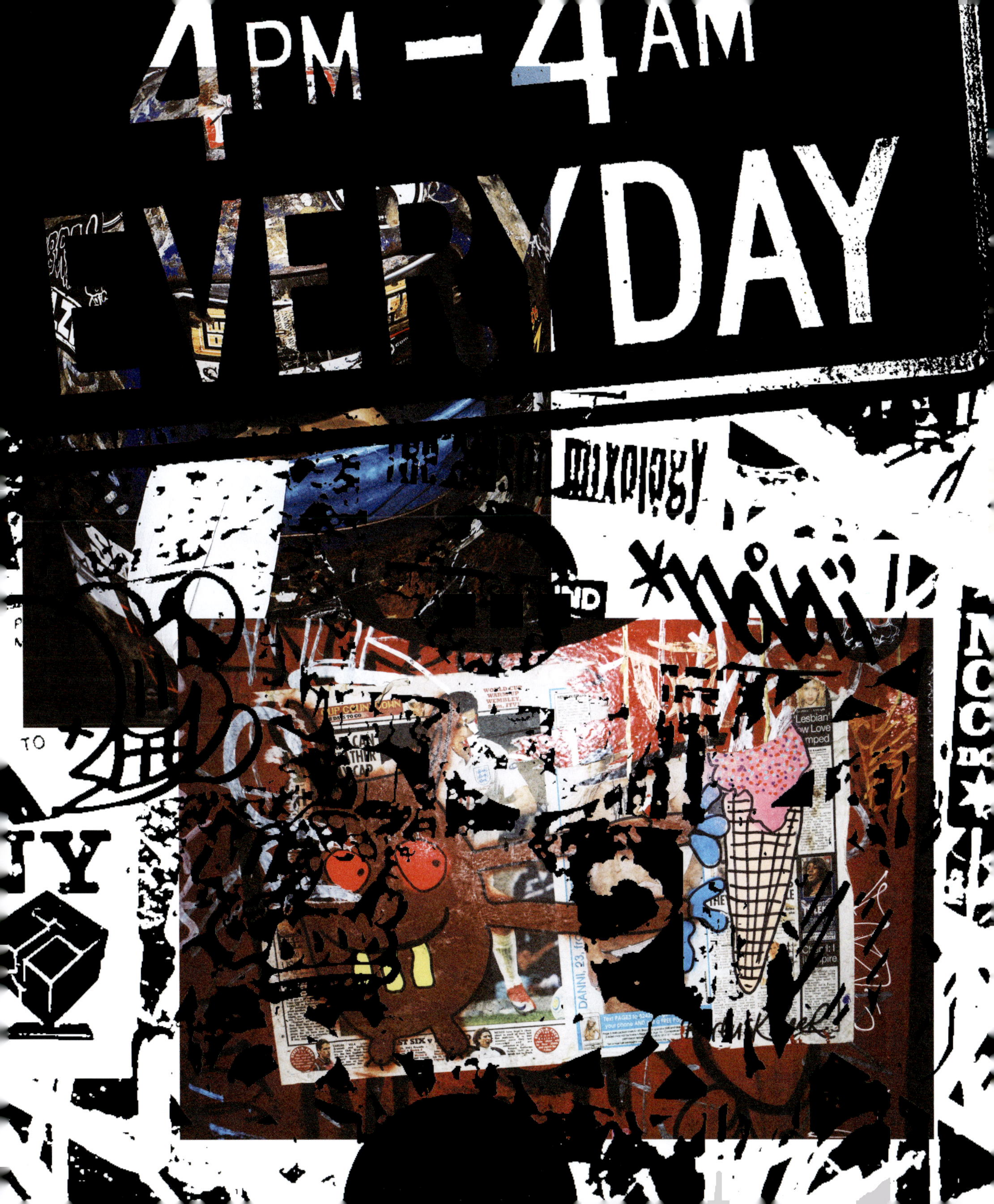

4PM - 4AM
EVERYDAY

PORT 41
POOL TABLES
FREE HOT DOG POOL
DART'S
PORT 41 CLUB
YOU WANT TO COME INSIDE
LOVE
LIFE
ART by CONSTANTINE LADIKOS

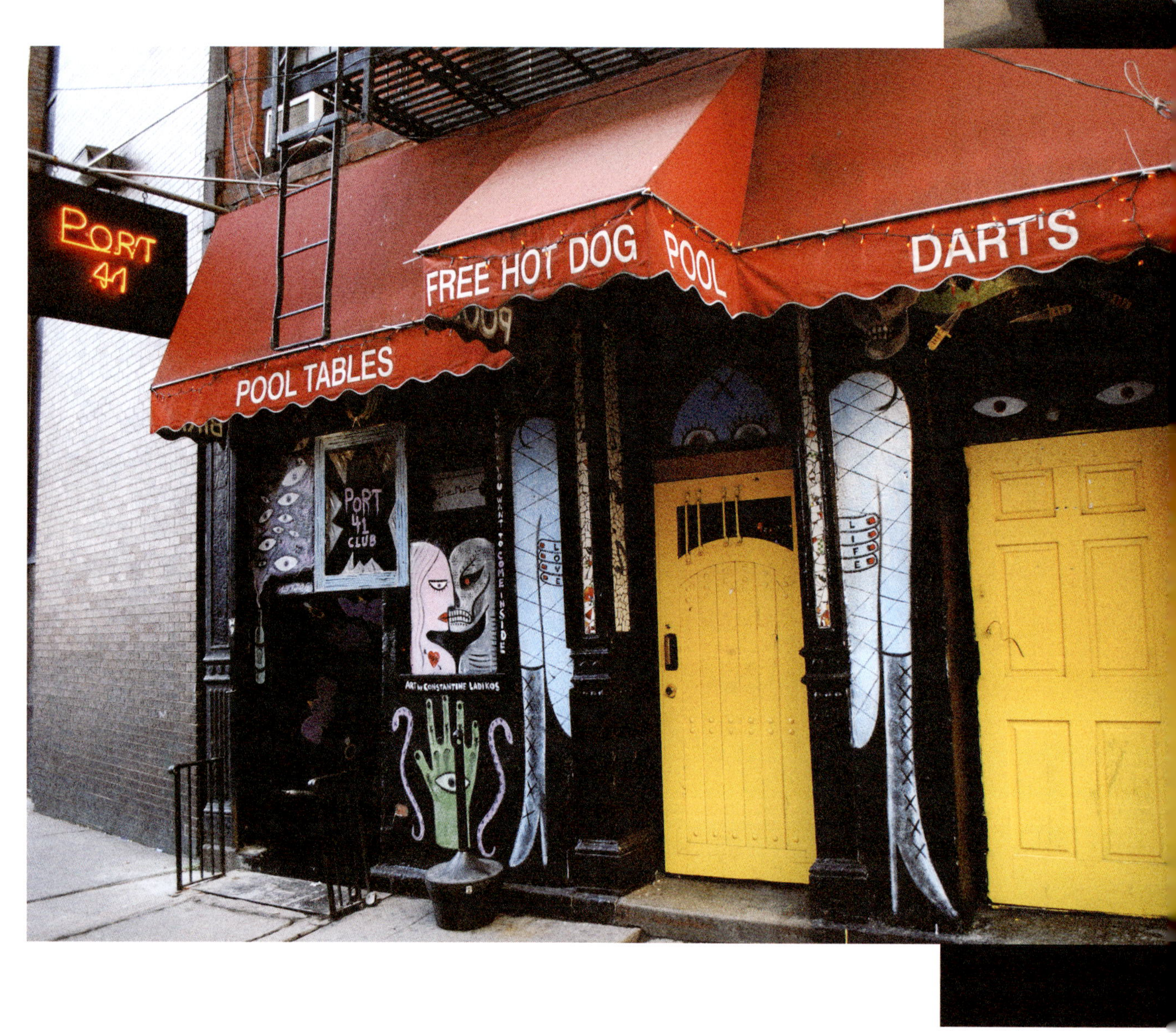

Port 41

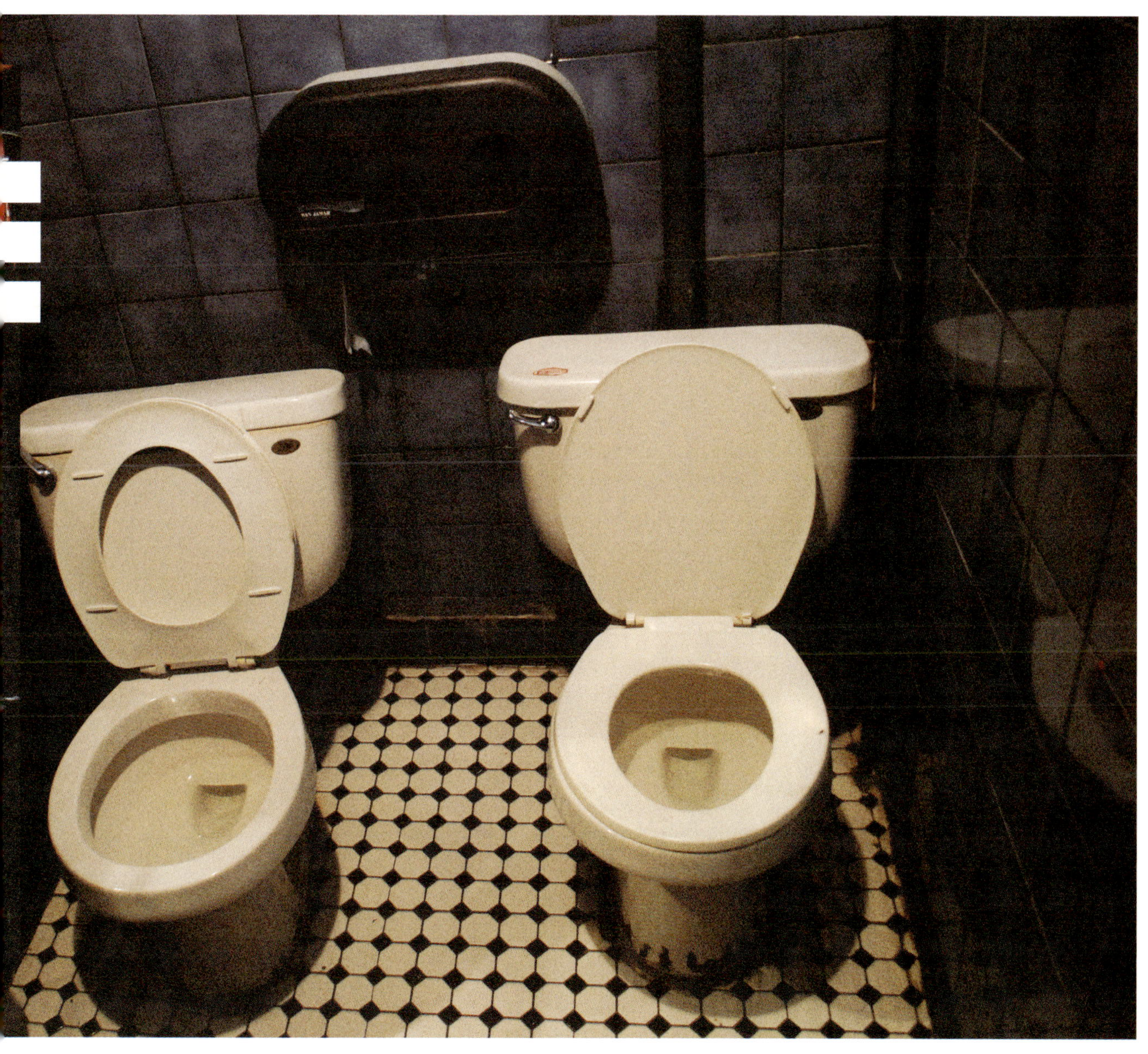

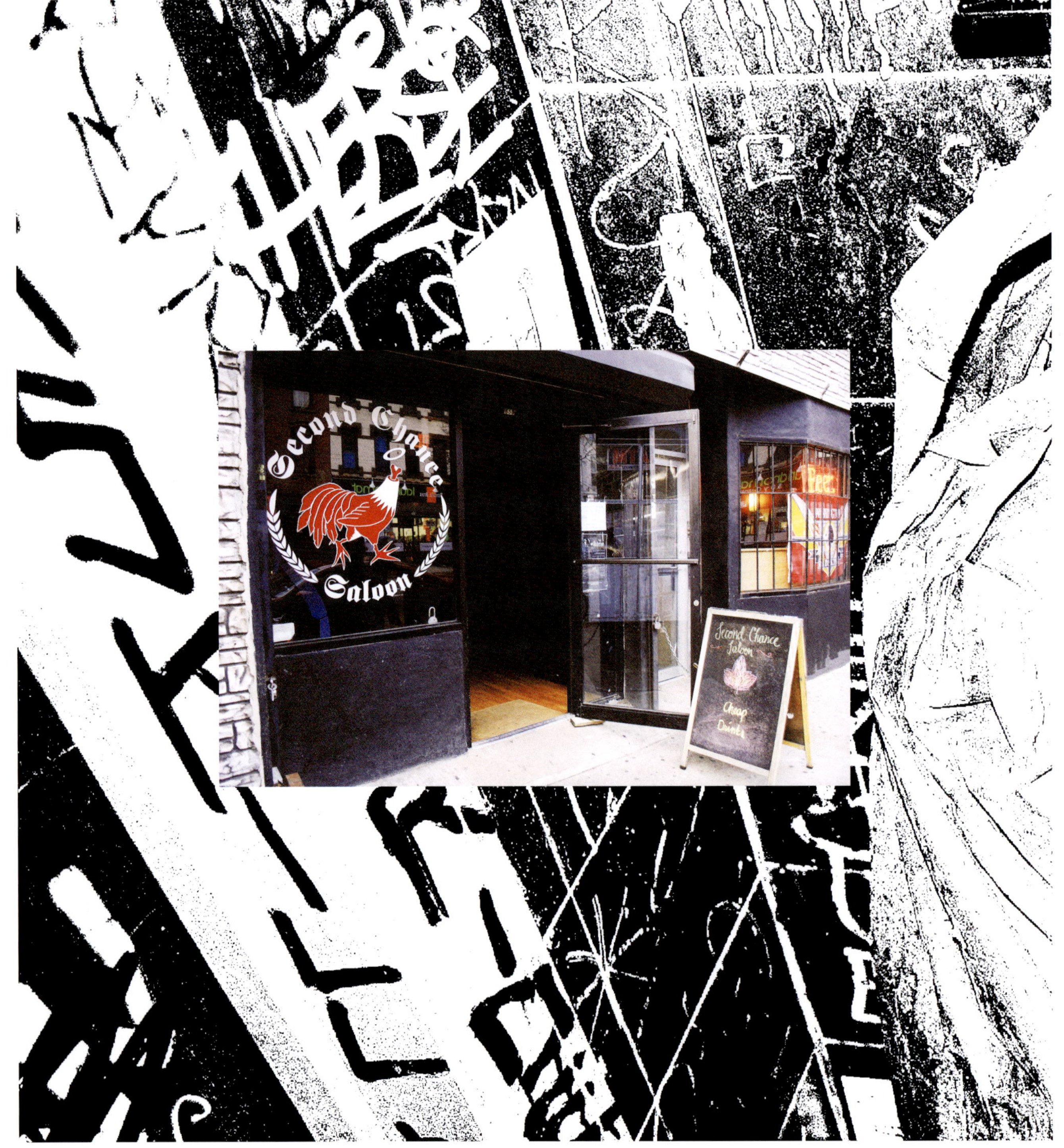

Second Chance
Saloon
Second Chance
Saloon
Cheap
Drinks

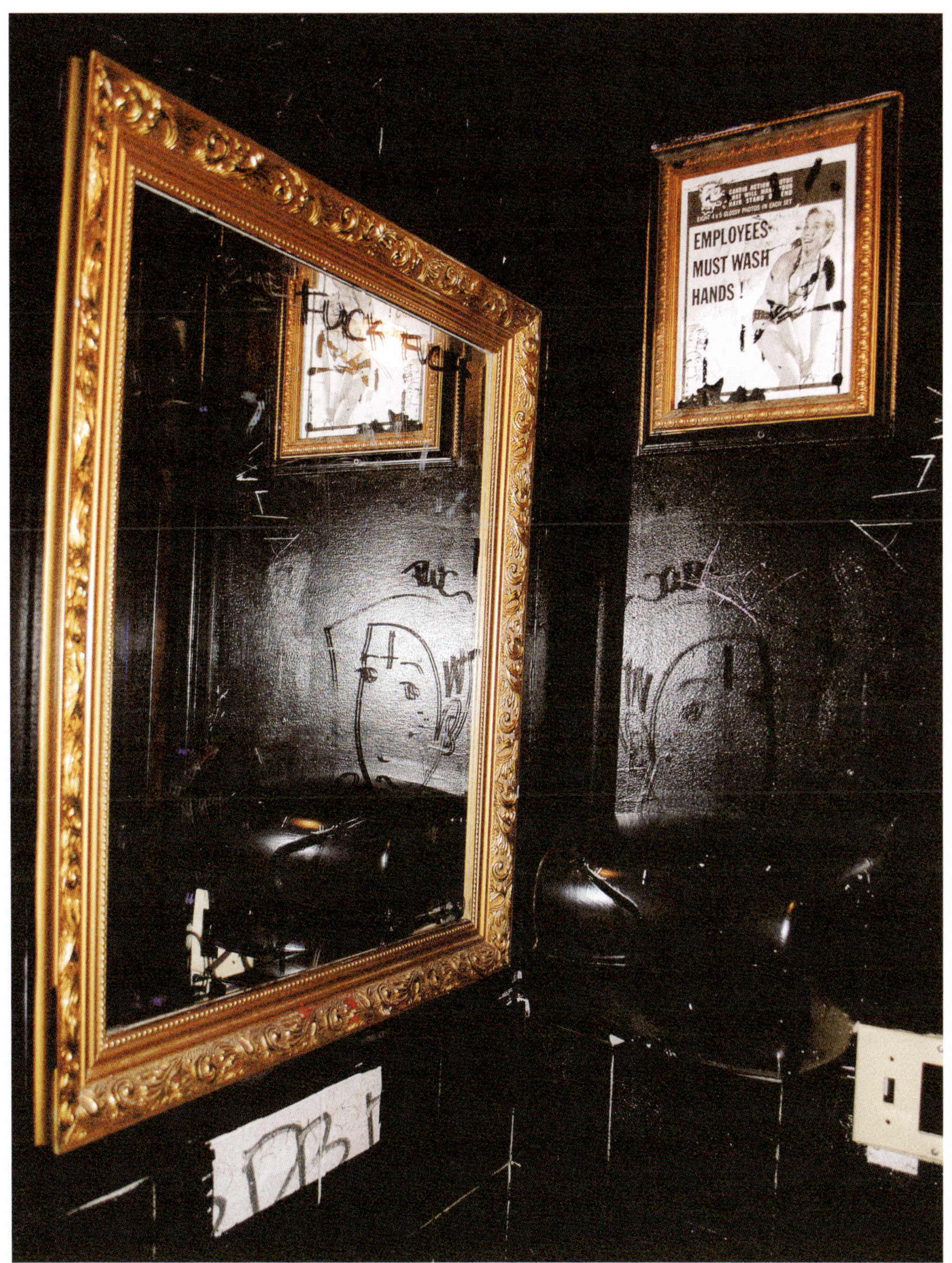
EMPLOYEES
MUST WASH
HANDS !

ROGER
NAEM
MOSHA
MOSHA
MOSHA
YOGA
EAGLES CANYON
UNITI PER VINCERE
BROOKLYN TATTOO
DIZZY WIZARD
HAIR
METAL

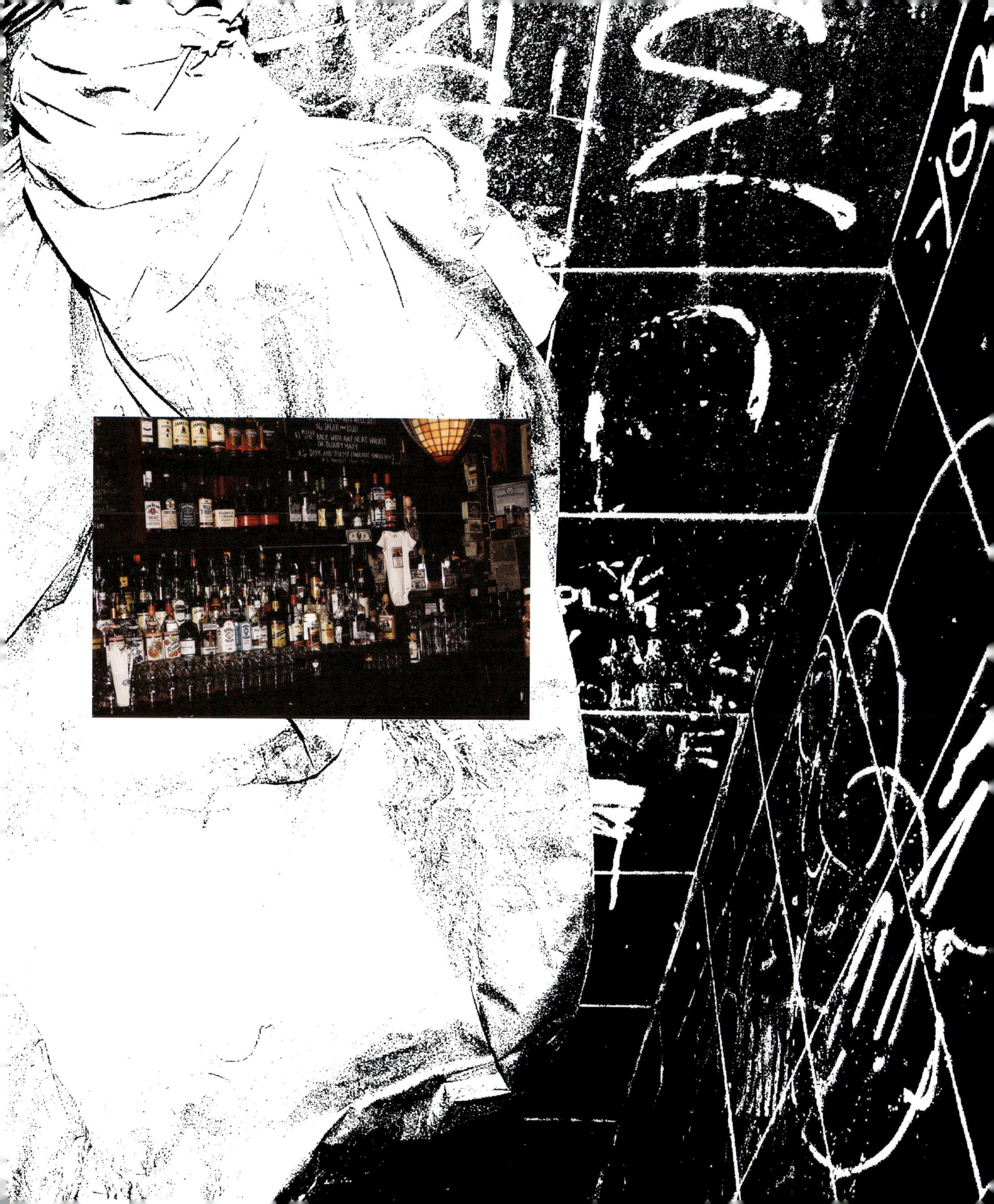
$6 JAGER and BUD
$1 MILLER LITE BACK WITH ANY NEAT WHISKEY
OR BLOODY MARY
$6 DARK AND STORMY (DARK RUM, GINGER BEER)

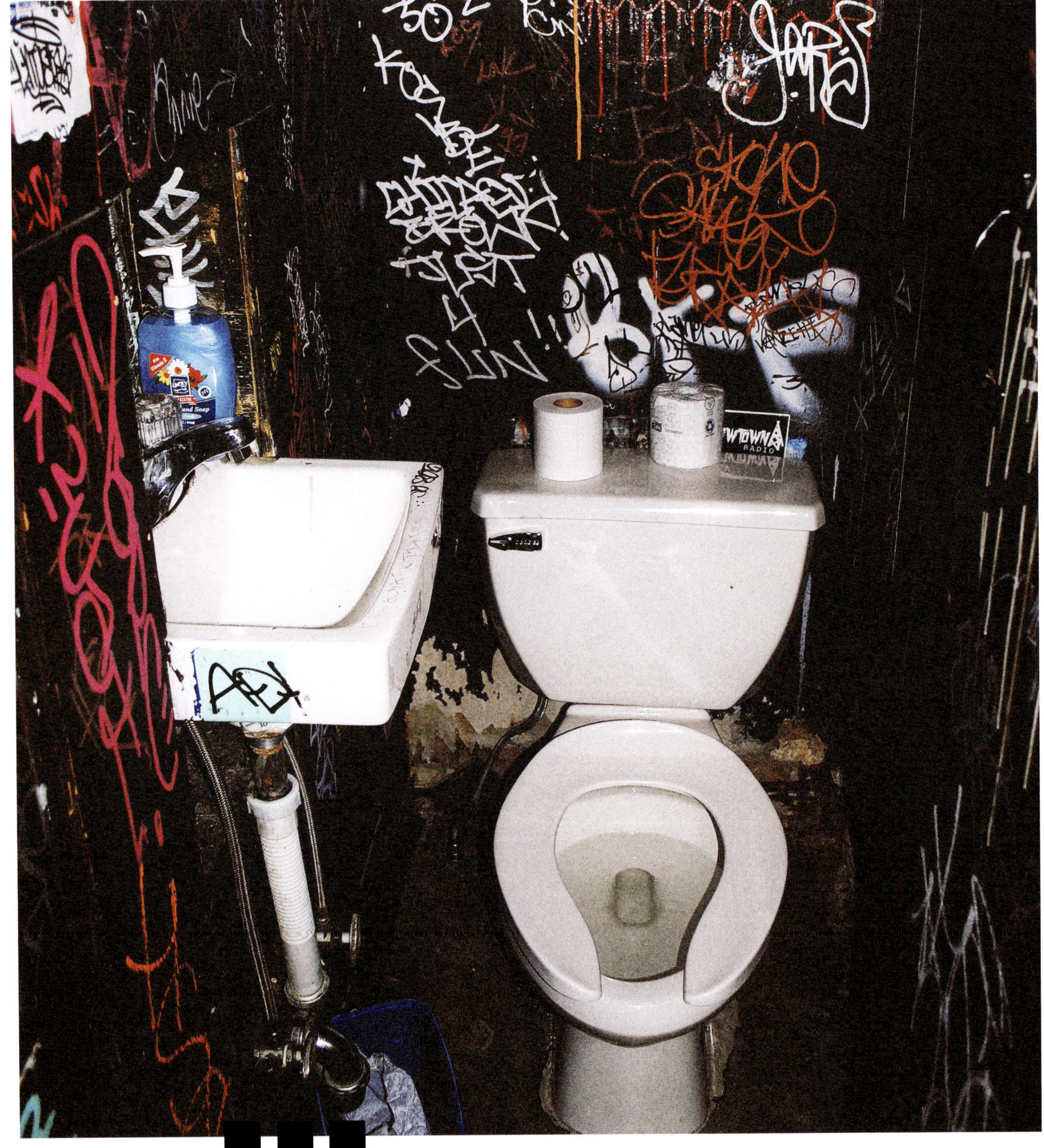

Welcome To The Johnsons

01.03.2011
08:44pm

Lower East Side
Manhattan

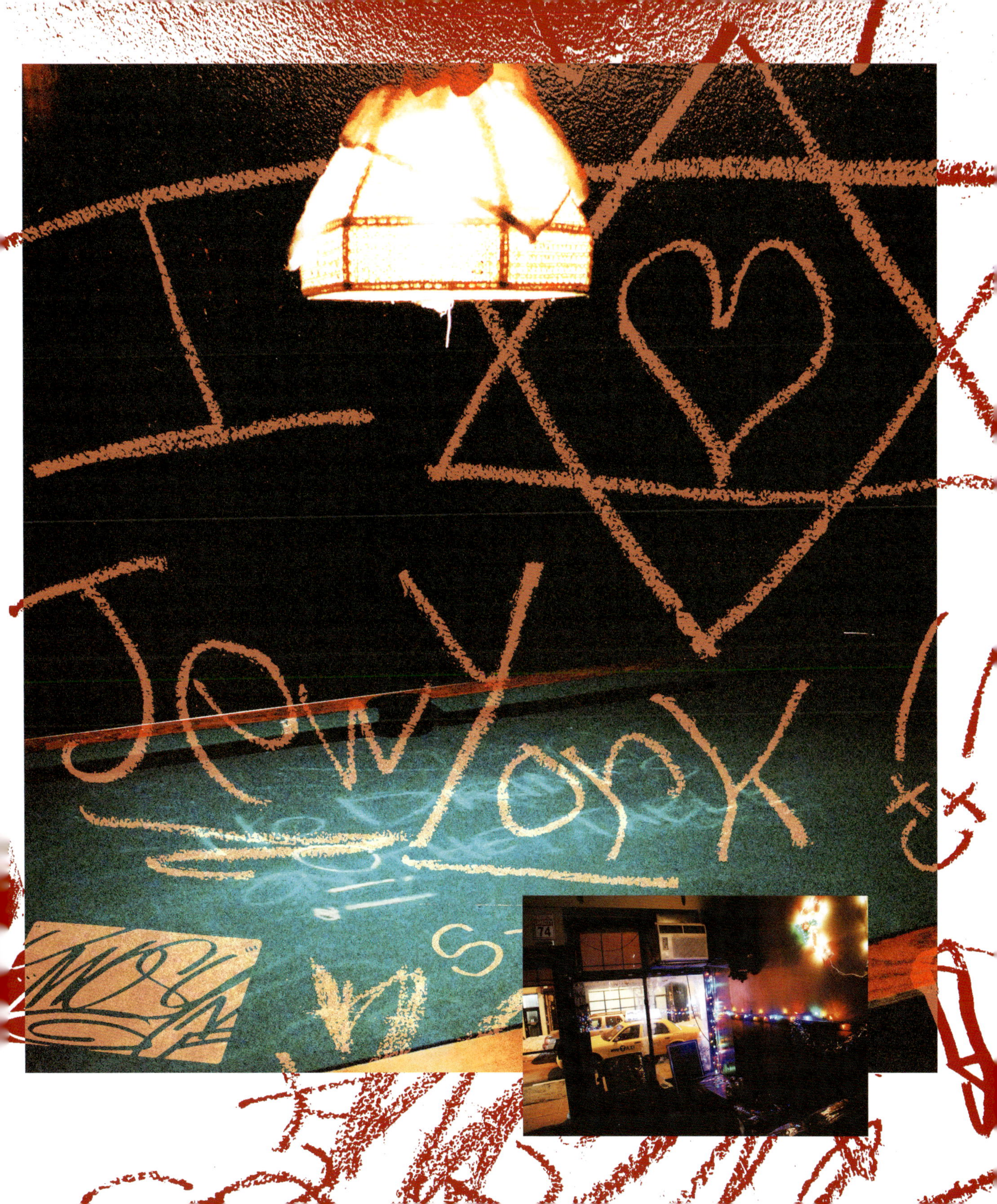

I ♥
Jew York !
74

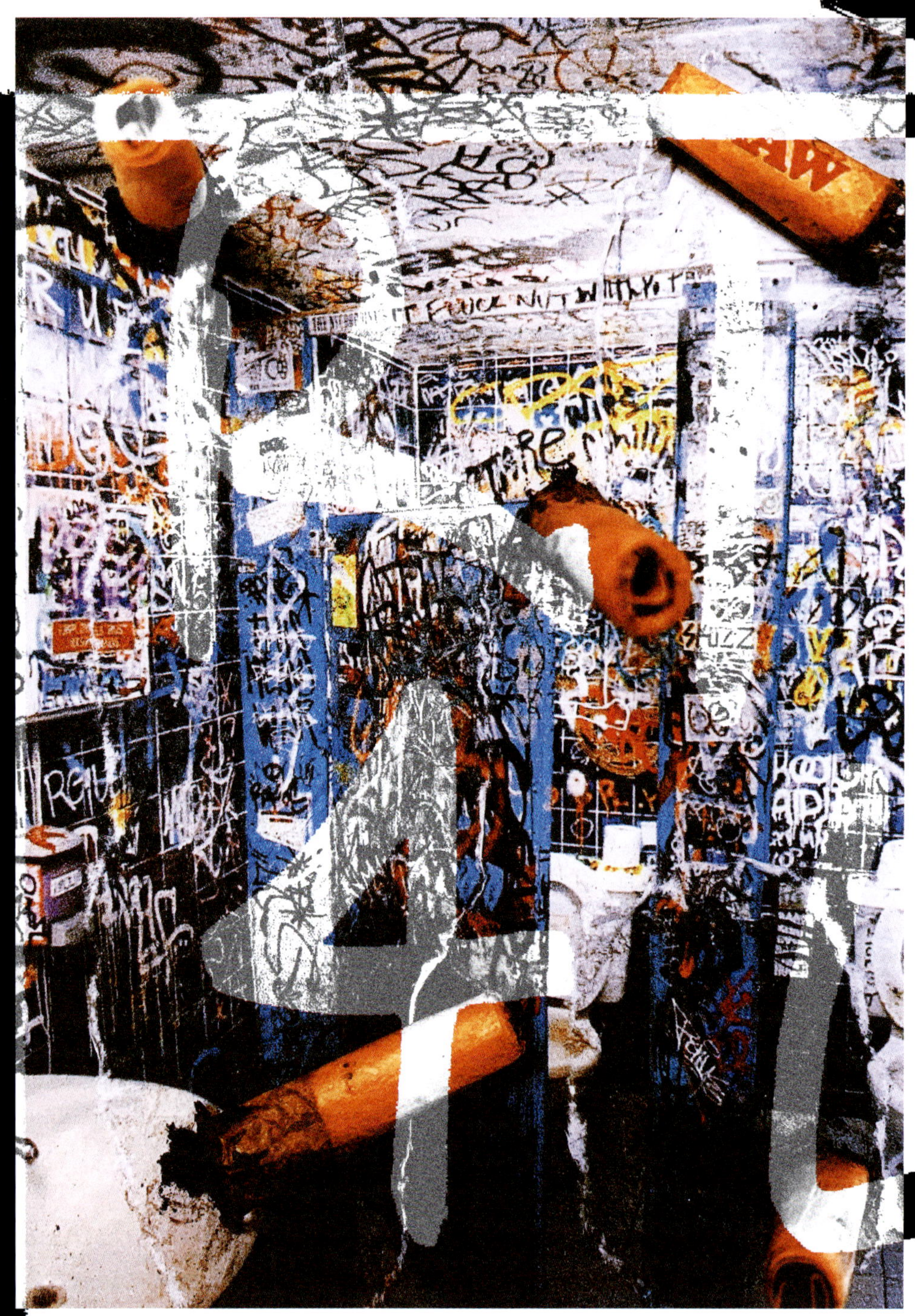

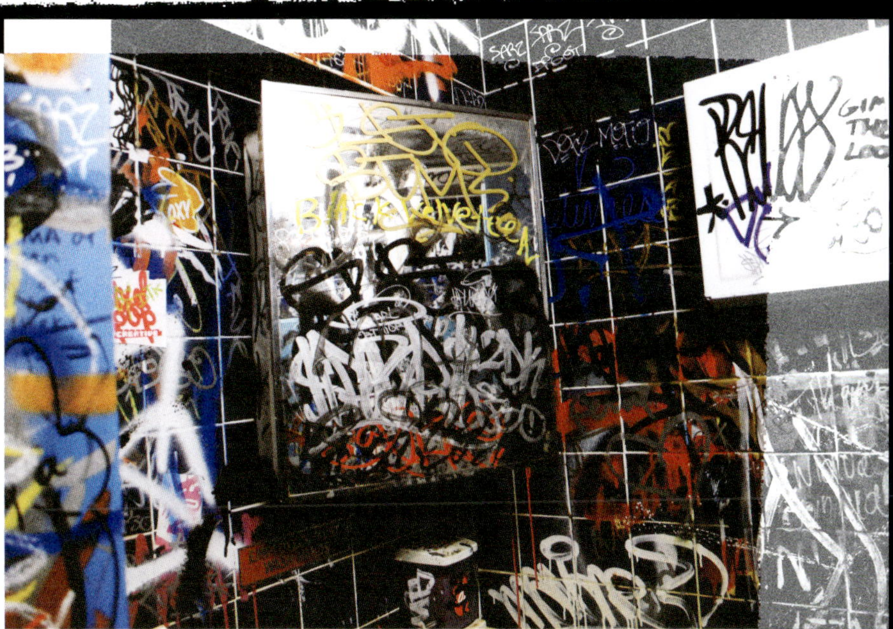

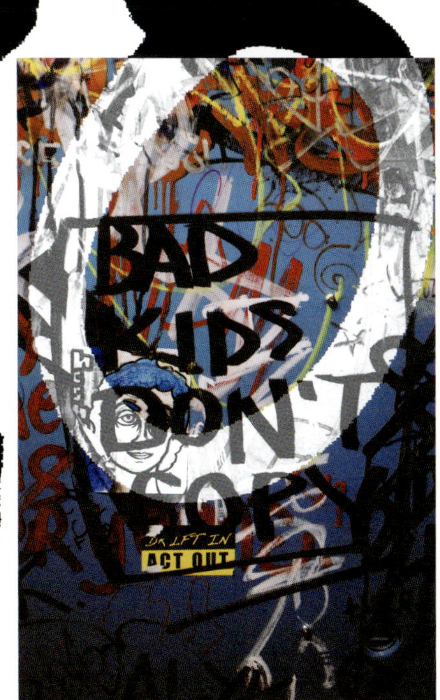
BAD
KIDS
DON'T
COPY
DRIFT IN
ACT OUT

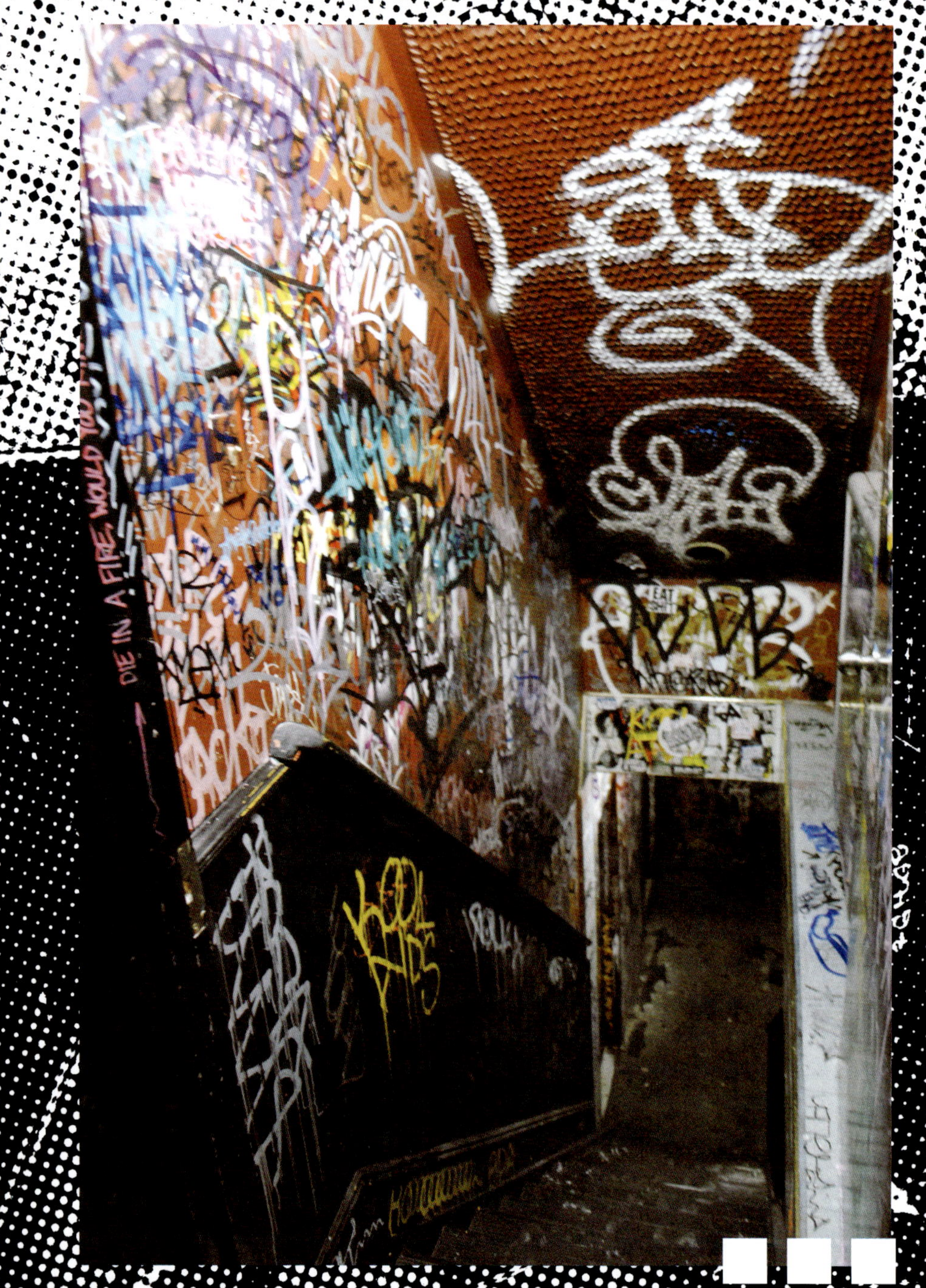

DIE IN A FIRE WOULD YOU

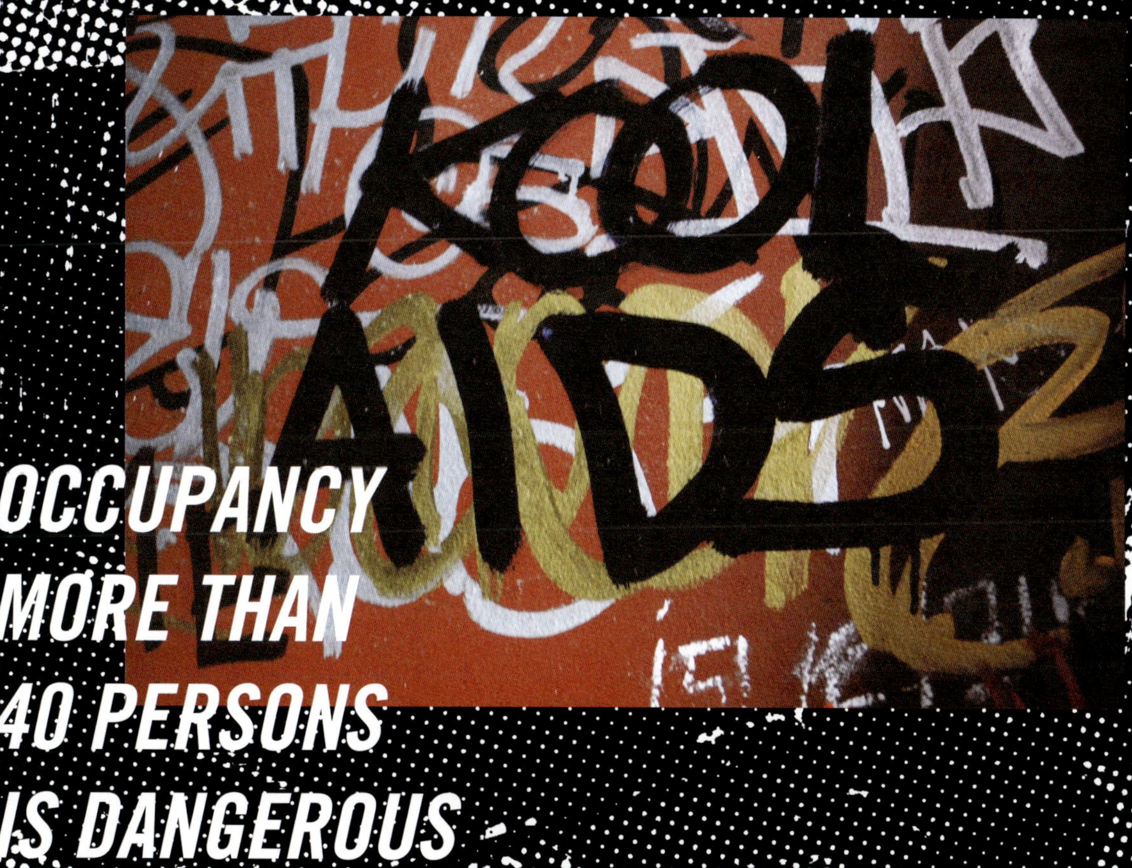

OCCUPANCY
MORE THAN
40 PERSONS
IS DANGEROUS
AND UNLAWFUL

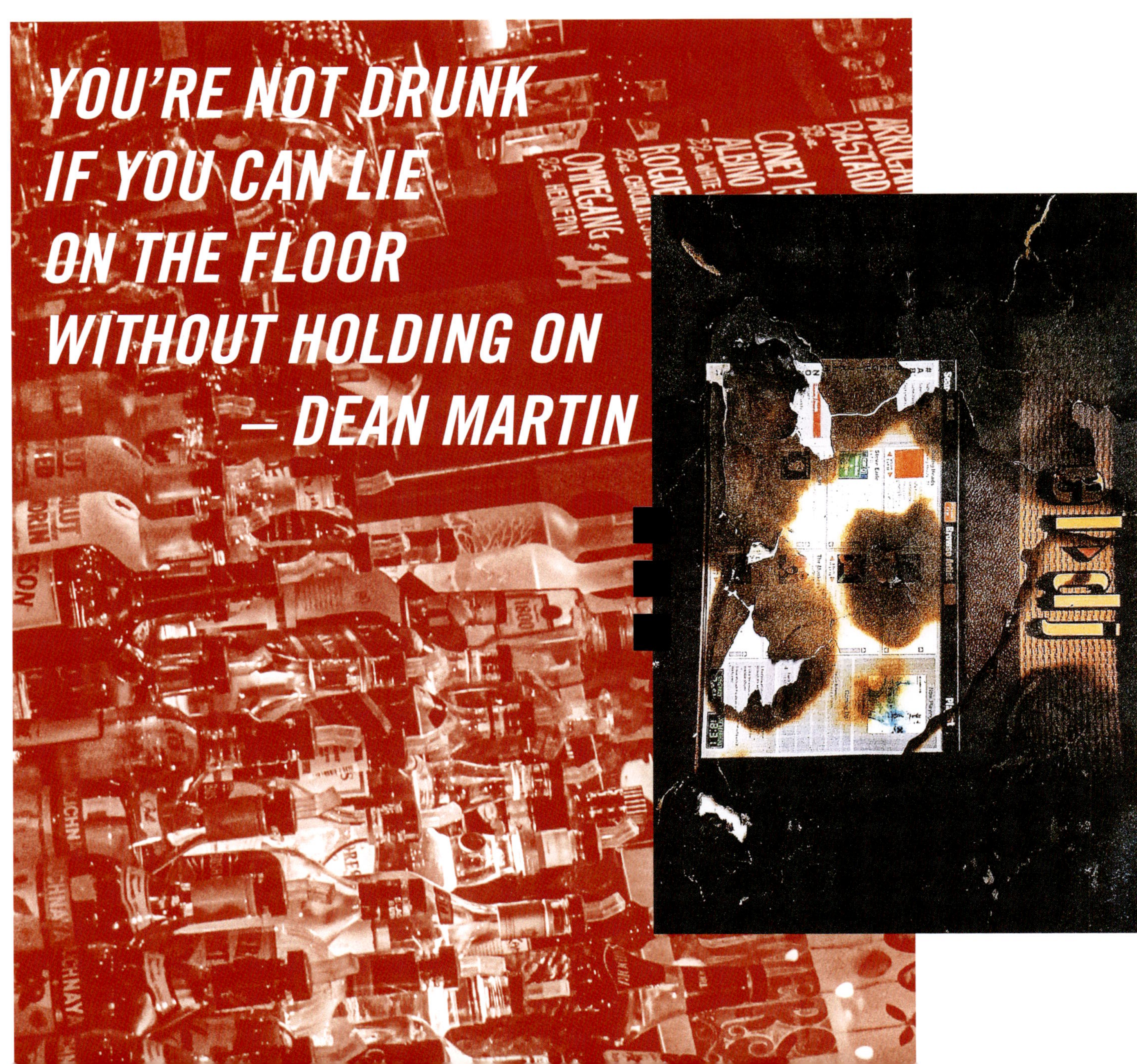
YOU'RE NOT DRUNK
IF YOU CAN LIE
ON THE FLOOR
WITHOUT HOLDING ON
— DEAN MARTIN

ARROGANT
BASTARD
CONEY I
ALBINO
ROGUE
OMMEGANG $14
HENNEPIN

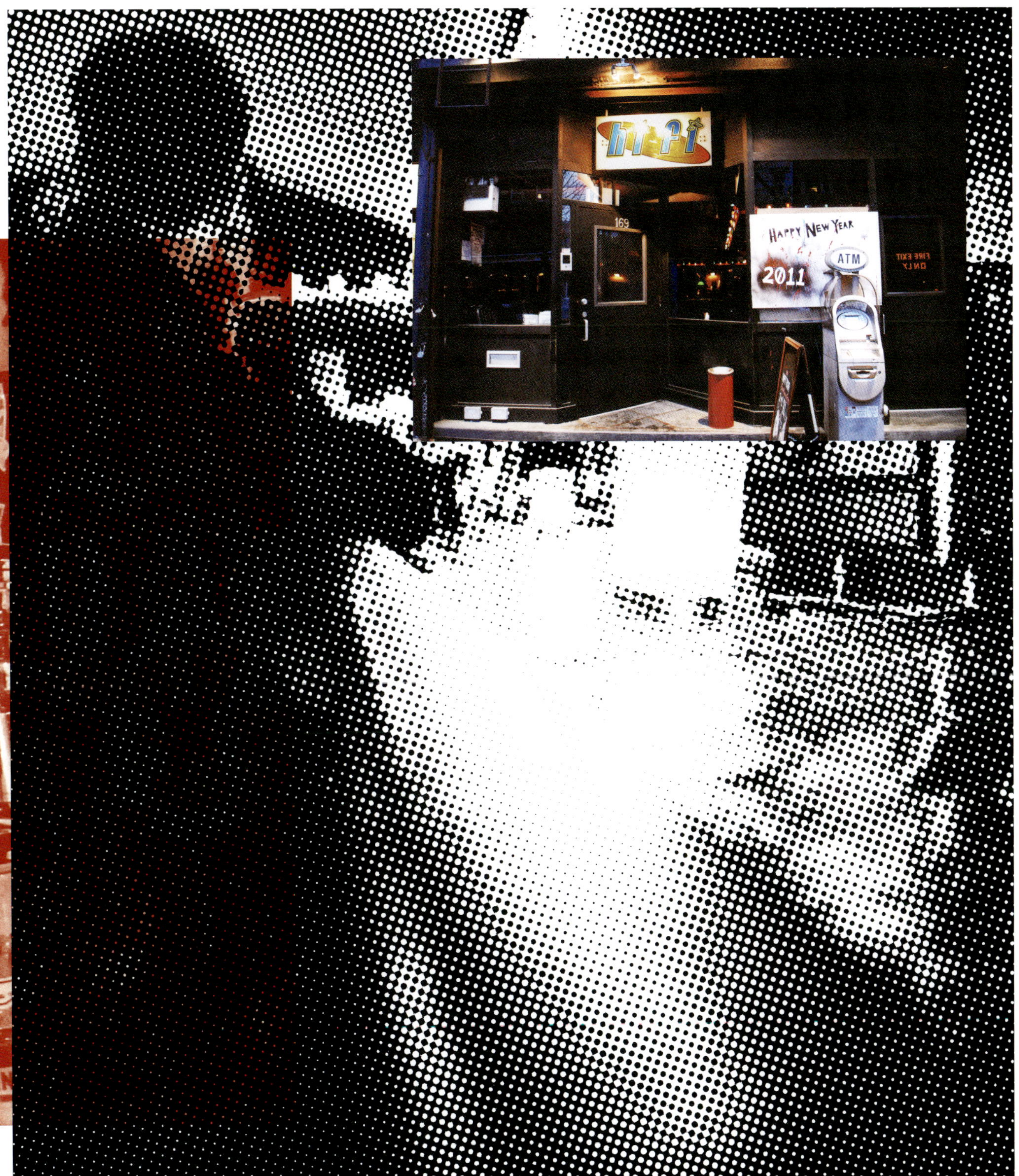
hi fi
169
HAPPY NEW YEAR
2011
ATM
FIRE EXIT
ONLY

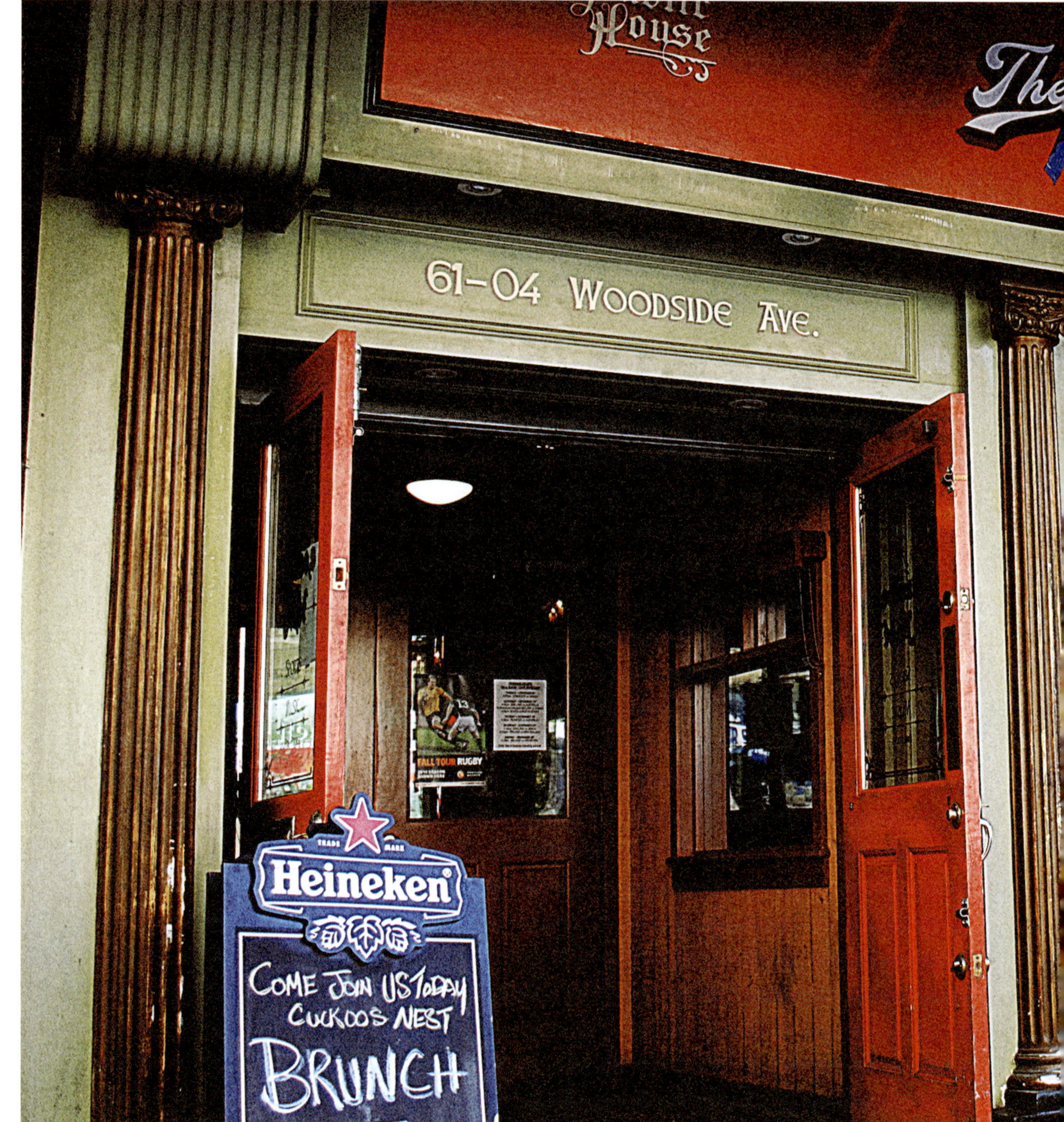

The Cuckoo's Nest

11.21.2010
02:22pm

Woodside
Queens

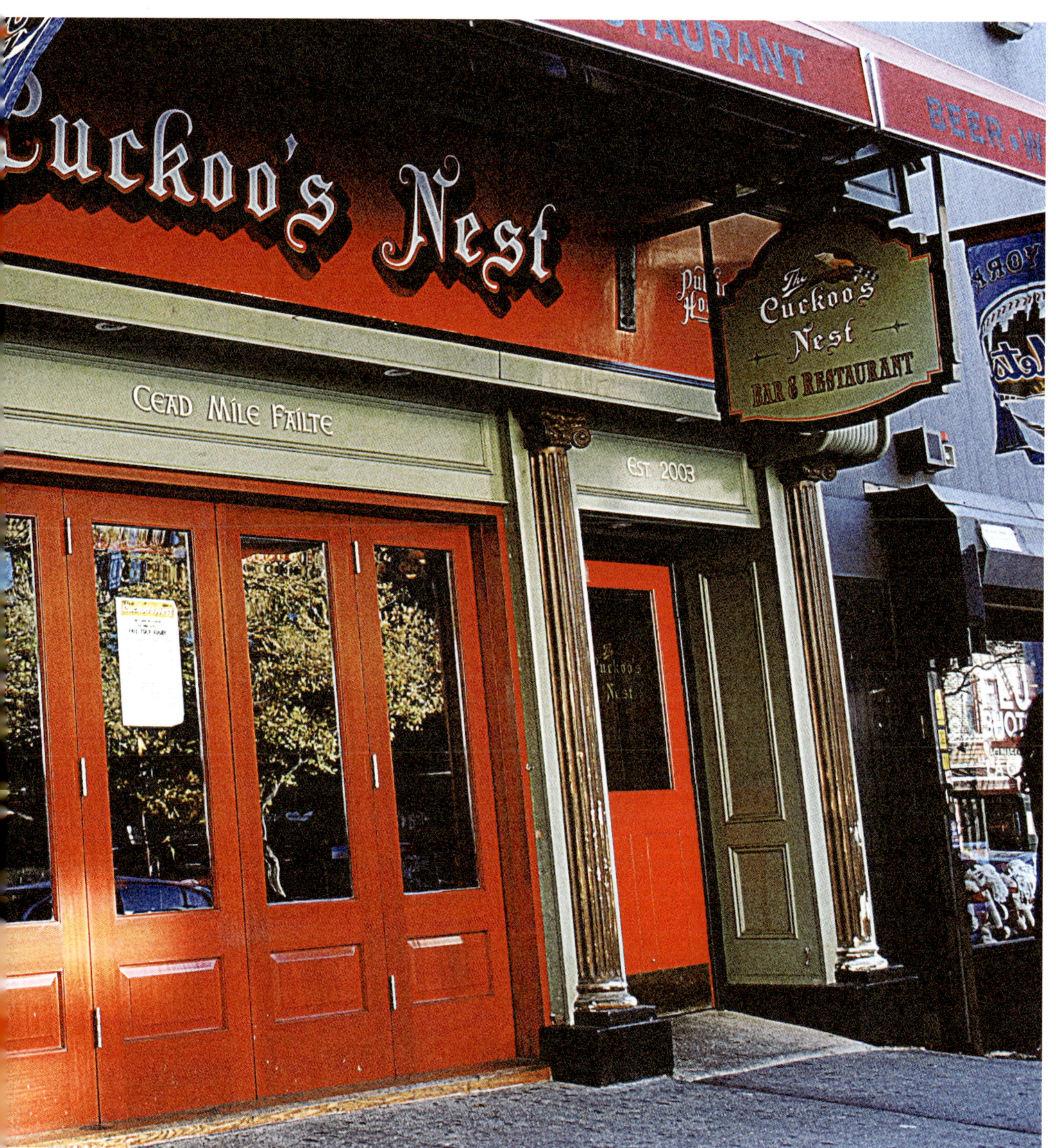
Cuckoo's Nest
RESTAURANT
BEER
The
Cuckoo's
Nest
BAR & RESTAURANT
Public House
CEAD MILE FAILTE
Est. 2003
Cuckoo's
Nest
FLU
SHOT

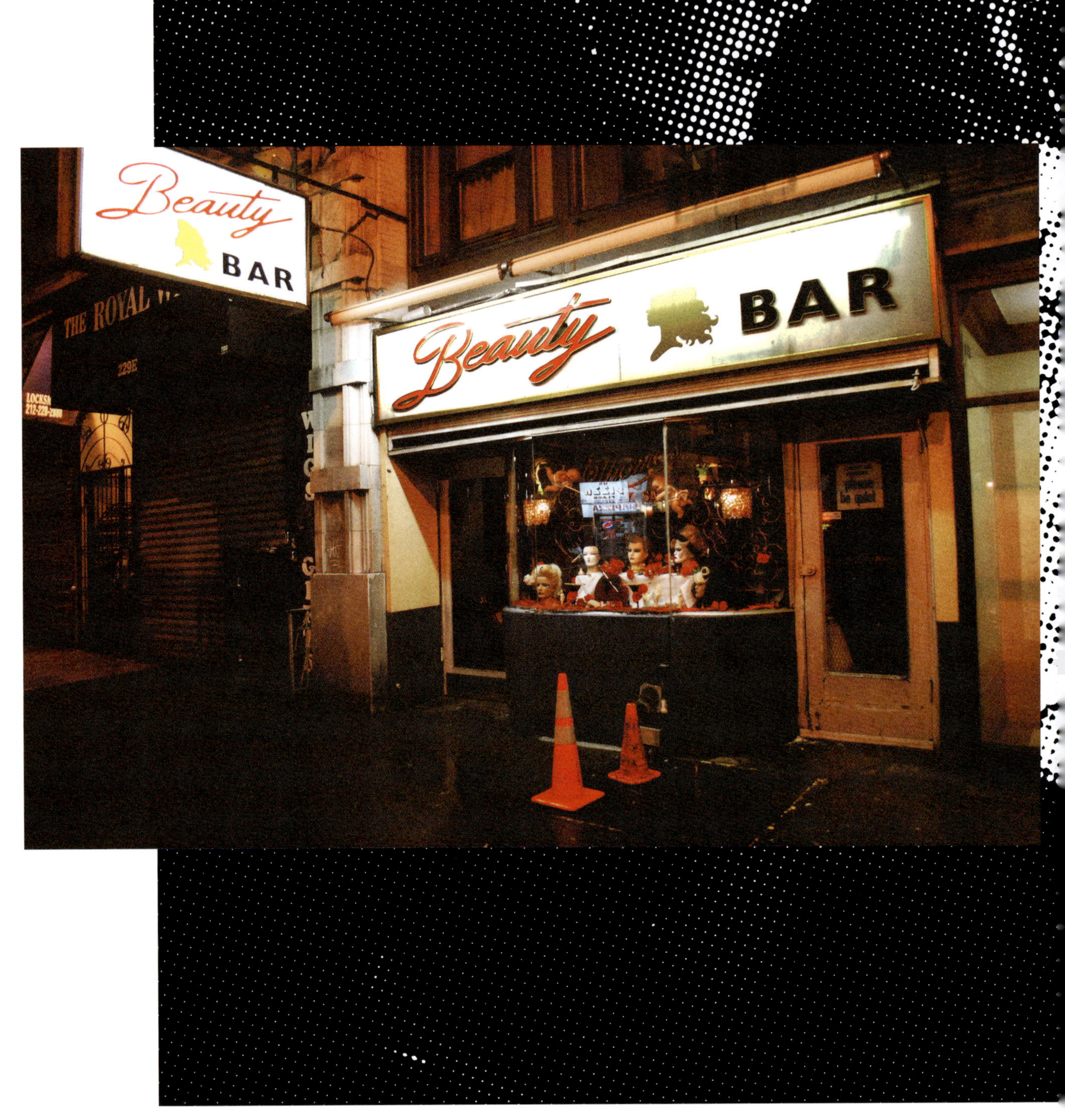

Beauty Bar

02.05.2011
08:28pm

East Village
Manhattan

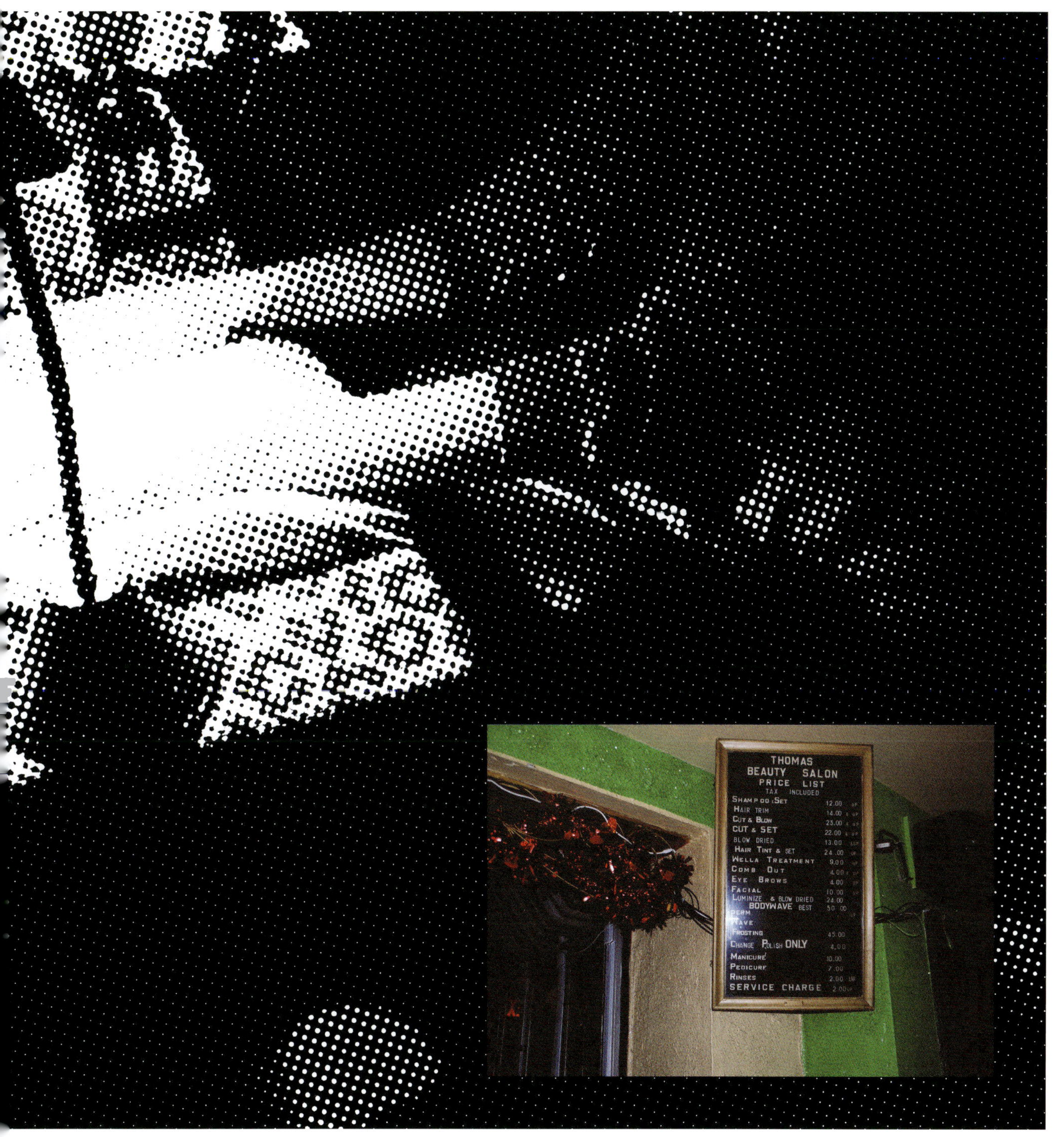

THOMAS
BEAUTY SALON
PRICE LIST
TAX INCLUDED
SHAMPOO & SET   12.00 UP
HAIR TRIM   14.00 & UP
CUT & BLOW   23.00 & UP
CUT & SET   22.00 & UP
BLOW DRIED   13.00 UP
HAIR TINT & SET   24.00 UP
WELLA TREATMENT   9.00 UP
COMB OUT   4.00 & UP
EYE BROWS   4.00 UP
FACIAL   10.00
LUMINIZE & BLOW DRIED 24.00
BODYWAVE BEST   50.00
PERM
WAVE
FROSTING   45.00
CHANGE POLISH ONLY   4.00
MANICURE   10.00
PEDICURE   7.00
RINSES   2.00 UP
SERVICE CHARGE   2.00 UP

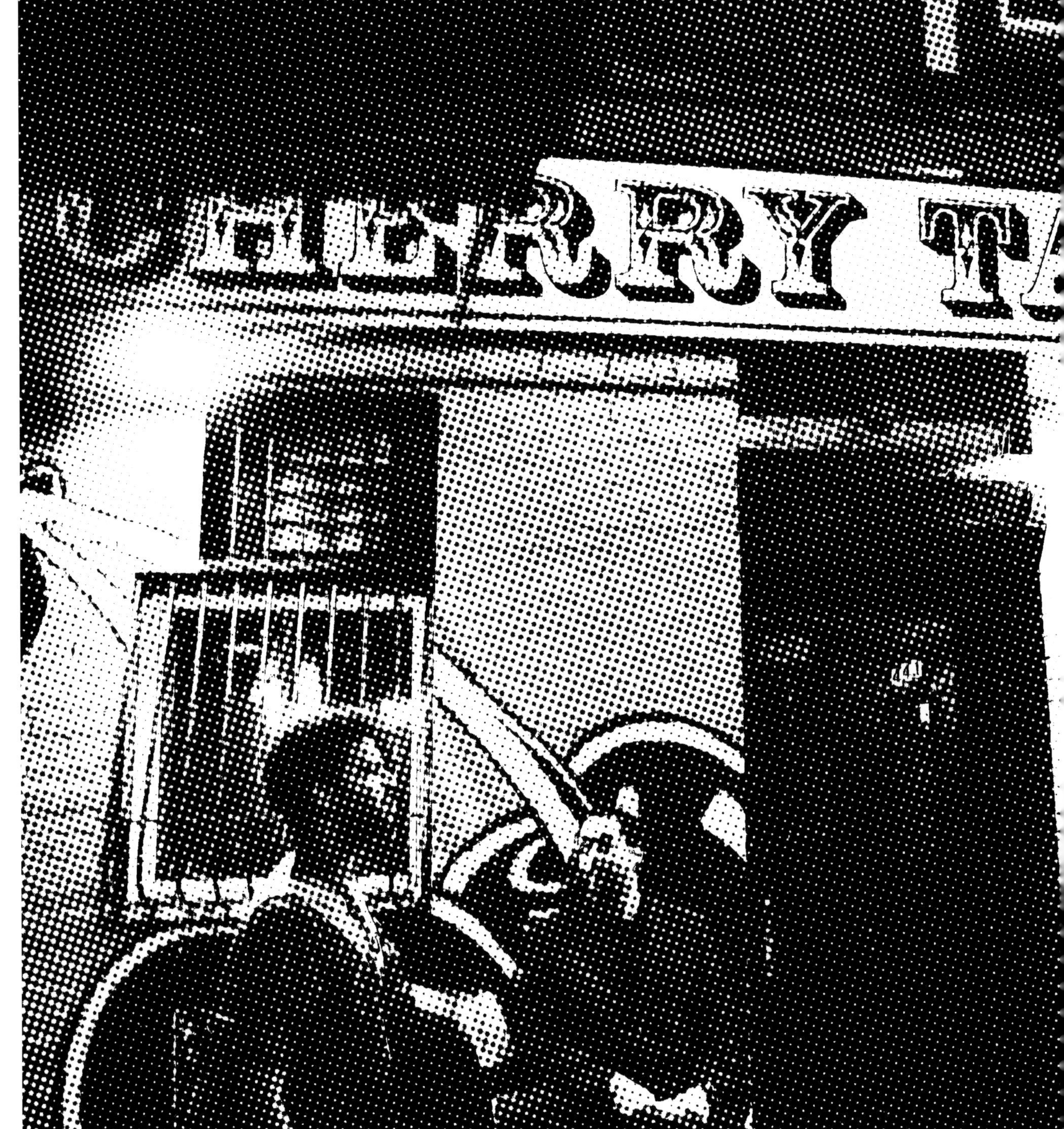CHERRY T

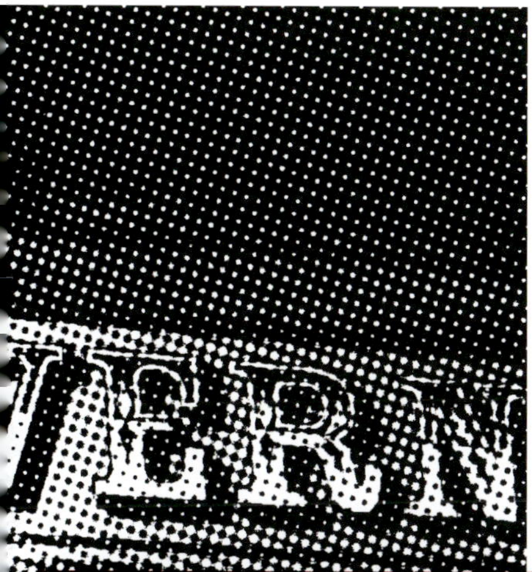

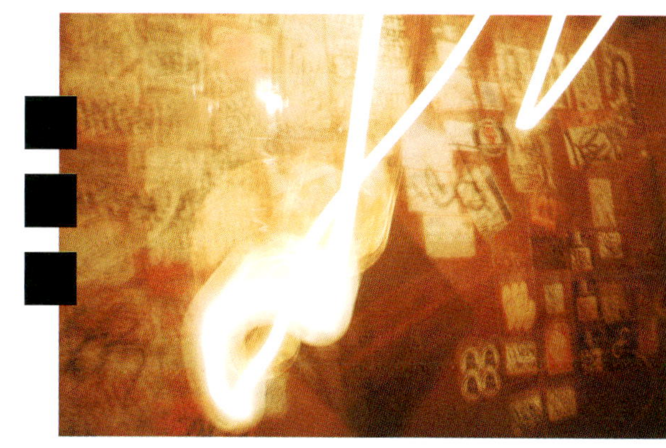

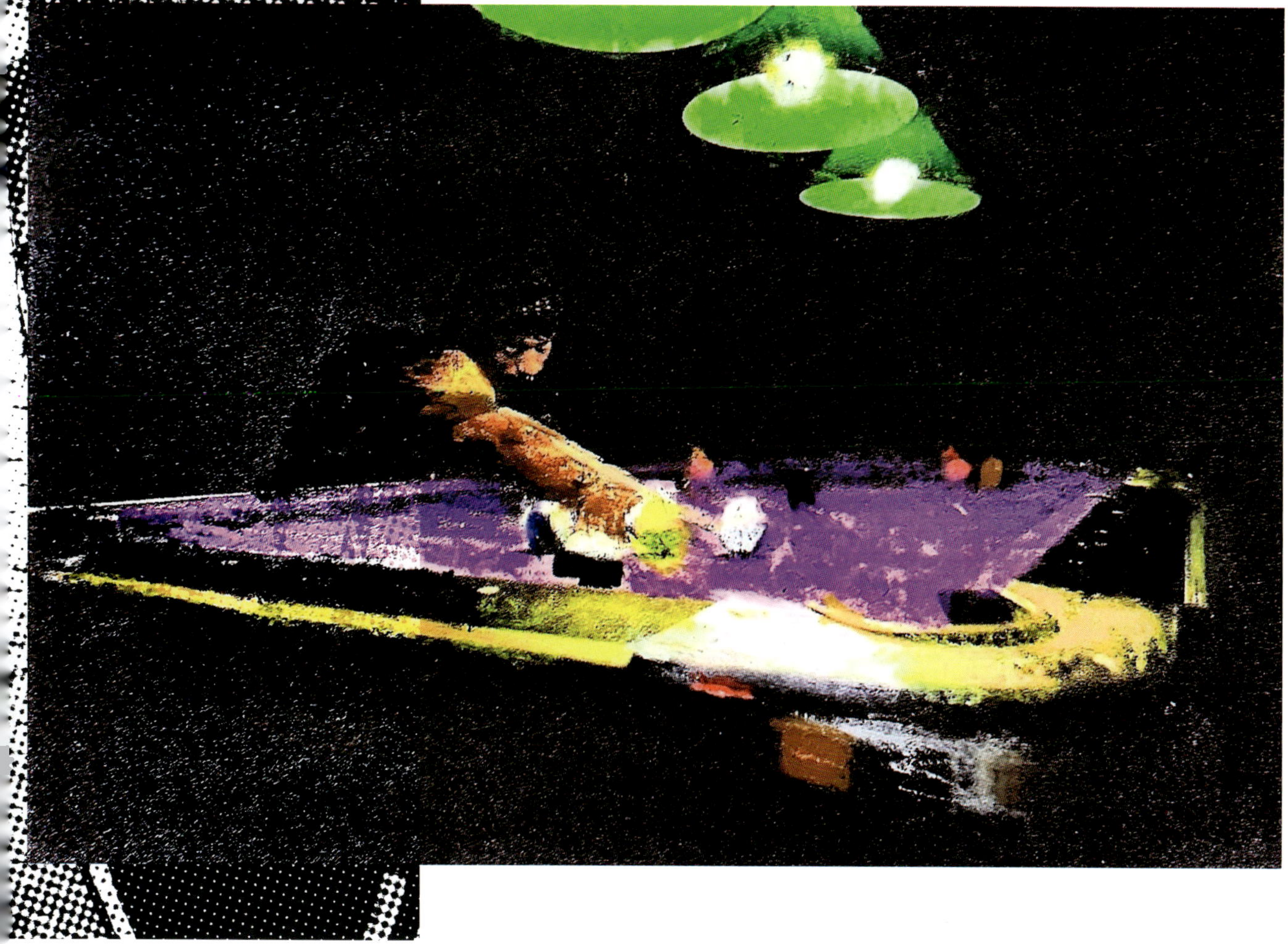

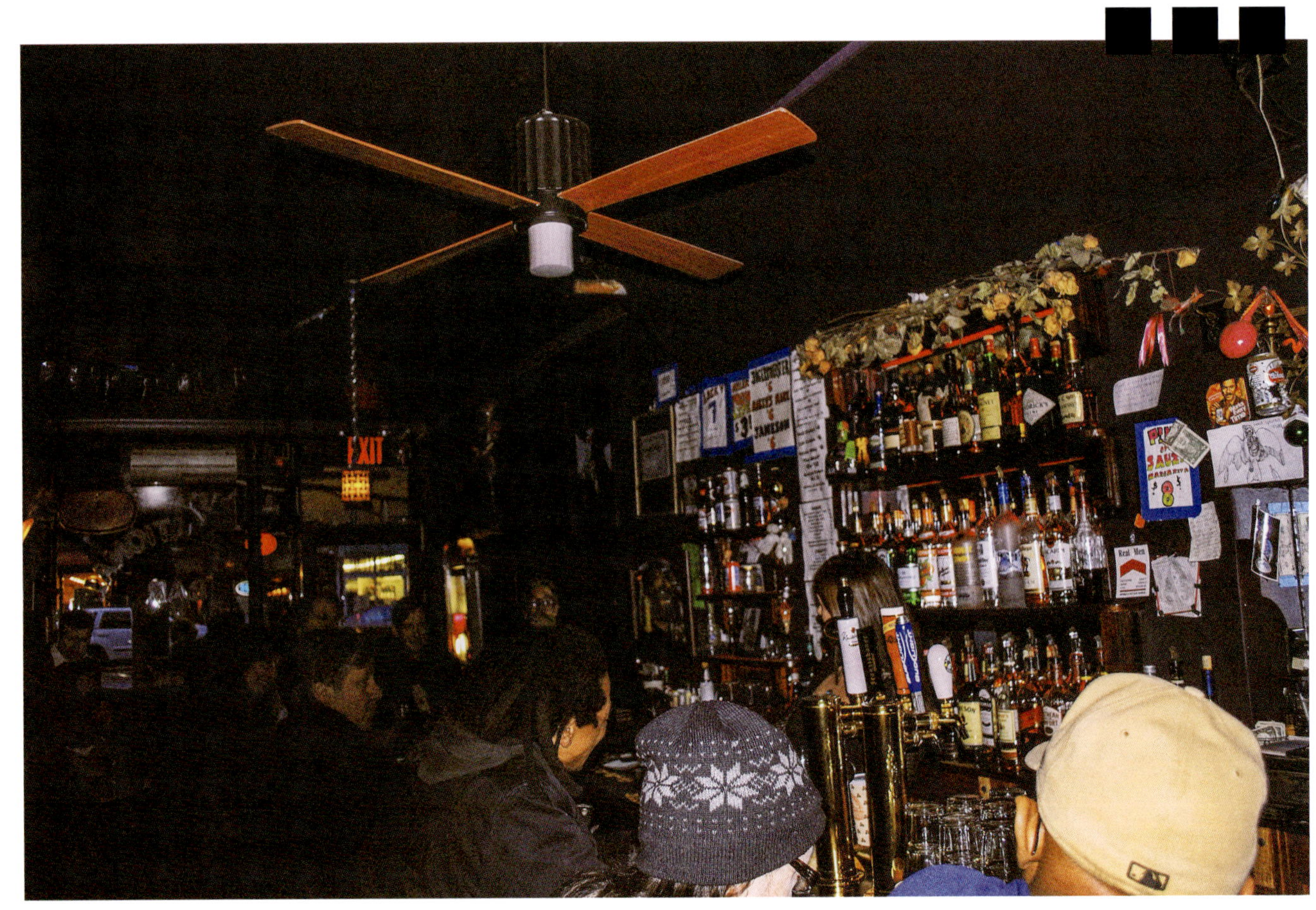

International Bar

04.02.2010
06:24pm

East Village
Manhattan

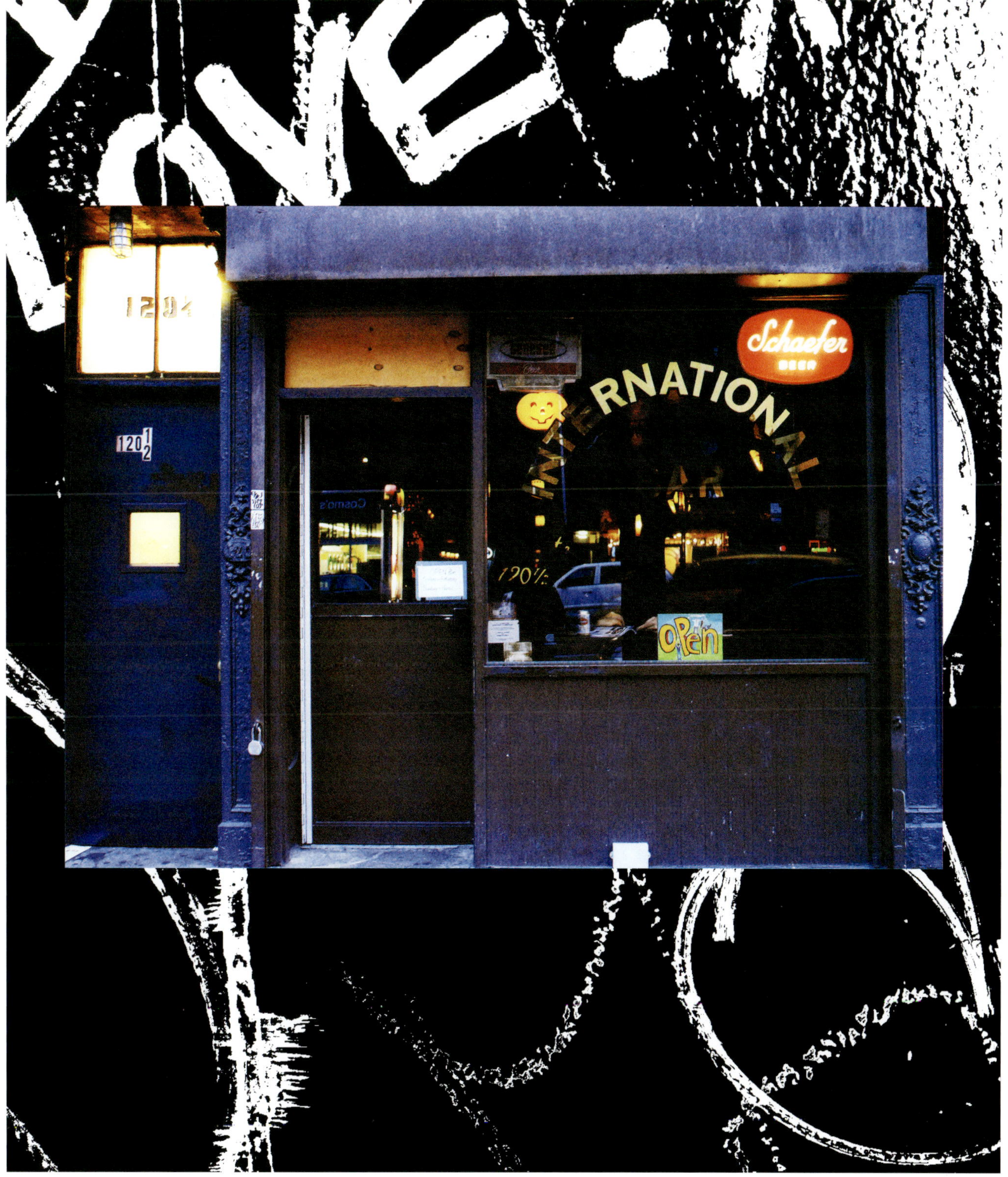

1204
120 1/2
Cosmo's
Schaefer
BEER
INTERNATIONAL
120 1/2
OPEN

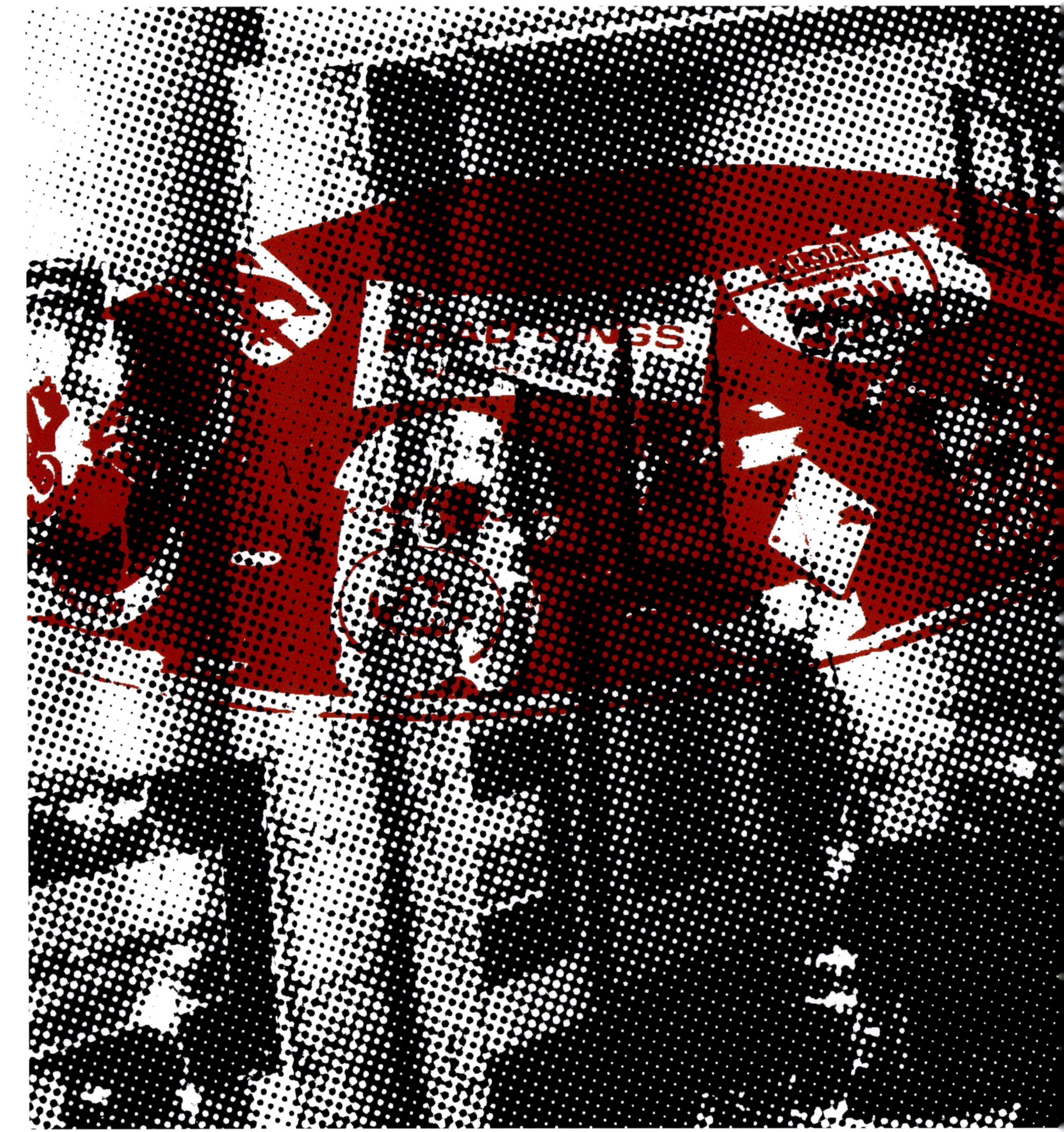

Ear Inn
02.20.2011
03:50pm
West Village
Manhattan

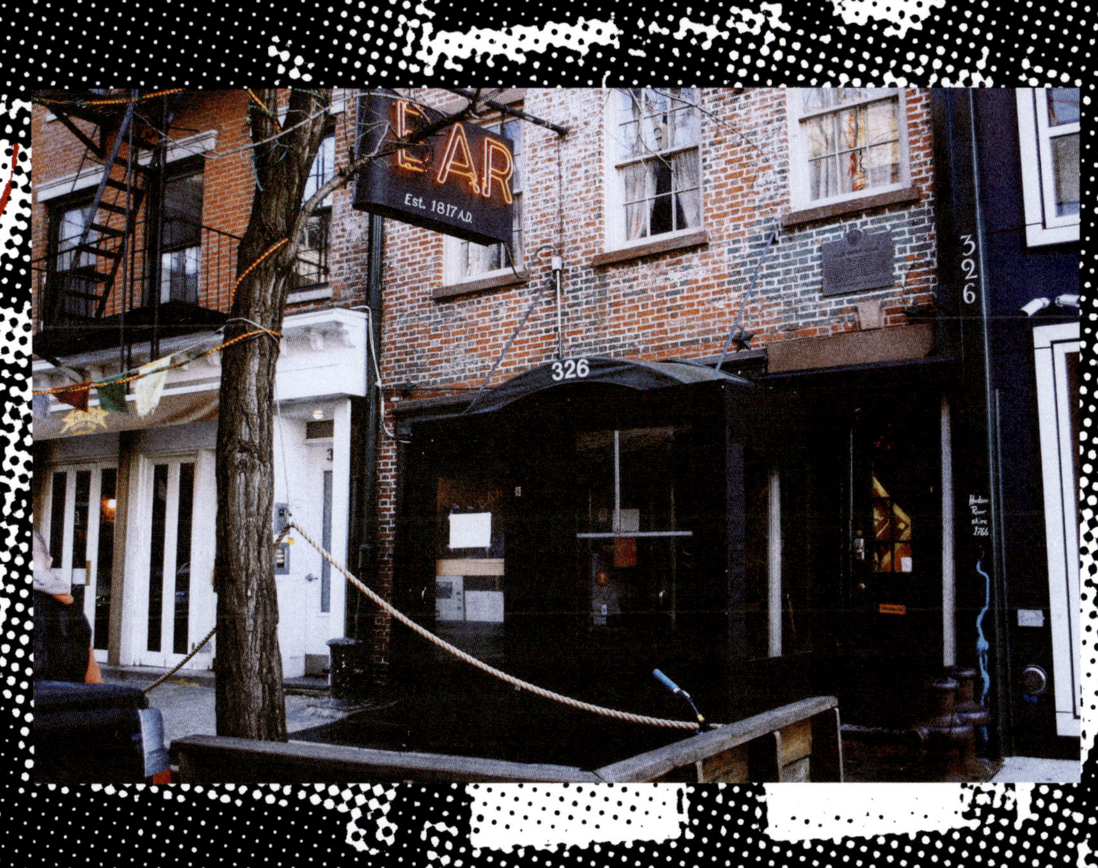
EAR
Est. 1817 A.D.
326
326

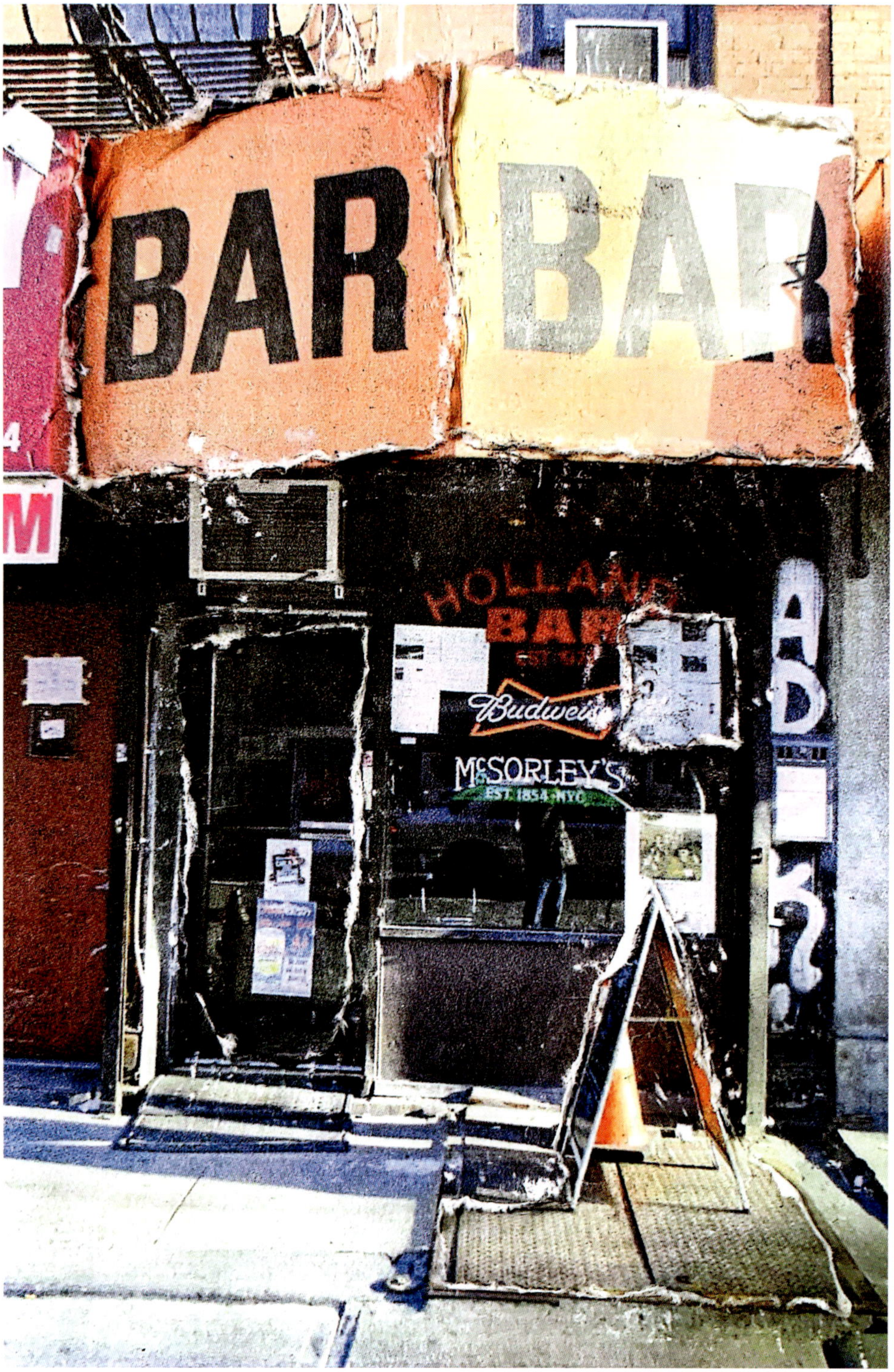

Holland Bar

01.10.2011
02:40pm

Hell's Kitchen
Manhattan

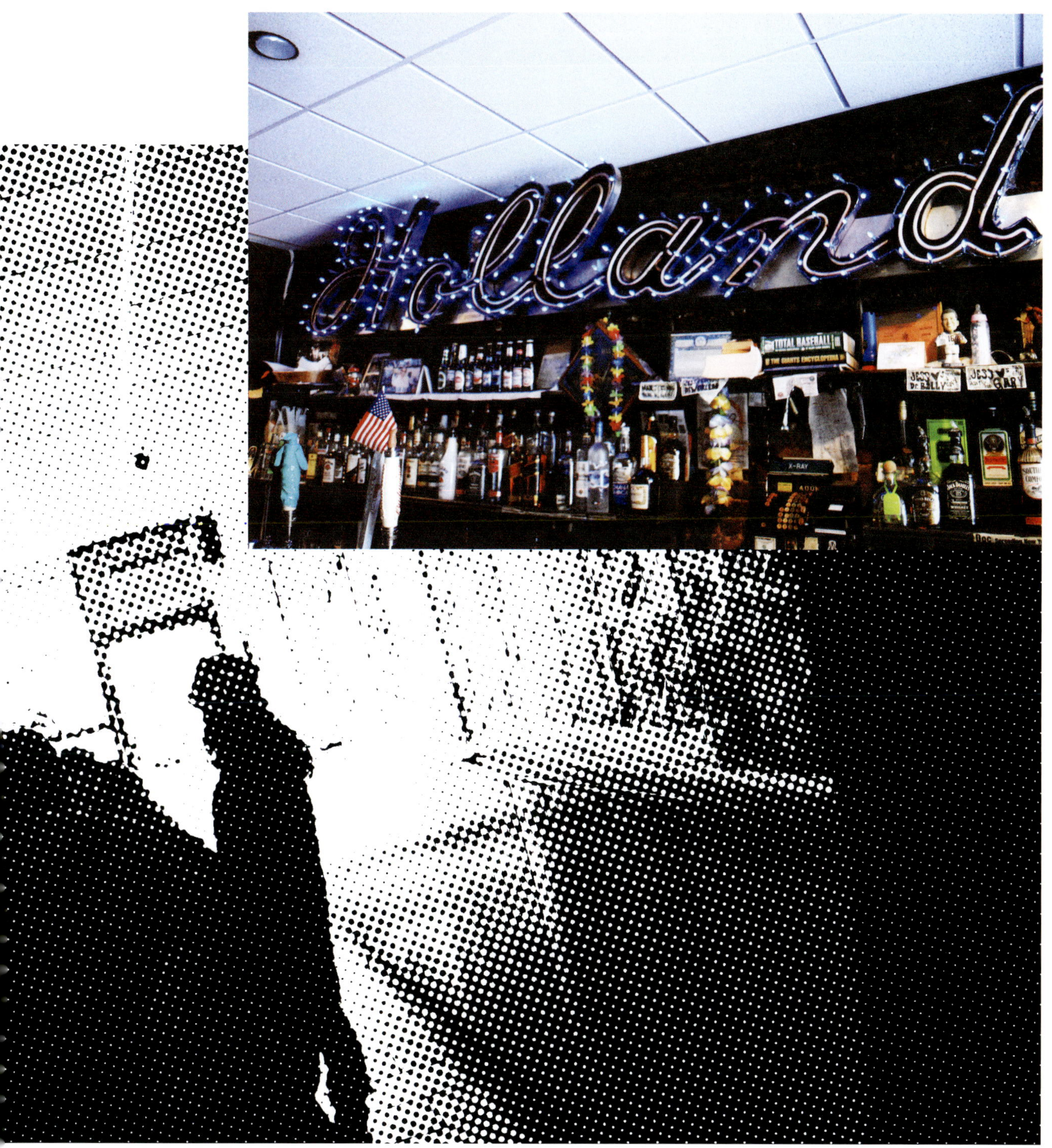

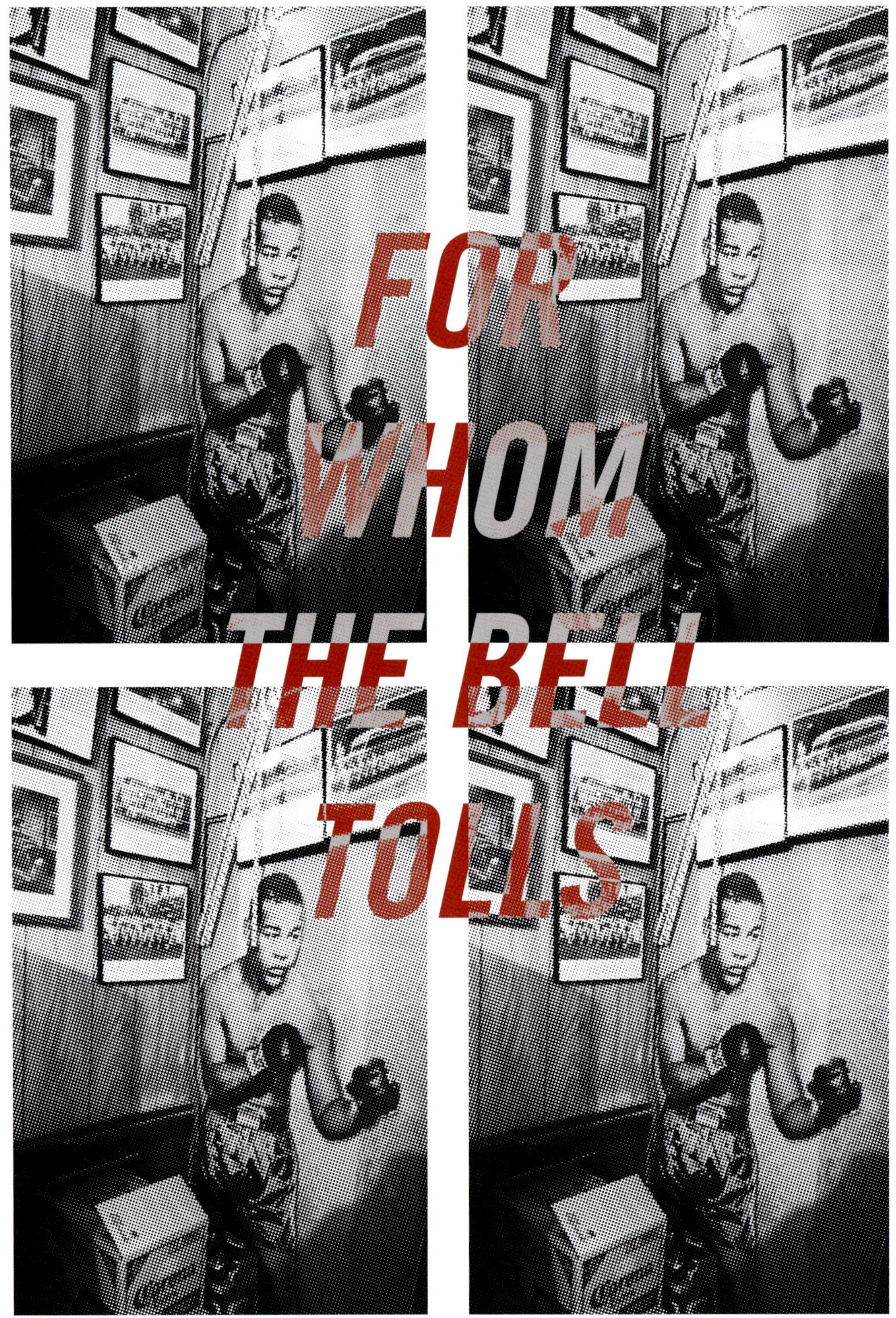
FOR
WHOM
THE BELL
TOLLS

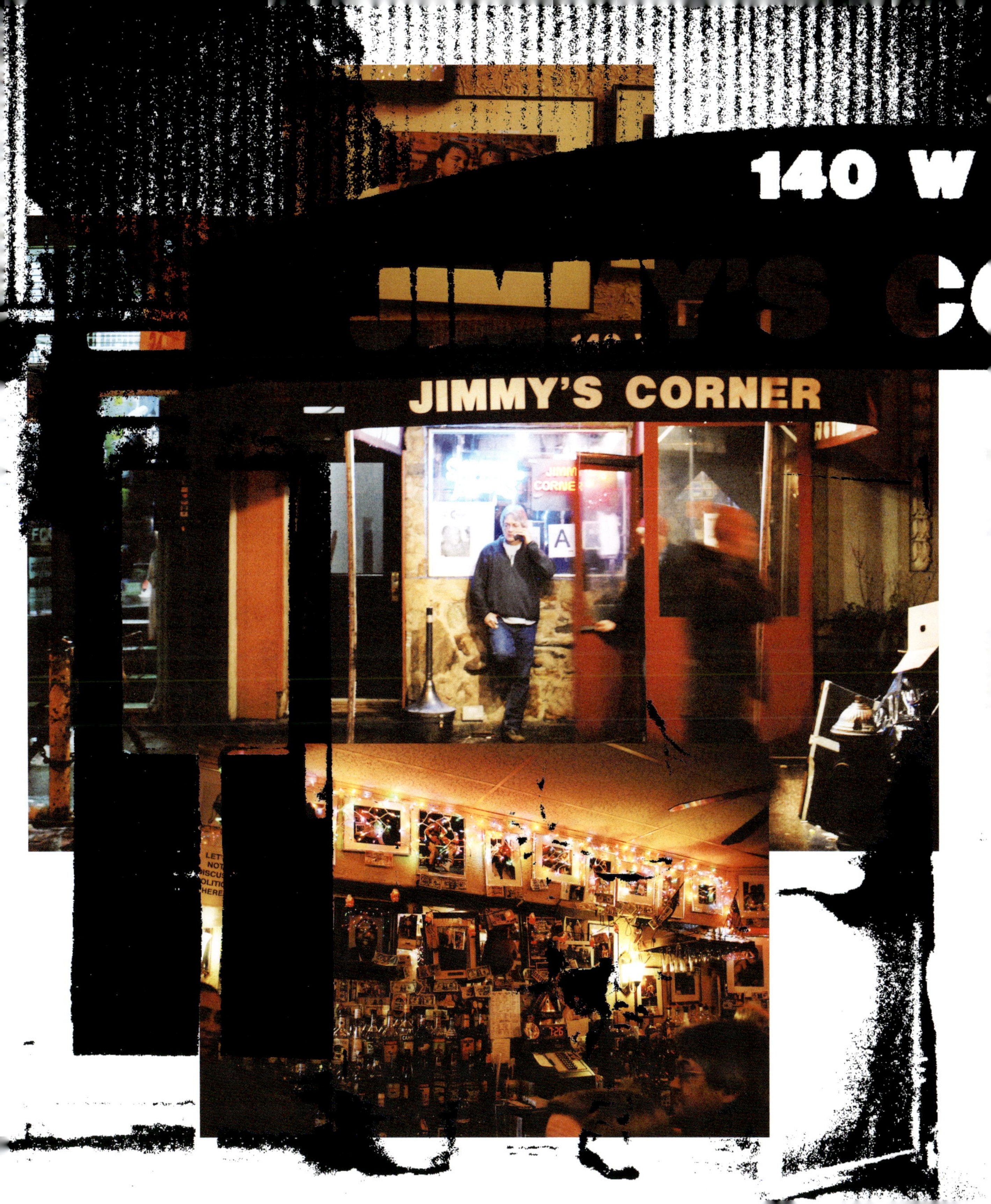

140 W
JIMMY'S CORNER
JIMMY'S CORNER

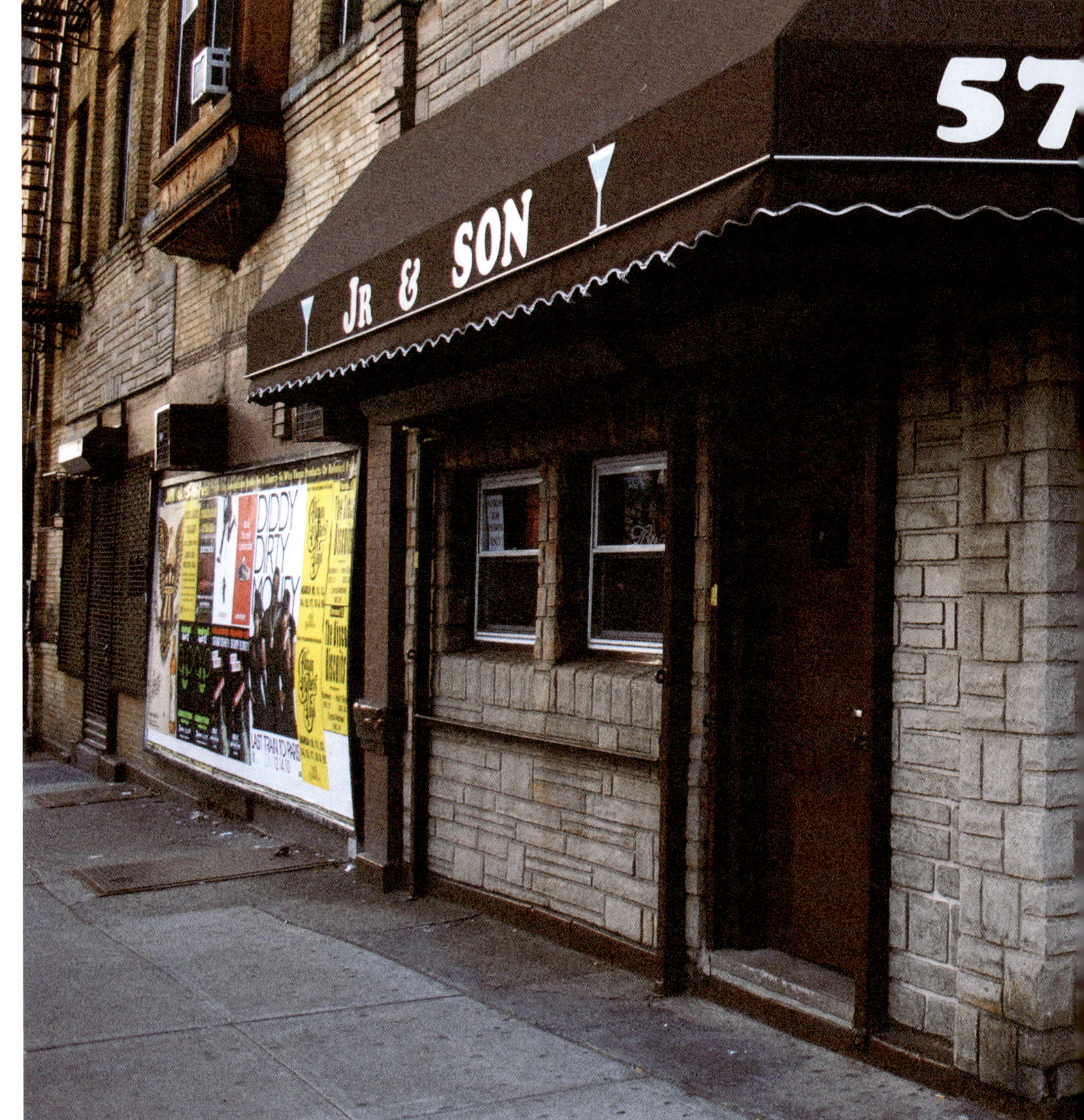

Junior & Son

12.05.2010
03:53pm

Williamsburg
Brooklyn

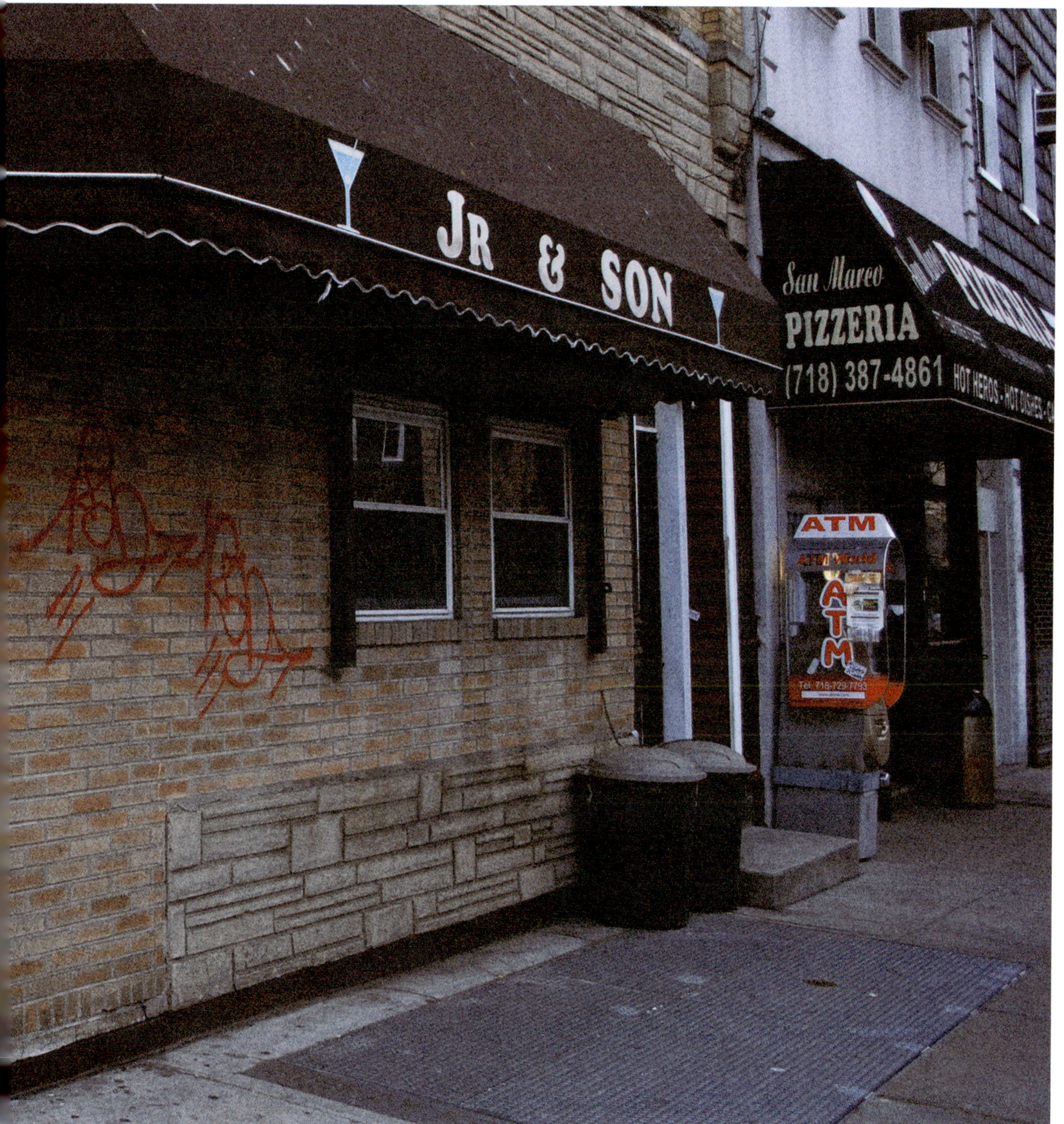
JR & SON
San Marco
PIZZERIA
(718) 387-4861 HOT HEROS · HOT DISHES ·
ATM
ATM
Tel: 718-729-7793

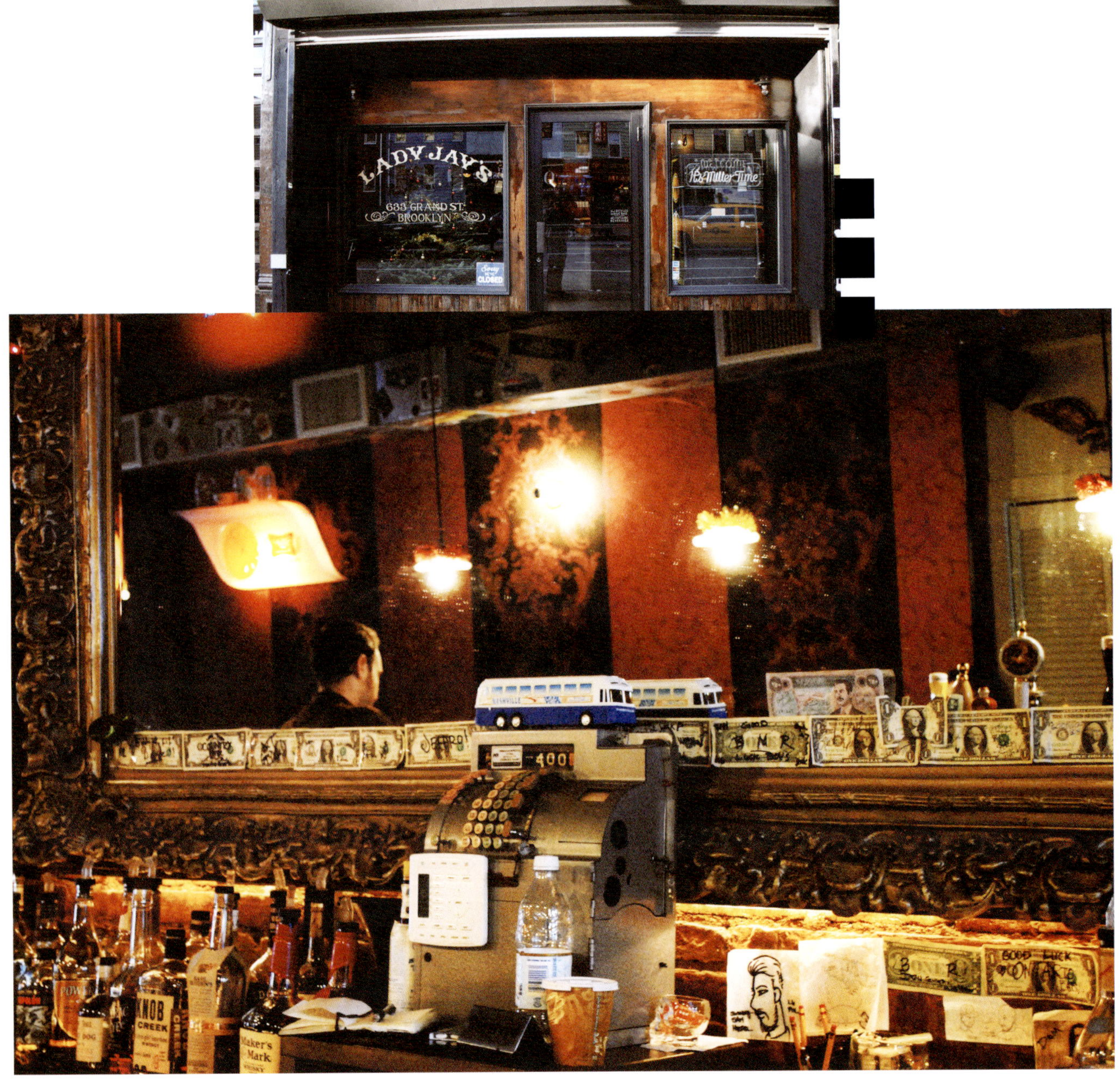

Lady Jay's

12.04.2010
03:27pm

**Williamsburg
Brooklyn**

Beauty behind the madness:

To the common eye, graffiti filled dive bars are an eyesore…and depending on the location, they can also contribute to the noise pollution. People in and out all times of the day, drunk revelvers, But there's something about raw aesthetics…dingy, chipped up bar tables, bathrooms where a woman wouldn't dare sit, sticker filled mirrors, lewd, yet comical messages on stalls & walls. Any dive in any city presents the same. Sometimes the locals like to keep their watering holes a secret… but like all things, influx brings pricing increases.

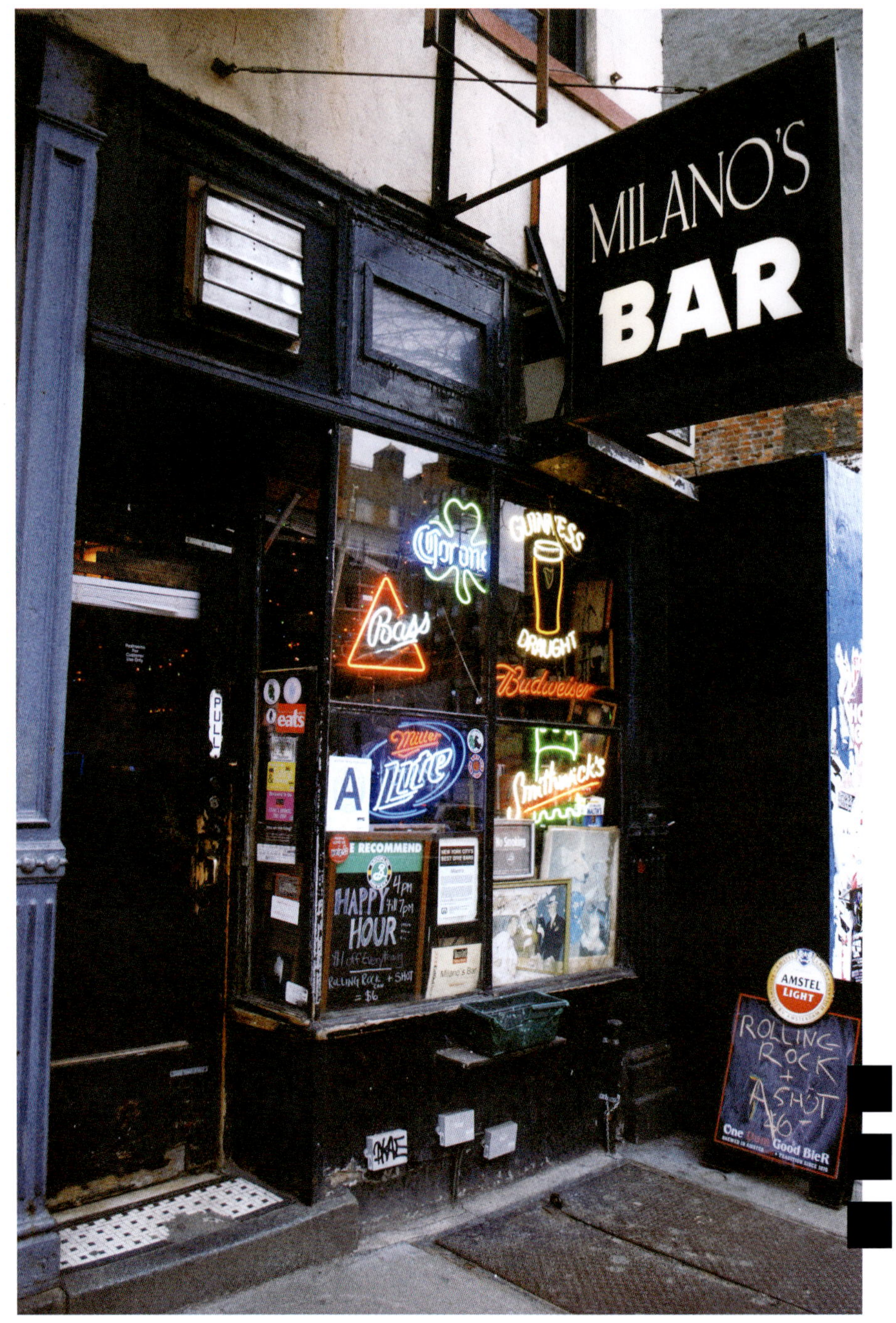
MILANO'S
BAR
Corona
GUINNESS
DRAUGHT
Bass
Budweiser
Miller Lite
Smithwick's
A
PULL
eats
E RECOMMEND
HAPPY 4PM
HOUR TILL 7PM
AMSTEL
LIGHT
ROLLING
ROCK
+
A SHOT
$6
One Damn Good BieR

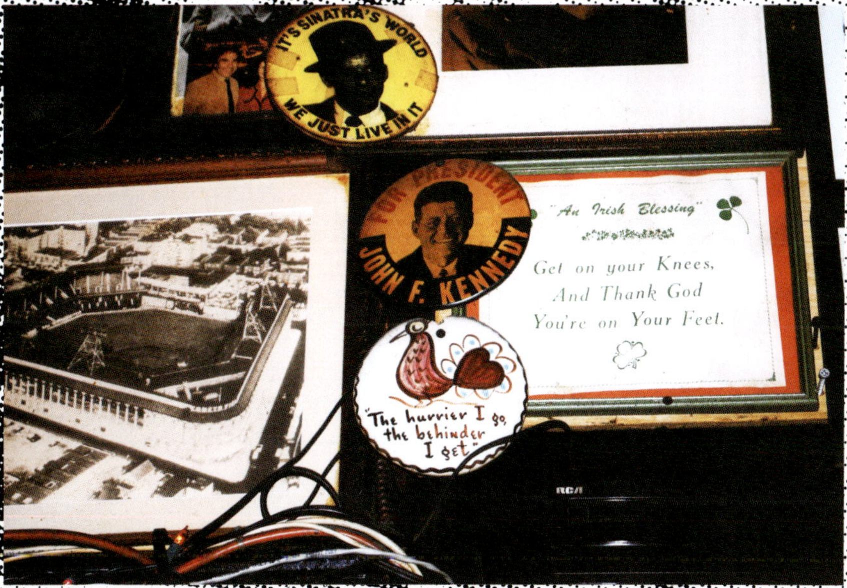

IT'S SINATRA'S WORLD
WE JUST LIVE IN IT
FOR PRESIDENT
JOHN F. KENNEDY
"An Irish Blessing"
Get on your Knees,
And Thank God
You're on Your Feet.
"The hurrier I go,
the behinder
I get"
RCA

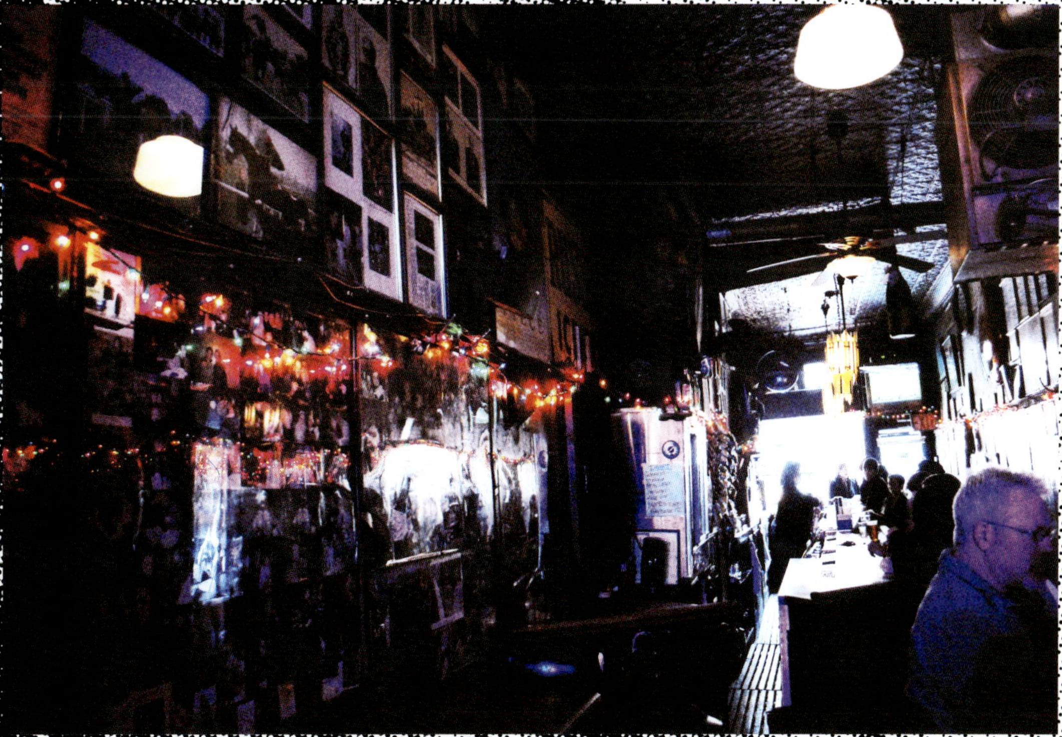

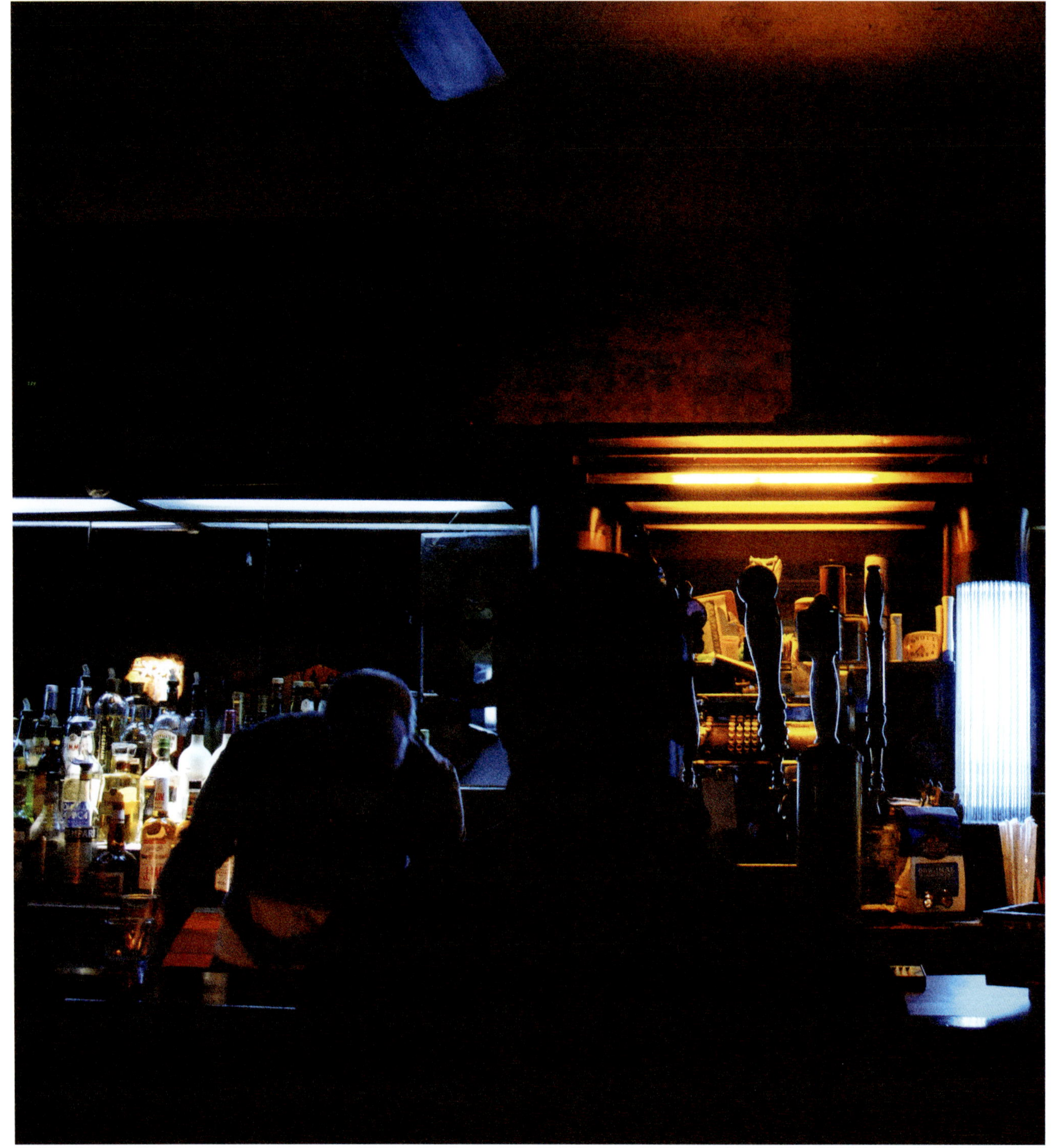

Mona's

03.03.2011
07:39pm

Alphabet City
Manhattan

I'M

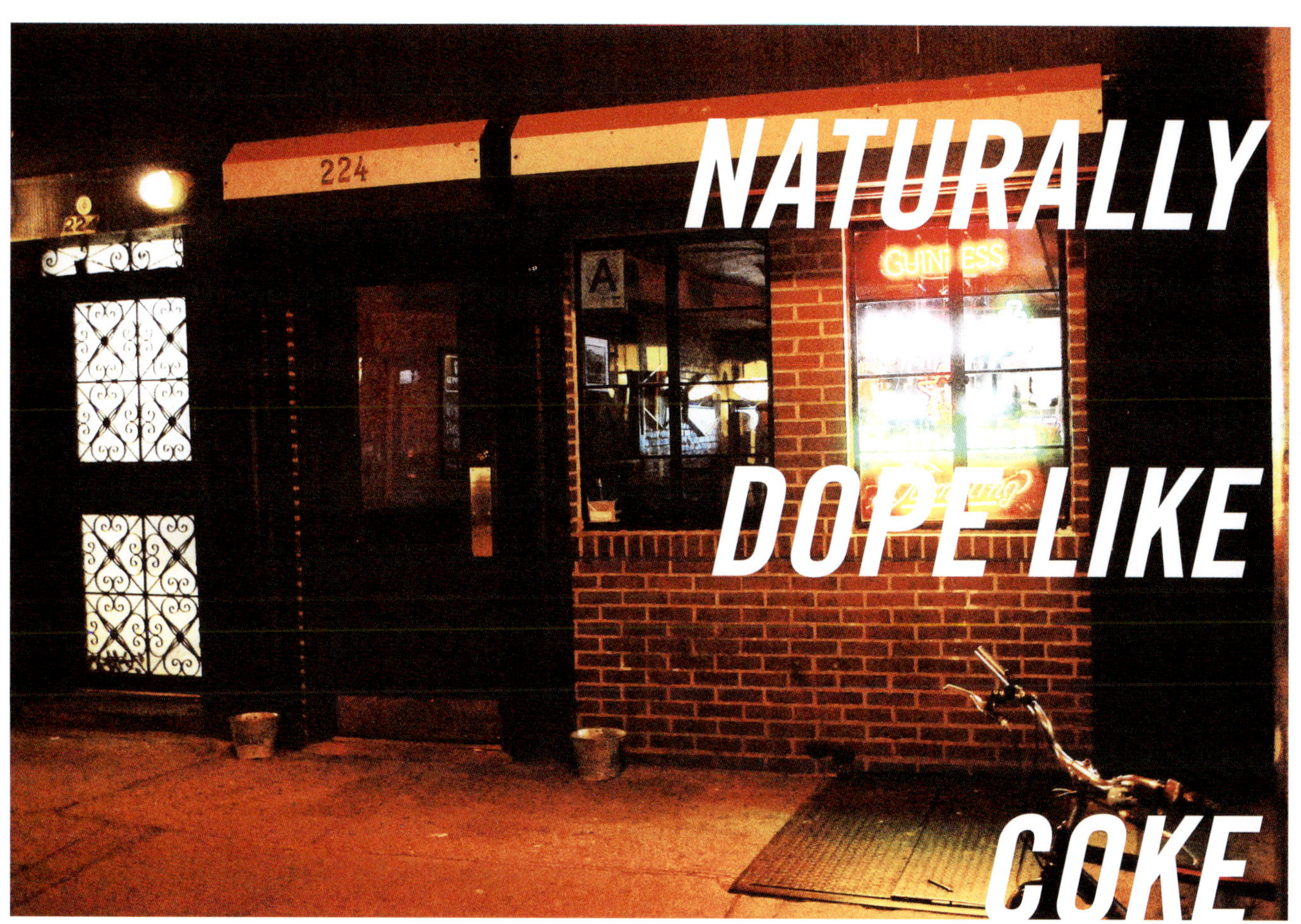
NATURALLY
GUINNESS
224
DOPE LIKE
COKE

BEFORE CRACK

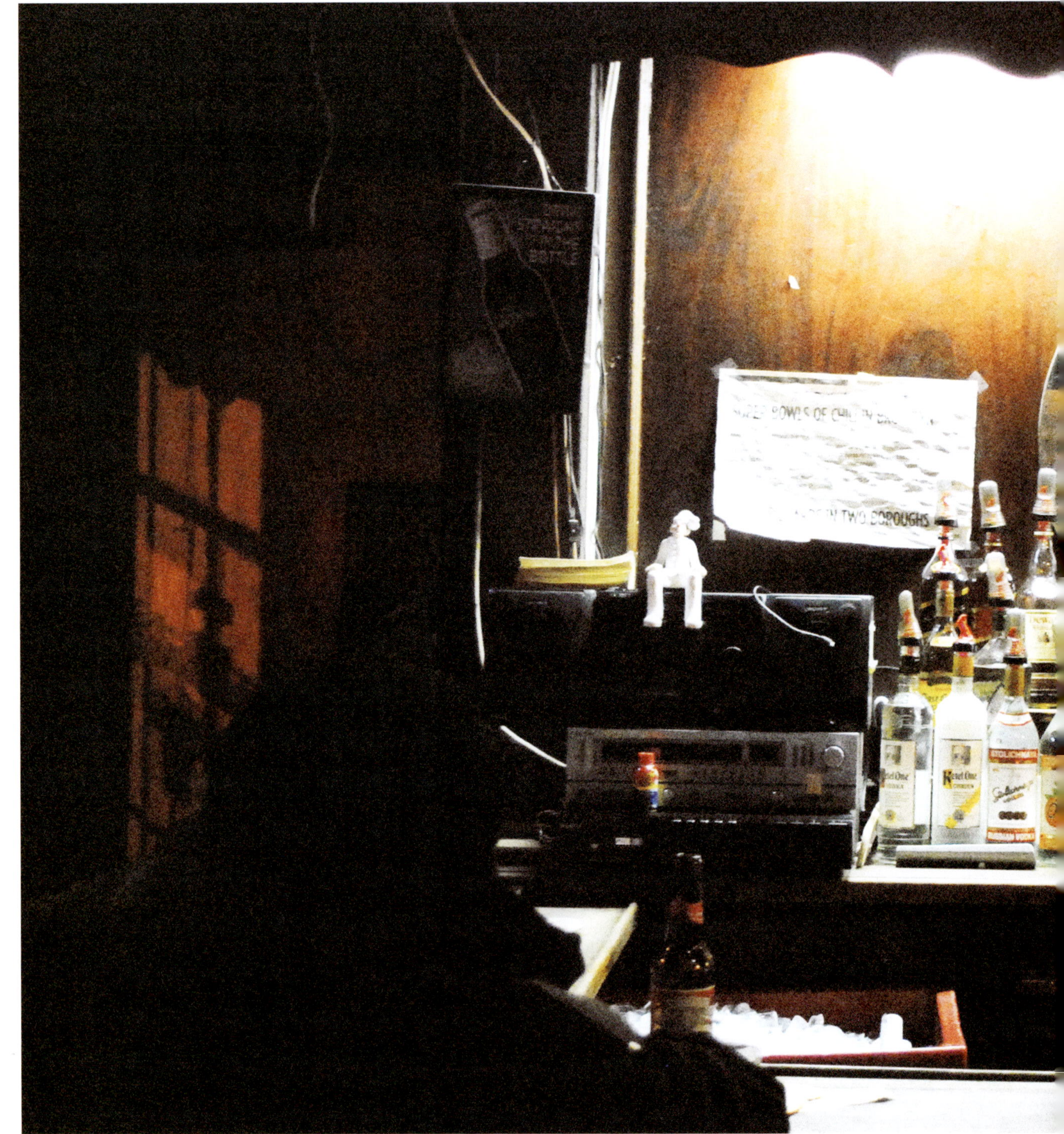

O'Conners

03.05.2011
06:54pm

Park Slope
Brooklyn

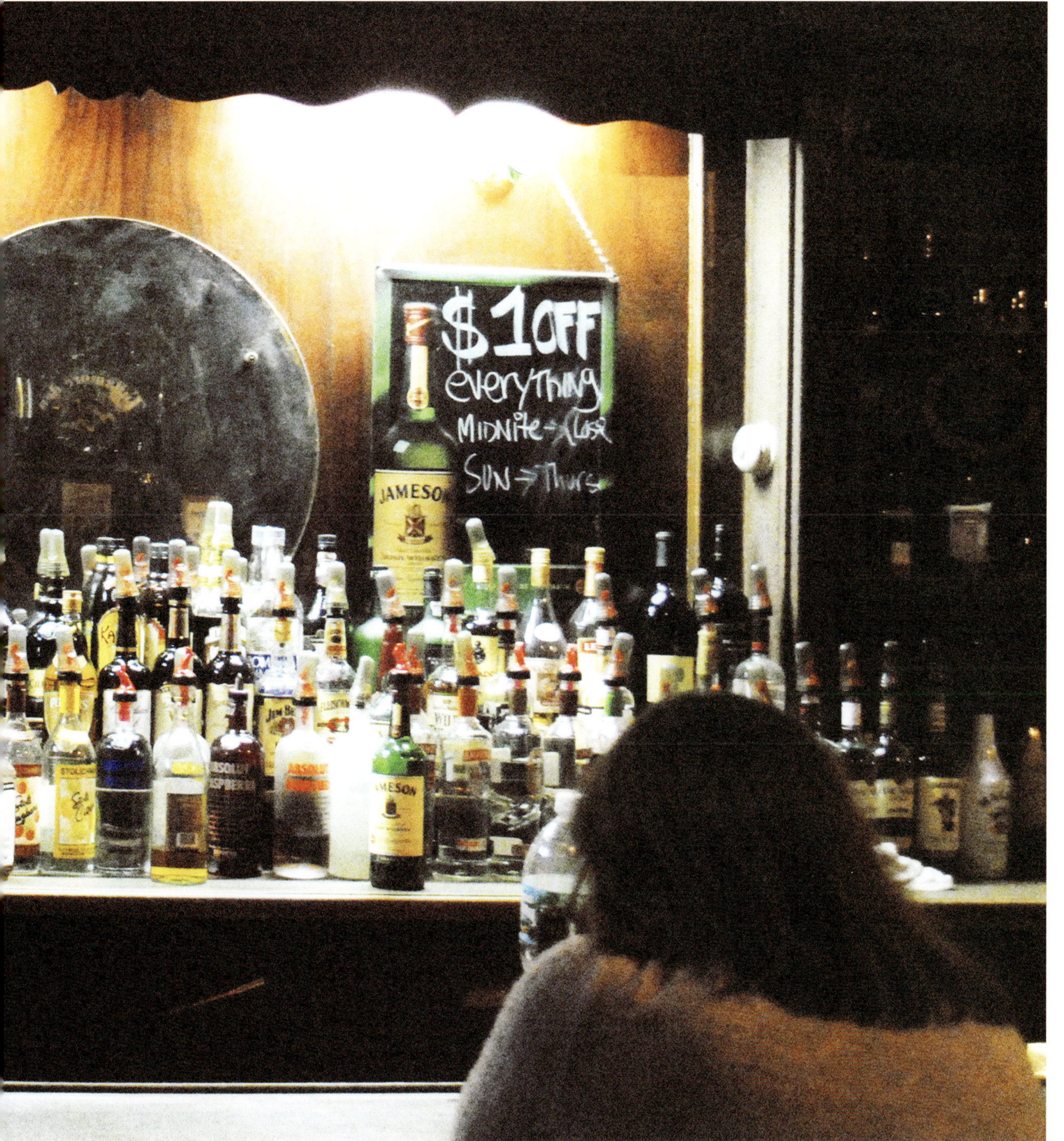

$1 OFF
everything
MIDNite → close
SUN → Thurs
JAMESON

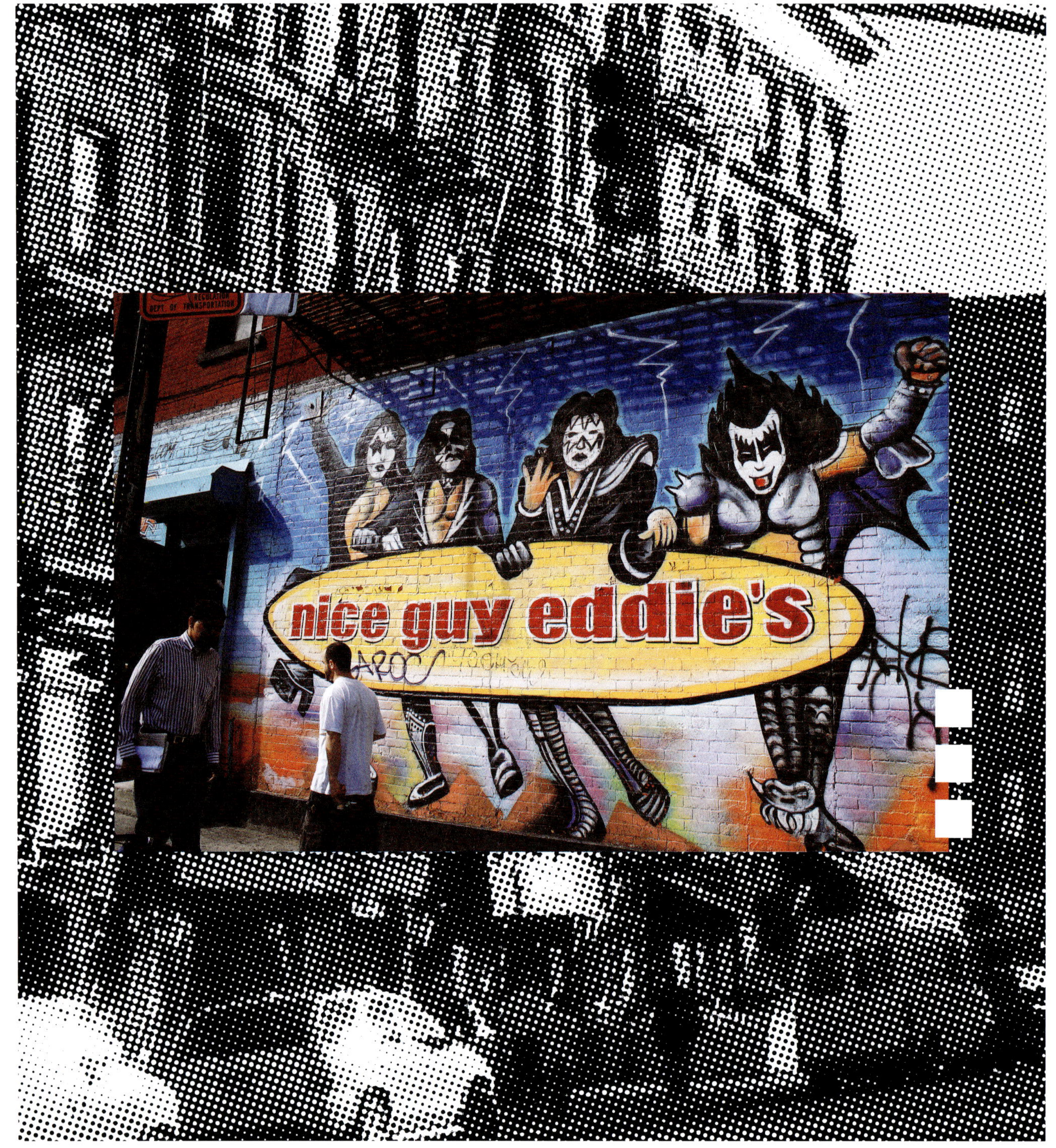

Nice Guy Eddie's

05.21.2011
04:49pm

Lower East Side
Manhattan

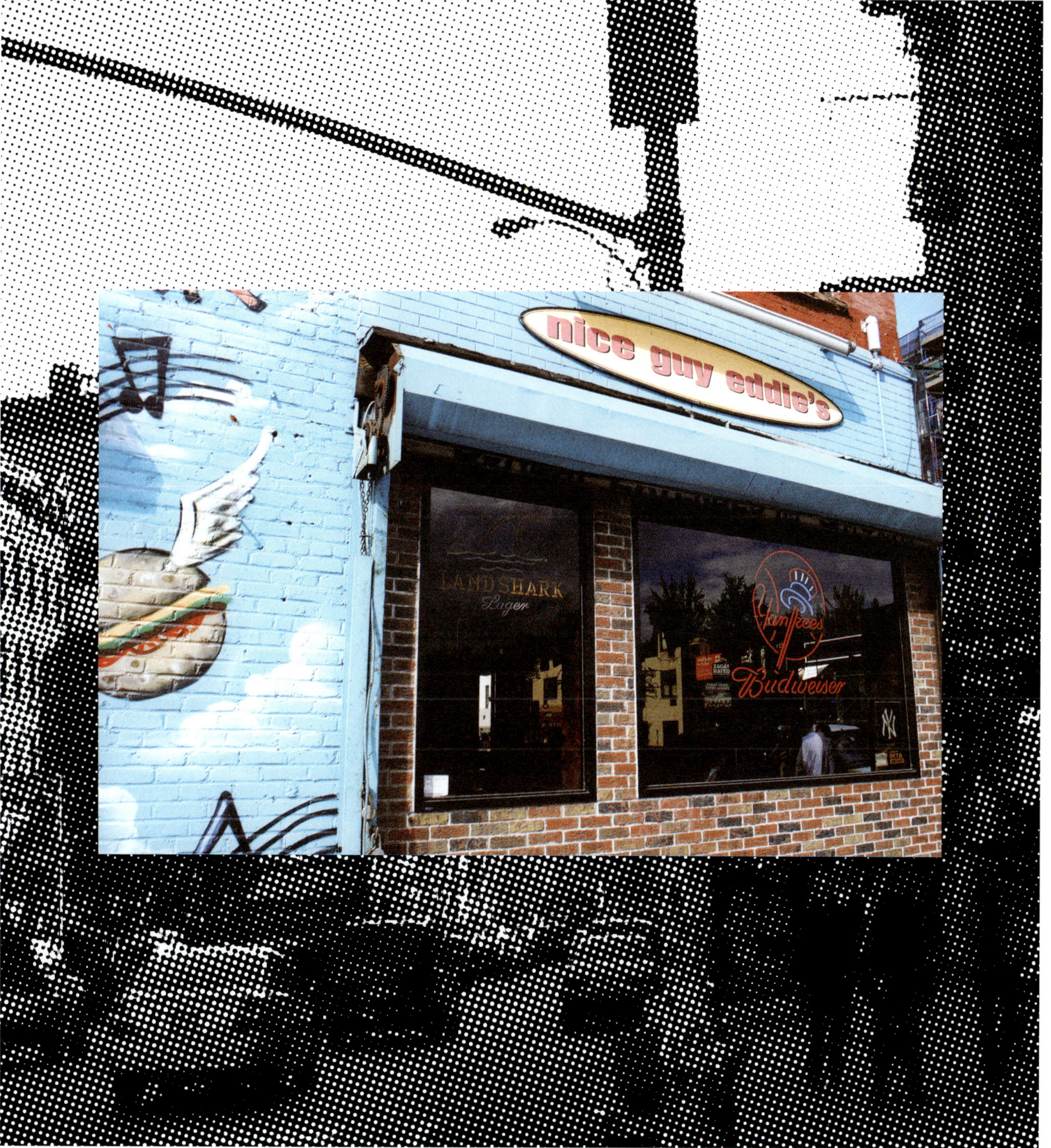

nice guy eddie's
LANDSHARK Lager
Yankees
Budweiser

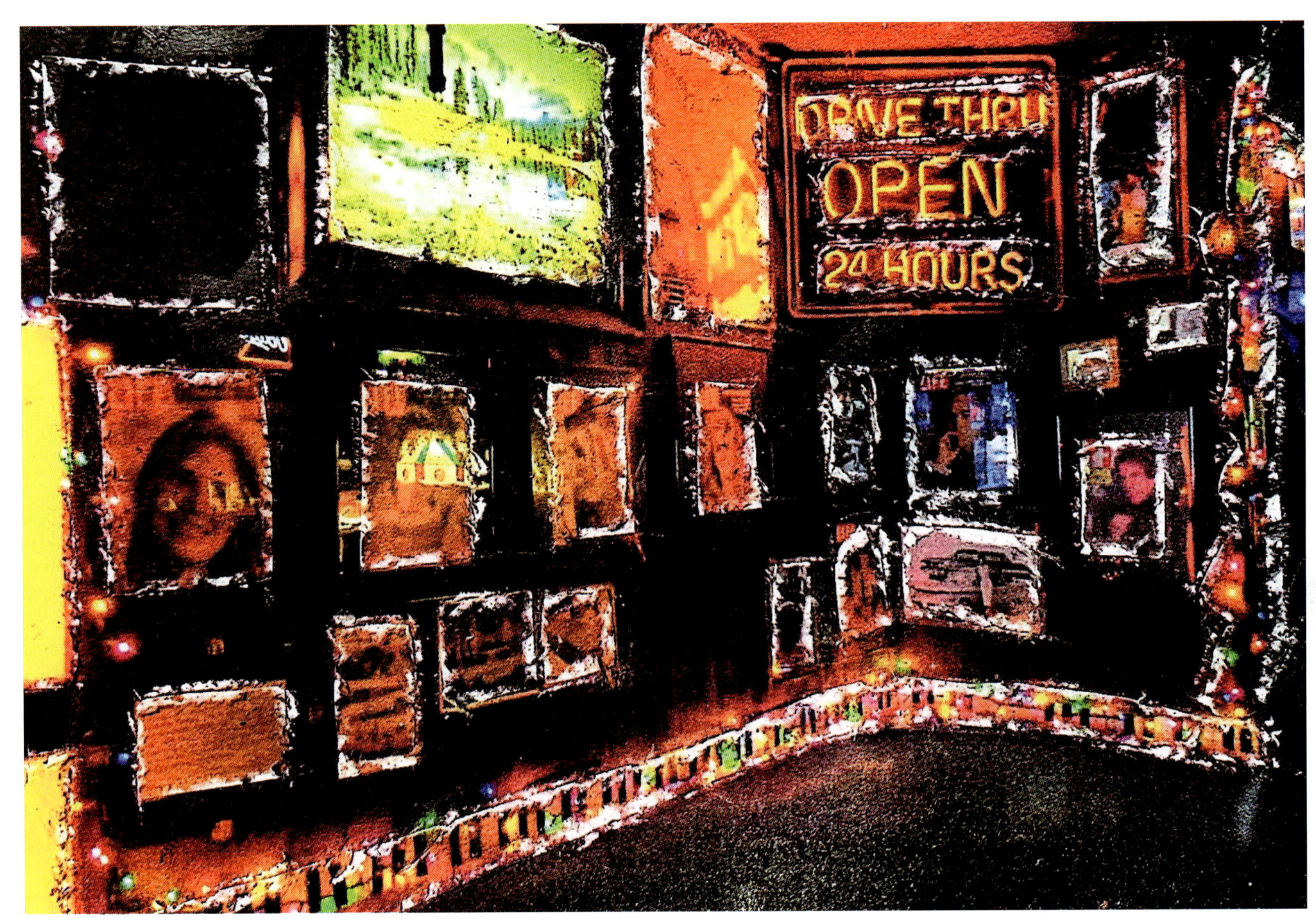

Parkside Lounge

12.11.2010
01:51pm

Lower East Side
Manhattan

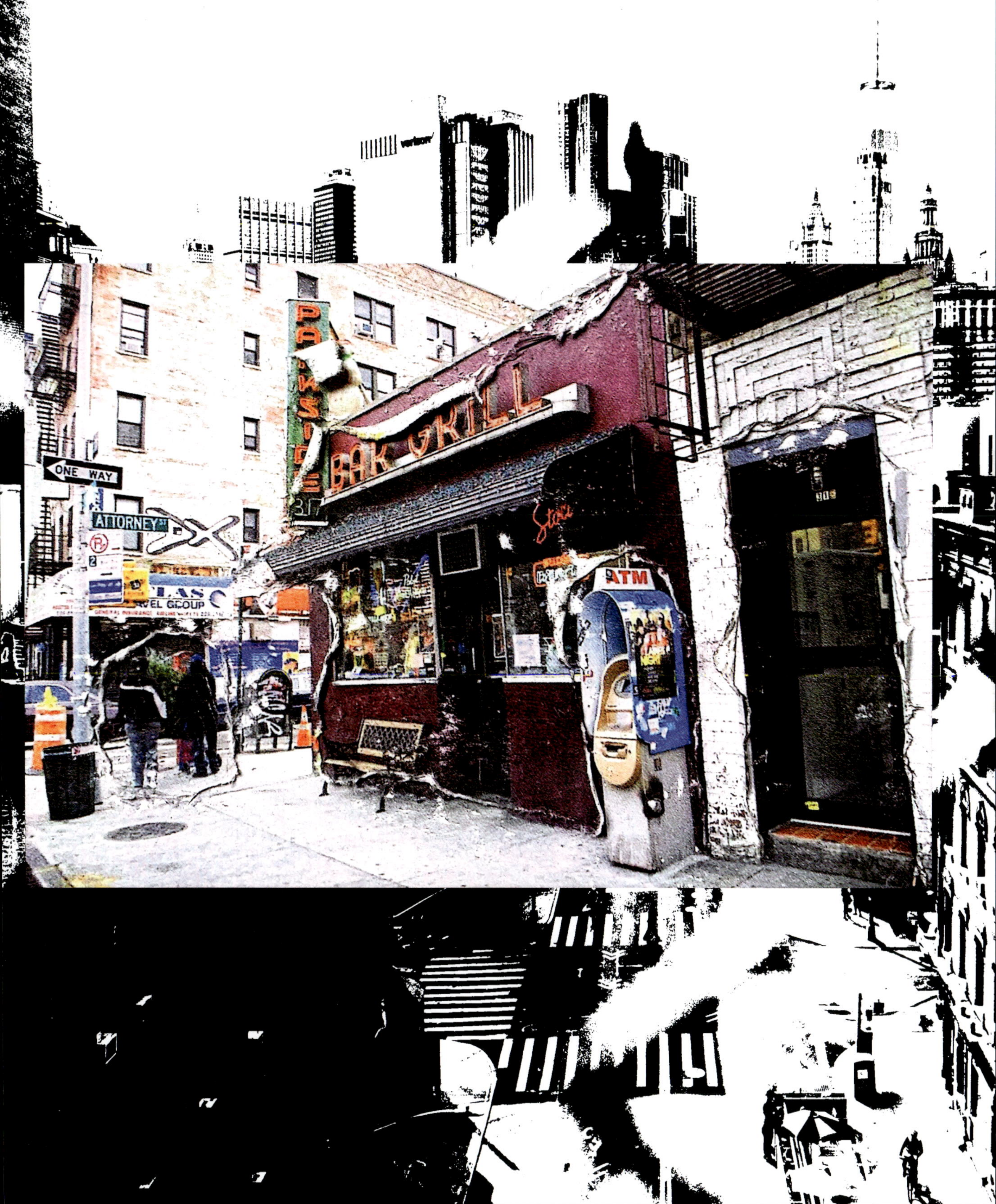

ONE WAY
ATTORNEY ST
PARKSIDE
BAR GRILL
Store
ATM
909
317

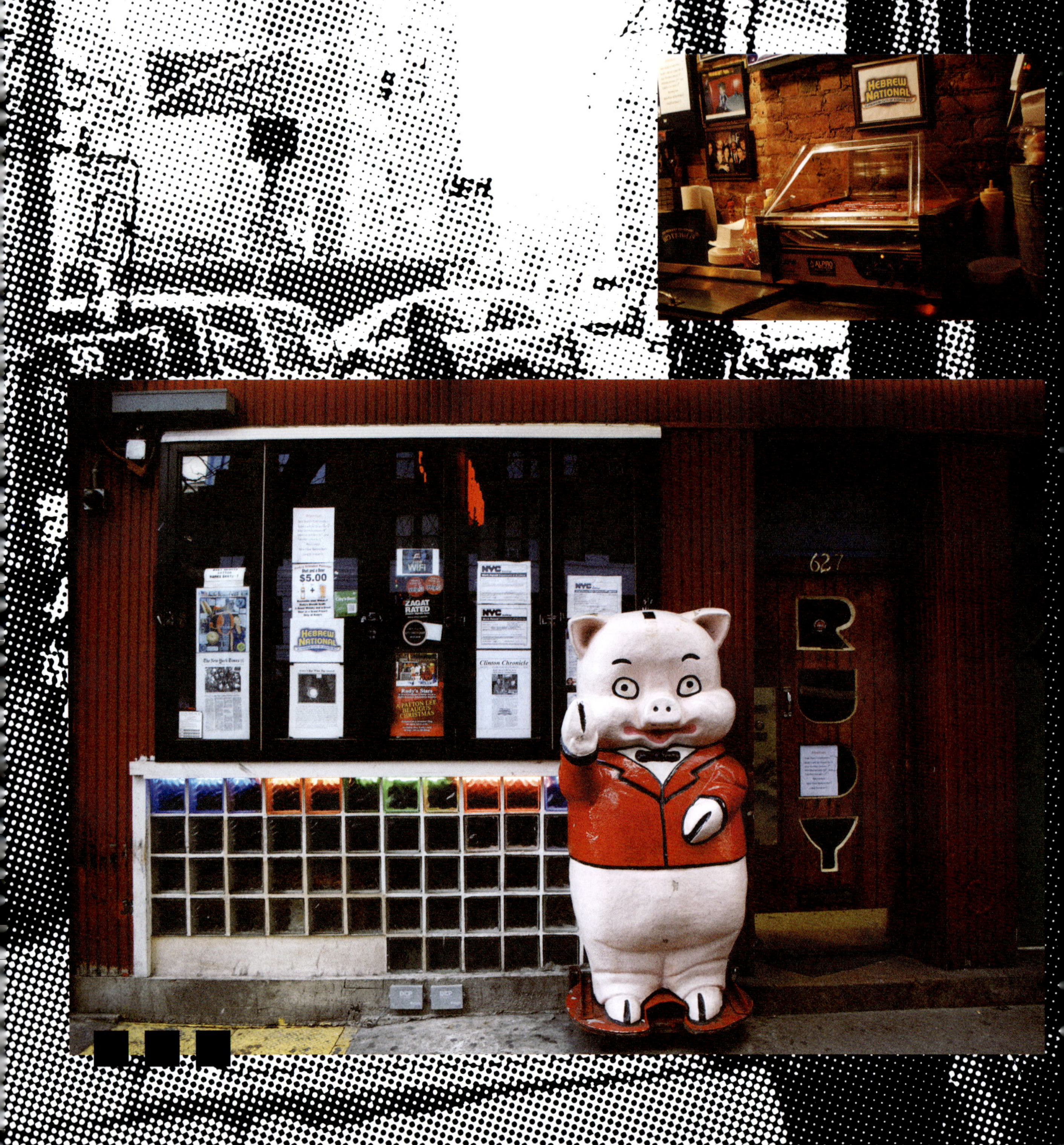

Rudy's

01.06.2011
03:23pm

Hell's Kitchen
Manhattan

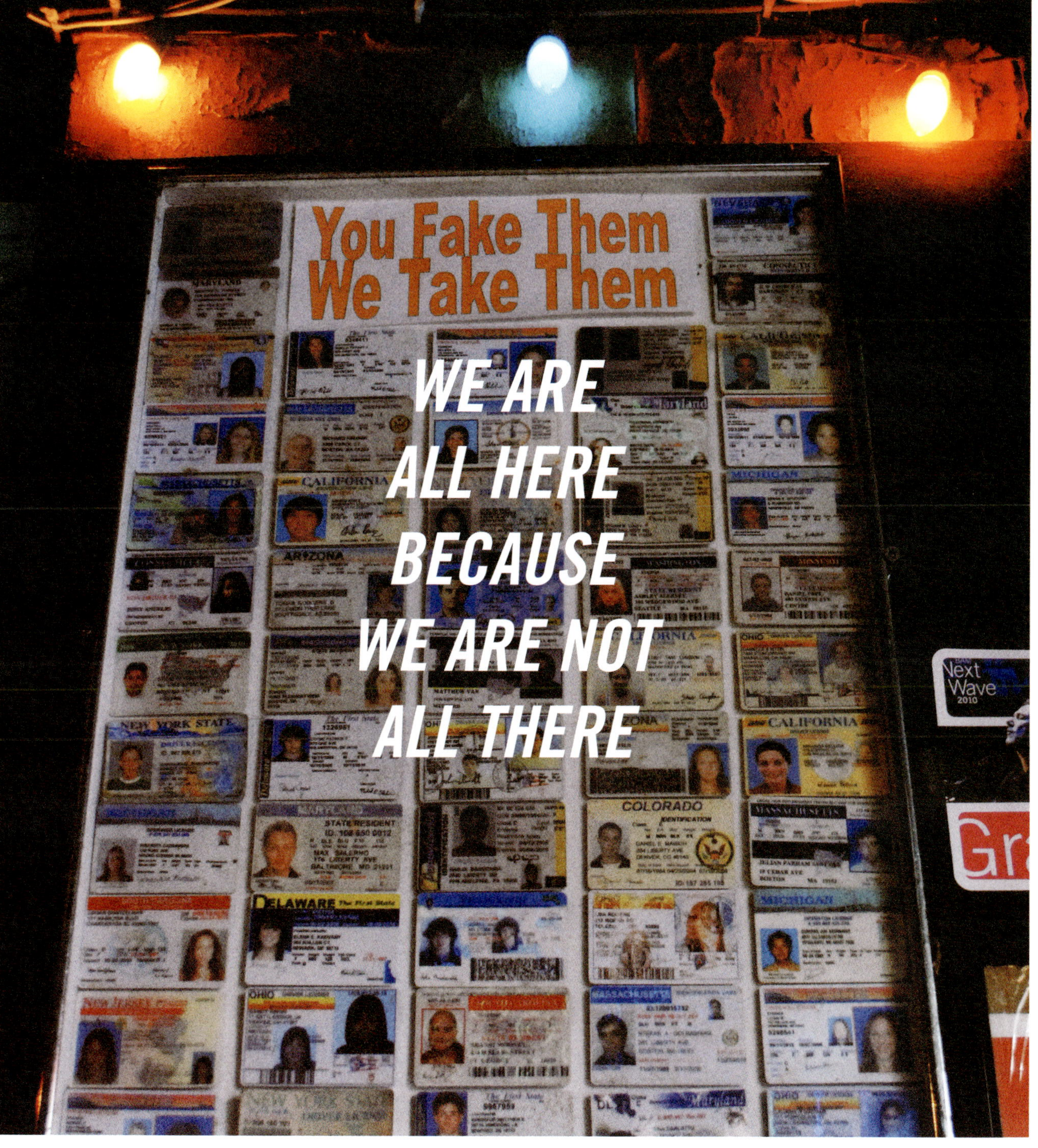
You Fake Them
We Take Them
WE ARE
ALL HERE
BECAUSE
WE ARE NOT
ALL THERE

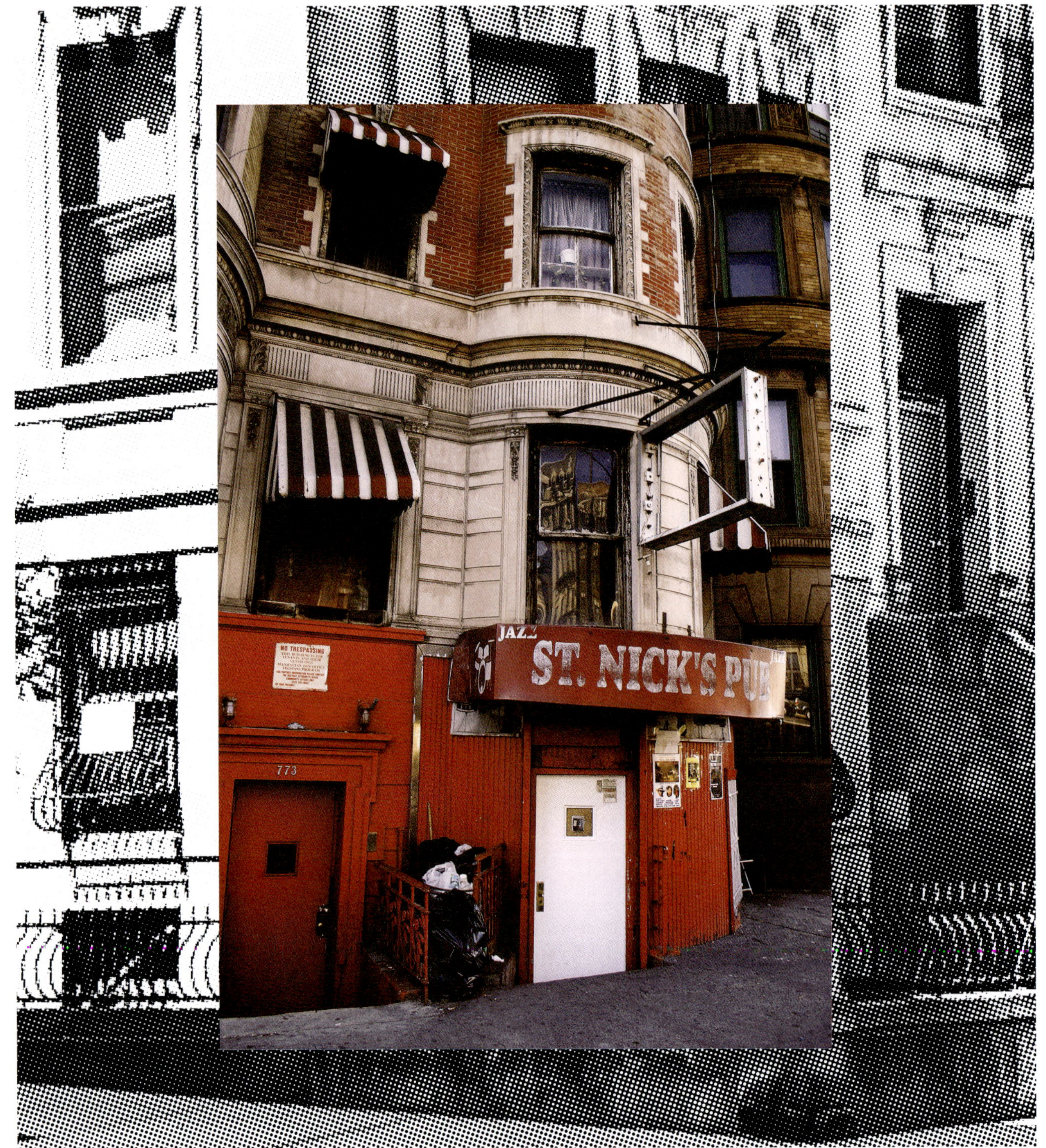

St. Nick's Pub

11.06.2010
05:21pm

Harlem
Manhattan

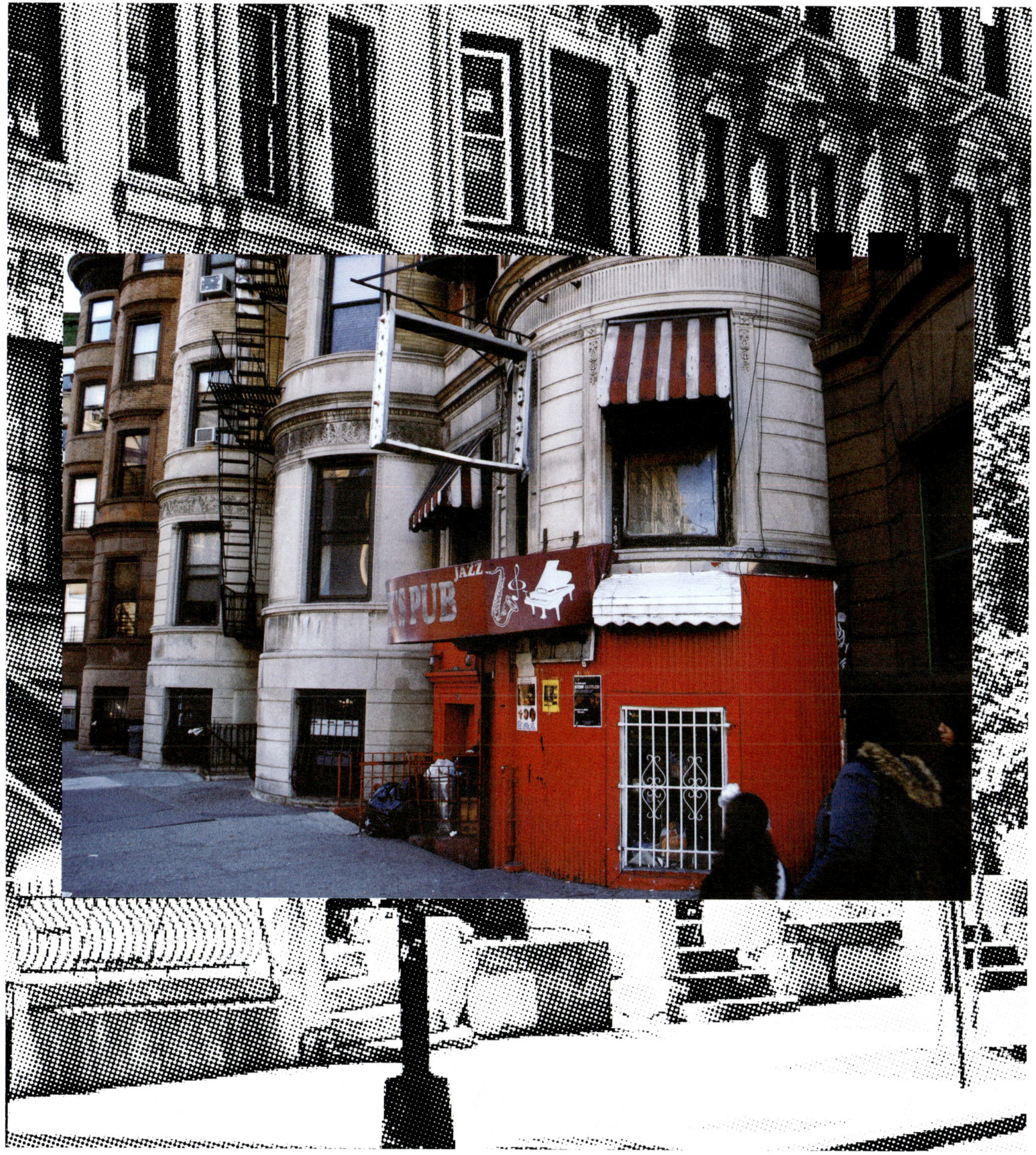
JAZZ
'S PUB

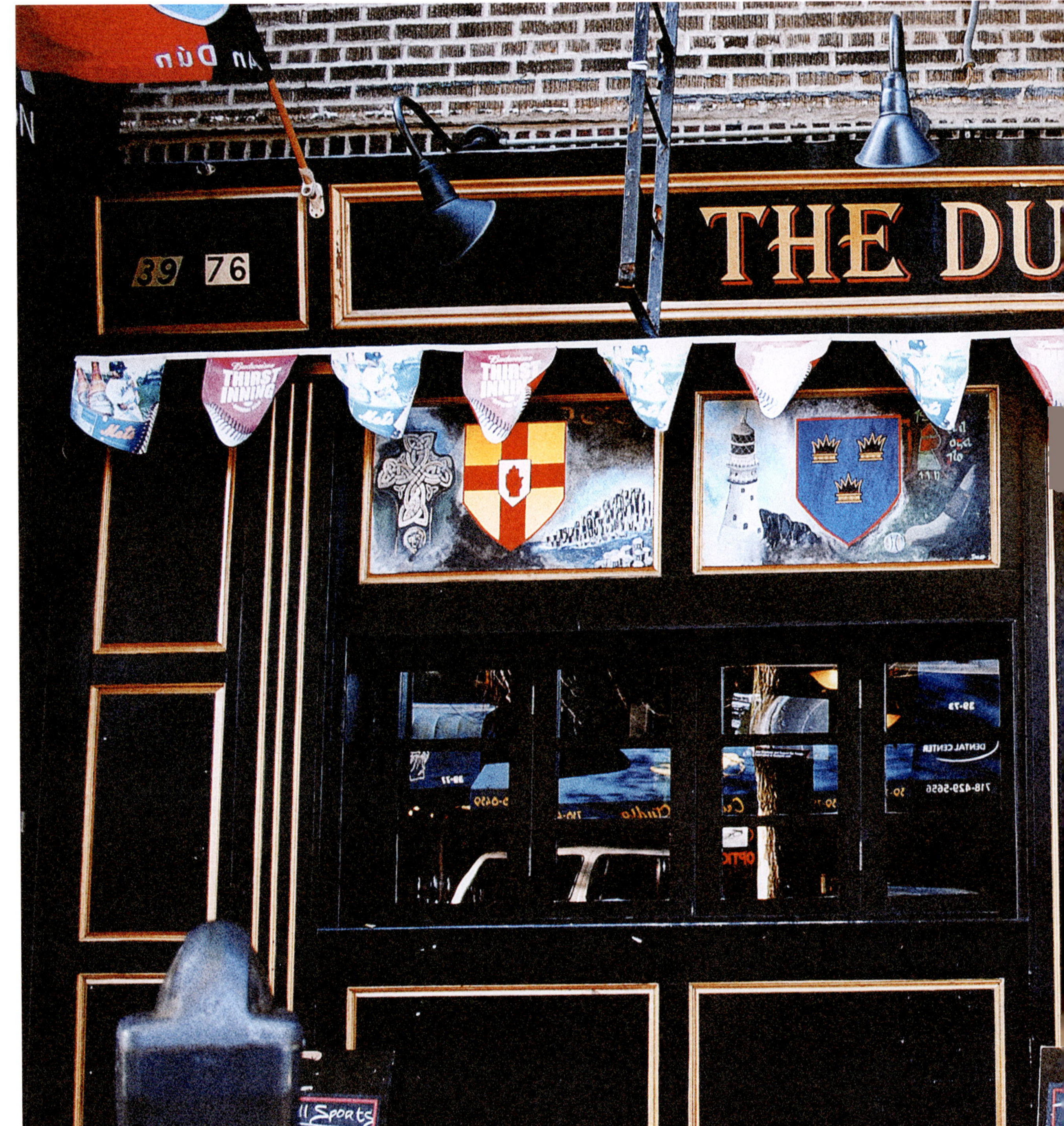

The Dugout

11.21.2010
01:30pm

Woodside
Queens

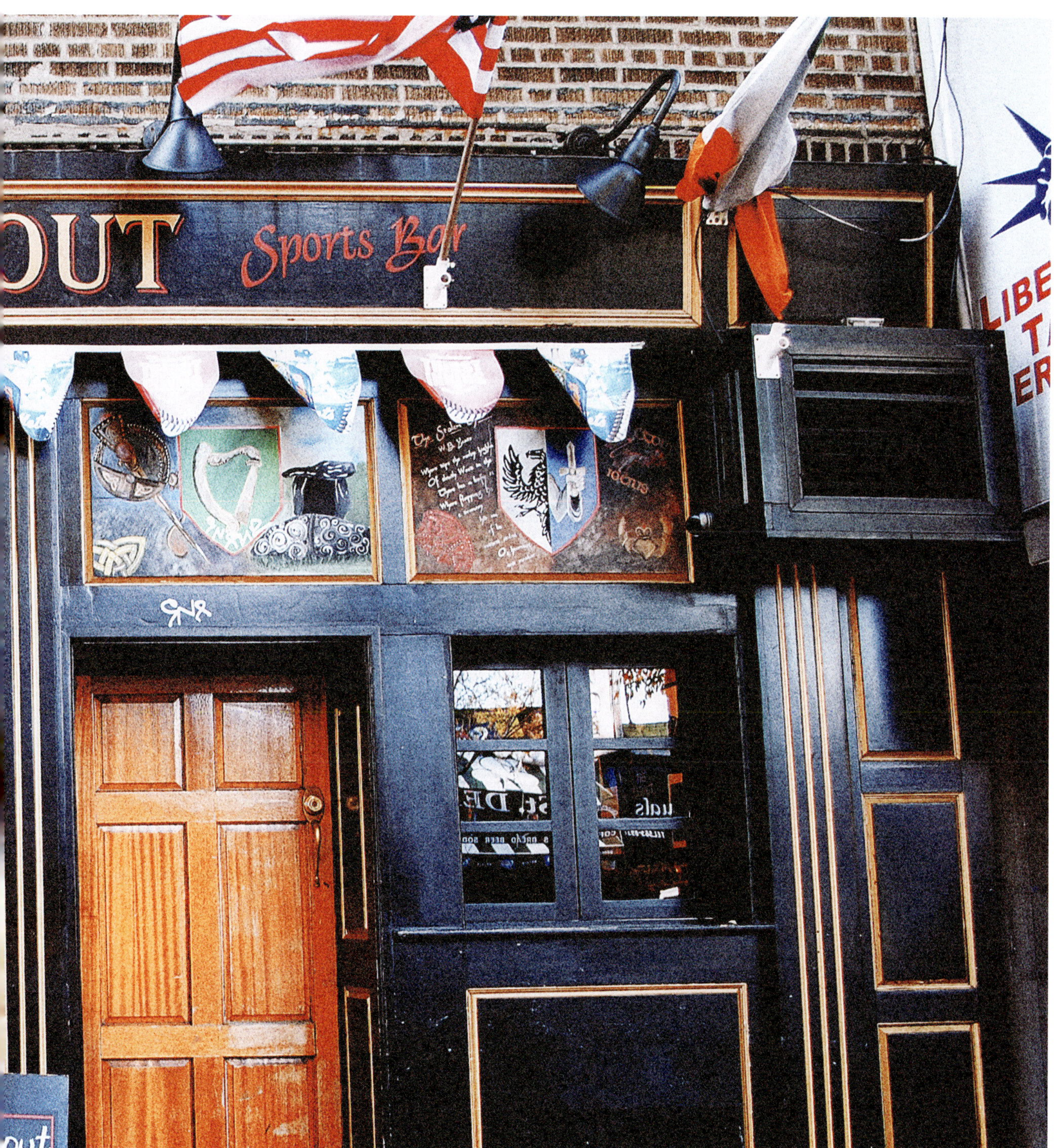
OUT
Sports Bar
LIBE
TA
ER
out

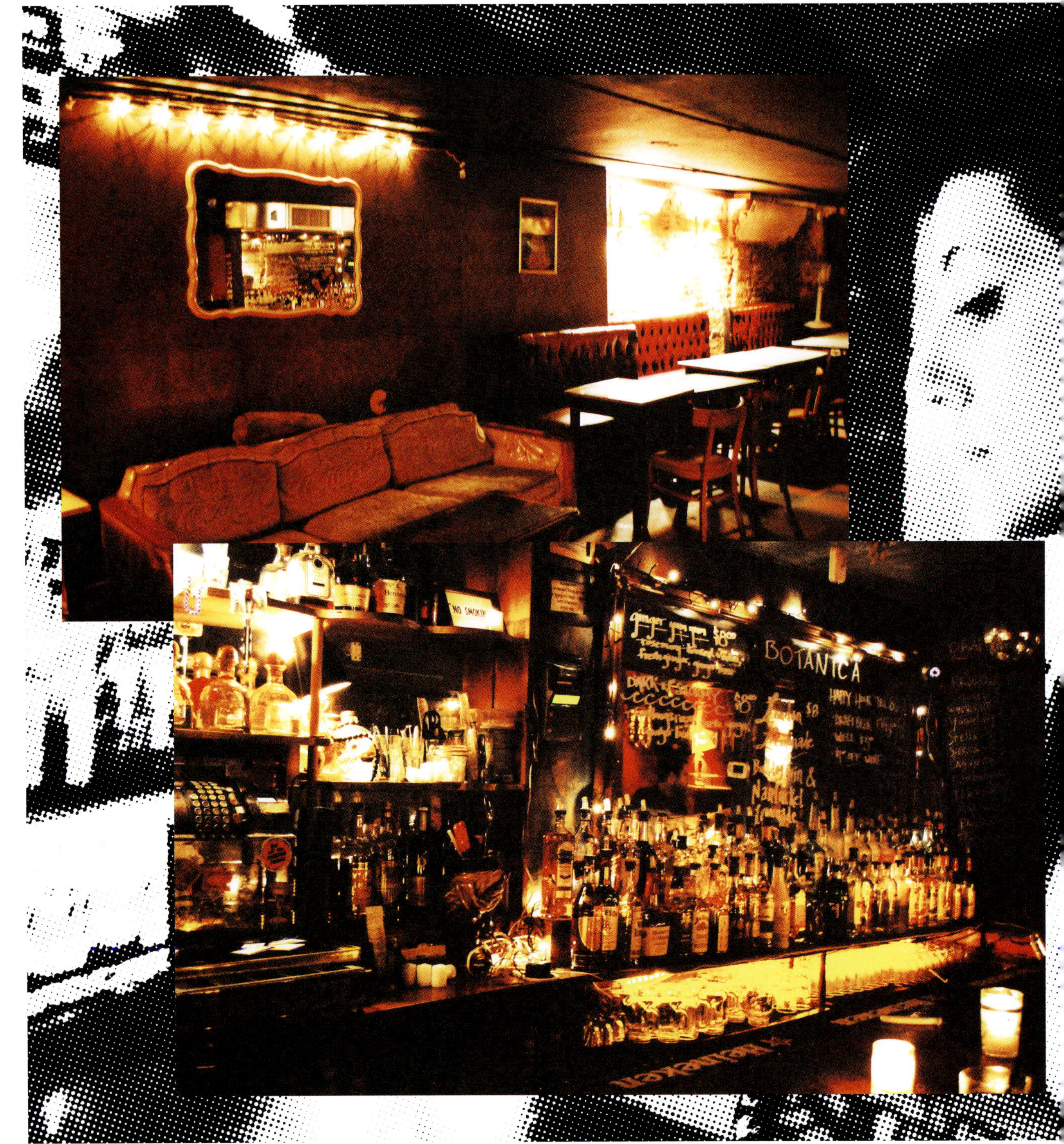

Botanica

02.12.2011
06:23pm

East Village
Manhattan

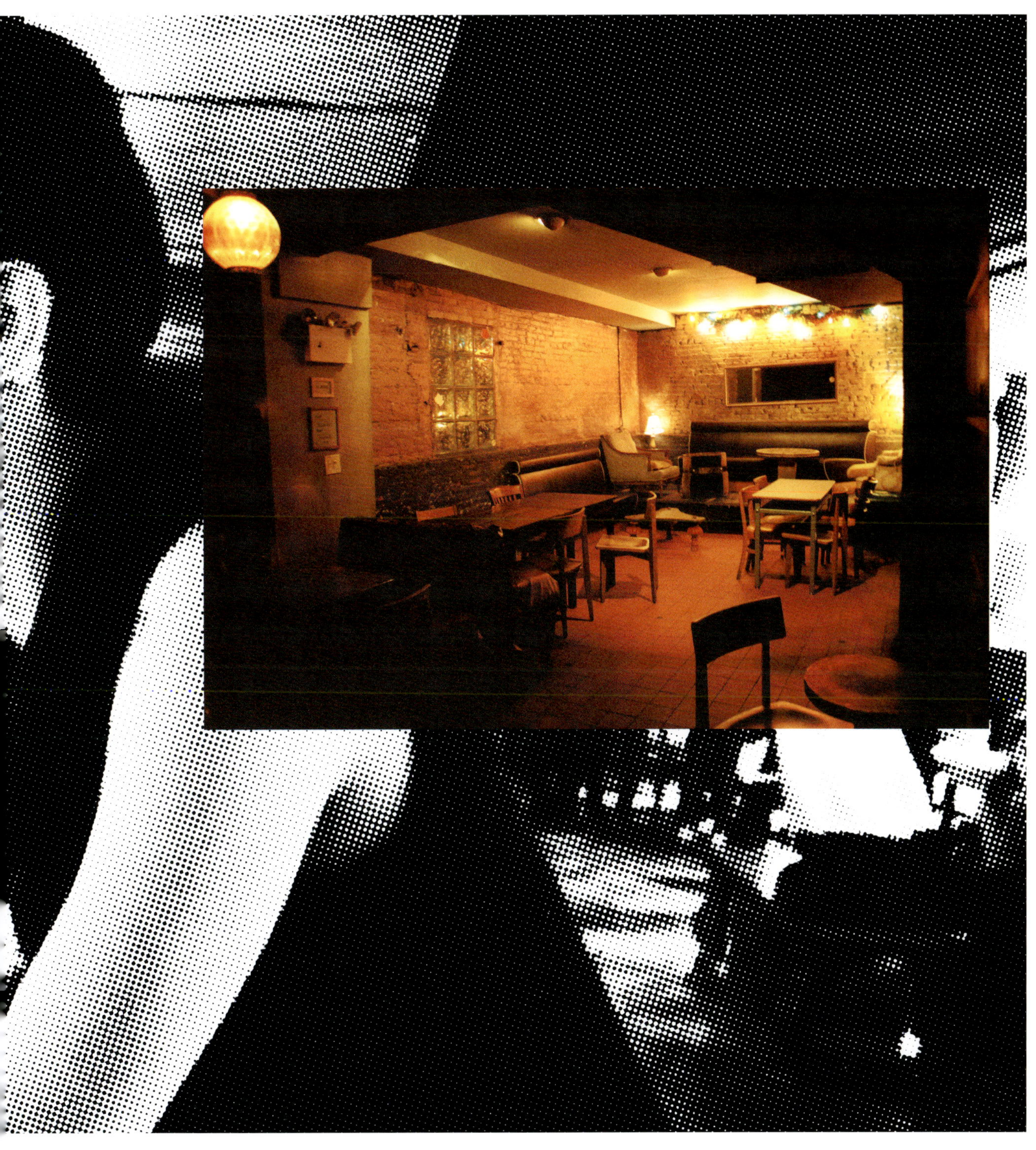

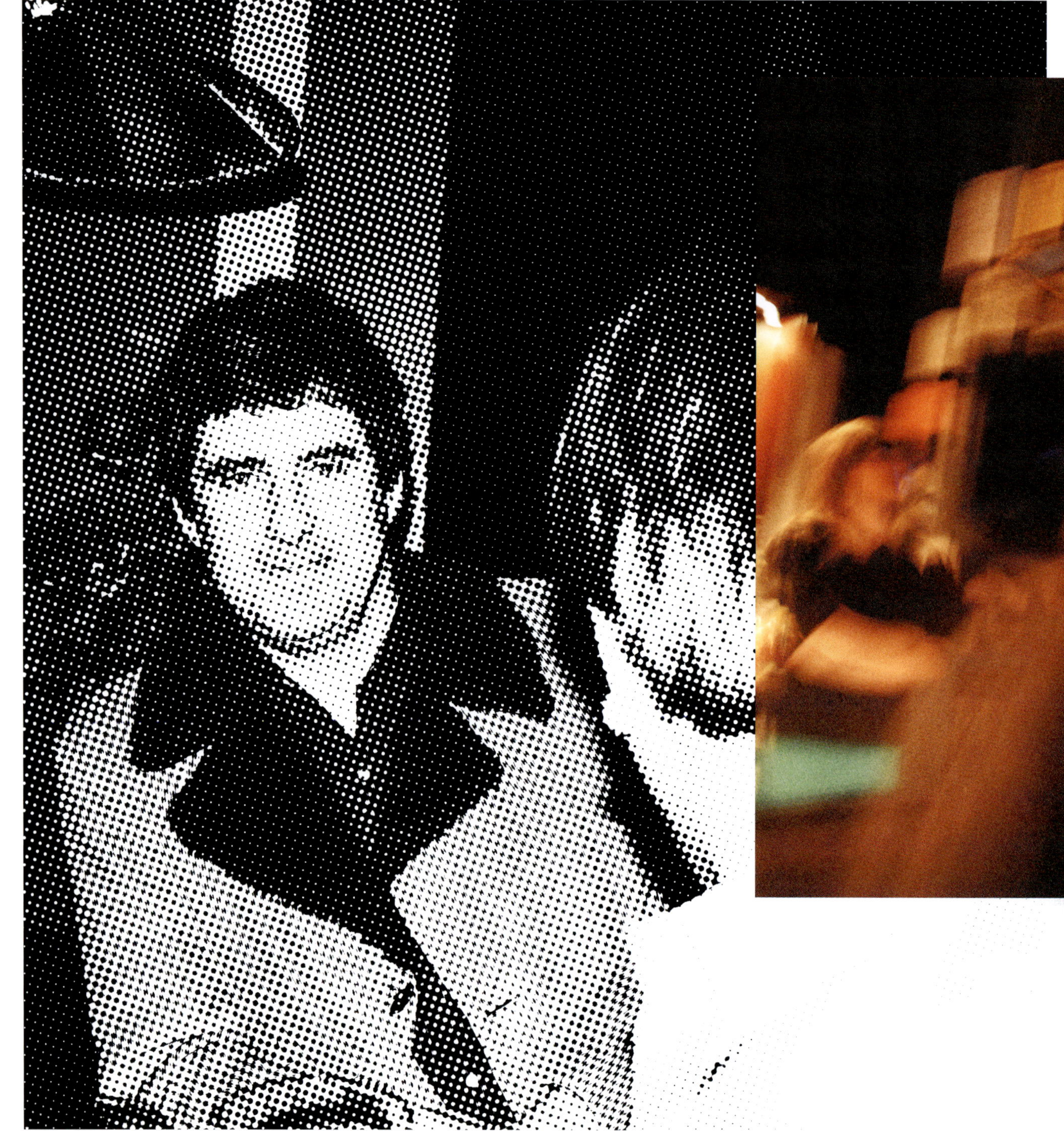

02.28.2011
10:55pm

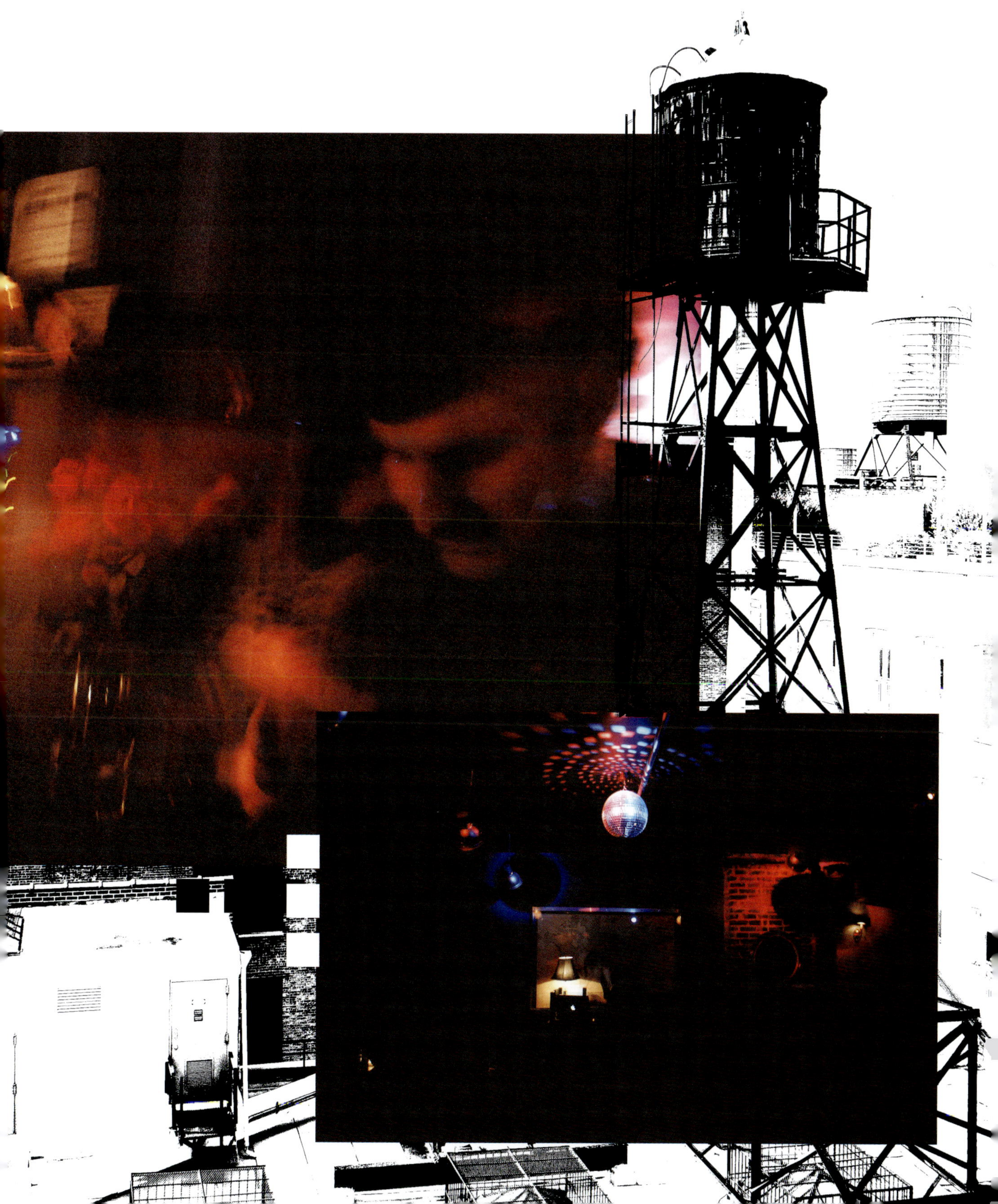

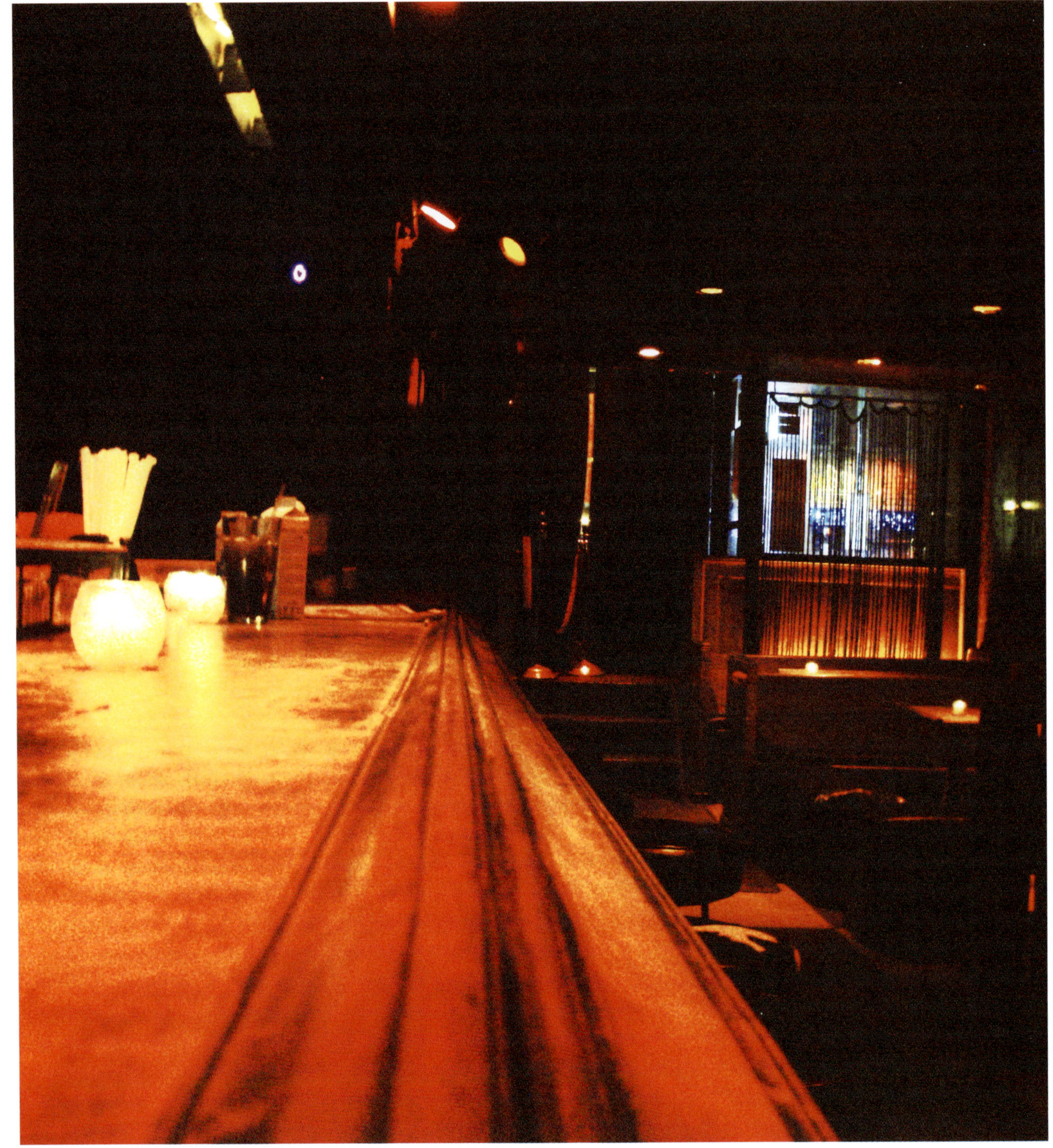

Lit Lounge
01.11.2012
08:24pm
East Village
Manhattan

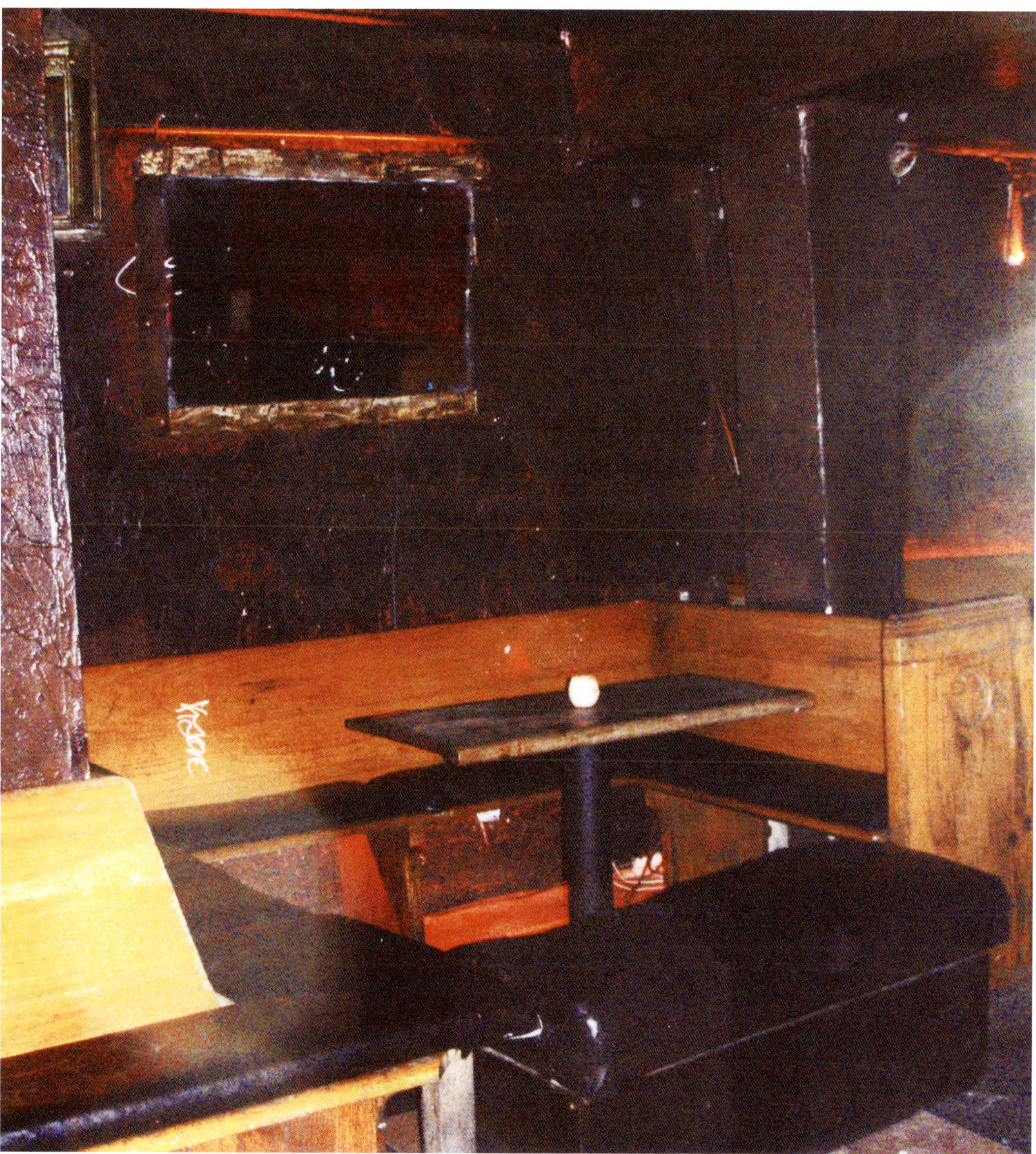

119	Manhattan / Union Square*
Alligator Bar	Williamsburg, Brooklyn
Barcade	Brooklyn
Bushwick Country Club	Bushwick, Brooklyn
Buttermilk Bar	Brooklyn
Ding Dong Lounge	Upper West Side*
Double Down Saloon	Lower East Side
Great Lakes	Park Slope*
Jackie's Fifth Amendment	Park Slope, Brooklyn*
J. Mac's Lounge	Midtown West*
Lakeside Lounge	Lower East Side/Alphabet City*
The Library	Lower East Side
Local 138	Lower East Side*
Lucy's	Lower East Side
Mama's Bar	Lower East Side/Alphabet City
Mars Bar	East Village*
Metropolitan Bar	Williamsburg, Brooklyn
M&S Front Line Co	Harlem*
Ontario Bar	Williamsburg, Brooklyn
Pat O'Briens	Upper East Side*
Dive Bar	Upper West Side
San Loco	East Village*
Sophies	Lower East Side
Union Pool	Williamsburg, Brooklyn
151 Bar	Lower East Side*
Max Fish	Lower East Side*
Motor City	Lower East Side*
Iggy's New York	Upper East Side

*CLOSED **ORIGINAL LOCATION CLOSED

Second Chance Saloo	**Williamsburg, Brooklyn***
Welcome To The Johnson's	Lower East Side
Wreck Room	Bushwick, Brooklyn*
HiFi Bar	Lower East Side*
The Cuckoo's Nest	**Woodside, Queens***
Beauty Bar	Union Square/East Village
Cherry Tavern	Lower East Side
International Bar	East Village**
Ear Inn	**West Village**
Holland Bar	**Hell's Kitchen***
Jimmy's Corner	Times Square
Jr. & Son	Williamsburg, Brooklyn**
Lady Jay's	Williamsburg, Brooklyn
Milano's Bar	East Village
Mona'a	**Alphabet City**
O'Connors	**Park Slope***
Nice Guy Eddie	East Village*
Parkside Lounge	**Lower East Side**
Ruby's	Hells Kitchen
St. Nick's Pub	Harlem*
The Dugout	Woodside, Queens
Botanica	East Village
Bowery Electric	**East Village**
Lit Lounge	**East Village***

*CLOSED   **ORIGINAL LOCATION CLOSED

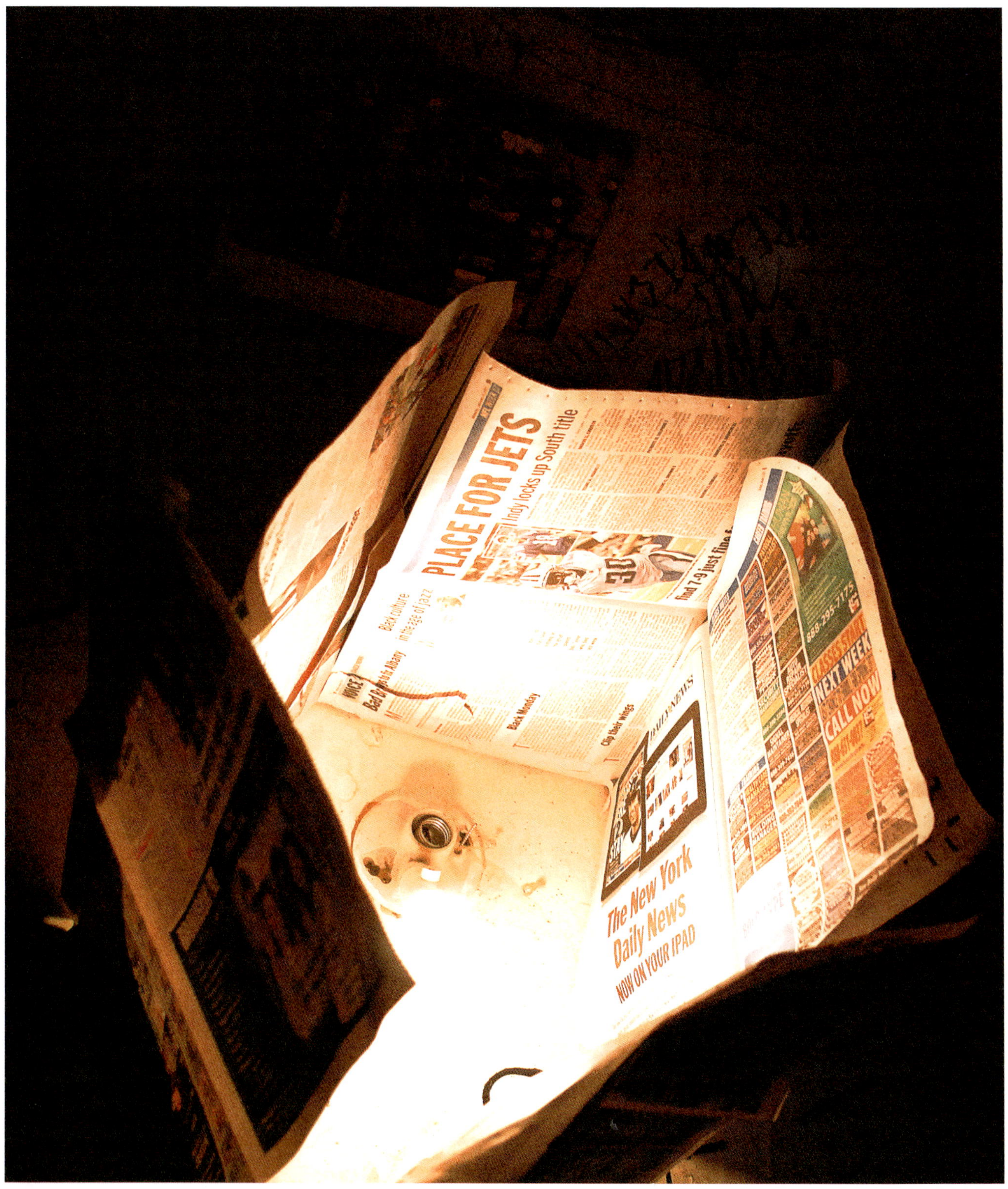
PLACE FOR JETS
Indy locks up South title
find 7-9 just fine
The New York
Daily News
NOW ON YOUR IPAD
CLASSES START
NEXT WEEK
CALL NOW!
888-295-1172